Strategies
in Prose

Strategies
in Prose
A THEMATIC READER
Fifth Edition

WILFRED A. FERRELL
NICHOLAS A. SALERNO
Arizona State University

Holt, Rinehart and Winston
New York   Chicago   San Francisco   Philadelphia
Montreal   Toronto   London   Sydney
Tokyo   Mexico City   Rio de Janeiro   Madrid

Library of Congress Cataloging in Publication Data
Main entry under title:

Strategies in prose.

1. College readers. I. Ferrell, Wilfred A. II. Sa-
lerno, Nicholas A.
PE1417.S766   1983   808'.0427   82–15501
ISBN   0-03-059324-7

CBS COLLEGE PUBLISHING
Holt, Rinehart and Winston
The Dryden Press
Saunders College Publishing

Preface

In preparing the fifth edition of *Strategies in Prose* we followed the same guidelines we had adopted for the earlier editions. These derive from the long-established fact that people best learn to write by writing. But the writing experience serves this purpose only when the writer has something to say and has a reason for saying it. Students in freshman composition courses may discover the substance for their writing by reading and discussing essays that lie within their range of interest and experience, engage their intellectual capabilities, and cause them to respond. By analyzing and studying *how* the various authors present their ideas, students may develop their own rhetorical strategies.

Of the seventy-four selections in this edition, forty are new. And following the recommendations of instructors who had used the fourth edition, we selected shorter essays, many of them light and humorous, to replace those we dropped from the last edition. Another major change, again at the reviewers' recommendations, was to drop the section on writing about literature.

But in all other aspects we have followed the format and guidelines we developed for the previous editions. We have retained the seven topical sections. Each section includes a pro and a con set of essays on a controversial subject or a cluster of essays dealing with a controversial issue. Each section includes a short story or narrative essay. Again, all selections are complete—there are no snippets or shortened versions of an essay.

For the Rhetorical Contents we have listed the selections according to the principal type of development used with each of them. Since any essay may incorporate more than one type of development, some of the essays are listed under more than one heading. The study questions at the end of each selection are intended to help students read the selection critically and to assist them in analyzing the writer's method and techniques. The questions are not intended to be exhaustive for these purposes, but merely suggest ways in which students may start to study and analyze the essays. For further exploration an Instructor's Manual is available from the English Editor, Holt, Rinehart and Winston, 383 Madison Avenue, New York, NY, 10017.

Many friends and colleagues have given us suggestions and recommendations for *Strategies in Prose,* and we wish to acknowledge their kind assistance. In particular we are grateful to Albert Adams, William Agopsowicz, Tom Allender, Richard S. Beal, Barbara Bixby, Anne Boynton-Trigg, Lynne Brewster, Bretty Brugh, William C. Creasy, Frank D'Angelo, Susan Ferrell, Nicholas D. Fratt, Leon Gatlin, George Haich, Ted Hann, Nancy J. Hawkey, Bruce Hollingsworth, Leonard Kulseth, Charles R. Lefcourt, Thom Martin, Rebecca Martino, R. Paul Murphy, Marjorie Neumann, Lorri Nivens, John Noll, Dixie Lee Powell, Peggy Pryzant, Daniel Quirk, Betty Renshaw, Clifford Roth, Richard Schroeder, Shelby Stephenson, James Van Pernis, Roger Widmeyer, and William H. Young.

We wish to thank the following reviewers for their work on the fifth edition: Barbara Dixon, Auburn University; Robert A. Gates, St. John's University; William J. Johnson, Augusta College; Lynn Kellerman, Rutgers University; Thomas Martinez, Villanova University; Sylvia G. O'Sullivan, University of Maryland; Eugenia Rossi, Modesto Junior College; Michael D. Shapiro, Hofstra University; Samuel J. Sinkovitz, Jackson Community College; and James T. Stewart, Furman University.

Tempe, Arizona   W.A.F.
                                                                    N.A.S.

Contents

5 Education:
UNWILLINGLY TO SCHOOL   229

6 Language:
THE SOUL OF WIT   275

7 Popular Culture and the Arts:
THE WINTER OF OUR DISCONTENT   317

Rhetorical Contents

(Many selections have been cross-listed because they illustrate more than one rhetorical method of development.)

Analysis

Classification

Comparison and Contrast

Exemplification

Cause and Effect

Definition

Strategies in Prose

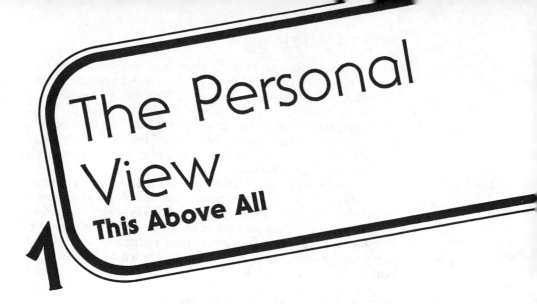

The Personal View

This Above All

1

Contemporary human problems and concerns seem ever more complex. Indeed, common goals now make cooperation so important that a section on the individual seems almost immoral. Yet some of the greatest human joys are strictly personal, and the dark night of the soul is essentially a private affair. Thus the necessity both to acknowledge our ever-expanding search for self-awareness and to provide a variety of rhetorical types has resulted in **The Personal View.**

Marya Mannes's "Who Am I?" opens this section with an inquiry into the search for a personal identity. Although Mannes makes it clear early on that the answer to the question can be found at any age, she writes for young adults. Her tone, structure, and style are colloquial and simple, probably because she has a youthful audience in mind. On the other hand, Eric Hoffer is more studied, more literary in his examination of the undesirables in society, and Martin Buber's contrasting of books and men is redolent of biblical language. Nothing bitter or sarcastic about these three. Exploratory, optimistic calls to action almost—urging us to find the potential within ourselves and in those around us. The tone, form, and style are sufficiently different to make the essays extremely useful for comparison and contrast.

The subsection on men and women offers variety in both form and content. Anthony Burgess seems to have arrived at a relationship with his wife that works. The lines of communication are open; the relationship flourishes, even over the long haul. Like Burgess, Ann Bayer uses the informal essay, but it's short-term relationships she opts for; she is droll but firm. Edna O'Brien and Woody Allen choose the short story for the battleground of the sexes. O'Brien's narrator is willing to make almost any number of concessions to get her affair under way, whereas Kugelmass wants out at the first taste of boredom. O'Brien's is clearly a first-person point of view, while Allen's is a third. Why, therefore, Allen's story seems more immediate will make for fruitful study. Then, Max Shulman's "logical" analysis of love demonstrates how humor and dialogue can be used in developing an argument.

The selections by Martin E. Marty, Langston Hughes, and Elisabeth Kübler-Ross probe our search for God and a reason for existence. Marty imitates the style and methodology of news analysts and gives us Jesus as a candidate for President. Hughes's is a first-person narrative of a young boy's supposedly personal encounter with Jesus. And Kübler-Ross offers advice on how to help the young cope with death and the idea of an afterlife. In each of these selections, form helps carry the message.

A careful analysis of the selections in this section reminds us that coming to grips with life, love, and death must be interpreted anew not only by each generation but also by each individual within that generation. The varieties of experience encountered and the strategies used may help the readers of this book bring the meaning of their own experiences into clearer focus.

Who Am I?

MARYA MANNES

Marya Mannes (1904–   ) was born in New York City. She holds an honorary L.H.D. from Hood College, Maryland. From 1942 to 1945 Mannes was an intelligence analyst for the United States government. Her television appearances, university lecture tours, and numerous periodical articles have made her a familiar figure to the American public. She has published *Message from a Stranger,* a novel (1948); *More in Anger* (1958); *Subverse,* satiric verse (1959); *The New York I Know* (1961); *But Will It Sell?* (1964); *They,* a novel (1968); and *Out of My Time* (1971).

1   Who are you? You singly, not you together. When did it start—that long day's journey into self? When do you really begin to know what you believe and where you're going? When do you know that you are unique—separate—alone?

2   The time of discovery is different for everybody. Some people find themselves in early childhood, some in middle age, some—the tragic ones—never.

3   I suggest that the first recognition comes when others try to tell you what you are. And although what happened in my generation is supposed to have no relevance to what happens in yours, I know when it happened to me.

4   I may have been six years old when aunts and uncles and cousins used to say: "You look just like your mother!" or "You're the image of your brother!"

5   Now for reasons that have nothing to do with duty or discipline in that distant day, I loved my family. I loved them because they were interesting, handsome, talented, and loving people. I was lucky. But in spite of that, I felt an immediate, instinctive resistance to any suggestion that I was like them or like anybody else. I didn't want to be like anybody else. I was Me. Myself. Separate. Alone.

6   This is probably as good a time as any to say that if I use the first-person pronoun—if I refer from time to time to my own long, arduous, bumbling journey into self—it is not because of narcissism, but because I have always believed that the particular is more illuminating than the general. Perhaps my dependence as a writer on direct observation rather than on scholarly research, on living example rather than on sociological method, is the natural result of illiteracy. I never went to college and therefore know much less than you people do. About books, I mean, or the sciences.

7   But since the laboratory for the study of man is clearly life itself,

Reprinted by permission.

then I have studied hard in the act of living, of looking, of feeling; involvement rather than detachment; doing as well as being.

We were talking of the first discoveries of uniqueness—of being 8 oneself and no one else. Not your father, not your mother, not your sister, not your brother. I. Me.

It is then—when you begin not only to know it, but act it—that 9 society moves in. Society says it wants people to be different but it doesn't really mean it. Parents like to believe their children are different from other children—smarter, of course, better-looking and so forth—but most parents are secretly disturbed when their children are *really* different—not like others at all. In fact, very early they start to pigeonhole you in certain ways.

Take the difference of sex, for instance. Little girls are pink, little 10 boys are blue. Little girls want dolls, little boys want trains.

For a long time, for instance, the word "tomboy" to a girl held 11 undertones of worry and disapproval. All it meant was that the girl liked to play ball, climb trees, and skin her knees instead of wearing frilly dresses and curtseying. The companion word for boys, of course, was "sissy"—meaning the kid liked music and poetry and hated fighting. These ignorant and damaging labels have now been discredited, thanks largely to you and the more enlightened members of our society. But there is still, alas, a large Squareland left where growing girls are told from the age of twelve onward not only by their mothers but by the mass media that marriage is the only valid female goal and that Career is a dirty word.

Even now—even when you here know how silly it is (at least, I 12 hope you do), most parents hear wedding bells the minute a girl is born, most parents see an executive office when a boy is born, and the relentless conditioning starts on its merry way. Educate a girl for the marriage market, educate a boy for success. That you, as a human being, as a separate identity, may not want or fit in with either of these goals is considered not a sign of independence but of deviation—pointing to the couch or—in social terms—failure.

That is why these same parents—and they are still a majority—are 13 bewildered, depressed, or plain horrified when their adolescents openly refuse to accept these goals or to share any common identity with any past. Who on earth, their parents moan, will marry this stringy girl with her false eyelashes and shuffling gait? Who will employ this bearded boy with his grunts and records, his pop and pot? On the other hand, how gratified are parents when their clean-cut athletic sons get high marks and their clean and pretty daughters marry the clean-cut boys who get good jobs?

You know, I pity you. I pity you for reasons you might not suspect. I 14 pity you because your search for self has been made so self-conscious. You are overexposed in and by the mass media, which never for one instant night and day stop telling you what you are and who you are. With us, decades ago, there was no radio and no television. As adolescents we seldom read papers (they never reported on us) or magazines. The word "teenager," thank God, never existed. From twelve to seventeen we were painful to our parents and not very attractive to ourselves. Our skins and bodies did strange things and we felt strange things. The world paid no attention to us. It didn't interview us, quote us, and ask our advice. We didn't expect it to. We had twenty-five to fifty cents a week to spend for allowance (rich kids got a dollar), but who needed it? Books were in the house or you could borrow them, movies were a quarter, and if you were lucky your family took you to occasional plays or concerts. School was sometimes boring, but we expected it to be. Nobody told us learning ought to be fun. When it was—well, great!

Nothing much external happened, except for trips with the family 15 and meetings with friends. There was a lot of unfilled, unstructured, unplanned free time—with no messages coming in from anywhere to distract us, no entertainment at arm's length, no guidance counselors or psychiatrists to tell us what was bugging us. We had a vast amount of inner space to fill by ourselves. In this inner space there was room and time for that very tender, very vulnerable thing called "I" to be born—and grow.

For there are really two births—the first physical, the second 16 spiritual. Both share something in common: Premature expulsion, premature exposure, can damage both foetus and soul. The prenatal fluid that protects the foetus until it is ready for air has its counterpart in the secret world of the yet unborn identity.

Now I want to make it quite clear that this secret world of child 17 and adolescent is not a matter of protection from reality. Just because a child may grow up in the relative security of home and school and neighborhood doesn't mean that the human comedy-tragedy is not a part of daily life. You are not cut off from experience because the world you live in is physically small. On the contrary, you can be put off from real experience because the world has become too large.

And that is precisely why I pity you. You stand naked and exposed 18 in too large a world, and that prenatal sac of your soul has been so repeatedly punctured by external influences, persuasions, and pressures that it must take superhuman will to keep yourself intact. Many of you don't. Or at least you find the only answer to a fragmented self in a fragmented life—or a withdrawal from life.

How, in any case, are you ever going to know what you are or who 19 you are when these hundreds of voices are doing the job *for* you? How do you know how much of what you think and do is what you *really* think and want to do, or how much is the feedback from what you hear about yourselves—daily, hourly? A lot of it, of course, is true.

You *are* the new power, if only in numbers. You *are* rich, if only in 20 dollars. You *are* smarter than your parents, if only in acquired knowledge. A lot of you take drugs and pills or cop out in communal huddles, living on handouts. I question whether you are more interested in sex than we were, or even more active. The difference here is that it's now so easy to come by, in beds as well as in books, that it may mean less. Obstacles are great aphrodisiacs.

I would like to think that those of you who hate war are a majority. 21

I would like to think that those of you who believe that sweeping changes must be made in our whole social, legal, political and economic life are a majority and an acting majority at that.

Whatever you are, you can't do anything about making a better **22** society and a better world until you are a productive human being. And you can't be a productive human being, sorting the world out, until you sort yourself out. Until you really attain an expansion of consciousness—not of another world, through hallucination, but of this world through illumination.

Not long ago Professor Lettwin, that dynamic free-wheeling bear **23** of M.I.T., told an audience of high school students and undergraduates in Boston that in order to do what they wanted to do—to change the disastrous drift of society—they would have to keep their wits about them. You must be conscious, he exhorted, you must at all times keep your sense of judgment intact. Anything that blurs, that weakens your judgmental values, will, in time, make you ineffective. Only your judgment, consciously arrived at, only the intellect and senses in the service of human compassion—will take you where you want to go—where this new society *must* go.

This I would also passionately advocate. As a long-time rebel, a **24** seeker of new adventures, a destroyer of old myths, I have come to believe that this total awareness is the greatest single attribute of identity, and most preciously to be guarded. That it can be chemically achieved I would very much doubt. For moments, maybe. For the long haul, no. It is one thing—and who doesn't need it?—to seek escape from the pain of total awareness—in drink or pot. It is another to take the quick exit from reality with the distinct possibility that you may not make the reentry back. Or that if you do, you may never be yourself—your real, your useful, your creative self—again. Fly Now—Pay Later.

The price of conscious awareness is stiff—but not that stiff. The **25** price is a very hard look at yourself—alone, and not bolstered by a crowd, a tribe—or even—a wife. And here is where I'm going to stick this already battered neck further out—on the institution of matrimony.

Your parents, I would imagine, consider your generation incom- **26** prehensible, sometimes frightening, and certainly unconventional. Everything you wear, grow on your face or head, think, believe, do, is way out of their norm.

Except marriage. In a world of undreamed-of scope and opportu- **27** nity and choice, most of you do exactly what your parents did in a much more limited world. You rush to the altar to tie the legal tie from the age of eighteen onward to a mate no older. Here you are in the full flower of body and mind (and I speak of both sexes) and with the only pure freedom of action you will ever know, and you tie yourself to one mate and one hearth before you know who you are.

If you're lucky, you will find yourselves *through* each other—the **28** ideal nature of love, the true—and rare—blessing of marriage.

If you're not lucky—and the evidence would call you a majority— **29** you will be two half-persons, half-grown, prematurely bound, inhibiting each other's growth, choking up the road to your full development as a human being.

Many of our laws and institutions, as you well know, have not yet 30 caught up with reality ... the fact that men and women cannot be codified. So long as we do others no harm, how we choose to live is our own affair, and ours alone. How *you* choose to live is yours alone. And if you are able to bring about an intelligent society—I avoid the word "great"—one of the most important things you will have to do is remove the senseless stigmas that still prevail against single men or single women, and against whatever kind of love is the product of deep inner need.

One of your great influences already is that in your new sense of 31 community—in part forced upon you by isolation from your elders— you have managed to blur already many of the lines of demarcation— between races, between sexes, between thought and feeling, between feeling and action—which have trapped the former generations in patterns of sterility. The best of you have not only discovered your conscience, but are living it.

But apart from the terrible issues of the day—to which the best of 32 you address your conscience—war in Vietnam, the brutal war in the streets—how much are you living it as individuals, how much in group conformity?

How brave, how independent are you when you are alone? I ask 33 this chiefly of my own sex, for I wonder whether girls now really know and want the chances and choices that are open to them, or whether they have been so conditioned by history and habit that they slip back into the old patterns of their mothers the minute they graduate. Oddly enough, this supposed choice between marriage and a career never bothered my generation as much as it seems to have bothered the postwar ones. And I lay the blame for it on a mass media—mainly television, advertising, and women's magazines—which maintain the fiction that the only valid goal for women is marriage and children and domesticity (with a little community work thrown in), and that women who demand and seek more than this from life are at best unfulfilled and at worst unfeminine. It is about time that we realized that many women make better teachers than mothers, better actresses than wives, better mistresses than housekeepers, better diplomats than cooks. Just as many men are better rakes than lawnmowers and better dreamers than providers. We have lost a great deal of talent and wasted a great many lives in the perpetuation of these myths that are called "the role of men" or "the role of women." And just as you have managed to dissipate some of them in your dress, I hope you will dissipate others in your lives. The only thing you need to aspire to, the only ultimate identity you must discover, is that of a human being. The sex, believe it or not, is secondary.

But in the search for this human identity, I urge you to remember 34 one thing. I said before that our first recognition of it comes when we know we are not like anybody else, that we are unique. That is so.

But we did not spring into this world through galactic 35
explosion—we did not even burst from the head of Zeus.

We came from somewhere. Not just the womb of our mothers and 36
the seeds of our fathers but from a long, long procession of
identities—whose genes we possess.

Whether we like it or not, we bear the past inside us. Good or bad, 37
it cannot be excised, it cannot be rejected ... it should not be.
Humanity is a continuous process, and without a past there is no
future.

In your worship of Now, in your fierce insistence that only the 38
present exists, that you are new on the face of the earth, owing nothing
to history—you are cheating yourself. You are not only denying
evolution but limiting your future.

You may say you have nothing in common with the preceding 39
generation, you may lay the blame for the present entirely on their
shoulders and on the mistakes of the past. But what of the others who
came before? What of the great rebels, the great innovators, the great
voices without which no light, no truth would ever have prevailed?
Much of what poets and philosophers and artists and scientists said ten
centuries ago is as valid now as it was then. Where would you be,
where would we be, without them?

On a much humbler level, I remember the photograph albums so 40
many families kept when I was a child. There, in our own, were these
strange faces and strange clothes of the dead who preceded me: the tall,
gaunt old baker in Poland, the opera singer in Germany, the immi-
grant furniture dealer in New York, the violinist in Breslau, the
General near Kiel, the incredible web of cells and genes contained in
my own self.

It took me more than twenty years to realize that they lived in me, 41
that I was part of them, and that in spite of distance, time, and
difference, I was part of them. I was not, in short, alone.

And neither are you. I suppose what I am asking for here is that, 42
along with your pride of generation, you somehow maintain compassion for those who preceded you as well as for those who will come after
you.

If you will, this is a community just as important as any living 43
community of your own age and time, and if you deny your connection
with it, you deny evolution, you deny the human race.

Don't play it too cool. The ultimate pattern of life is immense, there 44
are other worlds in other galaxies that may have far transcended ours,
and if you aren't turned on more by a shower of meteors than by an
electric circus, you're half dead already.

You won't find yourself in a crowded room. You may find yourself 45
under the crowded sky of night, where—if you attach yourself to a
single star—you will discover that you are one of many millions, but
still—One.

Listen to your own drum and march to it. You may fall on your 46
face—but then, anybody who never does is—Nobody!

Study Questions

1. For what kind of audience does Mannes write?
2. Is this essay propagandistic, trying to convert the reader to a point of view, or does it present an objective view of the subject, letting the reader reach his or her own conclusion?
3. What is Mannes's main point? Express it in one sentence.
4. Mannes uses short sentences to communicate quick judgments. Does this add to or detract from her main theme?
5. Comment on Mannes's use of sentence fragments and single words; on her use of exclamation points, question marks, dashes, and parentheses; on her use of italics.
6. How effective is Mannes's use of the first-person point of view, her directly addressing the reader, her use of the imperative?

The Role of the Undesirables
ERIC HOFFER

Eric Hoffer (1902–   ) was born in New York City. A philosophical writer who has had a lifelong passion for books, he has been compared to such diverse personalities as Machiavelli and the Duc de La Rochefoucauld. Hoffer early felt the stifling complexities of the big city and moved to California at the first opportunity. There he worked in a box factory, as a migrant field hand, in the gold mines and in construction, finally coming to rest in San Francisco, where he was a longshoreman for some twenty years. At present he holds weekly seminars at the University of California at Berkeley, where he has refused a full-time professorship. A logical, somewhat cold, and pessimistic writer, Hoffer nonetheless sees great potential for human growth. His first book, *The True Believer* (1951), won for him the Commonwealth Club of California Gold Medal in 1952. Other publications include *The Passionate State of Mind* (1955), *First Things, Last Things* (1971), *Reflections on the Human Condition* (1972), and *Before the Sabbath* (1976). *Working and Thinking on the Waterfront,* a journal of his experiences with longshoremen, was published in 1969.

In the winter of 1934, I spent several weeks in a federal **1** transient camp in California. These camps were originally established by Governor Rolph in the early days of the Depression to care for the single homeless unemployed of the state. In 1934 the federal government took charge of the camps for a time, and it was then that I first heard of them.

How I happened to get into one of the camps is soon told. Like **2** thousands of migrant agricultural workers in California I then followed the crops from one part of the state to the other. Early in 1934 I arrived in the town of El Centro, in the Imperial Valley. I had been given a free ride on a truck from San Diego, and it was midnight when the truck driver dropped me on the outskirts of El Centro. I spread my bedroll by the side of the road and went to sleep. I had hardly dozed off when the rattle of a motorcycle drilled itself into my head and a policeman was bending over me saying, "Roll up, Mister." It looked as though I was in for something; it happened now and then that the police got overzealous and rounded up the freight trains. But this time the cop had no such thought. He said, "Better go over to the federal shelter and get yourself a bed and maybe some breakfast." He directed me to the place.

I found a large hall, obviously a former garage, dimly lit, and **3** packed with cots. A concert of heavy breathing shook the thick air. In a small office near the door, I was registered by a middle-aged clerk. He informed me that this was the "receiving shelter" where I would get one night's lodging and breakfast. The meal was served in the camp nearby. Those who wished to stay on, he said, had to enroll in the camp. He then gave me three blankets and excused himself for not having a vacant cot. I spread the blankets on the cement floor and went to sleep.

I awoke with dawn amid a chorus of coughing, throat-clearing, the **4** sound of running water, and the intermittent flushing of toilets in the back of the hall. There were about fifty of us, of all colors and ages, all of us more or less ragged and soiled. The clerk handed out tickets for breakfast, and we filed out to the camp located several blocks away, near the railroad tracks.

From the outside the camp looked like a cross between a factory **5** and a prison. A high fence of wire enclosed it, and inside were three large sheds and a huge boiler topped by a pillar of black smoke. Men in blue shirts and dungarees were strolling across the sandy yard. A ship's bell in front of one of the buildings announced breakfast. The regular camp members—there was a long line of them—ate first. Then we filed in through the gate, handing our tickets to the guard.

It was a good, plentiful meal. After breakfast our crowd dispersed. I **6** heard some say that the camps in the northern part of the state were better, that they were going to catch a northbound freight. I decided to try this camp in El Centro.

My motives in enrolling were not crystal clear. I wanted to clean **7** up. There were shower baths in the camp and wash tubs and plenty of soap. Of course I could have bathed and washed my clothes in one of the irrigation ditches, but here in the camp I had a chance to rest, get the wrinkles out of my belly, and clean up at leisure. In short, it was the easiest way out.

A brief interview at the camp office and a physical examination **8** were all the formalities for enrollment.

There were some two hundred men in the camp. They were the **9** kind I had worked and traveled with for years. I even saw familiar faces—men I had worked with in orchards and fields. Yet my predominant feeling was one of strangeness. It was my first experience of life in intimate contact with a crowd. For it is one thing to work and travel with a gang, and quite another thing to eat, sleep, and spend the greater part of the day cheek by jowl with two hundred men.

I found myself speculating on a variety of subjects: the reasons for **10** their chronic bellyaching and beefing—it was more a ritual than the expression of a grievance; the amazing orderliness of the men; the comic seriousness with which they took their games of cards, checkers, and dominoes; the weird manner of reasoning one overheard now and then. Why, I kept wondering, were these men within the enclosure of a federal transient camp? Were they people temporarily hard up? Would jobs solve all their difficulties? Were we indeed like the people outside?

Up to then I was not aware of being one of a specific species of **11** humanity. I had considered myself simply a human being—not particularly good or bad, and on the whole harmless. The people I worked and traveled with I knew as Americans and Mexicans, whites and Negroes, Northerners and Southerners, etc. It did not occur to me that we were a group possessed of peculiar traits, and that there was something—innate or acquired—in our make-up which made us adopt a particular mode of existence.

It was a slight thing that started me on a new track.   **12**

I got to talking to a mild-looking, elderly fellow. I liked his soft **13** speech and pleasant manner. We swapped trivial experiences. Then he suggested a game of checkers. As we started to arrange the pieces on the board, I was startled by the sight of his crippled right hand. I had not noticed it before. Half of it was chopped off lengthwise, so that the horny stump with its three fingers looked like a hen's leg. I was mortified that I had not noticed the hand until he dangled it, so to speak, before my eyes. It was, perhaps, to bolster my shaken confidence in my powers of observation that I now began paying close attention to the hands of the people around me. The result was astounding. It seemed that every other man had had his hand mangled. There was a man with one arm. Some men limped. One young, good-looking fellow had a wooden leg. It was as though the majority of the men had escaped the snapping teeth of a machine and left part of themselves behind.

It was, I knew, an exaggerated impression. But I began counting **14** the cripples as the men lined up in the yard at mealtime. I found thirty (out of two hundred) crippled either in arms or legs. I immediately sensed where the counting would land me. The simile preceded the statistical deduction: we in the camp were a human junk pile.

I began evaluating my fellow tramps as human material, and for **15** the first time in my life I became face-conscious. There were some good

faces, particularly among the young. Several of the middle-aged and
the old looked healthy and well preserved. But the damaged and
decayed faces were in the majority. I saw faces that were wrinkled, or
bloated, or raw as the surface of a peeled plum. Some of the noses were
purple and swollen, some broken, some pitted with enlarged pores.
There were many toothless mouths (I counted seventy-eight). I noticed
eyes that were blurred, faded, opaque, or bloodshot. I was struck by the
fact that the old men, even the very old, showed their age mainly in the
face. Their bodies were still slender and erect. One little man over sixty
years of age looked a mere boy when seen from behind. The shriveled
face joined to a boyish body made a startling sight.

My diffidence had now vanished. I was getting to know everybody 16
in the camp. They were a friendly and talkative lot. Before many
weeks I knew some essential fact about practically everyone.

And I was continually counting. Of the two hundred men in the 17
camp there were approximately as follows:

Cripples	30
Confirmed drunkards	60
Old men (55 and over)	50
Youths under twenty	10
Men with chronic diseases, heart, asthma, TB	12
Mildly insane	4
Constitutionally lazy	6
Fugitives from justice	4
Apparently normal	70

(The numbers do not tally up to two hundred since some of the men
were counted twice or even thrice—as cripples and old, or as old and
confirmed drunks, etc.)

In other words: less than half the camp inmates (seventy normal, 18
plus ten youths) were unemployed workers whose difficulties would be
at an end once jobs were available. The rest (60 per cent) had handicaps
in addition to unemployment.

I also counted fifty war veterans, and eighty skilled workers 19
representing sixteen trades. All the men (including those with chronic
diseases) were able to work. The one-armed man was a wizard with the
shovel.

I did not attempt any definite measurement of character and 20
intelligence. But it seemed to me that the intelligence of the men in the
camp was certainly not below the average. And as to character, I found
much forbearance and genuine good humor. I never came across one
instance of real viciousness. Yet, on the whole, one would hardly say
that these men were possessed of strong characters. Resistance,
whether to one's appetites or to the ways of the world, is a chief factor
in the shaping of character; and the average tramp is, more or less, a
slave of his few appetites. He generally takes the easiest way out.

The connection between our makeup and our mode of existence as 21
migrant workers presented itself now with some clarity.

The majority of us were incapable of holding onto a steady job. We 22 lacked self-discipline and the ability to endure monotonous, leaden hours. We were probably misfits from the very beginning. Our contact with a steady job was not unlike a collision. Some of us were maimed, some got frightened and ran away, and some took to drink. We inevitably drifted in the direction of least resistance—the open road. The life of a migrant worker is varied and demands only a minimum of self-discipline. We were now in one of the drainage ditches of ordered society. We could not keep a footing in the ranks of respectability and were washed into the slough of our present existence.

Yet, I mused, there must be in this world a task with an appeal so **23** strong that were we to have a taste of it we would hold on and be rid for good of our restlessness.

My stay in the camp lasted about four weeks. Then I found a **24** haying job not far from town, and finally, in April, when the hot winds began blowing, I shouldered my bedroll and took the highway to San Bernardino.

It was the next morning, after I had got a lift to Indio by truck, that **25** a new idea began to take hold of me. The highway out of Indio leads through waving date groves, fragrant grapefruit orchards, and lush alfalfa fields; then, abruptly, passes into a desert of white sand. The sharp line between garden and desert is very striking. The turning of white sand into garden seemed to me an act of magic. This, I thought, was a job one would jump at—even the men in the transient camps. They had the skill and ability of the average American. But their energies, I felt, could be quickened only by a task that was spectacular, that had in it something of the miraculous. The pioneer task making the desert flower would certainly fill the bill.

Tramps as pioneers? It seemed absurd. Every man and child in **26** California knows that the pioneers had been giants, men of boundless courage and indomitable spirit. However, as I strode on across the white sand, I kept mulling the idea over.

Who were the pioneers? Who were the men who left their homes **27** and went into the wilderness? A man rarely leaves a soft spot and goes deliberately in search of hardship and privation. People become attached to the places they live in; they drive roots. A change of habitat is a painful act of uprooting. A man who has made good and has a standing in his community stays put. The successful businessmen, farmers, and workers usually stayed where they were. Who then left for the wilderness and the unknown? Obviously those who had not made good: men who went broke or never amounted to much; men who though possessed of abilities were too impulsive to stand the daily grind; men who were slaves of their appetites—drunkards, gamblers, and woman-chasers; outcasts—fugitives from justice and ex-jailbirds. There were no doubt some who went in search of health—men suffering with TB, asthma, heart trouble. Finally there was a sprinkling of young and middle-aged in search of adventure.

All these people craved change, some probably actuated by the **28** naive belief that a change in place brings with it a change in luck. Many wanted to go to a place where they were not known and there make a new beginning. Certainly they did not go out deliberately in search of hard work and suffering. If in the end they shouldered enormous tasks, endured unspeakable hardships, and accomplished the impossible, it was because they had to. They became men of action on the run. They acquired strength and skill in the inescapable struggle for existence. It was a question of do or die. And once they tasted the joy of achievement, they craved for more.

Clearly the same types of people which now swelled the ranks of 29 migratory workers and tramps had probably in former times made up the bulk of the pioneers. As a group the pioneers were probably as unlike the present-day "native sons"—their descendants—as one could well imagine. Indeed, were there to be today a new influx of typical pioneers, twin brothers of the forty-niners only in a modern garb, the citizens of California would consider it a menace to health, wealth, and morals.

With few exceptions, this seems to be the case in the settlement of 30 all new countries. Ex-convicts were the vanguard in the settling of Australia. Exiles and convicts settled Siberia. In this country, a large portion of our earlier and later settlers were failures, fugitives, and felons. The exceptions seemed to be those who were motivated by religious fervor, such as the Pilgrim Fathers and the Mormons.

Although quite logical, this train of thought seemed to me then a 31 wonderful joke. In my exhilaration I was eating up the road in long strides, and I reached the oasis of Elim in what seemed almost no time. A passing empty truck picked me up just then and we thundered through Banning and Beaumont, all the way to Riverside. From there I walked the seven miles to San Bernardino.

Somehow, this discovery of a family likeness between tramps and 32 pioneers took a firm hold on my mind. For years afterward it kept intertwining itself with a mass of observations which on the face of them had no relation to either tramps or pioneers. And it moved me to speculate on subjects in which, up to then, I had no real interest, and of which I knew very little.

I talked with several old-timers—one of them over eighty and a 33 native son—in Sacramento, Placerville, Auburn, and Fresno. It was not easy, at first, to obtain the information I was after. I could not make my questions specific enough. "What kind of people were the early settlers and miners?" I asked. They were a hard-working, tough lot, I was told. They drank, fought, gambled, and wenched. They were big-hearted, grasping, profane, and God-fearing. They wallowed in luxury, or lived on next to nothing with equal ease. They were the salt of the earth.

Still it was not clear what manner of people they were.   34

If I asked what they looked like, I was told of whiskers, broad- 35 brimmed hats, high boots, shirts of many colors, sun-tanned faces, horny hands. Finally I asked: "What group of people in present-day California most closely resembles the pioneers?" The answer, usually after some hesitation, was invariably the same: "The Okies and the fruit tramps."

I tried also to evaluate the tramps as potential pioneers by 36 watching them in action. I saw them fell timber, clear firebreaks, build rock walls, put up barracks, build dams and roads, handle steam shovels, bulldozers, tractors, and concrete mixers. I saw them put in a hard day's work after a night of steady drinking. They sweated and growled, but they did the work. I saw tramps elevated to positions of authority as foremen and superintendents. Then I could notice a remarkable physical transformation: a seamed face gradually smoothed out and the skin showed a healthy hue; an indifferent mouth became firm and expressive; dull eyes cleared and brightened; voices actually changed; there was even an apparent increase in stature. In almost no time these promoted tramps looked as if they had been on top all of their lives. Yet sooner or later I would meet up with them again in a railroad yard, on some skid row, or in the fields—tramps again. It was usually the same story: they got drunk or lost their temper and were fired, or they got fed up with the steady job and quit. Usually, when a tramp becomes a foreman, he is careful in his treatment of the tramps under him; he knows the day of reckoning is never far off.

In short, it was not difficult to visualize the tramps as pioneers. I **37** reflected that if they were to find themselves in a singlehanded life-and-death struggle with nature, they would undoubtedly display persistence. For the pressure of responsibility and the heat of battle steel a character. The inadaptable would perish, and those who survived would be the equal of the successful pioneers.

I also considered the few instances of pioneering engineered from **38** above—that is to say, by settlers possessed of lavish means, who were classed with the best where they came from. In these instances, it seemed to me, the resulting social structure was inevitably precarious. For pioneering deluxe usually results if a plantation society, made up of large landowners and peon labor, either native or imported. Very often there is a racial cleavage between the two. The colonizing activities of the Teutonic barons in the Baltic, the Hungarian nobles in Transylvania, the English in Ireland, the planters in our South, and present-day plantation societies in Kenya and other British and Dutch colonies are cases in point. Whatever their merits, they are characterized by poor adaptability. They are likely eventually to be broken up either by a peon revolution or by an influx of typical pioneers—who are usually of the same race or nation as the landowners. The adjustment is not necessarily implemented by war. Even our old South, had it not been for the complication of secession, might eventually have attained stability without war: namely, by the activity of its own poor whites or by influx of the indigent from other states.

There is in us a tendency to judge a race, a nation, or an **39** organization by its least worthy members. The tendency is manifestly perverse and unfair; yet it has some justification. For the quality and destiny of a nation is determined to a considerable extent by the nature and potentialities of its inferior elements. The inert mass of a nation is in its middle section. The industrious, decent, well-to-do, and satisfied middle classes—whether in cities or on the land—are worked upon and shaped by minorities at both extremes: the best and the worst.

The superior individual, whether in politics, business, industry, **40** science, literature, or religion, undoubtedly plays a major role in the shaping of a nation. But so do the individuals at the other extreme: the poor, the outcasts, the misfits, and those who are in the grip of some overpowering passion. The importance of these inferior elements as formative factors lies in the readiness with which they are swayed in any direction. This peculiarity is due to their inclination to take risks ("not giving a damn") and their propensity for united action. They crave to merge their drab, wasted lives into something grand and complete. Thus they are the first and most fervent adherents of new religions, political upheavals, patriotic hysteria, gangs, and mass rushes to new lands.

And the quality of a nation—its innermost worth—is made man- 41 ifest by its dregs as they rise to the top: by how brave they are, how humane, how orderly, how skilled, how generous, how independent or servile; by the bounds they will not transgress in their dealings with man's soul, with truth, and with honor.

The average American of today bristles with indignation when he 42 is told that this country was built, largely, by hordes of undesirables from Europe. Yet, far from being derogatory, this statement, if true, should be a cause for rejoicing, should fortify our pride in the stock from which we have sprung.

This vast continent with its towns, farms, factories, dams, 43 aqueducts, docks, railroads, highways, powerhouses, schools, and parks is the handiwork of common folk from the Old World, where for centuries men of their kind had been as beasts of burden, the property of the masters—kings, nobles, and priest—and with no will and no aspirations of their own. When on rare occasions one of the lowly had reached the top in Europe he had kept the pattern intact and, if anything, tightened the screws. The stuffy little corporal from Corsica harnessed the lusty forces released by the French Revolution to a gilded state coach, and could think of nothing grander than mixing his blood with that of the Hapsburg masters and establishing a new dynasty. In our day a bricklayer in Italy, a house painter in Germany, and a shoemaker's son in Russia have made themselves masters of their nations; what they did was to re-establish and reinforce the old pattern.

Only here, in America, were the common folk of the Old World 44 given a chance to show what they could do on their own, without a master to push and order them about. History contrived an earth-shaking joke when it lifted by the nape of the neck lowly peasants, shopkeepers, laborers, paupers, jailbirds, and drunks from the midst of Europe, dumped them on a vast, virgin continent and said: "Go to it, it is yours!"

And the lowly were not awed by the magnitude of the task. A 45 hunger for action, pent up for centuries, found an outlet. They went to it with ax, pick, shovel, plow, and rifle; on foot, on horse, in wagons, and on flatboats. They went to it praying, howling, singing, brawling, drinking and fighting. Make way for the people! This is how I read the statement that this country was built by hordes of undesirables from the Old World.

Small wonder that we in this country have a deeply ingrained faith **46** in human regeneration. We believe that, given a chance, even the degraded and the apparently worthless are capable of constructive work and great deeds. It is a faith founded on experience, not on some idealistic theory. And no matter what some anthropologists, sociologists, and geneticists may tell us, we shall go on believing that man, unlike other forms of life, is not a captive of his past—of his heredity and habits—but is possessed of infinite plasticity, and his potentialities for good and for evil are never wholly exhausted.

Study Questions

1. Hoffer's point is long in coming, in being expressed. Why? How does he nevertheless achieve immediacy in coming to that point?
2. Are the categories presented in paragraph 17 mutually exclusive? How important to the argument is your answer?
3. What function is served by the garden-desert images in paragraph 25?
4. Suggest any two paragraphs that could be effectively combined.
5. What does the first-person point of view contribute to the argument?
6. Hoffer's sentences frequently contain series or lists. What rhetorical purpose do such lists serve?
7. Make a list of noun substitutes for *undesirables*, i.e., *misfits, outcasts, dregs,* and show how Hoffer gives these words a positive connotation.
8. Examine paragraph 30 for sound patterns in Hoffer's style.
9. Comment on Hoffer's use of *undoubtedly* in paragraph 37.

Books and Men
MARTIN BUBER

Martin Buber (1878–1965) was born in Vienna. He studied at the universities of Vienna, Berlin, and Zurich. Although he is now considered one of the most important contemporary Jewish theologians and philosophers, he did not become publicly committed to the Zionist movement and Judaism until 1923, at the University of Leipzig. In Germany he edited *Der Welt, Der Jude,* and *Die Kreatur.* His first teaching position, in 1923, was at the University of Frankfurt. Buber left Germany in 1938 for Palestine, where he lived, teaching at the University of Jerusalem until his retirement in 1951. Among his honorary degrees is one from the University of Aberdeen, Scotland. His books include *I and Thou* (1937), *Between Man and Man* (1947), *Hasidism* (1948), *The Way of Man* (1950), *Israel and Palestine* (1950), *The Eclipse of God* (1952), *Images of Good and Evil* (1953), and *To Hallow This Life* (1958).

If I had been asked in my early youth whether I preferred to 1 have dealings only with men or only with books, my answer would certainly have been in favour of books. In later years this has become less and less the case. Not that I have had so much better experiences with men than with books; on the contrary, purely delightful books even now come my way more often than purely delightful men. But the many bad experiences with men have nourished the meadow of my life as the noblest book could not do, and the good experiences have made the earth into a garden for me. On the other hand, no book does more than remove me into a paradise of great spirits, where my innermost heart never forgets I cannot dwell long, nor even wish that I could do so. For (I must say this straight out in order to be understood) my innermost heart loves the world more than it loves the spirit. I have not, indeed, cleaved to life in the world as I might have; in my relations with it I fail it again and again; again and again I remain guilty towards it for falling short of what it expects of me, and this is partly, to be sure, because I am so indebted to the spirit. I am indebted to the spirit as I am to myself, but I do not, strictly speaking, love it, even as I do not, strictly speaking, love myself. I do not in reality love him who has seized me with his heavenly clutch and holds me fast; rather I love her, the "world," who comes again and again to meet me and extends to me a pair of fingers.

Both have gifts to share. The former showers on me his manna of 2 books; the latter extends to me the brown bread on whose crust I break my teeth, a bread of which I can never have enough: men. Aye, these tousle-heads and good-for-nothings, how I love them! I revere books— those that I really read—too much to be able to love them. But in the most venerable of living men I always find more to love than to revere: I find in him something of this world, that is simply there as the spirit never can be there. The spirit hovers above me powerfully and pours out his exalted gift of speech, books; how glorious, how weird! But she, the human world, needs only to cast a wordless smile, and I cannot live without her. She is mute; all the prattle of men yields no word such as sounds forth constantly out of books. And I listen to it all in order to receive the silence that penetrates to me through it, the silence of the creature. But just the human creature! That creature means a mixture. Books are pure, men are mixed; books are spirit and word, pure spirit and purified word; men are made up of prattle and silence, and their silence is not that of animals but of men. Out of the human silence behind the prattle the spirit whispers to you, the spirit *as soul*. She, she is the beloved.

Here is an infallible test. Imagine yourself in a situation where you 3 are alone, wholly alone on earth, and you are offered one of the two, books or men. I often hear men prizing their solitude, but that is only because there are still men somewhere on earth, even though in the far distance. I knew nothing of books when I came forth from the womb of my mother, and I shall die without books, with another human hand in my own. I do, indeed, close my door at times and surrender myself to a book, but only because I can open the door again and see a human being looking at me.

Study Questions

1. Buber contrasts books and men. Although his essay is entitled "Books and Men," most of it is a discussion of books *or* men. How do Buber's sentence patterns reinforce the contrast?
2. Find examples of metaphors and metaphorical language in the first paragraph.
3. Comment on the words with which Buber begins his sentences, particularly on his using *but*.
4. What does Buber mean in paragraph one by "him who has seized me with his heavenly clutch and holds me fast"?
5. Find examples of short sentences and comment on their effectiveness.
6. How "infallible" is the test posited in the last paragraph?
7. How do such words as *dwell, cleave,* and *sounds forth* contribute to the tone of Buber's essay?

The Private Dialect of Husbands and Wives

ANTHONY BURGESS

Anthony Burgess (1917–) was born in Manchester, England, and received a B.A. from Manchester University. He has taught school, served as an officer in Malaya and Borneo, produced plays, and been a jazz pianist. His critical works include *English Literature: A Survey for Students* (1958), *The Novel Today* (1963), *Language Made Plain* (1964), *Re Joyce* (1965), and *Shakespeare* (1970). His more important novels are *Time for a Tiger* (1956), *The Doctor Is Sick* (1960), *A Clockwork Orange* (1962), *Honey for the Bears* (1963), *Inside Mr. Enderby* (1963), *Nothing Like the Sun* (1964), *The Long Day Wanes* (1965), *A Vision of Battlements* (1966), *The Clockwork Testament, or Enderby's End* (1974), *The Napoleon Symphony* (1974), and *Moses* (1976). Burgess, who lives in Monte Carlo, provided the language for the apemen in the 1982 film *Quest for Fire*.

I remember an old film about Alcatraz or Sing Sing or 1
somewhere, in which Wallace Beery, having organized the killing of several wardens, broken up the prison hospital, and kicked the deputy governor in the guts, said in his defense: "I was only kiddin'." I've never gone so far, but I fear that my own kind of kidding may be the death of me. Like giving a college lecture on a purely fictitious Elizabethan dramatist called Grasmere Tadworth (1578–1621). Like writing a pseudonymous review of one of my own books. Like, when asked by the editors of *Who's Who* to give the names of my clubs, answering with Toby's Gym, the Nudorama Strip Club, the Naked City and so on. This is not really funny. When the same editors asked me for hobbies, I gave *wife* as one of them, and they let that go through. There it is now, perpetuated from edition to edition, waiting for *Who Was Who,* and sooner or later I was bound to be asked what the hell I meant, mean.

It's tempting to retreat into that high-school thicket of evasive- 2
ness, the dictionary. Thus, my wife is a small species of falcon, *falco subbuteo.* My wife is a horse of middle size, a pacing horse, a stick or figure of a horse on which boys ride. My wife is (Old French *hobin)* a stupid fellow. All right, all right, stop fooling about; try the definition "favourite pursuit" and don't for God's sake, say: "Ha, ha, I stopped pursuing her a long time ago."

Originally appeared in *Vogue Magazine,* June 1968. Reprinted by permission of the author.

I recognize a number of horrible possibilities, most of them 3
appropriate to the evenings and weekends after the honeymoon, but
those are not really applicable. The other possibilities are sentimental,
so I reject those too. Popular songs used to approach the woman-in-
one's-life as something of either gold or silver—nubile nymph or
fulfilled mother—but they never hymned her in middle age. In middle
age she has none of the properties of a cult. Not being an icon, she is not
a thing. She resists being used and she resists being worshiped; she is
at her most human.

My wife and I have now been married over twenty-six years, and I 4
recognize that by the standards of our milieu—an artistic one—we
have not played quite fair. We should have changed partners at least
once before now, and there was a time, just after World War Two, when
we tried. That was a period of almost mandatory disruption, and there
was no shortage of new marital opportunities. But things went wrong;
she and I found it more interesting to discuss what we proposed doing
than actually to do it. The prospect of learning somebody else's
language, of building up new mythologies from scratch, seemed shame-
fully wasteful. So we just carried on as we were, carry on as we are.

The lure of a fresh young body seems to me quite irrelevant to 5
questions of marriage; the desire to regenerate one's glands is only a
valid excuse for divorce in communities where adultery is a civil crime.
A marriage is really a civilization in miniature, and one breaks up a
civilization at the peril of one's soul. The vital element in any civilized
community is language, and without language there can be no marriage. By language I mean something more subtle, and much less
useful, than the signals of commerce and the directives of the law: I
mean sounds, noises, grunts, idioms, jokes, bits of silliness, inconse-
quential stupidities which affirm that a special *closed* community
exists. They are a sort of shorthand way of summing up a whole
complex of feelings; time (history, if you like) has given them a
meaning; they totally resist translation.

They can be explained, but then their significance disappears. 6
Explain a joke, and there is no laughter. Explain a poem, and the poem
dissolves into nonsense. If, at a party, I am asked to play the piano, and
if I play the piano for too long, my wife has only to call "Mary!" for me
to stop playing. The reference is to the scene in *Pride and Prejudice*
where Mr. Bennet says, to his piano-playing daughter, "Mary, you
have delighted us long enough." This is a fairly public example of
marital shorthand; the private ones tend to wither in the air of
disclosure. "Blue, honey?" doesn't mean what it says. It's a common
memory from some old trashy woman's magazine story, invoked in
mockery during a needless posture of depression. A reversion to dialect
(the Lancashire *aye*, for instance, instead of the Southern English *yes)*
denotes an instinctive testing of a metropolitan pretension (our own or
someone else's) against the earthier standards of my, or her, regional
background.

I needn't labour this point about the marital language, or about the 7
marital mythology which contains characters from literature or films,

real relatives, the fat Birmingham woman who said "I down't eat enough to keep a baird aloive," the man who comes into the pub belching, dead cats, living dogs, the Holy Ghost. Every married man or woman knows what I mean, but may not be willing to see the importance of it. It can only be built up over a long tract of time, and after a quarter of a century it can become rich, subtle and allusive as Shakespeare's English, though less long-winded. But, unlike literature, it is relaxed, and it promotes relaxation. It can even encompass long silences broken by noises, rude gestures, lines of filthy doggerel, rows of isolated vowel-sounds, bursts of *bel canto,* exaggerated toothpicking.

I seem to derive as much spare-time fulfillment from this sort of 8 unproductive communion as other men get from boats, golf, stamp collecting, and drilling holes in the kitchen wall. Working at home as I do, I'm prepared to waste a whole morning on it; it's a two-way communicative process, which is more than can be said for hammering at a typewriter. It can be helped along with games of Scrabble, gin, doing the crossword in the morning paper, kicking the dog's flank with one's bare foot, seeing how long one can hold one's breath. It ends with guilt and astonishment when the Angelus is tolled at midday from the nearby church; the shopping has not been done, lunch is unprepared (but does one deserve lunch?), not one word has been fired at the sheet in the typewriter. A hobby shouldn't get in the way of one's work.

Am I using this term *hobby* correctly? It probably denotes a 9 subcreative process, like constructing model cathedrals out of matches, and it goes more easily with plurals than with singulars. *Wives,* as with some notable serial polygamist, fits better than *wife,* and it connotes collection as well as sub-creation (very sub: a brief marriage is hardly worth the making). There's also a strong whiff of the impersonal, or depersonalized, about it. I see now that, hobbled by *hobby,* I've presented my wife as a very intricately programmed phatic communicatrix (or whatever the sociological jargon is). Let me straighten out my own usage.

We talk about our hobbies because we're shy of mentioning the 10 word *vocation*—unless we earn money from a vocation, when it promptly turns into a profession. And yet a lot of hobbies are true vocations—the fugues composed by the nightclub pianist, the paintings of a customs officer called Rousseau, the house that the bank clerk builds on summer evenings. In this term *vocation,* creation and religion combine. If one has a vocation for writing lyric poetry when the shop is shut for the day, one may also have a vocation for the priesthood. I think I have a vocation for gaining the maximal social fulfillment, which means communicative fulfillment, which means even a kind of spiritual fulfillment, out of living with a particular woman. But, frightened of the big words, and also incurably facetious, I have to talk of my wife as a hobby—the culminating item in a list that contains piano-playing, musical composition, and language-learning. Yet the term *hobby* is not really inept, since it implies enjoyment and not just, like *vocation,* a sort of pretension to uplift. One of Kingsley

Amis's characters talks about going to bed with his wife as being ennobling but also good fun—as though some stunning work of literature were also a good read. That will do pretty well for most levels of marital intercourse.

My *Who's Who* avowal has been taken by some people as a 11 misprint. Once I had to give an after-dinner speech, and the chairman, introducing me, said that *wife* was undoubtedly meant to be *wine*. The right facetious response is to say that a wife transubstantiates life into wine. The right highbrow response would take in the new communication philosophers—Marshall McLuhan in America and Roland Barthes in France—and point out that the basis of living is semiological, which means concerned with all possible modes of human signalling—from vulgar lip-noises to sublime poetry. In a marriage, you have an opportunity to erect the most subtle and exact semiological system civilization is capable of. It takes a long time, but it's worth it. So, apart from what else she is, my wife continues to be my non-professional vocation. Or, not to leave the fun out, my hobby. I hope to God I continue to be hers.

Study Questions

1. Identify the thesis statement of this essay.
2. How does the word *dialect* figure literally and whimsically in this essay?
3. To what end does the series of anecdotes in the opening paragraph lead? Are the introductory paragraphs genuinely funny or merely cute?
4. How would you describe the tone of Burgess's essay?
5. Can you find any puns?
6. Burgess uses parentheses more than most authors. Are they appropriate?
7. How does Burgess redefine *hobby, marriage, vocation?*
8. Does Burgess stop or provide a conclusion? How does the reversal in the last sentence alter the by now firmly established tone of the essay?

Love Me but Leave Me

ANN BAYER

Ann Bayer (1941–   ) was born in Cleveland, Ohio. She received
a B.A. from Sarah Lawrence College in 1963 and has made her
living as a free-lance writer ever since. "Department Store,"
originally published in *Harper's*, was included in the 1975 volume
of the O. Henry Memorial Award stories. Her stories and articles
have appeared in the *New York Times, Cosmopolitan, Seventeen,*
the *Saturday Evening Post,* and *Life,* where she is currently a staff
writer.

The other day in Bloomingdale's I happened to see a man I 1
had adored from November of 1968 through January of 1969. I was
riding the down escalator and he was riding the up, and as we neared
each other I experienced a feeling of giddiness, and my breathing
became rapid and shallow. Impulsively I laid my hand upon my heart.
"Feets, don't fail me now," I whispered. We passed without his even
seeing me. I considered racing up the down escalator and calling out to
him, but I'd forgotten his name.

Such chance encounters only remind me of how far I have come. 2
After that first shock of recognition, I soon regained my customary
composure and began to wonder how I ever could have eroticized what
was, after all, just another face in the crowd.

And conversely, how could *I* end up meaning nothing to a person to 3
whom I was once everything? Recently I boarded a crosstown bus and
sat down across from an ophthalmologist who, in 1971, rapturously
informed me that I was his Helen of Troy. Now, after giving me a
cursory glance, he returned his attention to the life insurance ad above
my head. This spring I went back to my hometown, Cleveland, and
phoned the boy in whose parked car I had spent most of the Eisenhower
Administration. "What did you say your name was?" he asked.
"Forgive me if I seem a little vague. Ronald is due home any minute
and my Bavarian cream *au chocolat* absolutely refuses to gel."

It has been my experience that falling in love is a matter of 4
proximity and timing, and has little—and often nothing—to do with
what the loved one is like. To me love is an illusion usually followed by
disillusion. Which is why, of all the reasons I'm grateful to the
women's movement, I'm grateful to it most for sanctioning spinster-

Reprinted by permission.

hood. If I weren't single, I'd be married, almost certainly to one of the men out of love with whom I have long since fallen.

I also want to thank the movement for showing me that just because I'm a member of the second sex, it doesn't mean I have to be the secondary half of the double standard. No longer am I susceptible to the charms of men who do me wrong. Take the fellow in Bloomingdale's. While I still cannot recall his name, I do recall that, at his urging, I once walked naked at midnight through the corridors of a Holiday Inn in North Platte, Nebraska, to fetch him a Coke from a vending machine. And I used my own quarter, too. That was over a decade ago. Today I'd never allow myself to be cast as the Lady Godiva of North Platte. As a feminist, I've become much more selective about the men in my past.

I believe in what Colette called "conjugal courtesy"—the determination of a husband and wife always to be at their best with each other. Only most of the conjugal courtesy I've observed has taken place between two people who, if they're married at all, are each married to somebody else.

I'm one of those people who likes her encounters brief and her obsessions magnificent. The long haul just isn't my style. As soon as the magic goes out of a relationship, I go with it. One summer on Martha's Vineyard I formed an attachment to a divorced poetry professor (July of 1974 to August of 1974). All was well until the afternoon he offered to drive me into town to buy groceries. I accepted, forgetting that the ambience of the A&P is not conducive to love. I wheeled my cart gaily up and down the aisles, selecting only those items that might betoken a woman of fascination—capers, Brie, leeks, club soda—while avoiding the paper products I desperately needed and the peanut butter I desperately wanted. Imagine my consternation when at the checkout counter I discovered my companion's cart piled high with toilet paper, Baggies, aluminum foil and a family-size jar of Jif. It was clear that my regard for his sensibilities far exceeded his for mine. The same was true that evening when we played Scrabble. How painstakingly I abstained from forming words that might make a negative impression, while he (a teacher of poetry) went right ahead and formed POLYP, OOZE, LEECH and the depressing seven-letter word DISEASE. By so doing, he managed to win the game and lose me.

Three years have passed since then and I'm back now on Martha's Vineyard. Occasionally I drop by to see the professor. We sit at his kitchen table, a sad-eyed Swinburne expert and an aging bachelorette, and talk about old times. "Why did you run away like that?" he asks me. I sigh. How can I explain that I wanted romance and he gave me Reynolds Wrap, that I wanted passion and he gave me POLYP?

Of course, as I become more particular, the men in my life become fewer and farther between. Even when a man is a pleasure to be with, I invariably find that when I am with him the pleasure quickly becomes too persistent. The most charming man I ever knew was a television quiz-show moderator (April of 1970 to June of 1970). At the time I had access to the Time Inc. morgue, and one day I signed out his file, which bulged with press releases and newspaper clippings. Spreading out everything in front of me, I gave myself over to the ecstatic contemplation of the beloved. The only trouble was that, once in possession of his vital statistics, I ceased having any need to possess *him*. He had turned out to be less than the sum of his parts. A little while later I gave him his walking papers. Sometimes as I'm twisting the channel turner, I see his face or hear his voice ("Okey-dokey, shall we have our first contestant?") and I'm astonished at the readiness with which I switch to another station.

I once read a play in which a missionary's wife says of her husband: 10 "To the presence of Mr. Banks, delightful as it is, I much prefer the absence of Mr. Banks." How well I know.

Study Questions

1. How does the passing of time, or the concept of time help organize Bayer's essay?
2. Pinpoint some of the sources of Bayer's humor.
3. Most good writers are specific. What do such specifics as the crosstown bus, the Holiday Inn, and Baggies contribute to the essay?
4. What is the topic sentence of paragraph 7?
5. Bayer thanks the women's movement. Does she seem liberated? Why or why not?

Violets

EDNA O'BRIEN

Edna O'Brien (1932–   ) was born in Ireland and was certified there as a pharmacist. Writing, however, took her out from behind the counter. She has published widely in all genres. Her novels include *The Country Girls* (1960), *Girls in Their Married Bliss* (1968), *Casualties of Peace* (1966), *A Pagan Place* (1970), *Nights* (1974), and *A Rose in The Heart* (1979). She has written for the stage, television, and the movies—such screenplays as *The Girl with Green Eyes, Three into Two Won't Go,* and *Zee & Co.* O'Brien's most recent collection of short stories was *Mrs. Reinhardt and Other Stories* (1980), and in 1981 she completed a biographical study of James and Nora Joyce.

In an hour he is due. In that hour I have tasks to perform 1
and they, of course, revolve around him. I shall lay the fire. I shall lay
it as I learned to as a child. I shall put on twists of paper, small pieces of
coal, and, last of all, a few dry logs. The kindling is a pale wooden chip
basket delivered from the vegetable shop. It was full of Clementines,
and their smell lingers in it like a presence. Christmas is but a month
gone. Then I did not know him; then I thought of myself as having
passed those seesaw states, subject to a man, maybe loving a man, on
tenterhooks because of a man.

Christmas I spent with my grownup children and several old 2
friends in a Tudor house in the North of England. We pulled crackers,
put on ridiculous paper hats, and marvelled at how happy one can be
ripping open packages or finding one's name crusted with a bit of silly
gold glitter. My younger son received a Russian sword and went about
the room lashing the uncomplaining air. We clapped and summoned up
adversaries for him, and he delighted in the game. Next day it snowed
and I thought, as I watched the swirl for an entire afternoon, that I
could watch forever because I had reached a plateau. It was quite
mesmerizing to see all those flakes coming vertically through the
hemisphere, then tilting sideways, and finally giving a beautiful suède
sheen to the gravelled earth, or to see them forming like small white
stones on the rhododendron bushes, and feathery plumes on the
branches of the fir trees.

That was only Christmas, and then came the meeting, and now he 3
is due to arrive. My next task is to plump cushions. A man I know said
that of all housewifely chores it is the most boring, the most monotonous, but still we do it, and the pink satin or the plum velvet or the
patchwork cushion sits there inflated, ridiculously waiting. Next thing
is to get more coal into the scuttle, to give the scuttle a bit of Brasso, to
sweep up the grains of coal that will have been spilled, and, if possible,
tighten the legs of the tongs so that they do not wobble and disgorge
the lumps of coal before they get to the fire.

You would think I have not had visitors for years, but I have—in 4
fact, they flock in all the time. But it is as if I see everything with a
ruthless clarity. It is the opposite of that vigil when I watched the snow
getting thicker and thicker, and saw the icicles extend from the roof,
until after some days they were like walking sticks or beautiful
javelins that one wanted to play with. I would paint a panel of this
sitting room in this one hour if I had time and a pot of emulsion. The
walls are apricot-colored, and in lamplight they are most pleasing
because so quietly they emit a glow. Sometimes I think of the yolk of a
gull's egg when I look at those walls, and the thought ushers me on to
the month of June, which for some reason I connect with happy and
graceful events. In England people give their annual ball, girls wear
myrtle in their hair, there are the races at Ascot, and even the most
unsumptuous garden has a display of tea roses or briar roses or
rambling roses, and if you stay in one of those lovely country houses
there is a vase of them on your bedside table, bright and wide open like
the eyes of watchful children.

But this is daylight and winter, and even the myriad bits of fluff on 5
the new Edith Piaf record have caught my eye, as they will undoubtedly catch his. So it's dusting time. I would make it night if I were
setting the appointment. Married men are lunchtime callers. I know
that. I know so much—albeit so little—about married men. I know how
divided they must be, and how cursory, and how mentally they must
brush off either her or her kiss as they step off the escalator to reach
the Underground, or as they step into their motorcars, or as they glide
through their own hallways, whistling or humming a familiar,
guarded tune. They deny. They could be called Judas.

I know the mistake I am making. I see the exits in life. It will be six 6
months or the proverbial nine months before it ends, and yet the
foreknowledge is as clear as the first meeting. It is just like lifting a
latch and seeing in to the blazing fire at the far end of the room, with
the passage in between, its carpet, its white rug, its chaise longue, its
birdcage, and its many secular delights. One day I will come to the
other end and I will perhaps get scorched. I was brought up to believe
in Hell and I was brought up to believe that men are masterful and
fickle. I could, of course, have said no, but I didn't. I demurred and then
I succumbed. Nevertheless, I am planning something new for myself. I
am putting my room in order. The smell of furniture wax, the
incenselike smell, will fill the air and complement the beautiful heady
innocent smell of the hyacinths that I have cultivated in a big bowl.
Their tubers are just visible above the clay, and they are the dreamiest
white, the palest blue, and a pink that looks artificial in color, like a
cake icing. They are like crests on the round table, and as I pass to do
this or that I want to bury my face in them, but there is no time and
also specks of pollen would stain the tip of my nose. There are only
thirty minutes left.

The soup that is supposed to be simmering on the kitchen stove is, 7
alas, boiling. I cry out, add cream, and beg all those little curds to
disappear as I stir it more and more in a circular motion. Then I cannot
find the embroidered cloth that I bought in Spain. Damn it. It is a
cream cloth with red appliqués stitched over it. It is both chaste and
gay. A stranger sitting down to eat might not only be surprised by it
but might in jest say, "Get me the castanets." I am resolved to be gay,
to show little of my inner self—no old sores or tragic portraits. The
cloth is not in the cupboard, and, with no time to spare, I ring up the
laundry. The laundry building is eight miles away, and one hundred
and thirty people are employed there, yet I am rash enough to think
that my Spanish cloth will be located and even delivered before one
o'clock.

It is in the middle of my conversation with an insolent girl at the 8
laundry that I realize that the soup is on the boil again. I run to turn
the gas off, and en route catch my knitted sleeve on the loose nail of the
cane chair. Things are getting bungled. These last minutes are the
worst. Hurry, Hurry.

But when I get out the cut-glass goblets, I remember my dead 9
mother. She gave them to me. Some are thickly cut with raised wedges
of glass, some have harps that seem to float inside the walls of the glass

itself, and three—the other three in the set got broken—have beautiful indentations to fit exactly the print of a thumb or a finger. I shall use them. I shall lay places for three. That will confuse him. I intend to confuse him. I intend to be someone else. The preparations are going against me—I have cut the bread too thick and the smoked salmon is in slithers. The shop has rooked me. I have met him, this caller, only once, and that was at a Christmas party, and our conversation was pure banter. Then, when he rang, he was crispness itself, and said such things as "Well, are we going to meet? Not that I think we should." I said that we need not meet, and, indeed, I meant it. But my stepping back from him whetted his interest. He invited himself to this lunch. "I shall come and lift lunch off you" was what he said. So English. So arch. I have made a cucumber salad. I pressed it all morning between two platters. Each disc of cucumber is softness itself, and even the green has been drained out of it. I sprinkle the salad with parsley. Soon I shall have to take off the cardigan, because I am wearing a new black dress. It fits me as if I were poured into it, as if I were molded to it.

Busy men often cancel at the last minute. Maybe he won't come; **10** maybe he will ring and cancel. He is a company director, he is married, he has a chauffeur, and I gather that his wife and he made it from scratch. He probably got a scholarship and went to Oxford or Cambridge. Now he has two houses and a croft in Scotland. I expect he is used to servants; maybe they have a cook. . . . Good God! I left the phone off the hook when I ran from it to save the soup. He may have tried to ring and decided that the phone is out of order, so that he need not ring again to account for his non-appearance. And here all this food, the lovely wine, pellucid, like liquid sun, into which who knows how many precious grapes have gone. The fruits of the earth. I have on black mesh stockings and a pair of lace suspenders that I found in my mother's drawer after she had died. They were wrapped up in a bolster case along with other things—necklaces, veiling, and some velvet flowers. They shocked me, and yet I said, "They will come in handy one day," and put them in my suitcase.

Opening the wine, I gauge my strength by pulling the cork out. My **11** strength is monumental. He will see me as some monster, devouring. I leave the ladle near the stove and turn the gas down until it shudders and shows signs of extinguishment. The clock has not chimed, but it is about to. It is in the next room, but I know that it has entered that spate of hesitancy that prevails just before it strikes. It broke once, but I had a man in from the city to repair it. He was actually called Mr. Goldsmith. I am superstitious about it and pray that it will not ever again expire.

My God, there is the doorbell. I know that I must answer it, but I **12** cannot. I am unable to move. I am upstairs. I cannot descend. I read something last night when I was unable to sleep. It has affected me. I read that the only paradise is the paradise lost. Proust. I read it years ago, but I had not absorbed it, and last night, after rereading it, I tossed and turned in my wide bed and thought of my caller and how I would seduce him. I saw our little drama as if on a picture postcard: a naked couple oblivious of the serpent that lies between them. And I thought that I could think of him to my heart's delight, and that he need never know, that he must never know, that I could paint postcard after postcard and give to skin the tints and the textures that I love, and give to speech and action all that I ever desire. I could ordain it regardless of him, and of course I thought how futile that would be in the end.

His finger is on the bell. He certainly is not timid—not as timid as I 13 would be entering a paramour's house and not quite knowing what to expect. For God's sake, I must do something. I can't just stand here. After all, I have an intercom. I can pick it up and say, "Go away," or "She's not here," or "Just a minute." But I do not pick it up. I lean against the wall. I am wobbling. I go down the stairs to let him in. He is just leaving. He seems surly. We do not kiss in the hall. I take his tweed coat and very formally lay it sideways on the prayer chair. As he comes into the sitting room, I see his evident pleasure as he takes stock of things.

"Nice room you've got," he says.   14

"We like it," I say.   15

"We?"   16

"Yes, we are a we."   17

I have set the course. I shall lie. I shall invent a lover, a mysterious 18 one who comes at night rather than at noon, a privileged one who is allowed to share the secrets of my soul, as this one must never be. Perhaps in this way I shall have my little Paradise Lost, yet I wonder if one has to enter it in order to find it, in order to lose it.

"Do you always dress like this?" he asks. The question bristles with 19 attraction and reproof.

"If I feel like it."   20

I am pouring the wine. He says that he does not drink but that he 21 will drink with me. I say there is apple juice, and point to it, on the beautiful gallery tray. He accepts the wine. He puts his tongue out in an involuntary gesture to taste whatever there is to taste.

"You don't know how lucky you are," he tells me.   22

"Why?" I ask.   23

"Because I like black stockings and black satin, for some odd 24 reason."

"In that case, you are the lucky one."   25

His eyes are like violets, but his skin is bleached. There is 26 something frozen about him. Life, too, has left its cold claws on his shoulder. But I will never know. No more than he will ever know about me. He is about to kiss me. I wonder if one has to enter the gates of paradise, even the tiniest adulterous little paradise, in order to find it, in order to lose it, in order to refind it, in perpetuity. And, wondering, I float into the first bewildered kiss.

Study Questions

1. Characterize the narrator on the basis of what she says about herself.

2. How does O'Brien use the woman's "tasks" to organize the story?
3. What is stream-of-consciousness and is this an example of it? Where and why does the narrator drift off from the tasks at hand?
4. A question to be considered in the light of current debate on sexist writing: If the personal pronouns were changed, could this story be about a man? if you didn't know a woman had written it, would you assume that one had? Why or why not? Why do you feel that way?
5. The story is named for a flower. What other flowers figure in the story? What significance is there in them?
6. Comment on the structure and meaning of the simile in paragraph 6.

The Kugelmass Episode
WOODY ALLEN

Woody Allen, or Allen Stewart Konigsberg (1935–) was born in Brooklyn. Although he has described himself as a student at both the Neighborhood School of Bit Players and the House of Vocal Cords, Allen actually attended New York University and the City College of New York. Best known as a writer and the star of such films as *Bananas, Play It Again, Sam, Sleeper, Love and Death, Annie Hall,* and *Manhattan,* Allen has also written for television and the stage. *Annie Hall* was Allen's greatest film success, earning for him both money and Academy Awards. He contributes to magazines, notably the *New Yorker* and *Playboy.* Collections of his magazine pieces include *Getting Even* (1971), *Without Feathers* (1975), and *Side Effects* (1980). In the playbill for *Play It Again, Sam,* Allen claimed to have played the title role in *Lady Windemere's Fan,* Porgy in *Porgy and Bess,* and Willy Loman in *Mr. Roberts.*

Kugelmass, a professor of humanities at City College, was   1
unhappily married for the second time. Daphne Kugelmass was an oaf. He also had two dull sons by his first wife, Flo, and was up to his neck in alimony and child support.

Reprinted by permission of *The New Yorker* and Woody Allen.

"Did I know it would turn out so badly?" Kugelmass whined to his   2
analyst one day. "Daphne had promise. Who suspected she'd let herself
go and swell up like a beach ball? Plus she had a few bucks, which is
not in itself a healthy reason to marry a person, but it doesn't hurt,
with the kind of operating nut I have. You see my point?"

Kugelmass was bald and as hairy as a bear, but he had soul.   3

"I need to meet a new woman," he went on. "I need to have an   4
affair. I may not look the part, but I'm a man who needs romance. I
need softness, I need flirtation. I'm not getting younger, so before it's
too late I want to make love in Venice, trade quips at '21,' and
exchange coy glances over red wine and candlelight. You see what I'm
saying?"

Dr. Mandel shifted in his chair and said, "An affair will solve   5
nothing. You're so unrealistic. Your problems run much deeper."

"And also this affair must be discreet," Kugelmass continued. "I   6
can't afford a second divorce. Daphne would really sock it to me."

"Mr. Kugelmass—"   7

"But it can't be anyone at City College, because Daphne also works   8
there. Not that anyone on the faculty at C.C.N.Y. is any great shakes,
but some of those coeds . . ."

"Mr. Kugelmass—"   9

"Help me. I had a dream last night. I was skipping through a   10
meadow holding a picnic basket and the basket was marked 'Options.'
And then I saw there was a hole in the basket."

"Mr. Kugelmass, the worst thing you could do is act out. You must   11
simply express your feelings here, and together we'll analyze them.
You have been in treatment long enough to know there is no overnight
cure. After all, I'm an analyst, not a magician."

"Then perhaps what I need is a magician," Kugelmass said, rising   12
from his chair. And with that he terminated his therapy.

A couple of weeks later, while Kugelmass and Daphne were   13
moping around in their apartment one night like two pieces of old
furniture, the phone rang.

"I'll get it," Kugelmass said. "Hello."   14

"Kugelmass?" a voice said. "Kugelmass, this is Persky."   15

"Who?"   16

"Persky. Or should I say The Great Persky?"   17

"Pardon me?"   18

"I hear you're looking all over town for a magician to bring a little   19
exotica into your life? Yes or no?"

"Sh-h-h," Kugelmass whispered. "Don't hang up. Where are you   20
calling from, Persky?"

Early the following afternoon, Kugelmass climbed three flights of   21
stairs in a broken-down apartment house in the Bushwick section of
Brooklyn. Peering through the darkness of the hall, he found the door
he was looking for and pressed the bell. I'm going to regret this, he
thought to himself.

Seconds later, he was greeted by a short, thin, waxy-looking man.   22

"*You're* Persky the Great?" Kugelmass said.   23

"The Great Persky. You want a tea?"   24

"No, I want romance. I want music. I want love and beauty." 25

"But not tea, eh? Amazing. O.K., sit down." 26

Persky went to the back room, and Kugelmass heard the sounds of 27
boxes and furniture being moved around. Persky reappeared, pushing
before him a large object on squeaky roller-skate wheels. He removed
some old silk handkerchiefs that were lying on its top and blew away a
bit of dust. It was a cheap-looking Chinese cabinet, badly lacquered.

"Persky," Kugelmass said, "what's your scam?" 28

"Pay attention," Persky said. "This is some beautiful effect. I 29
developed it for a Knights of Pythias date last year, but the booking fell
through. Get into the cabinet."

"Why, so you can stick it full of swords or something?" 30

"You see any swords?" 31

Kugelmass made a face and, grunting, climbed into the cabinet. He 32
couldn't help noticing a couple of ugly rhinestones glued onto the raw
plywood just in front of his face. "If this is a joke," he said.

"Some joke. Now, here's the point. If I throw any novel into this 33
cabinet with you, shut the doors, and tap it three times, you will find
yourself projected into that book."

Kugelmass made a grimace of disbelief. 34

"It's the emess," Persky said. "My hand to God. Not just a novel, 35
either. A short story, a play, a poem. You can meet any of the women
created by the world's best writers. Whoever you dreamed of. You could
carry on all you like with a real winner. Then when you've had enough
you give a yell, and I'll see you're back here in a split second."

"Persky, are you some kind of outpatient?" 36

"I'm telling you it's on the level," Persky said. 37

Kugelmass remained skeptical. "What are you telling me—that 38
this cheesy homemade box can take me on a ride like you're describing?"

"For a double sawbuck." 39

Kugelmass reached for his wallet. "I'll believe this when I see it," 40
he said.

Persky tucked the bills in his pants pocket and turned toward his 41
bookcase. "So who do you want to meet? Sister Carrie? Hester Prynne?
Ophelia? Maybe someone by Saul Bellow? Hey, what about Temple
Drake? Although for a man your age she'd be a workout."

"French. I want to have an affair with a French lover." 42

"Nana?" 43

"I don't want to have to pay for it." 44

"What about Natasha in *War and Peace*?" 45

"I said French. I know! What about Emma Bovary? That sounds to 46
me perfect."

"You got it, Kugelmass. Give me a holler when you've had 47
enough." Persky tossed in a paperback copy of Flaubert's novel.

"You sure this is safe?" Kugelmass asked as Persky began shutting 48
the cabinet doors.

"Safe. Is anything safe in this crazy world?" Persky rapped three 49
times on the cabinet and then flung open the doors.

Kugelmass was gone. At the same moment, he appeared in the 50 bedroom of Charles and Emma Bovary's house at Yonville. Before him was a beautiful woman, standing alone with her back turned to him as she folded some linen. I can't believe this, thought Kugelmass, staring at the doctor's ravishing wife. This is uncanny. I'm here. It's her.

Emma turned in surprise. "Goodness, you startled me," she said. 51 "Who are you?" She spoke in the same fine English translation as the paperback.

It's simply devastating, he thought. Then, realizing that it was he 52 whom she had addressed, he said, "Excuse me. I'm Sidney Kugelmass. I'm from City College. A professor of humanities. C.C.N.Y.? Uptown. I—oh, boy!"

Emma Bovary smiled flirtatiously and said, "Would you like a 53 drink? A glass of wine, perhaps?"

She is beautiful, Kugelmass thought. What a contrast with the 54 troglodyte who shared his bed! He felt a sudden impulse to take this vision into his arms and tell her she was the kind of woman he had dreamed of all his life.

"Yes, some wine," he said hoarsely. "White. No, red. No, white. 55 Make it white."

"Charles is out for the day," Emma said, her voice full of playful 56 implication.

After the wine, they went for a stroll in the lovely French 57 countryside. "I've always dreamed that some mysterious stranger would appear and rescue me from the monotony of this crass rural existence," Emma said, clasping his hand. They passed a small church. "I love what you have on," she murmured. "I've never seen anything like it around here. It's so . . . so modern."

"It's called a leisure suit," he said romantically. "It was marked 58 down." Suddenly he kissed her. For the next hour they reclined under a tree and whispered together and told each other deeply meaningful things with their eyes. Then Kugelmass sat up. He had just remembered he had to meet Daphne at Bloomingdale's. "I must go," he told her. "But don't worry, I'll be back."

"I hope so," Emma said. 59

He embraced her passionately, and the two walked back to the 60 house. He held Emma's face cupped in his palms, kissed her again, and yelled, "O.K., Persky! I got to be at Bloomingdale's by three-thirty."

There was an audible pop, and Kugelmass was back in Brooklyn. 61

"So? Did I lie?" Persky asked triumphantly. 62

"Look, Persky, I'm right now late to meet the ball and chain at 63 Lexington Avenue, but when can I go again? Tomorrow?"

"My pleasure. Just bring a twenty. And don't mention this to 64 anybody."

"Yeah. I'm going to call Rupert Murdoch." 65

Kugelmass hailed a cab and sped off to the city. His heart danced 66 on point. I am in love, he thought, I am the possessor of a wonderful secret. What he didn't realize was that at this very moment students in various classrooms across the country were saying to their teachers, "Who is this character on page 100? A bald Jew is kissing Madame Bovary?" A teacher in Sioux Falls, South Dakota, sighed and thought,

Jesus, these kids, with their pot and acid. What goes through their minds!

Daphne Kugelmass was in the bathroom-accessories department **67** at Bloomingdale's when Kugelmass arrived breathlessly. "Where've you been?" she snapped. "It's four-thirty."

"I got held up in traffic," Kugelmass said.   **68**

Kugelmass visited Persky the next day, and in a few minutes was **69** again passed magically to Yonville. Emma couldn't hide her excitement at seeing him. The two spent hours together, laughing and talking about their different backgrounds. Before Kugelmass left, they made love. "My God, I'm doing it with Madame Bovary!" Kugelmass whispered to himself. "Me, who failed freshman English."

As the months passed, Kugelmass saw Persky many times and **70** developed a close and passionate relationship with Emma Bovary. "Make sure and always get me into the book before page 120," Kugelmass said to the magician one day. "I always have to meet her before she hooks up with this Rodolphe character."

"Why?" Persky asked. "You can't beat his time?"   **71**

"Beat his time. He's landed gentry. Those guys have nothing better **72** to do than flirt and ride horses. To me, he's one of those faces you see in the pages of *Women's Wear Daily*. With the Helmut Berger hairdo. But to her he's hot stuff."

"And her husband suspects nothing?"   **73**

"He's out of his depth. He's a lacklustre little paramedic who's **74** thrown in his lot with a jitterbug. He's ready to go to sleep by ten, and she's putting on her dancing shoes. Oh, well . . . See you later."

And once again Kugelmass entered the cabinet and passed in- **75** stantly to the Bovary estate at Yonville. "How you doing, cupcake?" he said to Emma.

"Oh, Kugelmass," Emma sighed. "What I have to put up with. Last **76** night at dinner, Mr. Personality dropped off to sleep in the middle of the dessert course. I'm pouring my heart out about Maxim's and the ballet, and out of the blue I hear snoring."

"It's O.K., darling. I'm here now," Kugelmass said, embracing her. **77** I've earned this, he thought, smelling Emma's French perfume and burying his nose in her hair. I've suffered enough. I've paid enough analysts. I've searched till I'm weary. She's young and nubile, and I'm here a few pages after Léon and just before Rodolphe. By showing up during the correct chapters, I've got the situation knocked.

Emma, to be sure, was just as happy as Kugelmass. She had been **78** starved for excitement, and his tales of Broadway night life, of fast cars and Hollywood and TV stars, enthralled the young French beauty.

"Tell me again about O. J. Simpson," she implored that evening, as **79** she and Kugelmass strolled past Abbé Bournisien's church.

"What can I say? The man is great. He sets all kinds of rushing **80** records. Such moves. They can't touch him."

"And the Academy Awards?" Emma said wistfully. "I'd give **81** anything to win one."

"First you've got to be nominated."   **82**

"I know. You explained it. But I'm convinced I can act. Of course, **83**

I'd want to take a class or two. With Strasberg maybe. Then, if I had
the right agent—"

"We'll see, we'll see. I'll speak to Persky."   84

That night, safely returned to Persky's flat, Kugelmass brought up   85
the idea of having Emma visit him in the big city.

"Let me think about it," Persky said. "Maybe I could work it.   86
Stranger things have happened." Of course, neither of them could
think of one.

"Where the hell do you go all the time?" Daphne Kugelmass   87
barked at her husband as he returned home late that evening. "You got
a chippie stashed somewhere?"

"Yeah, sure, I'm just the type," Kugelmass said wearily. "I was   88
with Leonard Popkin. We were discussing Socialist agriculture in
Poland. You know Popkin. He's a freak on the subject."

"Well, you've been very odd lately," Daphne said. "Distant. Just   89
don't forget about my father's birthday. On Saturday?"

"Oh, sure, sure," Kugelmass said, heading for the bathroom.   90

"My whole family will be there. We can see the twins. And Cousin   91
Hamish. You should be more polite to Cousin Hamish—he likes you."

"Right, the twins," Kugelmass said, closing the bathroom door and   92
shutting out the sound of his wife's voice. He leaned against it and took
a deep breath. In a few hours, he told himself, he would be back in
Yonville again, back with his beloved. And this time, if all went well,
he would bring Emma back with him.

At three-fifteen the following afternoon, Persky worked his wiz-   93
ardry again. Kugelmass appeared before Emma, smiling and eager.
The two spent a few hours at Yonville with Binet and then remounted
the Bovary carriage. Following Persky's instructions, they held each
other tightly, closed their eyes, and counted to ten. When they opened
them, the carriage was just drawing up at the side door of the Plaza
Hotel, where Kugelmass had optimistically reserved a suite earlier in
the day.

"I love it! It's everything I dreamed it would be," Emma said as she 94
swirled joyously around the bedroom, surveying the city from their
window. "There's F.A.O. Schwarz. And there's Central Park, and the
Sherry is which one? Oh, there—I see. It's too divine."

On the bed there were boxes from Halston and Saint Laurent.   95
Emma unwrapped a package and held up a pair of black velvet pants
against her perfect body.

"The slacks suit is by Ralph Lauren," Kugelmass said. "You'll look   96
like a million bucks in it. Come on, sugar, give us a kiss."

"I've never been so happy!" Emma squealed as she stood before the   97
mirror. "Let's go out on the town. I want to see *Chorus Line* and the
Guggenheim and this Jack Nicholson character you always talk about.
Are any of his flicks showing?"

"I cannot get my mind around this," a Stanford professor said.   98
"First a strange character named Kugelmass, and now she's gone from
the book. Well, I guess the mark of a classic is that you can reread it a
thousand times and always find something new."

The lovers passed a blissful weekend. Kugelmass had told Daphne   99
he would be away at a symposium in Boston and would return Monday.
Savoring each moment, he and Emma went to the movies, had dinner
in Chinatown, passed two hours at a discothèque, and went to bed with
a TV movie. They slept till noon on Sunday, visited SoHo, and ogled
celebrities at Elaine's. They had caviar and champagne in their suite
on Sunday night and talked until dawn. That morning, in the cab
taking them to Persky's apartment, Kugelmass thought, It was hectic,
but worth it. I can't bring her here too often, but now and then it will be
a charming contrast with Yonville.

At Persky's, Emma climbed into the cabinet, arranged her new   100
boxes of clothes neatly around her, and kissed Kugelmass fondly. "My
place next time," she said with a wink. Persky rapped three times on
the cabinet. Nothing happened.

"Hmmm," Persky said, scratching his head. He rapped again, but   101
still no magic. "Something must be wrong," he mumbled.

"Persky, you're joking!" Kugelmass cried. "How can it not work?"   102

"Relax, relax. Are you still in the box, Emma?"   103

"Yes."   104

Persky rapped again—harder this time.   105

"I'm still here, Persky."   106

"I know, darling. Sit tight."   107

"Persky, we *have* to get her back," Kugelmass whispered. "I'm a   108
married man, and I have a class in three hours. I'm not prepared for
anything more than a cautious affair at this point."

"I can't understand it," Persky muttered. "It's such a reliable little   109
trick."

But he could do nothing. "It's going to take a little while," he said   110
to Kugelmass. "I'm going to have to strip it down. I'll call you later."

Kugelmass bundled Emma into a cab and took her back to the   111
Plaza. He barely made it to his class on time. He was on the phone all
day, to Persky and to his mistress. The magician told him it might be
several days before he got to the bottom of the trouble.

"How was the symposium?" Daphne asked him that night.   112

"Fine, fine," he said, lighting the filter end of a cigarette.   113

"What's wrong? You're as tense as a cat."   114

"Me? Ha, that's a laugh. I'm as calm as a summer night. I'm just   115
going to take a walk." He eased out the door, hailed a cab, and flew to
the Plaza.

"This is no good," Emma said. "Charles will miss me."   116

"Bear with me, sugar," Kugelmass said. He was pale and sweaty.   117
He kissed her again, raced to the elevators, yelled at Persky over a pay
phone in the Plaza lobby, and just made it home before midnight.

"According to Popkin, barley prices in Kraków have not been this   118
stable since 1971," he said to Daphne, and smiled wanly as he climbed
into bed.

The whole week went by like that. On Friday night, Kugelmass   119
told Daphne there was another symposium he had to catch, this one in
Syracuse. He hurried back to the Plaza, but the second weekend there

was nothing like the first. "Get me back into the novel or marry me," Emma told Kugelmass. "Meanwhile, I want to get a job or go to class, because watching TV all day is the pits."

"Fine. We can use the money," Kugelmass said. "You consume 120 twice your weight in room service."

"I met an Off Broadway producer in Central Park yesterday, and 121 he said I might be right for a project he's doing," Emma said.

"Who is this clown?" Kugelmass asked.   122

"He's not a clown. He's sensitive and kind and cute. His name's Jeff 123 Something-or-Other, and he's up for a Tony."

Later that afternoon, Kugelmass showed up at Persky's drunk.   124

"Relax," Persky told him. "You'll get a coronary."   125

"Relax. The man says relax. I've got a fictional character stashed 126 in a hotel room, and I think my wife is having me tailed by a private shamus."

"O.K., O.K. We know there's a problem." Persky crawled under the 127 cabinet and started banging on something with a large wrench.

"I'm like a wild animal," Kugelmass went on. "I'm sneaking 128 around town, and Emma and I have had it up to here with each other. Not to mention a hotel tab that reads like the defense budget."

"So what should I do? This is the world of magic," Persky said. "It's 129 all nuance."

"Nuance, my foot. I'm pouring Dom Pérignon and black eggs into 130 this little mouse, plus her wardrobe, plus she's enrolled at the Neighborhood Playhouse and suddenly needs professional photos. Also, Persky, Professor Fivish Kopkind, who teaches Comp Lit and who has always been jealous of me, has identified me as the sporadically appearing character in the Flaubert book. He's threatened to go to Daphne. I see ruin and alimony jail. For adultery with Madame Bovary, my wife will reduce me to beggary."

"What do you want me to say? I'm working on it night and day. As 131 far as your personal anxiety goes, that I can't help you with. I'm a magician, not an analyst."

By Sunday afternoon, Emma had locked herself in the bathroom 132 and refused to respond to Kugelmass's entreaties. Kugelmass stared out the window at the Wollman Rink and contemplated suicide. Too bad this is a low floor, he thought, or I'd do it right now. Maybe if I ran away to Europe and started life over ... Maybe I could sell the *International Herald Tribune,* like those young girls used to.

The phone rang. Kugelmass lifted it to his ear mechanically.   133

"Bring her over," Persky said. "I think I got the bugs out of it."   134

Kugelmass's heart leaped. "You're serious?" he said. "You got it 135 licked?"

"It was something in the transmission. Go figure."   136

"Persky, you're a genius. We'll be there in a minute. Less than a 137 minute."

Again the lovers hurried to the magician's apartment, and again 138 Emma Bovary climbed into the cabinet with her boxes. This time there was no kiss. Persky shut the doors, took a deep breath, and tapped the box three times. There was the reassuring popping noise, and when

Persky peered inside, the box was empty. Madame Bovary was back in her novel. Kugelmass heaved a great sigh of relief and pumped the magician's hand.

"It's over," he said. "I learned my lesson. I'll never cheat again, I **139** swear it." He pumped Persky's hand again and made a mental note to send him a necktie.

Three weeks later, at the end of a beautiful spring afternoon, **140** Persky answered his doorbell. It was Kugelmass, with a sheepish expression on his face.

"O.K., Kugelmass," the magician said. "Where to this time?" **141**

"It's just this once," Kugelmass said. "The weather is so lovely, and **142** I'm not getting any younger. Listen, you've read *Portnoy's Complaint?* Remember The Monkey?"

"The price is now twenty-five dollars, because the cost of living is **143** up, but I'll start you off with one freebie, due to all the trouble I caused you."

"You're good people," Kugelmass said, combing his few remaining **144** hairs as he climbed into the cabinet again. "This'll work all right?"

"I hope. But I haven't tried it much since all that unpleasantness." **145**

"Sex and romance," Kugelmass said from inside the box. "What we **146** go through for a pretty face."

Persky tossed in a copy of *Portnoy's Complaint* and rapped three **147** times on the box. This time, instead of a popping noise there was a dull explosion, followed by a series of crackling noises and a shower of sparks. Persky leaped back, was seized by a heart attack, and dropped dead. The cabinet burst into flames, and eventually the entire house burned down.

Kugelmass, unaware of this catastrophe, had his own problems. He **148** had not been thrust into *Portnoy's Complaint,* or into any other novel, for that matter. He had been projected into an old textbook, *Remedial Spanish,* and was running for his life over a barren, rocky terrain as the word *"tener"* ("to have")—a large and hairy irregular verb—raced after him on its spindly legs.

Study Questions

1. Analyze the construction of the single sentence which makes up the third paragraph. Is the sentence funny? If so, why?
2. How does Kugelmass's and Emma's use of language help form our judgments of them?
3. Find examples of Allen's satirizing literary critics and criticism.
4. Allen's story includes many questions and answers. How does Allen succeed in getting a laugh out of them?
5. Why is the story's conclusion funny? Why is the terrain barren and rocky, the verb large and hairy with spindly legs?

Love Is a Fallacy
MAX SHULMAN

Max Shulman (1919–   ) was born in St. Paul and received his
A.B. from the University of Minnesota (1942). He served with the
Army Air Force from 1942 to 1946. Later his short stories began
appearing in such periodicals as *The Saturday Evening Post, Good
Housekeeping, Esquire,* and *Mademoiselle.* His writing credits
include fiction—*Barefoot Boy With Cheek* (1943), *The Feather
Merchants* (1944), and *Rally Round the Flag, Boys!* (1957); movie
scripts—*Confidentially Connie, The Affairs of Dobie Gillis, Half a
Hero, The Tender Trap,* and *House Calls;* Broadway musical
comedies—*How Now Dow Jones* (1967) and *Potatoes Are Cheaper*
(1971); and the authorship of the "Dobie Gillis" television series.

Charles Lamb, as merry and enterprising a fellow as you
will meet in a month of Sundays, unfettered the informal
essay with his memorable *Old China* and *Dream Children.*
There follows an informal essay that ventures even beyond
Lamb's frontier. Indeed, "informal" may not be quite the
right word to describe this essay; "limp" or "flaccid" or
possibly "spongy" are perhaps more appropriate.

Vague though its category, it is without doubt an essay.
It develops an argument; it cites instances; it reaches a
conclusion. Could Carlyle do more? Could Ruskin?

Read, then, the following essay which undertakes to
demonstrate that logic, far from being a dry, pedantic
discipline, is a living, breathing thing, full of beauty, passion, and trauma.

—AUTHOR'S NOTE

Cool was I and logical. Keen, calculating, perspicacious,   1
acute and astute—I was all of these. My brain was as powerful as a
dynamo, as precise as a chemist's scales, as penetrating as a scalpel.
And—think of it!—I was only eighteen.

It is not often that one so young has such a giant intellect. Take, for   2
example, Petey Burch, my roommate at the University of Minnesota.
Same age, same background, but dumb as an ox. A nice enough fellow,
you understand, but nothing upstairs. Emotional type, unstable.
Impressionable. Worst of all, a faddist. Fads, I submit are the very
negation of reason. To be swept up in every new craze that comes

along, to surrender yourself to idiocy just because everybody else is doing it—this, to me, is the acme of mindlessness. Not, however, to Petey.

One afternoon I found Petey lying on his bed with an expression of such distress on his face that I immediately diagnosed appendicitis. "Don't move," I said. "Don't take a laxative. I'll get a doctor."   3

"Raccoon," he mumbled thickly.   4

"Raccoon?" I said, pausing in my flight.   5

"I want a raccoon coat," he wailed.   6

I perceived that his trouble was not physical, but mental. "Why do you want a raccoon coat?"   7

"I should have known it," he cried, pounding his temples. "I should have known they'd come back when the Charleston came back. Like a fool I spent all my money for textbooks, and now I can't get a raccoon coat."   8

"Can you mean," I said incredulously, "that people are actually wearing raccoon coats again?"   9

"All the Big Men on Campus are wearing them. Where've you been?"   10

"In the library," I said, naming a place not frequented by Big Men on Campus.   11

He leaped from the bed and paced the room. "I've got to have a raccoon coat," he said passionately. "I've got to!"   12

"Petey, why? Look at it rationally. Raccoon coats are unsanitary. They shed. They smell bad. They weigh too much. They're unsightly. They—"   13

"You don't understand," he interrupted impatiently. "It's the thing to do. Don't you want to be in the swim?"   14

"No," I said truthfully.   15

"Well, I do," he declared. "I'd give anything for a raccoon coat. Anything!"   16

My brain, that precision instrument, slipped into high gear. "Anything?" I asked, looking at him narrowly.   17

"Anything," he affirmed in ringing tones.   18

I stroked my chin thoughtfully. It so happened that I knew where to get my hands on a raccoon coat. My father had had one in his undergraduate days; it lay now in a trunk in the attic back home. It also happened that Petey had something I wanted. He didn't *have* it exactly, but at least he had first rights on it. I refer to his girl, Polly Espy.   19

I had long coveted Polly Espy. Let me emphasize that my desire for this young woman was not emotional in nature. She was, to be sure, a girl who excited the emotions, but I was not one to let my heart rule my head. I wanted Polly for a shrewdly calculated, entirely cerebral reason.   20

I was a freshman in law school. In a few years I would be out in practice. I was well aware of the importance of the right kind of wife in furthering a lawyer's career. The successful lawyers I had observed were, almost without exception, married to beautiful, gracious, intelli-   21 gent women. With one omission, Polly fitted these specifications perfectly.

Beautiful she was. She was not yet of pin-up proportions, but I felt   22
sure that time would supply the lack. She already had the makings.

Gracious she was. By gracious I mean full of graces. She had an   23
erectness of carriage, an ease of bearing, a poise that clearly indicated
the best of breeding. At table her manners were exquisite. I had seen
her at the Kozy Kampus Korner eating the speciality of the house—a
sandwich that contained scraps of pot roast, gravy, chopped nuts, and a
dipper of sauerkraut—without even getting her fingers moist.

Intelligent she was not. In fact, she veered in the opposite direc-   24
tion. But I believed that under my guidance she would smarten up. At
any rate, it was worth a try. It is, after all, easier to make a beautiful
dumb girl smart than to make an ugly smart girl beautiful.

"Petey," I said, "are you in love with Polly Espy?"   25

"I think she's a keen kid," he replied, "but I don't know if you'd call   26
it love. Why?"

"Do you," I asked, "have any kind of formal arrangement with her?   27
I mean are you going steady or anything like that?"

"No. We see each other quite a bit, but we both have other dates.   28
Why?"

"Is there," I asked, "any other man for whom she has a particular   29
fondness?"

"Not that I know of. Why?"   30

I nodded with satisfaction. "In other words, if you were out of the   31
picture, the field would be open. Is that right?"

"I guess so. What are you getting at?"   32

"Nothing, nothing," I said innocently, and took my suitcase out of   33
the closet.

"Where are you going?" asked Petey.   34

"Home for the weekend." I threw a few things into the bag.   35

"Listen," he said, clutching my arm eagerly, "while you're home,   36
you couldn't get some money from your old man, could you, and lend it
to me so I can buy a raccoon coat?"

"I may do better than that," I said with a mysterious wink and   37
closed my bag and left.

"Look," I said to Petey when I got back Monday morning. I threw   38
open the suitcase and revealed the huge, hairy, gamy object that my
father had worn in his Stutz Bearcat in 1925.

"Holy Toledo!" said Petey reverently. He plunged his hands into   39
the raccoon coat and then his face. "Holy Toledo!" he repeated fifteen or
twenty times.

"Would you like it?" I asked.   40

"Oh yes!" he cried, clutching the greasy pelt to him. Then a canny   41
look came into his eyes. "What do you want for it?"

"Your girl," I said, mincing no words.   42

"Polly?" he said in a horrified whisper. "You want Polly?"   43

"That's right."   44

He flung the coat from him. "Never," he said stoutly.   45

I shrugged. "Okay. If you don't want to be in the swim, I guess it's   46
your business."

I sat down in a chair and pretended to read a book, but out of the   47
corner of my eye I kept watching Petey. He was a torn man. First he
looked at the coat with the expression of a waif at a bakery window.
Then he turned away and set his jaw resolutely. Then he looked back
at the coat, with even more longing in his face. Then he turned away,
but with not so much resolution this time. Back and forth his head
swiveled, desire waxing, resolution waning. Finally he didn't turn
away at all; he just stood and stared with mad lust at the coat.

"It isn't as though I was in love with Polly," he said thickly. "Or   48
going steady or anything like that."

"That's right," I murmured.   49

"What's Polly to me, or me to Polly?"   50

"Not a thing," said I.   51

"It's just been a casual kick—just a few laughs, that's all."   52

"Try on the coat," said I.   53

He complied. The coat bunched high over his ears and dropped all   54
the way down to his shoe tops. He looked like a mound of dead
raccoons. "Fits fine," he said happily.

I rose from my chair. "Is it a deal?" I asked, extending my hand.   55

He swallowed. "It's a deal," he said and shook my hand.   56

I had my first date with Polly the following evening. This was in   57
the nature of a survey; I wanted to find out just how much work I had to
do to get her mind up to the standard I required. I took her first to
dinner. "Gee, that was a delish dinner," she said as we left the
restaurant. Then I took her to a movie. "Gee, that was a marvy movie,"
she said as we left the theater. And then I took her home. "Gee, I had a
sensaysh time," she said as she bade me good night.

I went back to my room with a heavy heart. I had gravely   58
underestimated the size of my task. This girl's lack of information was
terrifying. Nor would it be enough merely to supply her with information. First she had to be taught to *think*. This loomed as a project of no
small dimensions, and at first I was tempted to give her back to Petey.
But then I got to thinking about her abundant physical charms and
about the way she entered the room and the way she handled a knife
and fork, and I decided to make an effort.

I went about it, as in all things, systematically. I gave her a course   59
in logic. It happened that I, as a law student, was taking a course in
logic myself, so I had all the facts at my finger tips. "Polly," I said to her
when I picked her up on our next date, "tonight we are going over to
the Knoll and talk."

"Oo, terrif," she replied. One thing I will say for this girl: you   60
would go far to find another so agreeable.

We went to the Knoll, the campus trysting place, and we sat down   61
under an old oak, and she looked at me expectantly. "What are we
going to talk about?" she asked.

"Logic."   62

She thought this over for a minute and decided she liked it.   63
"Magnif," she said.

"Logic," I said, clearing my throat, "is the science of thinking.   64
Before we can think correctly, we must first learn to recognize the
common fallacies of logic. These we will take up tonight."

"Wow-dow!" she cried, clapping her hands delightedly.   65

I winced, but went bravely on. "First let us examine the fallacy   66
called Dicto Simpliciter."

"By all means," she urged, batting her lashes eagerly.   67

"Dicto Simpliciter means an argument based on an unqualified   68
generalization. For example: Exercise is good. Therefore everybody
should exercise."

"I agree," said Polly earnestly. "I mean exercise is wonderful. I   69
mean it builds the body and everything."

"Polly," I said gently, "the argument is a fallacy. *Exercise is good* is   70
an unqualified generalization. For instance, if you have heart disease,
exercise is bad, not good. Many people are ordered by their doctors *not*
to exercise. You must *qualify* the generalization. You must say
exercise is *usually* good, or exercise is good *for most people*. Otherwise
you have committed a Dicto Simpliciter. Do you see?"

"No," she confessed. "But this is marvy. Do more! Do more!"   71

"It will be better if you stop tugging at my sleeve," I told her, and   72
when she desisted, I continued. "Next we take up a fallacy called Hasty
Generalization. Listen carefully: You can't speak French. I can't speak
French. Petey Burch can't speak French. I must therefore conclude
that nobody at the University of Minnesota can speak French."

"Really?" said Polly, amazed. *"Nobody?"*   73

I hid my exasperation. "Polly, it's a fallacy. The generalization is   74
reached too hastily. There are too few instances to support such a
conclusion."

"Know any more fallacies?" she asked breathlessly. "This is more   75
fun than dancing even."

I fought off a wave of despair. I was getting nowhere with this girl,   76
absolutely nowhere. Still, I am nothing if not persistent. I continued.
"Next comes Post Hoc. Listen to this: Let's not take Bill on our picnic.
Every time we take him out with us, it rains."

"I know somebody just like that," she exclaimed. "A girl back   77
home—Eula Becker, her name is. It never fails. Every single time we
take her on a picnic—"

"Polly," I said sharply, "it's a fallacy. Eula Becker doesn't *cause* the   78
rain. She has no connection with the rain. You are guilty of Post Hoc if
you blame Eula Becker."

"I'll never do it again," she promised contritely. "Are you mad at   79
me?"

I sighed deeply. "No, Polly, I'm not mad."   80

"Then tell me some more fallacies."   81

"All right. Let's try Contradictory Premises."   82

"Yes, let's," she chirped, blinking her eyes happily.   83

I frowned, but plunged ahead. "Here's an example of Contradictory 84
Premises: If God can do anything, can He make a stone so heavy that
He won't be able to lift it?"

"Of course," she replied promptly. 85

"But if He can do anything, He can lift the stone," I pointed out. 86

"Yeah," she said thoughtfully. "Well, then I guess He can't make 87
the stone."

"But He can do anything," I reminded her. 88

She scratched her pretty, empty head. "I'm all confused," she 89
admitted.

"Of course you are. Because when the premises of an argument 90
contradict each other, there can be no argument. If there is an
irresistible force, there can be no immovable object. If there is an
immovable object, there can be no irresistible force. Get it?"

"Tell me some more of this keen stuff," she said eagerly. 91

I consulted my watch. "I think we'd better call it a night. I'll take 92
you home now, and you go over all the things you've learned. We'll
have another session tomorrow night."

I deposited her at the girl's dormitory, where she assured me that 93
she had had a perfectly terrif evening, and I went glumly home to my
room. Petey lay snoring in his bed, the raccoon coat huddled like a
great hairy beast at his feet. For a moment I considered waking him
and telling him that he could have his girl back. It seemed clear that
my project was doomed to failure. The girl simply had a logic-proof
head.

But then I reconsidered. I had wasted one evening; I might as well 94
waste another. Who knew? Maybe somewhere in the extinct crater of
her mind, a few embers still smoldered. Maybe somehow I could fan
them into flame. Admittedly it was not a prospect fraught with hope,
but I decided to give it one more try.

Seated under the oak the next evening I said, "Our first fallacy 95
tonight is called Ad Misericordiam."

She quivered with delight. 96

"Listen closely," I said. "A man applies for a job. When the boss 97
asks him what his qualifications are, he replies that he has a wife and
six children at home, the wife is a helpless cripple, the children have
nothing to eat, no clothes to wear, no shoes on their feet, there are no
beds in the house, no coal in the cellar, and winter is coming."

A tear rolled down each of Polly's pink cheeks. "Oh, this is awful, 98
awful," she sobbed.

"Yes, it's awful," I agreed, "but it's no argument. The man never 99
answered the boss's question about his qualifications. Instead he
appealed to the boss's sympathy. He committed the fallacy of Ad
Misericordiam. Do you understand?"

"Have you got a handkerchief?" she blubbered. 100

I handed her a handkerchief and tried to keep from screaming 101
while she wiped her eyes. "Next," I said in a carefully controlled tone,
"we will discuss False Analogy. Here is an example: Students should
be allowed to look at their textbooks during examinations. After all,

surgeons have X-rays to guide them during an operation, lawyers have briefs to guide them during a trial, carpenters have blueprints to guide them when they are building a house. Why, then, shouldn't students be allowed to look at their textbooks during an examination?"

"There now," she said enthusiastically, "is the most marvy idea 102 I've heard in years."

"Polly," I said testily, "the argument is all wrong. Doctors, lawyers, 103 and carpenters aren't taking a test to see how much they have learned, but students are. The situations are altogether different, and you can't make an analogy between them."

"I still think it's a good idea," said Polly. 104

"Nuts," I muttered. Doggedly I pressed on. "Next we'll try 105 Hypothesis Contrary to Fact."

"Sounds yummy," was Polly's reaction. 106

"Listen: If Madame Curie had not happened to leave a photo- 107 graphic plate in a drawer with a chunk of pitchblende, the world today would not know about radium."

"True, true," said Polly, nodding her head. "Did you see the movie? 108 Oh, it just knocked me out. That Walter Pidgeon is so dreamy. I mean he fractures me."

"If you can forget Mr. Pidgeon for a moment," I said coldly, "I 109 would like to point out that the statement is a fallacy. Maybe Madame Curie would have discovered radium at some later date. Maybe somebody else would have discovered it. Maybe any number of things would have happened. You can't start with a hypothesis that is not true and then draw any supportable conclusions from it."

"They ought to put Walter Pidgeon in more pictures," said Polly. "I 110 hardly ever see him any more."

One more chance, I decided. But just one more. There is a limit to 111 what flesh and blood can bear. "The next fallacy is called Poisoning the Well."

"How cute!" she gurgled. 112

"Two men are having a debate. The first one gets up and says, 'My 113 opponent is a notorious liar. You can't believe a word that he is going to say.' Now, Polly, think. Think hard. What's wrong?"

I watched her closely as she knit her creamy brow in concentration. 114 Suddenly a glimmer of intelligence—the first I had seen—came into her eyes. "It's not fair," she said with indignation. "It's not a bit fair. What chance has the second man got if the first man calls him a liar before he even begins talking?"

"Right!" I cried exultantly. "One hundred per cent right. It's not 115 fair. The first man has *poisoned the well* before anybody could drink from it. He has hamstrung his opponent before he could even start. . . . Polly, I'm proud of you."

"Pshaw," she murmured, blushing with pleasure. 116

"'You see, my dear, these things aren't so hard. All you have to do 117 is concentrate. Think—examine—evaluate. Come now, let's review everything we have learned."

"Fire away," she said with an airy wave of her hand. 118

Heartened by the knowledge that Polly was not altogether a cretin, 119
I began a long, patient review of all I had told her. Over and over and
over again I cited instances, pointed out flaws, kept hammering away
without let up. It was like digging a tunnel. At first everything was
work, sweat, and darkness. I had no idea when I would reach the light,
or even *if* I would. But I persisted. I pounded and clawed and scraped,
and finally I was rewarded. I saw a chink of light. And then the chink
got bigger and the sun came pouring in and all was bright.

Five grueling nights this took, but it was worth it. I had made a 120
logician out of Polly; I had taught her to think. My job was done. She
was worthy of me at last. She was a fit wife for me, a proper hostess for
my many mansions, a suitable mother for my well-heeled children.

It must not be thought that I was without love for this girl. Quite 121
the contrary. Just as Pygmalion loved the perfect woman he had
fashioned, so I loved mine. I determined to acquaint her with my
feelings at our very next meeting. The time had come to change our
relationship from academic to romantic.

"Polly," I said when next we sat beneath our oak, "tonight we will 122
not discuss fallacies."

"Aw, gee," she said, disappointed. 123

"My dear," I said, favoring her with a smile, "we have now spent 124
five evenings together. We have gotten along splendidly. It is clear
that we are well matched."

"Hasty Generalization," said Polly brightly. 125

"I beg your pardon," said I. 126

"Hasty Generalization," she repeated. "How can you say that we 127
are well matched on the basis of only five dates?"

I chuckled with amusement. The dear child had learned her 128
lessons well. "My dear," I said, patting her hand in a tolerant manner,
"five dates is plenty. After all, you don't have to eat a whole cake to
know that it's good."

"False Analogy," said Polly promptly. "I'm not a cake. I'm a girl." 129

I chuckled with somewhat less amusement. The dear child had 130
learned her lessons perhaps too well. I decided to change tactics.
Obviously the best approach was a simple, strong, direct declaration of
love. I paused for a moment while my massive brain chose the proper
words. Then I began:

"Polly, I love you. You are the whole world to me, and the moon 131
and the stars and the constellations of outer space. Please, my darling,
say that you will go steady with me, for if you will not, life will be
meaningless. I will languish. I will refuse my meals. I will wander the
face of the earth, a shambling, hollow-eyed hulk."

There, I thought, folding my arms, that ought to do it. 132

"Ad Misericordiam," said Polly. 133

I ground my teeth. I was not Pygmalion; I was Frankenstein, and 134
my monster had me by the throat. Frantically I fought back the tide of
panic surging through me. At all costs I had to keep cool.

"Well, Polly," I said, forcing a smile, "you certainly have learned 135
your fallacies."

"You're darn right," she said with a vigorous nod.   136

"And who taught them to you, Polly?"   137

"You did."   138

"That's right. So you do owe me something, don't you, my dear? If I 139
hadn't come along you never would have learned about fallacies."

"Hypothesis Contrary to Fact," she said instantly.   140

I dashed perspiration from my brow. "Polly," I croaked, "you 141
mustn't take all these things so literally. I mean this is just classroom
stuff. You know that the things you learn in school don't have anything
to do with life."

"Dicto Simpliciter," she said, wagging her finger at me playfully. 142

That did it. I leaped to my feet, bellowing like a bull. "Will you or 143
will you not go steady with me?"

"I will not," she replied.   144

"Why not?" I demanded.   145

"Because this afternoon I promised Petey Burch that I would go 146
steady with him."

I reeled back, overcome with the infamy of it. After he promised, 147
after he made a deal, after he shook my hand! "The rat!" I shrieked,
kicking up great chunks of turf. "You can't go with him, Polly. He's a
liar. He's a cheat. He's a rat."

"Poisoning the Well," said Polly, "and stop shouting. I think 148
shouting must be a fallacy too."

With an immense effort of will, I modulated my voice. "All right, I 149
said. "You're a logician. Let's look at this thing logically. How could
you choose Petey Burch over me? Look at me—a brilliant student, a
tremendous intellectual, a man with an assured future. Look at
Petey—a knothead, a jitterbug, a guy who'll never know where his
next meal is coming from. Can you give me one logical reason why you
should go steady with Petey Burch?"

"I certainly can," declared Polly. "He's got a raccoon coat." 150

Study Questions

1. Is this an essay or a short story? How do you know?
2. Shulman repeatedly inverts normal subject-verb order. What does he accomplish by doing this?
3. This selection is entitled "Love Is a Fallacy." The narrator tells Polly that her "argument is a fallacy." The statements are similar in form. Are their meanings similar? Why?
4. By what means does Shulman characterize Polly?
5. Analyze in detail any one of the narrator's "logical" statements.

The Best Man
MARTIN E. MARTY

Martin E. Marty (1928–   ) was born in West Point, Nebraska. He is now a Professor of the History of Modern Christianity at the University of Chicago and associate editor of the *Christian Century*. After receiving B.A. and D.B. degrees from Concordia Seminary (1949, 1952), he attended the Lutheran School of Theology (S.T.M., 1954) and received a Ph.D. from the University of Chicago (1956). A regular contributor to numerous religious periodicals, he has published *The Improper Opinion* (1961), *Varieties on Unbelief* (1964), *The Modern Schism* (1969), *You Are Promise* (1973), *The Pro and Con Book of Religious America* (1975), and *A Nation of Believers* (1977), among others. For *Righteous Empire* (1970), he received the National Book Award.

At 7:00 A.M. the networks broke the news simultaneously: 1
"What had been mere rumors when America retired last night 2 became confirmed as fact moments ago.

"The long convention deadlock was finally broken at dawn and the 3 veil of secrecy was lifted at the convention hall. The new candidate, identified first only as The Favorite Son, met with all delegations and caucuses, none of whom opposed him. He was nominated by all the deadlocked candidates and became the party's choice by acclamation. Party officials expressed delight that he had chosen their party.

"The candidate told network representatives, however, that he was 4 not showing favoritism. In fact, he reminded them, 'My kingdom is not of this world.' Why had he made an appearance in America's Bicentennial Year, and why had he agreed to run for office? 'Oh, because this time I thought I should "work within the system." ' Was he surprised when the bandwagon rolled for him? 'It's happened before.' Was he worried about possible voter rejection? 'It's happened before.'

"Legal experts advised that a constitutional amendment may be 5 necessary because the candidate, Jesus of Nazareth, was born in Israel. . . ."

The event brought disarray in the ranks of the other party. 6 Late-morning special editions of the newspapers, however, carried a statement signed by all members of the national committee saying that their campaign plans would go ahead. "We remain in the race out of a deep sense of responsibility to our wonderful American two-party system. But we will not vote for our candidate, and ask the American people not to. No one votes against Jesus." The public-relations people picked up that last sentence. It became the slogan. In the course of the day buttons and posters were ready: "NO ONE VOTES AGAINST JESUS."

By noon it dawned on the party chairman that he had a religious 7 issue on his hands. "We forgot to check this all out with the religious leaders!" But the leaders, it turns out, had taken care of the issue on their own. The Catholic bishops announced their delight that for a third time there was a Catholic candidate. Meanwhile the Houston Protestant clergy bulletined their approval. Since the candidate was a Protestant, they were sure he would veto any proposed support for parochial schools. The Central Conference of American Rabbis promised not to oppose a candidate who, after all, "was a Jew, a rabbi, a friend of Israel," and added: "We do not hold against him the almost unbroken bad record of his followers against his own people, the Jews." In response to a phone call, Mrs. Madlyn Murray O'Hair, who had been uncharacteristically silent all day, announced that she was coming out of her recent self-imposed retirement in order to organize Atheists for Jesus: "When religious people hear his positions they'll be embarrassed. But now that he has reappeared I cannot find anyone who admits to being atheist. No one votes against Jesus."

The last skeptic, an unnamed member of the liberal Eastern 8 Establishment in the media, checked out the candidate's identity with Billy Graham: "Is this really Jesus?" Billy: "Oh, yes, I'd know him anywhere." The computers at the National Opinion Research Center gave instant scientific support for these claims. The C.I.A. clearly agreed that this was Jesus and that he needed special protection. A Defense Department representative who had been contacted by the Secret Service and the C.I.A. announced: "Despite the candidate's well-known nonviolent position and over his protests, we want to make it clear that if Cuba tries any assassination activity, the full force of our nuclear capabilities will be unleashed on that hostile island."

The candidate rested the first day but began his campaign by 9 showing up late at the next morning's Congressional Prayer Breakfast. Reporters were barred, but they had no difficulty picking up leaks after a while. Jesus had begun: "My Father and I have little stomach for these events. Early in the morning we hear your prayers. They inform us of your desire to please us. Then you climb the Hill and vote against our poor." A Senator broke the ensuing silence. "If elected—I mean, when elected—will you re-establish worship in the White House East Room?" The response: "Beware of practicing your piety before men in order to be seen by them. I said that long ago. Matthew 6:1. You could look it up."

The postbreakfast exchanges were revealing. Since the candidate, 10 who had no problem with the recognition factor, had skipped the primaries, his positions were not well known. What was his own platform? "Oh, you've had my platform for almost 2,000 years. It's set forth in a well-enough-known set of writings. The Gospels."

Q: "Why are you here now?" 11

A: "Simple. The Bicentennial. While America does not have 'most 12 favored-nation' status, my Father and I have always looked kindly on it. Never much impressed by the 'In God We Trust' on your money, we have been attracted by some lines in your founding creed. My Father, for example, has always liked that line about all people being 'endowed by their Creator with certain unalienable rights.' For 200 years your politicians and preachers have been reminding us that you are a nation 'under God.' We cannot even escape such prayers when we look in on a televised professional football game. I knew, however, that you were in trouble. True, as recently as 1970, I heard your former President say, 'I know America, and the American heart is good." But I thought you should have a chance to show it."

The breakfast chaplain asked the candidate whether he thought 13 immoral America would respond to the principles of his ethical system. Jesus answered: "Here the nonbelievers and the scholars have it more correct than you do. I don't have a system of ethical principles. I left you with a set of active verbs: 'repent,' 'believe,' 'heal', 'love.' I announced a coming Kingdom. The Gospels do not provide general principles for everyone. True, I have always asked people to love everyone, including their enemies. That ought to keep this nation busy for a while. But if you'll reread them, you'll see that the Gospels are full of my announcement of the coming Kingdom. They are full of urgency and calls to change your ways. At such a time we don't set forth mild guidelines for living. I am aware that in these latter days there have been many bizarre best sellers that tell exactly what I would do if I returned to earth. Well, you can imagine: Each author has me saying exactly what he or she wants me to say. I rather think of myself as a misfit in any circumstance. It is your idea that your nation should be measured by my teachings. You say that often enough. So, for a few months or years, I'll play the game your way. How are you doing at feeding the hungry, peacemaking, loving your enemies?" The chaplain immediately pronounced the benediction.

One late afternoon, framed against the 10 story library mosaic   a 14 "poor likeness," everyone said—at Notre Dame stadium, the candidate appeared at the largest press conference in history. He was asked whether this was the Second Coming.

"No. The Second Coming is still waiting for some first-class 15 repentances. You'll recognize it when it occurs. The Gospels tell about angels and trumpets and clouds of power and glory and thrones. (We have a little taste for the theatrical at big occasions like Second Comings. This is only a dry run, a sort of trial balloon.)"

Patrick Buchanan spoke up. "Three urgent questions are left over 16 from the McGovern campaign. Alphabetically, how are you on abortion, acid and amnesty?"

"On abortion, I am, of course, prolife. I wish the prolife people were 17 prolife. We are pleased to see how solicitous many of them are about the life of fetuses. How many of them spoke up for life when you were bombing real, live, innocent babies back in Cambodia? We seldom heard a peep then. [A headline after that exchange was: "CANDI-DATE DUCKS ABORTION ISSUE."] Acid? I have a great concern for health and wholeness. Amnesty? My platform is quite clear. On almost every page there is something about being reconciled to your brother."

Sensing that the Buchanan alphabet was getting close to "bus- 18 ing," party officials decided not to test their "No One Votes Against Jesus" slogan, and adjourned the conference. As the 55,000 reporters hurried out, party leaders assessed the damage. Asked one: "Did you hear him sneak in that new line for a benediction? What's this 'Blessed are the peacemakers, for they shall be called sons of God' stuff? The peace issue is controversial enough, but this business about 'sons' will alienate the E.R.A. people."

The image experts tried a rescue job, and whisked the candidate 19 back to New York. Taken to the top of the World Trade Center, he looked down on all the kingdoms of the world. What he saw was New York. He wept. A press agent said, "Don't let that get out. You know what a good cry did to Ed Muskie four years ago. The people don't want a human candidate. We certainly don't dare let them think Jesus is one!" At a midnight reception, the candidate was asked by New York leaders what he would do about their debts. "Remember my counsel in Luke? 'For which of you, intending to build a tower, sitteth not down first, and counteth the cost, whether he hath sufficient to finish it?' The guests dispersed into the night.

In the midst of the night, there came to him a religious delegation. 20 "Aren't you at least pleased with our religious revival? Everyone is talking about you." Jesus answered them saying, "Not everyone that saith unto me, 'Lord Lord,' shall enter into the Kingdom of heaven, but he that doeth the will of my Father which is in heaven." Did he not like anything he'd seen in America? "Oh, yes, I am not hard to please, except when I use the drastic standards of the Kingdom for measurement. I enjoy the faith of children. Some people are not grim and despairing. I've looked in on a couple of good parties. I've seen some acts of grace in homes for the aged and heard a good choir or two. Some simple people say wonderful prayers and then share their bread. I even heard of an offended woman who forgave her husband."

Any complaints about organized religion and its role in the 21 campaign? "I am not enthusiastic about the 'Bingo for Jesus' support. I'd like redistribution of church wealth. Your churches own $80 billion in property. Couldn't a bit more of your income go for bread for the hungry?"

That $80 billion figure leaked out, and someone brought it up on 22 "Meet the Press" the next day. "Yes," the candidate agreed, "$80 billion is a lot for 300 years' worth of church building. It is almost as much as one year's defense budget and would more than pay for your next single weapon, the B-1 bomber. But my enemy—not the candidate of the other party, but The Enemy—need have no fear about your getting priorities confused. He and I both know that most of your funds will go into killing. Where your treasure is, there is your heart also."

That exchange inspired a question about defense and then about 23 detente. "We don't use that word. We speak of 'reconciliation.' " When he went on about "turning the other cheek" to the attacker, the party chairman, watching at home, turned off his television. "That crack will produce a million goddamn letters from the National Rifle Association."

No letters came in. No one was against Jesus. He could say 24
anything without provoking a negative response. The common people
heard him gladly. Columnists Evans and Novak were puzzled: "He
sounds conservative half the time and super-liberal the rest of the
time, but Gallup and Harris polls find no one ready to vote against
him. To date he has said things that ought to have provoked the
opposition of prayer breakfasters, the clergy, pro- and antiabortionists,
acid droppers, enemies of amnesty, New Yorkers, the military and
defense establishments, socialists and capitalists." At a party in his
home William F. Buckley whispered, "If you keep taking these
positions, my God, they'll *crucify* you!" He blanched as he heard
himself and gasped, "Oh, I'm sorry." His guest smiled. A knowing,
forgiving smile.

The months passed. It was a good year. People had been looking for 25
a candidate who favored small government and this one seemed to
favor no government at all. Voters wanted a candidate who was
compassionate, decent, trustworthy. He was all of these.

September and October produced two delicate moments. First, the 26
males in the antipornography movement brought their huge collections of hardcore materials to the candidate, asking him to condemn
those who produced them. But he, knowing their own hearts, said to
them that "everyone who looks at a woman lustfully has committed
adultery with her in his heart." He went on, "If your right eye causes
you to sin, pluck it out and throw it away." The National Conference of
Ophthalmologists announced that while they would still vote for Jesus,
they opposed this specific policy because of malpractice hazards. In any
case, after having confronted the candidate, the antipornography
forces themselves dispersed and the issue was dropped. In October the
Foundation for Christian Economic Freedom brought economic issues
to a head. The F.C.E.F. wanted the candidate to promise that he would
name Prof. Milton Friedman to be his chief economic adviser, since it
was clear that *this* candidate at last was one who would favor an
absolutely free market and permit unlimited accumulation of private
property, untrammeled by regulation or other concerns. The candidate's press aide put them off with a release that said simply: "If you
would be perfect, go, sell what you possess and give to the poor . . . and
come, follow me. Matthew 19:21."

Election Day came. How many would vote against Jesus? Now the 27
answer would be clear. The usual number of people went to cast
ballots. When the first returns—from Dixville Notch, N.H.—came in at
12:01 A.M. on Election Day, everyone got a hint of what was going on.
By 6:45 that evening, with the first projections in Kentucky and
Indiana, everyone was sure.

There was no winner of the Presidency. No one had voted against 28
Jesus. No one had voted *for* him, either.

Next morning, the cleaning woman began to work in the now- 29
vacant hotel room of the former candidate. He had left her a nice tip in

the ash tray. On the night stand she saw two scribbled notes. Both had references to Bible verses. One said "Matt. 15:8." The other: "Luke 23:34." The Gideon Bible was at hand, and she opened it. The first verse read, "This people draweth nigh unto me with their mouth, and honoureth me with their lips; but their heart is far from me." The one from Luke began, "Father, forgive. . . ." She crumpled the first, and pushed the second one, along with the tip, into her apron pocket. She wondered whether America would go four years without any President. If so, would anyone notice?

Two months later, Vogue's column began: "PEOPLE are talking 30 about . . . the impact left by America's first Presidential candidate who did not receive a single negative vote. Everyone liked him. He was loving. We remember a look of almost infinite tenderness in his eyes. We will never forget him. . . . THE NEW KICK: Bisexual parties for the Bicentennial. . . ."

Study Questions

1. Although this essay is written in the past tense, there is a real sense of immediacy, of the present, about it. Why?
2. What is the style an imitation of?
3. How does Marty manage to avoid writing in a strict Q. and A. format?
4. Many of the allusions are distinctly contemporary. Does that date the essay?
5. What is the effect of 'He wept' in paragraph 19?
6. What is "The Best Man"? Satire? Allegory? Parody? Parable?

Salvation
LANGSTON HUGHES

Langston Hughes (1902–1967) was born in Joplin, Missouri. After attending Columbia University, he received a B.A. from Lincoln University in 1929. His first poem, "The Negro Speaks of Rivers," was published in 1921 in *Crisis*. He drifted around the United States, to Europe and Africa, before poet Vachel Lindsay took an interest in his work and helped him get published. Thereafter Hughes wrote poetry, fiction, and drama, earning the title of "Poet Laureate of Harlem." In his newspaper columns in the *New York Post* and the Chicago *Defender,* he created Jesse B. Semple (generally called Simple), a character who was Hughes's persona for years thereafter. Among Hughes's books are *The Weary Blues* (1926), *The Dream Keeper* (1932), *Shakespeare in Harlem* (1942), *Simple Speaks His Mind* (1950), and his autobiography, *The Big Sea* (1940). As the editor of anthologies of works by other black writers, Hughes extended his own sphere of literary influence while continuing to champion his people.

1   I was saved from sin when I was going on thirteen. But not really saved. It happened like this. There was a big revival at my Auntie Reed's church. Every night for weeks there had been much preaching, singing, praying, and shouting, and some very hardened sinners had been brought to Christ, and the membership of the church had grown by leaps and bounds. Then just before the revival ended, they held a special meeting for children, "to bring the young lambs to the fold." My aunt spoke of it for days ahead. That night I was escorted to the front row and placed on the mourners' bench with all the other young sinners, who had not yet been brought to Jesus.

2   My aunt told me that when you were saved you saw a light, and something happened to you inside! And Jesus came into your life! And God was with you from then on! She said you could see and hear and feel Jesus in your soul. I believed her. I have heard a great many old people say the same thing and it seemed to me they ought to know. So I sat there calmly in the hot, crowded church, waiting for Jesus to come to me.

3   The preacher preached a wonderful rhythmical sermon, all moans and shouts and lonely cries and dire pictures of hell, and then he sang a song about the ninety and nine safe in the fold, but one little lamb was left out in the cold. Then he said: "Won't you come? Won't you come to Jesus? Young lambs, won't you come?" And he held out his arms to all

us young sinners there on the mourners' bench. And the little girls
cried. And some of them jumped up and went to Jesus right away. But
most of us just sat there.

A great many old people came and knelt around us and prayed, old   4
women with jet-black faces and braided hair, old men with work-
gnarled hands. And the church sang a song about the lower lights are
burning, some poor sinners to be saved. And the whole building rocked
with prayer and song.

Still I kept waiting to *see* Jesus.   5

Finally all the young people had gone to the altar and were saved,   6
but one boy and me. He was a rounder's son named Westley. Westley
and I were surrounded by sisters and deacons praying. It was very hot
in the church, and getting late now. Finally Westley said to me in a
whisper: "God damn! I'm tired o' sitting here. Let's get up and be
saved." So he got up and was saved.

Then I was left all alone on the mourners' bench. My aunt came   7
and knelt at my knees and cried, while prayers and songs swirled all
around me in the little church. The whole congregation prayed for me
alone, in a mighty wail of moans and voices. And I kept waiting
serenely for Jesus, waiting, waiting—but he didn't come. I wanted to
see him, but nothing happened to me. Nothing! I wanted something to
happen to me, but nothing happened.

I heard the songs and the minister saying: "Why don't you come?   8
My dear child, why don't you come to Jesus? Jesus is waiting for you.
He wants you. Why don't you come? Sister Reed, what is this child's
name?"

"Langston," my aunt sobbed.   9

"Langston, why don't you come? Why don't you come and be saved?   10
Oh, Lamb of God! Why don't you come?"

Now it was really getting late. I began to be ashamed of myself,   11
holding everything up so long. I began to wonder what God thought
about Westley, who certainly hadn't seen Jesus either, but who was
now sitting proudly on the platform, swinging his knickerbockered
legs and grinning down at me, surrounded by deacons and old women
on their knees praying. God had not struck Westley dead for taking his
name in vain or for lying in the temple. So I decided that maybe to save
further trouble, I'd better lie, too, and say that Jesus had come, and get
up and be saved.

So I got up.   12

Suddenly the whole room broke into a sea of shouting, as they saw   13
me rise. Waves of rejoicing swept the place. Women leaped in the air.
My aunt threw her arms around me. The minister took me by the hand
and led me to the platform.

When things quieted down, in a hushed silence, punctuated by a   14
few ecstatic "Amens," all the new young lambs were blessed in the
name of God. Then joyous singing filled the room.

That night, for the last time in my life but one—for I was a big boy   15
twelve years old—I cried. I cried, in bed alone, and couldn't stop. I
buried my head under the quilts, but my aunt heard me. She woke up

and told my uncle I was crying because the Holy Ghost had come into my life, and because I had seen Jesus. But I was really crying because I couldn't bear to tell her that I had lied, that I had deceived everybody in the church, that I hadn't seen Jesus, and that now I didn't believe there was a Jesus any more, since he didn't come to help me.

Study Questions

1. Does Hughes tell of our salvation from a child's point of view or that of an adult looking back at a childhood incident?
2. Is the situation Hughes describes funny? Does he at any point write humorously?
3. Consider the first word of each paragraph. How many of them are concerned with the concept of time? What does this tell you about how Hughes organized this section of his autobiography?
4. Traditionally, pronouns are capitalized when referring to God or Christ. Hughes does not do this. Why not?
5. How can you tell that Hughes the boy saw himself as part of a group from which girls were excluded?

Facing Up to Death
ELISABETH KÜBLER-ROSS

Elisabeth Kübler-Ross (1926–   ) was born in Zurich, Switzerland. Her medical degree is from the University of Zurich, and she has received honorary degrees from Smith College and the University of Notre Dame, among others. She has said that her preoccupation with death is the result of her experiences during World War II and the Holocaust. A series of seminars for the staff at Billings Hospital in Chicago, in 1965, resulted in a very influential group of essays and books on the experience of death. Among Kübler-Ross's full-length studies are *On Death and Dying* (1969) and *Death: The Final Stage* (1974).

People used to be born at home and die at home. In the old   1
days, children were familiar with birth and death as part of life. This is perhaps the first generation of American youngsters who have never

From *Today's Education*, January 1972. Published by the National Education Association. Reprinted by permission of *Today's Education* and Elisabeth Kübler-Ross.

been close by during the birth of a baby and have never experienced the death of a beloved family member.

Nowadays when people grow old, we often send them to nursing 2 homes. When they get sick, we transfer them to a hospital, where children are usually unwelcome and are forbidden to visit terminally ill patients—even when those patients are their parents. This deprives the dying patient of significant family members during the last few days of his life and it deprives the children of an experience of death, which is an important learning experience.

At the University of Chicago's Billings Hospital, some of my 3 colleagues and I interviewed and followed approximately 500 terminally ill patients in order to find out what they could teach us and how we could be of more benefit, not just to them but to the members of their families as well. We were most impressed by the fact that even those patients who were not told of their serious illness were quite aware of its potential outcome. They were not only able to say that they were close to dying, but many were able to predict the approximate time of their death.

It is important for next of kin and members of the helping 4 professions to understand these patients' communications in order to truly understand their needs, fears, and fantasies. Most of our patients welcomed another human being with whom they could talk openly, honestly, and frankly about their predicament. Many of them shared with us their tremendous need to be informed, to be kept up-to-date on their medical condition, and to be told when the end was near. We found out that patients who had been dealt with openly and frankly were better able to cope with the imminence of death and finally to reach a true stage of acceptance prior to death.

Two things seem to determine the ultimate adjustment to a 5 terminal illness. When patients were allowed hope at the beginning of a fatal illness and when they were informed that they would not be deserted "no matter what," they were able to drop their initial shock and denial rather quickly and could arrive at a peaceful acceptance of their finiteness.

Most patients respond to the awareness that they have a terminal 6 illness with the statement, "Oh no, this can't happen to me." After the first shock, numbness, and need to deny the reality of the situation, the patient begins to send out cues that he is ready to "talk about it." If we, at that point, need to deny the reality of the situation, the patient will often feel deserted, isolated, and lonely and unable to communicate with another human being what he needs so desperately to share.

When, on the other hand, the patient has one person with whom he 7 can talk freely, he will be able to talk (often for only a few minutes at a time) about his illness and about the consequences of his deteriorating health, and he will be able to ask for help. Sometimes, he'll need to talk about financial matters; and, toward the end of the life, he will frequently ask for some spiritual help.

Most patients who have passed the stage of denial will become 8 angry as they ask the question, "Why me?" Many look at others in their environment and express envy, jealousy, anger, and rage toward those who are young, healthy, and full of life. These are the patients who make life difficult for nurses, physicians, social workers, clergymen, and members of their families. Without justification they criticize everyone.

What we have to learn is that the stage of anger in terminal illness 9 is a blessing, not a curse. These patients are not angry at their families or at the members of the helping professions. Rather, they are angry at what these people represent: health, pep, energy.

Without being judgmental, we must allow these patients to express 10 their anger and dismay. We must try to understand that the patients have to ask, "Why me?" and that there is no need on our part to answer this question concretely. Once a patient has ventilated his rage and his envy, then he can arrive at the bargaining stage. During this time, he's usually able to say, "Yes, it is happening to me—*but.*" The *but* usually includes a prayer to God: "If you give me one more year to live, I will be a good Christian (or I'll go to the synagogue every day)."

Most patients promise something in exchange for prolongation of 11 life. Many a patient wants to live just long enough for the children to get out of school. The moment they have completed high school, he may ask to live until the son gets married. And the moment the wedding is over, he hopes to live until the grandchild arrives. These kinds of bargains are compromises, the patient's beginning acknowledgement that his time is limited, and an expression of finiteness, all necessary in reaching a stage of acceptance. When a patient drops the *but,* then he is able to say, "Yes, me." At this point, he usually becomes very depressed. And here again we have to allow him to express his grief and his mourning.

If we stop and think how much we would grieve if we lost a beloved 12 spouse, it will make us realize what courage it takes for a man to face his own impending death, which involves the loss of everyone and everything he has ever loved. This is a thousand times more crushing than to become a widow or a widower.

To such patients, we should never say, "Come on now, cheer up." 13 We should allow them to grieve, to cry. And we should even convey to them that "it takes a brave person to cry," meaning that it takes courage to face death. If the patient expresses his grief, he will feel more comfortable, and he will usually go through the stage of depression much more rapidly than he will if he has to suppress it or hide his tears.

Only through this kind of behavior on our part are our patients 14 able to reach the stage of acceptance. Here, they begin to separate themselves from the interpersonal relationships in their environment. Here, they begin to ask for fewer and fewer visitors. Finally, they will require only one beloved person who can sit quietly and comfortably near.

This is the time when a touch becomes more important than words, 15 the time when a patient may simply say one day, "My time is very close now, and it's all right." It is not necessarily a happy stage, but the patient now shows no more fear, bitterness, anguish, or concern over unfinished business. People who have been able to sit through this stage with patients and who have experienced the beautiful feeling of inner and outer peace that they show will soon appreciate that working with terminally ill patients is not a morbid, depressing job but can be an inspiring experience.

The tragedy is that in our death-denying society, people grow up 16 uncomfortable in the presence of a dying patient, unable to talk to the terminally ill and lost for words when they face a grieving person.

We tried to use dying patients as teachers. We talked with these 17 patients so they could teach our young medical students, social work students, nurses, and members of the clergy about one part of life that all of us eventually have to face. When we interviewed them, we had a screened window setup in which we were able to talk with them in privacy while our students observed and listened. Needless to say this observation was done with the knowledge and agreement of our patients.

This teaching by dying patients who volunteered this service to us 18 enabled them to share some of their turmoil and some of their needs with us. But perhaps more important than that, they were able to help our own young students to face the reality of death, to identify at times with our dying patients, and to become aware of their own finiteness.

Many of our young students who originally were petrified at the 19 thought of facing dying patients were eventually able to express to us their own concerns, their own fears, and their own fantasies about dying. Most of our students who have been able to attend one quarter or perhaps a semester of these weekly death-and-dying seminars have learned to come to grips with their own fears of death and have ultimately become good counselors to terminally ill patients.

One thing this teaches us is that it would be helpful if we could 20 rear our children with the awareness of death and of their own finiteness. Even in a death-denying society, this can be and has been done.

In our hospital we saw a small child with acute leukemia. She 21 made the rounds and asked the adults, "What is it going to be like when I die?" The grown-ups responded in a variety of ways, most of them unhelpful or even harmful for this little girl who was searching for an answer. The only message she really received through the grown-ups' response was that they had a lot of fear when it came to talking about dying.

When the child confronted the hospital chaplain with the same 22 question, he turned to her and asked, "What do you think it's going to be like?" She looked at him and said, "One of these days I'm going to fall asleep and when I wake up I'm going to be with Jesus and my little sister." He then said something like "That should be very beautiful." The child nodded and happily returned to play. Perhaps this is an exaggerated example, but I think it conveys how children face the reality even of their own death if the adults in their environment don't make it a frightening, horrible experience to be avoided at all costs.

The most forgotten people in the environment of the dying patient 23 are the brothers and sisters of dying children. We have seen rather tragic examples of siblings who were terribly neglected during the terminal illness of a brother or a sister. Very often those children are left alone with many unanswered questions while the mother attends the dying child in the hospital and the father doesn't come home from work because he wants to visit the hospital in the evening.

The tragedy is that these children at home not only are anxious, 24 lonely, and frightened at the thought of their sibling's death, but they also feel that somehow their wish for a sibling to "drop dead" (which all children have at times) is being fulfilled. When such a sibling actually dies, they feel responsible for the death, just as they do when they lose a parent during the preschool years. If these children receive no help prior to, and especially immediately after, the death of a parent or a sibling, they are likely to grow up with abnormal fears of death and a lot of unresolved conflicts that often result in emotional illness later on in life.

We hope that teachers are aware of the needs of these children and 25 can make themselves available to them in order to elicit expression of their fears, their fantasies, their needs. If they're allowed to express their anger for being neglected and their shame for having "committed a crime," then these children can be helped before they develop permanent emotional conflict.

A beautiful example of death education in an indirect way is 26 expressed in a letter I received from a man who became aware of my work and felt the need to convey some of his life experiences to me. I will quote his letter verbatim because it shows what an early childhood memory can do for a man when he's faced with the imminent death of his own father.

> Dear Dr. Ross: May I commend you and your colleagues who took part in 27 the Conference on "death   "
>
> I am a production-line brewery worker here in Milwaukee who feels 28 strongly on this subject. Because of your efforts, maybe one day we can all look death in the eye. . . . In reading and rereading the enclosed account of your meeting, I found myself with the urge to relate to you a personal experience of my own.
>
> About six years ago, my dad was a victim of terminal cancer. He was a 29 tough, life-loving 73-year-old father of 10 with 10 grandchildren who kept him aglow and always on the go. It just couldn't be that his time had come. The last time I saw him alive was the result of an urgent phone call from my sister. "You'd better come home as soon as possible; it's Pa."
>
> The 500-mile drive to northern Minnesota wasn't the enjoyable trip 30 that so many others had been. I learned after I arrived that he wasn't in the hospital, but at home. I also learned that "he didn't know." The doctor told the family that it was up to us to tell him or not tell him. My brother and sisters who live in the area thought it best "not to" and so advised me.
>
> When I walked in on him, we embraced as we always did when we'd 31 visit about twice or so each year. But this time it was different—sort of restrained and lacking the spirit of earlier get-togethers; and each of us, I know, sensed this difference.
>
> Then, some hours later, after the usual kinds of questions and 32 answers and talk, it was plain to me that he appeared so alone and

withdrawn, almost moody or sulking. It was scary to see him just sitting there, head in hand, covering his eyes. I didn't know what to say or do. I asked if he'd care for a drink—no response. Something had to give. It all seemed so cruel. So I stepped into the kitchen and poured me a good one—and another. This was it, and if he didn't "know," he would now.

I went over and sat down beside and sort of facing him, and I was 33 scared. I was always scared of my father, but it was a good kind of fear, the respectful kind. I put one hand on his shoulder and the other on his knee. I said, "Pa, you know why I came home, don't you? This is the last time we will be together." The dam burst. He threw his arms around me, and just hung on.

And here's the part I'll never forget and yet always cherish. I 34 remember when our tears met, I recalled, in a sort of vivid flashback, a time 30 years before when I was five or six and he took me out into the woods to pick hazelnuts. My very first big adventure! I remembered being afraid of the woods. Afraid of bears or monsters or something that would eat me up. But even though I was afraid, I at the same time was brave, because my big strong daddy was with me.

Needless to say, thanks to that hazelnut hunt, I knew how my dad was 35 feeling at that moment. And I could only hope that I gave him some small measure of courage; the kind he had given me. I do know he was grateful and appreciated my understanding. As I remember, he regained his composure and authority enough to scold *me* for crying. It was at the kitchen table, after a couple or three fingers of brandy, that we talked and reminisced and planned. I would even guess he was eager to start a long search for his wife, who also had known how to die. . . .

What I am trying to convey is that everything depends on the way 36 we rear our children. If we help them to face fear and show them that through strength and sharing we can overcome even the fear of dying, then they will be better prepared to face any kind of crisis that might confront them, including the ultimate reality of death.

Study Questions

1. This essay was originally printed in *Today's Education.* At what point do you realize that Kübler-Ross addresses her remarks to those who teach children? How effective is the final paragraph?
2. Use examples of Kübler-Ross's diction to comment on her tone in the essay.
3. How many "stages" do the dying go through? Where is each of these stages discussed in the essay?
4. Examine paragraphs 3–16. Is this section of the essay conventionally organized? Are there subunits, groupings of paragraphs within this section? What transitional devices does Kübler-Ross use?
5. Find examples such as those in paragraph 11 which help make this essay more vivid.
6. Are you surprised to find that the letter Kübler-Ross quotes was written by a production-line brewery worker? Why or why not?

Modern Social Problems

SOME MUST WATCH

2

The category of modern social problems admits such a wide range of topics that a limited number of selections can represent only a small part of the whole. That part covered by the nine essays and one short story chosen for this section includes topics familiar to most people, either indirectly through observation and the experience of others or through personal involvement. It would be surprising if anyone did not have an opinion or ideas on most of the topics included: rape, unwed mothers, divorce, problems of retirement, the threat of the bomb, life in the suburbs.

Norman Cousins's "Unwed Mothers in America" deals with a problem that has become a major concern in our society. Describing the magnitude of the increasing numbers of unwed mothers, especially young ones, he states that "a bomb has already fallen on America, the effects of which touch all of us." He offers no remedy, only a proposal for the first step to place this problem higher on our priorities for national concern.

Retirement, the American dream that has become a nightmare for many people, is Kenneth Bernard's concern in "The First Step to the Cemetery." Contrary to what we are led to believe, retirement today means a wretched existence, according to Bernard. In pungent prose he describes the pitfalls and conditions that await the retired person in these times of inflation. Worse than the financial plight, the retired person becomes an outcast, a member of an unwanted minority. Although students are too far from retirement to share these concerns, they will have opinions based on what they know about older relatives who have retired.

In sharp contrast to Cousins's and Bernard's serious and alarming tones, Russell Baker's "Son of H-Bomb" is a light and lively account of how the author regards the specter that has grown more terrifying for all of us—the threat of nuclear war. Beneath the surface of his humor, Baker satirizes the logic used to justify the growing number and types of nuclear armament.

Gloria Steinem's "Wonder Woman" is an account of her early introduction to feminism and all it implies. Surprisingly, she found it in the comic book *Wonder Woman,* created by psychologist William Moulton Marston. This is a provocative essay that should appeal to students who have found serious social implications in comic books and comic strips. In contrast to Steinem's tone and presentation, Art Buchwald's "Acid Indigestion" and Erma Bombeck's "Super Mom in the Suburbs" illustrate how a subject ordinarily treated seriously can be written in a light and humorous style. They also demonstrate different modes of development that may be used as models for students to follow in writing on similar subjects.

For an example of irony at its classic best, Swift's "A Modern Proposal" is retained from earlier editions of *Strategies in Prose.* Although written for another time and audience, it deals with topics that trouble our age. In addition to offering students the opportunity to analyze masterfully written prose, it may be used to suggest ways students can deal with similar topics.

The pro-and-con essays in this section are Roy Schenk's "So Why Do Rapes Occur?" and Gina Allen's "A Reply to Roy Schenk." They write on a topic that is another of society's major concerns. Schenck's position is that one cause of rape is female chauvinism. This and other arguments he advances will provoke analyses and rebuttals far more vigorous than Allen's.

The John Updike story concerns one of the most appropriate topics for this section. "Separating" is a sensitive and gracefully structured story about divorce and its effects upon the various members of the family, especially the young son who wants to know why. Divorce is so common today that many students will identify with the situation described in the story and with the reactions of the children. In addition to its other qualities to be noted in an analysis, this story illustrates how intense feelings and emotional situations can be handled with restraint and detachment.

Unwed Mothers in America

NORMAN COUSINS

Norman Cousins (1915–   ) was born in New Jersey. He received a Litt.D. from the American Univerity in 1948, and has been awarded honorary degrees by many other colleges and universities, including Notre Dame, Brandeis, and Washington and Jefferson. Although probably best known as the editor of *Saturday Review*, Cousins has performed in a similar capacity for *Current History* and served as chairman of programming for PBS. He has received awards too numerous to list for journalism, and for his efforts in education and humanitarian endeavors. His works include *Talks with Nehru* (1951), *Who Speaks for Man?* (1952), *Doctor Schweitzer of Lambarene* (1960), and *The Celebration of Life* (1975).

The grimmest statistics of 1979 have nothing to do with 1 inflation or even the cost of the arms race. Nothing about the year now ending deserves greater concern and scrutiny than the fact that almost a million babies were born to unwed women. Equally startling and disturbing is a statistic showing that about 600,000 teenagers become mothers each year. Of these, more than 10,000 are 14 years of age or younger.

The problem is compounded when many of the unwed mothers, 2 especially the teenagers, go on to have additional children. One of the reasons behind that decision is that the mothers cannot support themselves and are attracted to the added welfare payments given for each family member.

Inevitably, the immediate question raised by these developments 3 concerns the economic cost. The Population Resource Center has estimated that the bill for the first 10 years of life of each child born to a teenager will be $18,710. This translates into more than $8 billion for the entire group. If these figures are projected to all the children born of unwed and economically dependent mothers during the next 20 years, assuming the total number of babies each year is no greater than it is now, the eventual cost could be in excess of $100 billion. Inflation could add another $20 billion to the total expenditure.

But the economic cost, catastrophic though it is, may actually be 4 the minor part of the problem. Far more serious is the social, moral, and psychological impact on life in America. What happens to a nation when the family ceases to exist as the central and stabilizing unit of society? Underlining and magnifying this problem is the current divorce rate, now approaching 40 percent.

In this light, there is something almost bizarre about the preoccu- 5 pation of the American people with military security from external sources. A bomb has already fallen on America. The shattering effect is reaching into every aspect and corner of our lives. It doesn't take much imagination to visualize the disfiguration of a society when a large percentage of the population requires government support. Moreover, government is being forced not just to assume the financial burden but to provide the kind of care that in many cases is beyond the capacity of many mothers. Doctors report that a horrendously high number of teenage mothers are emotionally and intellectually incapable of bringing up their children. The same failure applies to many older women. Social-welfare agencies are therefore confronted with the need to fill the roles of both mother and father on a day-to-day basis. The pressure on schools and particularly on teachers is correspondingly great.

How did we come to this point?   6

It will be said that the decline of religion in American life in the 7 past 20 or 30 years may account for a large part of the problem. Yet many unwed mothers identify themselves as members of religious denominations. Nor do all the girls come from broken homes. What we are dealing with here is a complex equation involving many factors, not all of them readily identifiable. Certainly it is true that moral and social restraints no longer have a presiding presence in American life. Marriage is no longer universally considered an indispensable or even desirable condition of a full and ongoing relationship between the sexes. Explicit love scenes between young people—or people of any age, for that matter—are commonplace in almost every form of entertainment, especially in film and print. Unfortunately, no one has yet figured out a way to control pornography without touching off perhaps even greater problems in government thought control; but it is absurd to contend that the kind of exploitation of sex that now abounds in society does not produce desensitization and casualness about the prime elements of life. It is similarly irresponsible to contend that there is no connection between the saturating violence in the entertainment media and the lack of respect for human emotions and for life in general.

One of the dangers in the present situation is that if it continues 8 unchecked, a demand will go up for the sterilization of unwed mothers with more than one child—with their consent if possible but without their consent if necessary. Before the problem deteriorates to that level, it would be useful if a presidential commission could examine every aspect of the question and its long-term implications. Such a study should look into all the interacting factors of home background, housing, community experience, quality of education, church influence, economic conditions, and so forth. A report by itself would not solve the problem, but it might succeed at least in getting the issue into the American consciousness and putting it at the top of the national agenda, where it belongs.

Study Questions

1. What effect does the author achieve by using statistics in the opening paragraph?
2. What is the rhetorical function of the one-sentence paragraph 6?
3. Analyze the way the sentences in paragraph 7 are linked.
4. Note the metaphor in paragraph 5. In what ways is it appropriate?
5. How does the author establish and maintain a voice of authority?
6. Analyze the structure of the last sentence of the essay. What is the author's strategy?

The First Step to the Cemetery
KENNETH BERNARD

Kenneth Bernard (1930–   ) was born in Brooklyn, received a B.A. from the City College of New York, and an M.A. and Ph.D. from Columbia University. An indefatigable writer, he has published fiction, drama, poetry, and critical articles, especially on the theater. His published books include *The Maldive Chronicles*, a novel (1970); *Night Club and Other Plays* (1971); *Two Stories* (1973); and *The Magic Show of Dr. Magico* (1979). Bernard's work has appeared in the *New American Review*, the *Paris Review*, *Harper's*, and *Tri-Quarterly*, and he has served as fiction editor for *Confrontation*. He has received writing grants from the Guggenheim and Rockefeller Foundations as well as the National Endowment for the Arts.

The prevailing vision of the good life in America has for 1 some time included early retirement. Numerous voices speak in its behalf, from insurance companies to unions to government agencies. Quit while you're ahead, still healthy and young enough to enjoy a generous spread of the sunset years. Not only should you enjoy the fruit of your labors in this most bountiful of countries, say the many voices, but you should also give the young folk their chance to move up by exiting gracefully. There are, you are told, numerous benefits—tax, medical, recreational, psychological. It is not only foolish to overlook the opportunity; it is downright un-American. So why not do it? Why not? Because it will probably be the worst decision you have ever made. Here's why.

To begin, it is an immediate, and usually irrevocable, step into 2 second-class citizenship. Once retired, you are one with blacks, Hispanics, the handicapped, homosexuals, jailbirds, the insane, the retarded, children and women: America's Third World hordes. America doesn't like old people, and retired people are old people, whether they are 45, 55 or 65. Old people clutter up the landscape. Their families don't want them. Their communities don't want them. They are a nightmare vision of everyone's future. They are of interest mainly to doctors and hospitals, real-estate brokers and travel agents—but not as people, rather as bodies from whom some final payments can still be exacted.

Colonies: In America you are primarily valued not for your good 3 deeds or your good character. You are valued for the money you command. The more money you have, the better you are treated by everyone from your local cop to your congressman. If you doubt this, go to any store or social agency. Go, for example, to any urban clinic and see what it is like to be old, sick and poor. There is a living hell. You get neither kindness nor respect nor service. To voluntarily take a step toward that condition you have to be either blind or mad. For as your ability to command money decreases, so too does your stature as a human being. To doctors, you are less important than the forms they must process to get money for their services. To landlords, you are a barrier to higher rents. Small wonder that retirees band together in colonies, in clubs, homes and hospitals. They want to belong, and they can do so only with their own kind. Everywhere else, their money will be taken, but they will be shut out.

What are these colonies like? To be sure, just as there are decent 4 people who respect old people, so too there are homes, hospitals and communities that are genuinely humanitarian, that perform genuine functions. But how many? Our public knowledge of old-age homes is that they are less clean and only slightly less efficient than slaughterhouses, dismal halfway houses to the grave: turnover is profit.

In some societies where people live to be very old, it is observable 5 that they, whatever their age, have useful, needed work to perform. In America, activities for old people are manufactured. People get degrees in how to occupy old people with busy-work. But this has nothing to do with life; it is all meaningless filler. These people are out of it. Although everyone knows it, everyone lies about it and society conspires to keep them there. It is a not so genteel form of genocide. The old people know it, too; and, knowing it (and often being very gracious), they cooperate: they begin to die in spirit and then bodily. And no amount of shuffleboard, creative writing, canasta or sight-seeing can hide the unpleasant truth. Society's message is: spend money, but stay out of the way, and make no demands.

Old people are besieged by indifference, loneliness and uselessness. **6** They are also physically assaulted by toughs and criminals. They are, understandably, fearful. Often they are imprisoned in their own homes. Yes, the perpetrators are few in number, but the assaults could not take place without a climate of sentiment, a cast of mind, that allowed for them. Our society fears the natural extinction of life so much that it behaves grotesquely. After all, with luck we will all grow old someday. Thus the mistreatment of the old is a form of self-mutilation. Nevertheless, the cruelty persists.

Faced with such barbarism, why join the legions of the doomed and **7** damned? All your life you maintain a certain schedule. You break that routine once or twice a year. You go on this way 30 or 40 years. Your heart, your bowels, your mind keep time with it. And then you stop. You leave your pleasures, your sorrows, your family, everything. You might as well run full speed into a brick wall. No body or mind was meant to stop like that. Things have to go wrong—your heart, your bowels, your mind. It is the first giant step to the cemetery. Why take it? What's the percentage? Why, indeed, do it younger and younger when people are living to be older and older? Would you invest money with the same logic? Does it make any sense? Perhaps it would if there were alternatives (for example, working less) but there aren't any alternatives for most of us. It's out, totally out, out all the way, and don't try to get back in.

Don't Quit: In our society, life is useful work and continuing **8** income. Even what seems like a large retirement income is to be regarded with deep suspicion in this day of inflation. Life and respect are work and money. It shouldn't be so, but it is.

There is something suicidal in retirement, just as there is something suicidal in society's callousness toward the old. So forget the young. You worked to get what you have. Keep it; enjoy it. They are young and strong; let them struggle. It isn't your problem, you shouldn't take the rap. Don't leave your job one minute before you have to—even if you hate it—unless you can't get out of bed. You have something to give. It isn't true that to be old is to be incompetent. Fight. Don't quit. Elect your own to legislative office. Band together: the old-age party, the life party. Don't let them convince you that the "golden years" await you. It's a lie. No one should go down without a struggle. Kick. Scream. Be heard all the way to Washington. You have nothing to lose but your dignity and your life.

Study Questions

1. What effect does the author achieve by the preponderance of short sentences? Analyze the sentence structure in paragraphs 2, 7, and 9.
2. What tone is established by the diction and sentence structure?

3. What is the author's strategy in the development of the first paragraph?
4. Note the various times the author uses questions (paragraphs 1, 4, and 7). What is his purpose?
5. Does the humor blur or enhance what may be a serious intent in this essay? Explain.

Son of H-Bomb
RUSSELL BAKER

Russell Baker (1925–   ) was born in Virginia and graduated from Johns Hopkins in 1947. As a newspaperman, he has served on *The Baltimore Sun* and *The New York Times* for which he writes the "Observer" column. His many awards include a Pulitzer Prize in 1976. Baker has published *An American in Washington* (1961), *No Cause for Panic* (1964), *All Things Considered* (1965), *Our Next President* (1968), *Poor Russell's Almanac* (1972), and *The Upside Down Man* (1977).

Although I don't exactly love the H-bomb, it comes close to   1
my idea of what a bomb should be. First, it fulfills the human need to have a bomb. Second, of all the bombs in circulation these days, it is the one you are least likely to be assaulted with.

In the more than thirty years since it became popular, it has never   2
been used against anybody. A person could get fond of a bomb like that. There is no other bomb with a comparable safety record.

Twentieth-century humanity has many destinies, and while get-   3
ting bombed is only one of them, it is also one of the more unpleasant. You can get firebombed, napalm-bombed, fragmentation-bombed or just plain old dynamite-bombed. You can get bombed in an Irish pub, a Manhattan office, a London restaurant or an Arab bazaar. You can get bombed by large governmental institutions which are bombing you to improve world society. You can get bombed by blithering maniacs. You can get bombed by patriotic heroes who are bombing you to fight injustices you have never heard of.

These possibilities leave me with mixed feelings about bombs. As a   4
man of the twentieth century, I accept the need for bombs. There is something about them that fulfills people of our time and makes whole nations feel better. Show a nation that's got bombs a nation without bombs and right away the nation that has bombs wants to bomb the nation that hasn't. It's human nature, twentieth-century-style.

At the same time, I would prefer not to be bombed. The trick about 5 bombs, it seems to me, is to satisfy the human craving for bombs while making sure that nobody is going to be bombed with them. This, of course, is what the H-bomb does and why it is the best of all possible bombs.

Now we have the neutron bomb, an offspring of the H-bomb, and a 6 nasty little fellow it is, if my understanding is correct. The great charm of its sire is its ferocity. The H-bomb makes such a mess that nobody wants to clean up after it, and nobody, therefore, uses it.

The people who invent bombs, unhappy with such perfection, went 7 back to the atom and came up with the neutron bomb. Their aim was a nuclear bomb that would leave less mess, the sort of bomb which, after being exploded, would leave the premises neat. If it was just a question of scrubbing down with extra-strength detergent to remove the after-bombing equivalent of waxy buildup on the linoleum, they reasoned, then the world could have a nuclear bomb it wouldn't mind using.

The neutron bomb is said to do this by killing only people—that's 8 us, folks—with heavy doses of rapid-fade radiation while leaving the local property in reasonably good condition. I want to like this bomb as much as I like its progenitor, the H-bomb, but it isn't easy, and the Government's arguments about why I should are not persuasive.

The Government says it is really quite a decent bomb because it is 9 only "tactical." If the Russian Army starts invading Germany, says the Government, the neutron bomb will be exploded over the invaders and they will be wiped out without damage to nearby towns and farms. This is "tactical" bombing.

The illustration asks us to believe the Russians might be dumb 10 enough to expose their army in an invasion of Germany, all the time knowing that they were marching into the jaws of the neutron bomb. For thirty-five years the Russians haven't made a military move into Western Europe, despite the fact that our best deterrent has been that old pussycat, the H-bomb.

One should never exclude madness as a factor in foreign affairs, 11 but the likelihood of Moscow's risking the ultimate mess by advancing an army to be neatly dispatched with N-bombs seems farfetched, particularly since after the hypothetical liquidation of the invaders an exchange of H-bombs would remain a lively possibility.

One suspects that what the bomb people have in mind is something 12 else. If all parties to the H-bomb were to be armed with N-bombs, and if the present understanding that the H-bomb can be used only at the brink of doom remained effective, the tidiness of the N-bomb would make it possible for big powers to develop nuclear weapons which they could use as real bombs in real wars of the kind we used to enjoy in the days of the great old wars.

The threat of the neutron bomb is that it makes nuclear war thinkable at last. Do we really need that? Possibly. Bombs seem to be embedded in the psyche of the race, and something in us is soured by the fact that the H-bomb has never been any good for expressing ourselves on ourselves.

Study Questions

1. How does the first sentence of the essay function to indicate the tone?
2. In what specific ways does the sentence structure of this essay differ from the sentence structure of Cousins's essay?
3. Analyze the way paragraph 3 is developed. What effect is achieved by the series of parallel sentences?
4. Is the metaphor in paragraph 7 appropriate to the general tone of the essay? Explain.
5. Underline the words and phrases that link the paragraphs of the essay.
6. Identify the elements that produce the tone of this essay.

Wonder Woman
GLORIA STEINEM

Gloria Steinem (1936–   ) was born in Ohio. After graduating from Smith College *magna cum laude,* she became a Chester Bowles Asian Fellow at the universities of Delhi and Calcutta. A free-lance writer, Steinem founded *Ms.* magazine in 1972. One of the foremost proponents of the women's liberation movement, she was a founding member of the National Women's Political Caucus and has been chairperson and a member of the board of the Women's Action Alliance. Her awards include the Penney-Missouri journalism award (1970) and Doctor of Human Justice from Simmons College (1973). Steinem has contributed to many magazines, among them *Esquire, Ms., Vogue, Cosmopolitan,* and *Time.* Additional writings include *The Thousand Indias* (1957), *The Beach Book* (1963), and parts of the series "That Was the Week That Was" and other scripts for television.

Comic books were not quite respectable, which was a large   1
part of the reason I read them: under the covers with a flashlight, in the car while my parents told me I was ruining my eyes, in a tree or some other inaccessible spot; any place that provided sweet privacy and independence. Along with cereal boxes and ketchup labels, they

were the primers that taught me how to read. They were even cheap enough to be the first items I could buy on my own; a customer whose head didn't quite reach the counter but whose dignity was greatly enhanced by making a selection (usually after much agonizing) and offering up money of her own.

If as I have always suspected children are simply short people— ancient spirits who happen to be locked up in bodies that aren't big enough or skillful enough to cope with the world—then the superhuman feats in comic books and fairy tales become logical and necessary. It's satisfying for anyone to have heroes who can see through walls or leap over skyscrapers in a single bound. But it's especially satisfying if our worldview consists mostly of knees, and tying our shoes is still an exercise in frustration.

2

The trouble is that the comic book performers of such superhuman feats—and even of only dimly competent ones—are almost always heroes, literally. The female child is left to believe that, even when her body is as grown-up as her spirit, she will still be in the childlike role of helping with minor tasks, appreciating men's accomplishments, and being so incompetent and passive that she can only hope some man can come to her rescue. Of course, rescue and protection are comforting, even exhilarating experiences that should be and often are shared by men and boys. Even in comic books, the hero is frequently called on to protect his own kind in addition to helpless women. But dependency and zero accomplishments get very dull as a steady diet. The only option for a girl reader is to identify with the male characters—pretty difficult, even in the adrogynous years of childhood. If she can't do that, she faces limited prospects: an "ideal" life of sitting around like a technicolor clothes horse, getting into jams with villains, and saying things like "Oh, Superman! I'll always be grateful to you," even as her hero goes off to bigger and better adventures. It hardly seems worth learning to tie our shoes.

3

I'm happy to say that I was rescued from this plight at about the age of seven or eight; rescued (Great Hera!) by a woman. Not only was she as wise as Athena and as lovely as Aphrodite, she had the speed of Mercury and the strength of Hercules. Of course, being an Amazon, she had a head start on such accomplishments, but she had earned them in a human way by training in Greek-style contests of dexterity and speed with her Amazon sisters. (Somehow it always seemed boring to me that Superman was a creature from another planet, and therefore had bullet-proof skin, X-ray vision, and the power to fly. Where was the contest?) This beautiful Amazon did have some fantastic gadgets to help her: an invisible plane that carried her through dimensions of time and space, a golden magic lasso, and bullet-proof bracelets. But she still had to get to the plane, throw the lasso with accuracy, and be agile enough to catch bullets on the steel-enclosed wrists.

4

Her creator had also seen straight into my heart and understood the secret fears of violence hidden there. No longer did I have to pretend to like the "pow!" and "crunch!" style of Captain Marvel or the Green Hornet. No longer did I have nightmares after reading ghoulish

5

comics filled with torture and mayhem, comics made all the more horrifying by their real-life setting in World War II. (It was a time when leather-clad Nazis were marching in the newsreels *and* in the comics, and the blood on the pages seemed frighteningly real.) Here was a heroic person who might conquer with force, but only a force that was tempered by love and justice. She converted her enemies more often than not, and if they were destroyed, they did it to themselves, usually in some unbloody accident.

She was beautiful, brave, and explicitly out to change "a world torn 6
by the hatreds and wars of men."

She was Wonder Woman.   7

Looking back now at these Wonder Woman stories from the '40's, I   8
am amazed by the strength of their feminist message. One typical story centers on Prudence, a young pioneer in the days of the American frontier. (Wonder Woman is transported there by her invisible plane, of course, which also served as a time machine.) Rescued by Wonder Woman, Prudence realizes her own worth and the worth of all women: "I've learned my lesson," she says proudly in the final scene. "From now on, I'll rely on myself, not on a man." In yet another episode, Wonder Woman herself says, "I can never love a dominant man who is stronger than I am." And throughout the strips, it is only the destructive, criminal woman—the woman who has brought the whole idea that male means aggression and female means submitting—who says "Girls want superior men to boss them around."

Many of the plots revolve around evil men who treat women as   9
inferior beings. In the end, all are brought to their knees and made to recognize women's strength and value. Some of the stories focus on weak women who are destructive and confused. These misled females are converted to self-reliance and self-respect through the example of Wonder Woman. The message of the strips is sometimes inconsistent and always oversimplified (these are, after all, comics), but it is still a passable version of the truisms that women are rediscovering today: that women are full human beings; that we cannot love others until we love ourselves; that love and respect can only exist between equals.

Wonder Woman's family of Amazons on Paradise Island, her band 10
of college girls in America, and her efforts to save individual women are all welcome examples of women working together and caring about each other's welfare. The idea of such cooperation may not seem particularly revolutionary to the male reader: men are routinely depicted as working well together. But women know how rare and therefore exhilarating the idea of sisterhood really is.

Wonder Woman's mother, Queen Hippolyte, offers yet another 11
welcome example to young girls in search of strong identity. Queen Hippolyte founds nations, wages war to protect Paradise Island, and sends her daughter off to fight the forces of evil in the world. Perhaps most impressive in an age fraught with Freudian shibboleths, she also marshals her queenly strength to protect her daughter in bad times. How many girl children grew to adulthood with no experience of a courageous and worldly mother, except in these slender stories? How

many adult women disdain the birth of a female child, believe it is "better" to bear male children, and fear the competition and jealousy they have been conditioned to believe is "natural" to a mother and daughter? Feminism is just beginning to uncover the sense of anger and loss in girls whose mothers had no power to protect them in the world, and so trained them to be victims, or left them to identify with their fathers if they had any ambitions outside the traditional female role.

Wonder Woman symbolizes many of the values of the women's 12 culture that feminists are now trying to introduce into the mainstream: strength and self-reliance for women; sisterhood and mutual support among women; peacefulness and esteem for human life; a diminishment both of "masculine" aggression and of the belief that violence is the only way of solving conflicts.

Of course, the Wonder Woman stories are not admirable in all 13 ways. Many feminist principles are distorted or ignored. Thus, women are converted and saved. Mad scientists, foreign spies, criminals, and other male villains are regularly brought to the point of renouncing violence and, more often, of saying, "You're right, Wonder Woman. I'll never make the mistake of thinking women are inferior again." Is the reader supposed to conclude women are superior? The Wonder Woman stories not only depict women as culturally different (in ways that are sometimes constructive and sometimes not), they also hint that women are biologically, and therefore immutably, superior to men.

Few modern feminists would agree. There are as yet no perfectly 14 culture-free tests to prove to us which traits come from conditioning and which do not, but the consensus seeems to be that society, not biology, assigns some human traits to males and others to females. Women have suffered from being taught to develop what society considers the less-valued traits of humanity, but this doesn't mean we want to switch to a sole claim on the "more valuable" ones either. That might accomplish nothing more than changing places with men in the hierarchy. Most feminist philosophy supposes that the hierarchy itself must be eliminated; that individuals who are free of roles assigned because of sex or race will also be free to develop the full range of human qualities. It's the multitudinous differences in individuals that count, not the localized differences of sex or race.

For psychologist William Moulton Marston—who, under the pen 15 name of "Charles Moulton," created Wonder Woman—females were sometimes romanticized as biologically and unchangeably superior. "Women," he wrote, "represent love; men represent force. Man's use of force without love brings evil and unhappiness. Wonder Woman proves that women are superior to men because they have love in addition to force." If that's the case, then we're stuck with yet another social order based on birth.

For the purposes of most Wonder Woman stories, however, the 16 classic argument of nature versus nurture is a mere intellectual quibble. Just helping women to respect themselves, to use their strength and refuse domination by men is time-consuming enough:

Wonder Woman rarely has the leisure to hint at what the future social order ought to be. As for men, we do get the idea that they have some hope—even if vague—of collective redemption. "This man's world of yours," explains Wonder Woman, "will never be without pain and suffering until it learns respect for human rights." Put in more positive terms, this does seem to indicate that humanized men will have full membership in the new society.

Some of the Wonder Woman stories preach patriotism in a false 17 way, but much of the blame rests with history. Wonder Woman was born in 1941, just about the time that World War II became a reality for most Americans, and she therefore had to spend much of her time protecting this country from foreign threats. Usually, that task boiled down to proving that women could be just as brave and loyal as men in the service of their country. Even when her adventures took place in other countries or at other times, they still invariably ended with simplistic commercials about democracy. Although Wonder Woman was shocked by America's unjust patriarchal system—a shock she recorded on her arrival here from Paradise Island—she never had much opportunity to follow up on it; a nation mobilized for war is not a nation prepared to accept criticism. In fact, her costume was patterned after the American flag, and her wartime adventures sometimes had highly jingoistic and even racist overtones, especially when she was dealing with Japanese and Germans.

Compared to the other comic book characters of the period, 18 however, Wonder Woman is still a relief. Marston invented her as a counter to the violence and "bloodcurdling masculinity" that pervaded most comic books, and he remained true to his purpose. Wonder Woman and her sisters were allowed to use violence, but only in self-defense and only if it stopped short of actually killing someone. Most group conflicts between men and women were set not in America, but in a mythological past. Thus Mars, the God of War, periodically endangered the Amazon community and sometimes tried to disarm Queen Hippolyte through the ruses of love. Mars, of course, was the "heavy." He preached that women "are the natural spoils of war" and must remain at home, the helpless slaves of the male victors. Marston used Mars as the symbol of everything Wonder Woman must fight against, but he also gave the God of War a rationale for his beliefs that was really the female superiority argument all over again: If women were allowed to become warriors like the Amazons, they would grow stronger than men, and put an end to war. What future for an unemployed god?

The inconsistencies in Wonder Woman's philosophy are especially 19 apparent in her love life. It is confused, to say the least. Sometimes her adventures with Steve, the pilot she is supposedly "in love" with, bear a feminist message. And sometimes they simper and go conventional in a way that contradicts everything that has gone before. In her American disguise as mild-mannered Diana Prince (a clear steal from Superman), she plays the classic feminine role: secretary, nurse, and worshipful, unrequited sidekick to Steve. The implicit moral is that, at least as Wonder Woman, she can love only an equal. But an equal never turns up, and sometimes she loses her grip on herself and falls for the masculine notion that there must be a permanent winner and a permanent loser, a conqueror and a conquered. "Some girls love to have a man stronger than they are to make them do things," she muses aloud. "Do I like it? I don't know, it's sort of thrilling. But isn't it more fun to make a man obey?"

I remember being worried by these contradictions. How could 20 Wonder Woman be interested in Steve, who seemed so weak and so boring? Did women really have to live in a community by themselves—a separate country like Paradise Island—in order to be both happy and courageous? The very fact that the ideal was an island—insular, isolated, self-contained, cut-off—both pleased and bothered me. And why, when she chose an earthly disguise, did Wonder Woman have to pick such a loser? How could she bear to be like Diana Prince? Did that mean that all women really had to disguise their true selves in weak feminine stereotypes in order to survive?

But all these doubts paled beside the relief, the sweet vengeance, 21 the toe-wriggling pleasure of reading about a woman who was strong, beautiful, courageous, and a fighter for social justice. A woman who strode forth, stopping wars and killing with one hand, distributing largesse and compassionate aid with the other. A Wonder Woman.

In 1947, William Marston died, leaving his heroine in the hands of 22 writers who didn't really understand her spirit. Gradually, her feminist orientation began to wane. She became simultaneously more submissive to men. I don't remember the transition very well, possibly because I myself was on the verge of adolescence and was therefore putting comic books behind me. Or possibly because the comparatively free years of my childhood were at an end. Like Wonder Woman, the full impact of the feminine role was beginning to close around me. Now I was thirteen and made to see that the idea of accomplishing anything on my own was at best eccentric and at worst impossible. Recognition and status through men was the best possibility; it was also socially rewarded and socially enforced. Both Wonder Woman and I fell into some very hard times in the '50's.

Looking at her most recent adventures is even more discouraging. 23 By 1968, she had given up her magic lasso, her bracelets, her invisible plane, and all her superhuman Amazonian powers. She had become Diana Prince, a mere mortal who walked about in boutique clothes and took the advice of a male mastermind named "I Ching." She still had adventures and she had learned something about karate, but any attractive man could disarm her. She was a female James Bond—but far more boring since she was denied his sexual freedom. She had become a simpleminded "good girl."

In 1973, Wonder Woman comics will be born again; I hope with the 24 feminism and strength of the original Wonder Woman—my Wonder Woman—restored. But regardless of her future, these selections from the original adventures of the golden forties will remain classics for children, boys as well as girls. And perhaps for many heroine-starved

and nostalgic grownups as well. If we had all read more about Wonder
Woman and less about Dick and Jane, the new wave of the feminist
revolution might have happened less painfully and sooner.

Wonder Woman is a comic book character. She and her Amazon 25
sisters are fictional creations. Indeed, Amazons have generally been
considered figments of the imagination, perhaps the mythological
evidence of man's fear of woman. Yet there is a tentative but growing
body of anthropological and archeological evidence to support the
theory that Amazon societies were real; they did exist. German and
Brazilian scientists exploring the jungles of Brazil, for instance,
recently came upon the caves of what appears to have been an
all-female society. The caves are strikingly devoid of the usual phallic
design and theme; they feature, instead, the triangular female symbol.
(The only cave that does bear male designs is believed to have been the
copulatorium.)

Though the Brazilian research is still too indefinite for conclu- 26
sions, there are many evidences of the existence of Amazon societies in
all parts of the world. Dr. Phyllis Chesler details them in her book to
mind-blowing effect and with great scholarship. Being a writer, not a
scientist tied to proven fact, I have fused the sometimes contradictory
versions of Amazonia into one amalgam; into a story that sounds right
to me in the way that a dream interpretation or a race-memory seems
suddenly, thuddingly right as it strikes off our subconscious. Much of it
has been proved, but I tell it as a story.

Once upon a time, the many cultures of this world were all part of 27
the Gynocratic Age. Paternity had not yet been discovered, and it was
thought (as it still is in some tribal cultures) that women bore fruit like
trees—when they were ripe. Childbirth was mysterious. It was vital.
And it was envied. Women were worshipped because of it, were
considered superior because of it. Men prayed to female gods and, in
their religious ceremonies, imitated the act of birth (as many tribes-
men still do). In such a world, the only clear grouping was that of
mothers and children. Men were on the periphery—an interchangeable
body of workers for, and worshippers of, the female center, the
principle of life.

The discovery of paternity, of sexual cause and childbirth effect, 28
was as cataclysmic for society as, say, the discovery of fire or the
shattering of the atom. Gradually, the idea of male ownership of
children took hold; with it came the idea of private property that could
be passed down to children. If paternity was to be unquestioned, then
women had to be sexually restricted. That was the origin of marriage.

Gynocracy also suffered from the periodic invasions of nomadic 29
tribes. Gynocracies were probably stable and peaceful agricultural
societies since agriculture was somewhat more—though not totally—a
female occupation. Nomadic tribes survived by hunting, which was
somewhat more—though not totally—a male occupation. The conflict
between the hunters and the growers was really the conflict between
male-dominated and female-dominated cultures.

Restricted by new systems of marriage as well as by occasional 30 pregnancies, women gradually lost their freedom, mystery, and superior position. For five thousand years or more, the Gynocratic Age had flowered in peace and productivity. Slowly, in varying stages and in different parts of the world, the social order was painfully reversed. Women became the underclass, marked by their visible differences regardless of whether they had children. Often, the patriarchal take-over of female-dominated societies was accomplished violently. Everywhere, fear of goddesses, of women's magical procreative powers, and of the old religions caused men to suppress the old social order very cruelly indeed.

Some women resisted the patriarchal age. They banded together to 31 protect their female-centered culture and religions from a more violent, transient, and male-centered way of life. Men were dangerous, to be tolerated only during periodic mating ceremonies. The women themselves became adept at self-defense.

These were backlash cultures, doomed by their own imbalance. 32 But they did survive in various groupings on every continent for many thousands of years. Why don't they turn up in history? For one reason, most of their existence was lived in those thousands of years dismissed as *pre*-history—that is, preliterate. The few records that are available to us were written under the patriarchal assumptions of a much later age. Even archeology and anthropology have suffered from the fundamental, almost subconscious assumption that male and female roles as we see them in the patriarchal age are "natural"; therefore, they must have been the same in the prehistoric past. Only lately have we begun to question and check out those assumptions. Large, strong, and presumably male skeletons from prehistoric sites, for instance, have turned out on closer examination to be female after all.

Perhaps the mystery story Dr. Chesler traces through history and 33 mythology is soon to be solved. After all, mythology is a collective human memory that has, on other occasions, turned out to be accurate about invasions, great floods, the collision of stars. The Amazon cultures may also one day be proven as fact. Meanwhile, the fascination that brings them up as fantasy again and again may itself be some psychic evidence of their existence.

If so, Wonder Woman becomes just one small, isolated outcropping 34 of a larger human memory. And the girl children who love her are responding to one small echo of dreams and capabilities in their own forgotten past.

Study Questions

1. What is the thesis of this essay and at what point is it apparent?
2. Identify the four major sections of this essay. Analyze each section to determine its purpose in developing the thesis.

3. The punctuation of the first sentence is unconventional. What effect is achieved by this punctuation?
4. What method does Steinem use in the introductory section to gain the reader's interest? What effect is achieved by withholding the identity of the comic book character?
5. What type of analysis does the author use in paragraphs 8–24? What is the unifying element?
6. How does Steinem lend authority to the account she presents in paragraphs 27–32?

Acid Indigestion
ART BUCHWALD

Art Buchwald (1925–   ) was born in Mt. Vernon, New York, and attended the University of Southern California for three years. His syndicated column appears daily in hundreds of newspapers and has made him one of the most popular American humorists. His recent books include *And Then I Told the President* (1965), *The Establishment Is Alive and Well in Washington* (1969), *I Never Danced at the White House* (1973), *I Am Not a Crook* (1974), *Down the Seine and Up the Potomac* (1977), and *The Buchwald Stops Here* (1979).

America is an abundant land that seems to have more of   1
everything than anybody else. And if one were to ask what we have the most of the answer would be acid indigestion.

No country can touch us when it comes to heartburn and upset   2
stomachs. This nation, under God, with liberty and justice for all, neutralizes more stomach acid in one day than the Soviet Union does in a year. We give more relief from discomfort of the intestinal tract than China and Japan combined.

They can say what they will about us, but we Americans know   3
what to do with our excess gas.

It is no accident that the United States became the largest   4
producer of acid indigestion in the world. When the first settlers came to the New World they found their lives fraught with danger. First they had to worry about Indians, then they had to worry about their crops. Afterward they had to worry about witches. This played hell

Reprinted from *Esquire,* December 1975, with permission.

with everyone's stomach and the early settlers realized if they ever hoped to survive they would have to come up with a cure for acid indigestion.

Providence was on their side, because amongst the early settlers 5 were two brothers, Alka and Bromo Seltzer. They were both chemists who had experimented with various potions that had been given to them by the Indians.

One potion was a white powder that the Indians used for athlete's 6 foot. Why, asked the Seltzer brothers, couldn't the same powder be used for upset stomachs. Al was neater than Bromo and rolled his powder into a tablet which he then dropped into a mug of water where it immediately fizzed. Bromo said it was too expensive to make tablets, and it was much easier just to dump the powder into the water, which would produce the same effect.

The brothers split in anger, and Al put out his product under the 7 name Alka-Seltzer, while Bromo put his out as Bromo-Seltzer. Fortunately for the country, both methods worked, and as soon as the cure for acid indigestion had been concocted the New World could be settled once and for all.

You would think that after we killed all the Indians and won the 8 West and became a large industrial nation Americans would have stopped having queasy stomachs. But the truth is we suffer more from the blaahhs now than we ever did before. Some of it still comes from fear, some of it comes from ambition, and some of it comes from eating the whole thing.

As a people who strive for the best we must accept the fact that it 9 takes a cup of acid for every step we take up the ladder of success. It is no accident that the men and women who run our corporations and our advertising agencies and our networks and our government are the same people who keep the Maalox, Pepto-Bismol, Bisodol, Tums, and Rolaid companies alive.

Show me a man who has to drink milk instead of wine with his 10 meals and I'll show you a titan of American industry.

For years other nations have tried to catch up with us when it came 11 to sour stomachs and heartburn. But they never had the drive to produce a good case of acid indigestion. They never understood what it takes to keep up with the Joneses or outdo the Smiths. They don't realize that in order to live in the best of all possible worlds you have to have a certain amount of stomach discomfort to go with it.

If there is anything that shows up our system to that of the 12 Communist nations, it is that we Americans can not only live with acid indigestion but we have three thousand different remedies to give us relief. In a Communist society the state decides what you should coat your digestive tract with, and if it doesn't soothe you, the state couldn't care less if you burp all night long.

Acid indigestion is as American as Mom's apple pie (which is one of 13 the reasons we get it) and as long as there is enough heartburn to go around, we, as a great nation, will survive.

Study Questions

1. Although written primarily to entertain, does this essay have a serious intent? If so, summarize it in a thesis sentence.
2. What effect does Buchwald achieve by using one-sentence paragraphs?
3. What is the tone of this essay and how is it expressed by the diction and sentence structure?
4. What purpose is served by the account about the Seltzer brothers?
5. Count the commas Buchwald uses in this essay. Would you say he uses more or fewer commas than most writers represented in this reader? Explain.

Super Mom in the Suburbs
A Cautionary Tale About How to Be Neat, Clean, Cheerful, Organized—and Friendless
ERMA BOMBECK

Erma Bombeck (1927–   ) was born in Dayton, Ohio, and graduated from the University of Dayton in 1949. Her newspaper column, "At Wit's End," was begun in 1965 and is now syndicated in over 500 newspapers; she also contributes "Up the Wall" to *Good Housekeeping*. Numerous American schools have awarded her honorary degrees, among them a doctorate from Bowling Green. Her popular books include *Just Wait Till You Have Children of Your Own* (1971), *The Grass Is Always Greener Over the Septic Tank* (1976), *If Life Is a Bowl of Cherries, What Am I Doing in the Pits?* (1979), and *Aunt Erma's Cope Book* (1979). In 1978 she was appointed to the President's National Advisory Committee for Women.

Suburban mothers are divided into two distinct groups: The 1
Super Moms and the Interim Mothers.

The Super Moms are faster than a speeding bullet, more powerful 2
than a harsh laxative, and able to leap six shopping carts on double-
stamp day. They are a drag for all seasons.

Super Moms are the product of isolation, a husband who is rarely 3
home and a clean-oven wish. There is a waiting list for canonization.

The Interim Mothers are just biding their time until the children 4
are grown. They never give their right name at PTA meetings, hide
candy under the dish towels so the kids will never find it, have
newspapers lining the cupboard shelves that read MALARIA STOPS
WORK ON THE CANAL, and secretly believe that someday they will
be kissed by an ugly meter reader and turned into Joey Heatherton.

There are no restrictions in our suburb. Super Moms are free to 5
integrate at any time they wish, and when one moved in across the
street, I felt the only decent thing to do was welcome her to the
neighborhood.

The moving van hadn't been gone a minute when we saw her in the 6
yard waxing her garden hose. I walked over with my nine-bean salad
and knocked on the door. Her name was Estelle. I could not believe the
inside of her house. The furniture was shining and in place, the mirrors
and pictures were hung, there was not a cardboard box in sight, the
books were on the shelves, there were fresh flowers on the kitchen
table and she had an iron tablet in her hand, ready to pop into her
mouth.

"I know things are an absolute mess on moving day," I fumbled. 7

"Are people ever settled?" she asked, picking a piece of lint off the 8
refrigerator.

Then she waltzed in the children and, seeing one lock of hair in her 9
son's eyes, grimaced and said, "Boys will be boys!"

If my kids looked that good, I'd have sold them. 10

"Hey, if you need anything from the store, I go every three hours," I 11
offered.

"I shop once a month," she said. "I find I save money that way by 12
buying in quantity and by planning my meals. Besides, I'm a miser
with my time. I read voraciously—right now I'm into Cather—and try
to go three or four places a week with the children. They're very aware
of contemporary art. Now they're starting the romantics. Could I get
you something?" she asked softly. "I just baked a chiffon cake."

I felt my face break out. 13

"The doctor said I have to put on some weight," she went on, "and I 14
try desperately . . . I really do."

I wanted to smack her right across the mouth. 15

Frankly, what it boiled down to was this: Could a woman who dyed 16
all her household linens black to save time find happiness with a
woman who actually had a baby picture of her last child?

The Interim Mothers tried to get along with Estelle, but it wasn't 17
easy. There was just no getting ahead of her.

She cut the grass, baked her own bread, shoveled the driveway, 18
grew her own herbs, made the children's clothes, altered her husband's
suits, played the organ at church, planned the vacation, paid the bills,
was on three telephone committees, five car pools, two boards, took her
garden hose in during the winter, took her ironing board down every
week, stocked the freezer with sides of beef, made her own Christmas
cards, voted in every election, saw her dentist twice a year, assisted in
the delivery of her dog's puppies, melted down old candles, saved the
antifreeze and had a pencil by her telephone.

"Where is Estelle?" asked my friend Helen when she dropped by 19
one day.

"Who knows? Probably painting her varicose veins to make them 20
look like textured stockings. I tell you that woman gets on my nerves."

"She is a bit much," said Helen.   21

"A bit much! Would you trust a woman who always knows where 22
her car keys are?"

"I think she'd like to be your friend."   23

"It wouldn't work."   24

"You could try."   25

"You don't know what you are saying. She's so . . . so organized. 26
Hers is the only house on the block that has fire drills. Take the other
day—the school called to tell her Kevin had been hurt. Do you
remember what happened when the school called me when my son
flunked his eye test?"

"You became hysterical and had to be put under sedation."   27

"Right. Not Estelle. She calmly got her car keys off the hook, threw 28
a coordinated sweater over her coordinated slacks, put the dinner in
the oven on 'warm,' picked up that pencil by the phone, wrote a note,
went to school to pick up Kevin and drove him to the emergency ward."

"So. You could have done that."   29

"I'm not finished. In the emergency ward, she deposited Kevin, 30
remembered his birth date, his father's name, and recited their
hospitalization number from *memory*."

"I remember when you took Andy to the hospital."   31

"I don't want to talk about it."   32

"You had to write a check for a dime to make a phone call."   33

"Okay. I remember."   34

Actually, Estelle didn't bother anyone. She wasn't much more than 35
a blur, whipping in and out of the driveway each day. I was surprised
when she appeared at my mailbox. "Erma," she said, "what's wrong
with me?"

"Nothing," I hedged. "Why?"   36

"Be honest with me. I don't fit into the neighborhood. Why?"   37

"I don't know how to explain it," I faltered. "It's just that . . . you're 38
the type of woman you'd call from the drugstore and ask what you use
for your irregularities."

"All I want is to be someone's friend."   39

"I know you do, Estelle, and I'd like to help you, but first you have 40
to understand what a friend is."

"Tell me." 41

"It's sorta hard to understand. But a friend doesn't go on a diet 42
when you are fat. A friend never defends a husband who gets his wife
an electric skillet for her birthday by saying, 'At least, he's not one to
carouse around at night.'

"A friend will tell you she saw your old boyfriend . . . and he's a 43
priest.

"A friend will baby-sit your children when they are contagious. 44

"A friend when asked what she thinks of a home permanent will 45
lie. A friend will threaten to kill anyone who tries to come into the
fitting room when you are trying on bathing suits. But, most of all, a
friend will not make each minute of every day count and screw it up for
the rest of us."

From then on, Estelle, neighborhood Super Mom, began to change. 46
Not all at once. But week by week we saw her learning how to
compromise with herself. At first, she did little things like buying a
deodorant that wasn't on sale and scraping the list of emergency
numbers off the phone with her fingernail.

One morning one of her children knocked on my door and asked to 47
use our bathroom. He said his mommy had locked him out.

The next week Estelle ran out of gas while making the Girl Scout 48
run. A few days later she forgot to tie her garbage cans together, and
the dogs dragged TV-dinner boxes all over her lawn for the world to
see.

You could almost see her image beginning to crumble. She dropped 49
in unexpectedly one afternoon and leaned over the divider to confide, "I
have come to the conclusion there is an afterlife."

"An afterlife?" 50

"Right. I think life goes on after the children are grown." 51

"Who told you that?" 52

"I read it on a vitamin label." 53

"What are you trying to say, Estelle?" 54

"I am trying to tell you that I am going to run away from home. 55
Back to the city. There's a life for me back there."

"Don't talk crazy," I said. 56

"I've tried to be so perfect," she sobbed. 57

"I know. I know." 58

At that moment one of Estelle's children ran excitedly into the 59
room. "Mommy! Mommy!" she said wildly. "I was on the team that
used a toothpaste with fluoride and I only have one cavity."

Estelle looked at her silently for a full minute, then said, "Who 60
cares?"

She was one of us. 61

Study Questions

1. What is the method Bombeck uses to develop her subject?
2. How does she use comparison and contrast? What is the advantage of this type of development?
3. What method of identification is used to define "a friend" in paragraphs 43–45?
4. What are the implied topics of paragraphs 6 and 18?
5. What is the basic difference in the presentations of Bombeck's and Buchwald's essays?

A Modest Proposal
JONATHAN SWIFT

Jonathan Swift (1667–1745) is recognized as one of England's greatest prose writers. He was born in Dublin, Ireland, and was educated there at Trinity College. The fact that he was a priest in the Church of England did not prevent him from becoming involved in politics, first as a Whig, then a Tory. However, Queen Anne disapproved of *A Tale of a Tub* (1704), and Swift was given the deanery of St. Patrick's, Dublin, instead of the English preferment he wanted. Among his now-classic works are *The Battle of the Books* (1970), *Gulliver's Travels* (1726), *A Modest Proposal* (1729), and *Journal to Stella* (1766).

It is a melancholly Object to those, who walk through this 1
great Town or travel in the Country, when they see the Streets, the Roads and Cabbin-doors crowded with Beggars of the Female Sex, followed by three, four, or six Children, all in Rags, and importuning every Passenger for an Alms. These Mothers instead of being able to work for their honest livelyhood, are forced to employ all their time in Stroling to beg Sustenance for their helpless Infants, who, as they grow up, either turn Thieves for want of Work, or leave their dear Native Country, to fight for the Pretender in Spain, or sell themselves to the Barbadoes.

I think it is agreed by all Parties, that this prodigious number of 2
Children in the Arms, or on the Backs, or at the Heels of their Mothers, and frequently of their Fathers, is in the present deplorable state of the Kingdom, a very great additional grievance; and therefore whoever

First published in 1729.

could find out a fair, cheap and easy method of making these Children sound and useful Members of the Common-wealth, would deserve so well of the publick, as to have his Statue set up for a Preserver of the Nation.

But my Intention is very far from being confined to provide only for 3 the Children of professed Beggers, it is of a much greater Extent, and shall take in the whole Number of Infants at a certain Age, who are born of Parents in effect as little able to support them, as those who demand our Charity in the Streets.

As to my own part, having turned my Thoughts, for many Years, 4 upon this important Subject, and maturely weighed the several Schemes of other Projectors, I have always found them grossly mistaken in their computation. It is true, a Child just dropt from its Dam, may be supported by her Milk, for a Solar Year with little other Nourishment, at most not above the Value of two Shillings, which the Mother may certainly get, or the Value in Scraps, by her lawful Occupation of Begging; and it is exactly at one Year Old that I propose to provide for them in such a manner as, instead of being a Charge upon their Parents, or the Parish, or wanting Food and Raiment for the rest of their Lives, they shall, on the Contrary, contribute to the Feeding and partly to the Cloathing of many Thousands.

There is likewise another great Advantage in my Scheme, that it 5 will prevent those voluntary Abortions, and that horrid practice of Women murdering their Bastard Children, alas! too frequent among us, Sacrificing the poor innocent Babes, I doubt, more to avoid the Expense than the Shame, which would move Tears and Pity in the most Savage and inhuman breast.

The number of Souls in this Kingdom being usually reckoned one 6 Million and a half, Of these I calculate there may be about two hundred thousand Couples whose Wives are Breeders; from which number I subtract thirty Thousand Couples, who are able to maintain their own Children, although I apprehend there cannot be so many, under the present Distresses of the Kingdom; but this being granted, there will remain an hundred and seventy thousand Breeders. I again Subtract fifty Thousand, for those Women who miscarry, or whose Children die by accident, or disease within the Year. There only remain an hundred and twenty thousand Children of poor Parents annually born: The question therefore is, How this number shall be reared, and provided for? which, as I have already said, under the present Situation of Affairs, is utterly impossible by all the Methods hitherto proposed; for we can neither employ them in Handicraft or Agriculture; we neither build Houses, (I mean in the Country) nor cultivate Land: They can very seldom pick up a Livelihood by Stealing till they arrive at six years Old; except where they are of towardly parts; although, I confess, they learn the Rudiments much earlier; during which time they can however be properly looked upon only as Probationers; as I have been informed by a principal Gentleman in the County of Cavan, who protested to me, that he never knew above one or two Instances under the Age of six, even in a part of the Kingdom so renowned for the quickest proficiency in that Art.

I am assured by our Merchants, that a Boy or Girl before twelve 7 years Old, is no saleable Commodity, and even when they come to this Age, they will not yield above three Pounds, or three Pounds and half a Crown at most, on the Exchange; which cannot turn to Account either to the Parents or Kingdom, the Charge of Nutriment and Rags having been at least four times that Value.

I shall now therefore humbly propose my own Thoughts, which I 8 hope will not be liable to the least Objection.

I have been assured by a very knowing American of my acquain- 9 tance in London, that a young healthy Child well Nursed is at a year Old a most delicious nourishing and wholesome Food, whether Stewed, Roasted, Baked, or Boiled; and I make no doubt that it will equally serve in a Fricasie, or a Ragout.

I do therefore humbly offer it to publick consideration, that of the 10 Hundred and twenty thousand Children, already computed, twenty thousand may be reserved for Breed, whereof only one fourth part to be Males; which is more than we allow to Sheep, black Cattle, or Swine, and my Reason is, that these Children are seldom the Fruits of Marriage, a Circumstance not much regarded by our Savages, there- fore, one Male will be sufficient to serve four Females. That the remaining Hundred thousand may at a year Old be offered in Sale to the Persons of Quality and Fortune, through the Kingdom, always advising the Mother to let them Suck plentifully in the last Month, so as to render them Plump, and Fat for a good Table. A Child will make two Dishes at an Entertainment for Friends, and when the Family dines alone, the fore or hind Quarter will make a reasonable Dish, and seasoned with a little Pepper or Salt will be very good Boiled on the fourth Day, especially in Winter.

I have reckoned upon a Medium, that a Child just born will weigh 11 12 pounds, and in a solar Year, if tolerably nursed, encreaseth to 28 Pounds.

I grant this food will be somewhat dear, and therefore very proper 12 for Landlords, who, as they have already devoured most of the Parents seem to have the best Title of the Children.

Infant's flesh will be in Season throughout the Year, but more 13 plentiful in March, and a little before and after; for we are told by a grave Author, an eminent French Physician, that Fish being a pro- lifick Dyet, there are more Children born in Roman Catholic Countries about nine Months after Lent, than at any other Season; therefore reckoning a Year after Lent, the Markets will be more glutted than usual, because the Number of Popish Infants, is at least three to one in this Kingdom, and therefore it will have one other Collateral advan- tage, by lessening the Number of Papists among us.

I have already computed the Charge of nursing a Begger's Child 14 (in which List I reckon all Cottagers, Labourers, and four fifths of the Farmers) to be about two Shillings per Annum, Rags included; and I believe no Gentleman would repine to give Ten Shillings for the Carcass of a good fat Child, which, as I have said will make four Dishes of excellent Nutritive Meat, when he hath only some particular Friend, or his own family to dine with him. Thus the Squire will learn to be a good Landlord, and grow popular among his Tenants, the Mother will have Eight Shillings neat Profit, and be fit for Work till she produces another Child.

Those who are more thrifty (as I must confess the Times require) may flay the Carcass; the Skin of which, Artificially dressed, will make admirable Gloves for Ladies, and Summer Boots for fine Gentlemen. **15**

As to our City of Dublin, Shambles may be appointed for this purpose, in the most convenient parts of it, and Butchers we may be assured will not be wanting; although I rather recommend buying the Children alive, and dressing them hot from the Knife, as we do roasting Pigs. **16**

A very worthy Person, a true Lover of his Country, and whose Virtures I highly esteem, was lately pleased, in discoursing on this matter, to offer a refinement upon my Scheme. He said, that many Gentlemen of this Kingdom, having of late destroyed their Deer, he conceived that the Want of Venison might be well supply'd by the Bodies of young Lads and Maidens, not exceeding fourteen Years of Age, nor under twelve; so great a Number of both Sexes in every Country being now ready to Starve, for want of Work and Service: And these to be disposed of by their Parents if alive, or otherwise by their nearest Relations. But with due deference to so excellent a Friend, and so deserving a Patriot, I cannot be altogether in his Sentiments; for as to the Males, my American acquaintance assured me from frequent Experience, that their Flesh was generally Tough and Lean, like that of our Schoolboys, by continual exercise, and their Taste disagreeable, and to fatten them would not answer the Charge. Then as to the Females, it would, I think with humble Submission, be a Loss to the Publick, because they soon would become Breeders themselves: And besides it is not improbable that some scrupulous People might be apt to Censure such a Practice, (although indeed very unjustly) as a little bordering upon Cruelty, which I confess, hath always been with me the strongest Objection against any Project, how well soever intended. **17**

But in order to justify my Friend, he confessed, that this expedient was put into his Head by the famous Sallmanaazor, a Native of the Island Formosa, who came from thence to London, above twenty Years ago, and in Conversation told my Friend, that in his Country when any young Person happened to be put to Death, the Executioner sold the Carcass to Persons of Quality, as a prime Dainty, and that, in his Time, the Body of a plump Girl of fifteen, who was crucified for an attempt to poison the Emperor, was sold to his Imperial Majesty's prime Minister of State, and other great Mandarins of the Court, in Joints from the Gibbet, at four hundred Crowns. Neither indeed can I deny, that if the same Use were made of several plump young Girls in this Town, who, without single Groat to their Fortunes, cannot stir **18** abroad without a Chair, and appear at a Play-house, and Assemblies in Foreign fineries, which they never will pay for; the Kingdom would not be the worse.

Some Persons of a desponding Spirit are in great concern about 19 that vast Number of poor People, who are Aged, Diseased, or Maimed, and I have been desired to imploy my Thoughts what Course may be taken, to ease the Nation of so grevious an Incumbrance. But I am not in the least Pain upon that matter, because it is very well known, that they are every Day dying, and rotting, by cold and famine, and filth, and vermin, as fast as can be reasonably expected. And as to the younger Labourers, they are now in almost as hopeful a Condition. They cannot get Work, and consequently pine away for want of Nourishment, to a degree, that if at any Time they are accidentally hired to common Labour, they have not Strength to perform it, and thus the Country and themselves are happily delivered from the Evils to come.

I have too long digressed, and therefore shall return to my Subject. 20 I think the Advantages by the Proposal which I have made are obvious and many, as well as of the highest Importance.

For *First,* as I have already observed, it would greatly lessen the 21 Number of Papists, with whom we are Yearly over-run, being the principal Breeders of the Nation, as well as our most dangerous Enemies, and who stay at home on purpose with a Design to deliver the Kingdom to the Pretender, hoping to take their Advantage by the Absence of so many good Protestants, who have chosen rather to leave their Country, than stay at home, and pay Tithes against their conscience, to an Episcopal Curate.

Secondly, The poorer Tenants will have something valuable of 22 their own which by Law may be made lyable to Distress, and help to pay their Landlord's Rent, their Corn and Cattle being already seized, and Money a Thing unknown.

Thirdly, Whereas the Maintenance of a hundred thousand Chil- 23 dren, from two Years old, and upwards, cannot be computed at less than Ten Shillings a Piece per Annum, the Nation's Stock will be thereby increased fifty thousand Pounds per Annum, beside the Profit of a new Dish, introduced to the Tables of all Gentlemen of Fortune in the Kingdom, who have any Refinement in Taste, and the Money will circulate among our Selves, the Goods being entirely of our own Growth and Manufacture.

Fourthly, The constant Breeders besides the gain of eight Shillings 24 Sterling per Annum, by the Sale of their Children, will be rid of the Charge of maintaining them after the first Year.

Fifthly, This Food would likewise bring great Custom to Taverns, 25 where the Vintners will certainly be so prudent as to procure the best Receipts for dressing it to Perfection; and consequently have their Houses frequented by all the fine Gentlemen, who justly value themselves upon their Knowledge in good Eating; and a skillful Cook, who understands how to oblige his Guests, will contrive to make it as expensive as they please.

Sixthly, This would be a great Inducement to Marriage, which all 26 wise Nations have either encouraged by Rewards, or enforced by Laws and Penalties. It would encrease the Care and Tenderness of Mothers towards their Children, when they were sure of a Settlement for Life, to the poor Babes, provided in some Sort by the Publick, to their annual Profit instead of Expence; we should soon see an honest Emulation among the married Women, which of them could bring the fattest Child to the Market. Men would become as fond of their Wives, during the Time of their Pregnancy, as they are now of their Mares in Foal, their Cows in Calf, or Sows when they are ready to farrow, nor offer to beat or kick them (as is too frequent a Practice) for fear of a Miscarriage.

Many other Advantages might be enumerated. For Instance, the 27 Addition of some thousand Carcasses in our Exportation of Barrel'd Beef: The Propagation of Swine's Flesh, and Improvement in the Art of making good Bacon, so much wanted among us by the great Destruction of Pigs, too frequent at our Tables, which are no way comparable in Taste, or Magnificence to a well grown, fat yearling Child, which roasted whole will make a considerable Figure at a Lord Mayor's Feast, or any other Publik Entertainment. But this, and many others, I omit, being studious of Brevity.

Supposing that one thousand Families in this City, would be 28 constant Customers for Infant's Flesh, besides others who might have it at merry Meetings, particularly at Weddings and Christenings. I compute that Dublin would take off Annually about twenty thousand Carcasses, and the rest of the Kingdom (where probably they will be sold somewhat cheaper) the remaining eighty Thousand.

I can think of no one Objection, that will possibly be raised against 29 this Proposal, unless it should be urged, that the Number of People will be thereby much lessened in the Kingdom. This I freely own, and 'twas indeed one principal Design in offering it to the World. I desire the Reader will observe, that I calculate my Remedy for this one individual Kingdom of Ireland, and for no Other that ever was, is, or I think, ever can be upon Earth. Therefore let no man talk to me of other Expedients: Of taxing our Absentees at five Shillings a Pound: Of using neither Cloaths, nor Household Furniture, except what is of our own Growth and Manufacture: Of utterly rejecting the Materials and Instruments that promote Foreign Luxury: Of curing the Expensiveness of Pride, Vanity, Idleness, and Gaming in our Women: Of introducing a Vein of Parcimony, Prudence and Temperance: Of learning to love our Country, wherein we differ even from Laplanders, and the Inhabitants of Topinamboo: Of quitting our Animosities, and Factions, nor act any longer like the Jews, who were murdering one another at the very Moment their City was taken: Of being a little cautious not to sell our Country and Consciences for nothing: Of teaching Landlords to have at least one Degree of Mercy towards their Tenants. Lastly, Of putting a Spirit of Honesty, Industry, and Skill into our Shop-keepers, who, if a Resolution could now be taken to buy only our Native Goods, would immediately unite to cheat and exact upon us in the Price, the Measure, and the Goodness, nor could ever yet be brought to make one fair Proposal of just Dealing, though often and earnestly invited to it.

Therefore I repeat, let no Man talk to me of these and the like 30 Expedients, till he hath at least some Glimpse of Hope, that there will ever be some hearty and sincere Attempt to put them in Practice.

But as to my self, having been wearied out for many Years with 31 offering vain, idle, visionary Thoughts, and at length utterly despairing of Success, I fortunately fell upon this Proposal, which as it is wholly new, so it hath something Solid and Real, of no Expence and little Trouble, full in our own Power, and whereby we can incur no Danger in disobliging England. For this kind of Commodity will not bear Exportation, the Flesh being of too tender a Consistence, to admit a long Continuance in Salt, although perhaps I cou'd name a Country, which wou'd be glad to eat up our whole Nation without it.

After all, I am not so violently bent upon my own Opinion, as to 32 reject any Offer, proposed by wise Men, which shall be found equally Innocent, Cheap, Easy and Effectual. But before something of that Kind shall be advanced in Contradiction to my Scheme, and offering a better, I desire the Author or Authors, will be pleased maturely to consider two Points. *First,* As Things now stand, how they will be able to find Food and Raiment for a hundred Thousand useless Mouths and Backs. And *Secondly,* There being a round Million of Creatures in Human Figure, throughout this Kingdom, whose whole Subsistence put into a common Stock, would leave them in Debt two Millions of Pounds Sterling, adding those, who are Beggers by Profession, to the Bulk of Farmers, Cottagers, and Labourers, with their Wives and Children, who are Beggers in Effect; I desire those Politicians, who dislike my Overture, and may perhaps be so bold to attempt an Answer, that they will first ask the Parents of these Mortals, Whether they would not at this Day think it a great Happiness to have been sold for Food at a Year Old, in the manner I prescribe, and thereby have avoided such a perpetual Scene of Misfortunes, as they have since gone through, by the Oppression of Landlords, the Impossibility of paying Rent without Money or Trade, the Want of common Sustenance, with neither House nor Cloaths to cover them from the Inclemencies of the Weather, and the most inevitable Prospect of intailing the like, or greater Miseries, upon their Breed for ever.

I profess in the Sincerity of my Heart, that I have not the least 33 Personal Interest in endeavoring to promote this Necessary Work, having no other Motive than the Publick Good of my Country, by advancing our Trade, providing for infants, relieving the Poor, and giving some Pleasure to the Rich. I have no Children, by which I can propose to get a single Penny; the youngest being nine Years Old, and my Wife past Childbearing.

Study Questions

1. What is Swift's strategy in describing the advantages of his proposal in paragraphs 1–8?
2. At what point in the essay is it evident that Swift is not to be taken literally in his proposal?
3. What do the statistics in paragraphs 6 and 10 and in other paragraphs contribute to the tone of the essay?
4. What is Swift's strategy in citing authorities and sources of his information?
5. What types of arguments does Swift use to advance his proposal?

So Why Do Rapes Occur?

ROY U. SCHENK

Roy U. Schenk (1929–   ) was born in Evansville, Illinois. He attended Purdue University, where he earned a B. S.; and Cornell University, from which he received both an M. S. and a Ph. D. He currently works as a Senior Researcher for a small laboratory in Madison, Wisconsin. However, he also has a private corporation that includes Bioenergetics Press, Creative Industries, and Enterprising Real Estate units. He says that *The Other Side of the Coin: Causes and Consequences of Men's Oppression* (1982) is his "most significant accomplishment." Schenk feels that his ideas are opposed because they do not represent a feminist perspective.

Rape and the threat of rape cause serious and quite 1 legitimate concern among women. And any suggestions that women, by their dress or actions, in any way contribute to the occurrence of rape is met with intense, even violent, reactions from women, particularly, it seems, from feminists. An illusion of this is the recent recall election in Madison (Dane County), Wisconsin, of Judge A. Simonson who dared to suggest that this is so.

It does seem important to try to understand what the basic causes 2 of this violent treatment of women are, rather than merely to expend

This article first appeared in the *Humanist* Mar./Apr. 1979 and is reprinted by permission.

enormous effort in trying to prevent rapes. We have to understand the nature of the problem before we can remove the causes. Otherwise it is like treating a cancer-caused headache without trying to understand and treat the basic disease that caused the headache.

It appears to be rather well accepted by persons who have studied   3
the occurrence of rape that given the right circumstances any woman is at the risk of being raped and that given the right circumstances any man is apt to assault a woman. Yet as feminist Freda Salzman insists in a recent article, probably correctly, there are no clear genetic differences that make men more aggressive than women. This leads me to believe that there is something in the male-female relationship that sets up the dynamic which causes rape to occur; just as Dr. Paul Kaunitz recently pointed out: there is a dynamic in sado-masochistic marriages that causes the battering of wives (or occasionally of husbands).

In a search for the causes of rape, it seems appropriate to start by   4
stating what I believe are well-known and accepted facts, and then to develop further from these statements. Fact 1: Men rape women. Seldom do women even attempt to rape men. Fact 2: Women can sell sex (prostitution). Seldom do men even try to sell sex, except to other men. Fact 3: Women are neither more good nor more evil than men are. Fact 4: Men tend to take out their anger in more physically violent ways than women do.

From these facts, I believe we can deduce other facts. For example,   5
if women can sell sex and men can't, then sex must be less readily available, on the average, to men than to women. Of course, this is well known because women are socially conditioned to believe they don't need sex, while men are conditioned to actively pursue sex. As a result of this, women seeking sex at any one time can usually secure a sexual partner whenever they want one, so they really don't have any need to pursue sex. The argument that sex usually involves one man and one woman and so must be equally available, which I often hear, is fallacious simply because at any one time there are far more men seeking sex than there are women. So, on the average, sex is far more readily available to women than to men.

A psychiatric study of men who have raped women, which I read   6
about several years ago but have not been able to locate, reported that in about 70 percent of rapes the primary motivating emotion was *rage*. One must necessarily understand the causes of this rage, then, to understand why rapes happen. Many, if not most, feminists apparently believe that rage occurs because men perceive women as sexual objects that men have a right to have sex with, and that the rage occurs when women reject them. Here we see an expression of what I refer to as the Innocent Victim Syndrome—the perception of women as innocent victims of evil men—which seems to be prevalant among women, feminists and nonfeminists alike. But I think the facts contradict the idea that women are so blameless, so morally superior to men.

So what *does* cause this rage? If we can return to our earlier   7
gathered facts, we established that, on the average, sex is far more

readily available to women than to men; indeed it can be said that women have a surplus of sexually available partners and men have a deficit of sexually available partners; that is, women can usually get all the sex they want and have even more offered and pushed on them, whereas men do not.

Developing this idea further, some time ago, on the same day, a 8 fellow said to me: "I don't see why women think jobs are so important," and a women said to me: "I don't know why men think sex is so important." Here we see serious insensitivity; each one failing to recognize that relative unavailability increases importance, just as water becomes far more important in a desert.

It's time that women recognize that sex, because of this unavail- 9 ability, is far more important to men than it is to women. So sexual teasing and manipulation is a far more serious provocation, more serious violence, than most women seem to recognize. The best analogy I can think of is when men dangle job promises and manipulate women with threats to their jobs—behavior which certainly enrages women.

As we are surely all aware, the results of sexual inequality are that 10 women are socially conditioned in practice to use sex and the direct or indirect promise of sex (flirting, teasing, and so on) to control and manipulate men. Unfortunately this manipulative behavior is accepted as normal behavior in our society. But in my opinion, if this manipulative kind of treatment of men by women were directed against any other creature, it would be labeled for what it is—namely, cruel and sadistic. For example, a person who dangled a beefsteak in front of a hungry dog time after time, and then yanked it away when the dog reached out for it, would certainly be called cruel and sadistic. His actions would be considered violent and the dog would ultimately become enraged. But dangling sex in front of sex-hungry men and yanking it away are practiced routinely by women. And rage by men is a most natural response to this cruelty, this violence.

I think it would not be surprising if a dog, enraged at the violence 11 of humans who have teased and tantalized it, given the opportunity, would respond in a violent manner by attacking a human, and the behavior, dress, and so on of that particular person would probably be largely irrelevant. I think it is not surprising that an occasional man, enraged at the violence of women who have teased and tantalized him, might, if the opportunity occurred, attack a woman, and the behavior, dress, and so on of that particular person might be largely irrelevant. Since the rage was generated by sexual manipulation, it would frequently be directed toward the sexuality of the woman.

It is a common human experience that violence begets violence. If a 12 person hits another person, there is a strong likelihood that the second person will strike back. Of, if he cannot, he will likely react violently to someone or something else. What also needs to be recognized is that not all violence is physical. An insulting put-down can be as violent as, or even more violent than, a physical blow.

I think it is important to recognize that rape is a violent response 13 to violence. But I do not believe that sexual teasing and tantalizing by women is the only or perhaps even the primary violence that causes the violent response of rape. I believe there is an even more serious form of violence that women do to men.

Returning now to another fact, the relative moral goodness or evil 14 of men and women. This is probably the most-likely-to-be-challenged issue of this essay, because, just as we have been socially conditioned to perceive men as superior in leadership ability, job skills, and so on, so have we also been socially conditioned to perceive women as morally and spiritually superior to men. For example, women are perceived as the peace lovers and men as the aggressors and warmakers; women are also perceived as maintaining higher sexual moral standards than men do.

My feminist associates define chauvinism as an attitude of 15 superiority of one group over another, so it seems only reasonable to conclude that all of these perceptions of superiority are chauvinistic. And if male-chauvinist attitudes are sexist, it certainly seems appropriate that we recognize that these female-chauvinist attitudes are also sexist behavior.

This attitude of moral superiority is probably the cause for the 16 harpylike response by some feminists that I have regularly experienced and observed when I or anyone else even hints that women's behavior may in any way contribute to the occurrence of rape (for example, the Simonson affair). It appears that these women want to retain at all costs the image that women are innocent victims of evil men. I suggest that this attitude of moral superiority and of women as innocent victims is obviously sexist and should be labeled as such.

A recent radio advertisement encouraged people to be sure to buy 17 enough photographic film so that they could get plenty of pictures of their little angels—and also their little devils. It doesn't take a degree in psychology to perceive that the angels are girls and the devils are boys.

This perception of girls as sugar and spice and everything nice, and 18 boys as dirty, vulgar, evil, and unnice, pervades our whole culture and the upbringing of our children. But somehow it has escaped the consciousness of almost everyone that the perception of boys through their upbringing as morally inferior, by their nature, to girls must have a psychologically devastating effect on boys and ultimately on the men they become, when they continue to carry the same negative perceptions of themselves. Just as women's negative attitudes toward themselves in other areas have had psychologically devastating effects on women, these social attitudes about moral inferiority hurt men.

Actually, the devastating effects on men are quite evident in the 19 ease with which women can use shame and guilt-feelings to manipulate men. They are further manifest in the quoted remarks of men when they rape women, remarks about bringing women down, of the woman not being able to be so high and mighty anymore; and also the remarks of raped women themselves, remarks of feeling degraded, unclean, and lowered parallel the attitude.

The damage to men's egos resulting from their social conditioning 20 as morally inferior persons needs to be recognized as a destructive form of violence. Indeed, if one can seriously hear what Fredric Storaska, executive director of the National Organization for the Prevention of Rape and Assault says, this is evidently the major violence to men that is countered by men through the violence of rape.

Storaska, in his book *How to Say No to a Rapist—and Survive,* 21 reports that a sure way to prevent rape is to treat the man as a human being. What Storaska, in his guilt-laden male state, fails to perceive is the obvious fact that if this is so, then women must not normally treat men as human beings, that is, as morally equal to women. Rather, many women treat men as dirt, as morally inferior, as beings to be used and manipulated and walked over, as economic objects—violence of a severity so great that only men laden with intense moral guilt feelings, would tolerate.

But violence begets violence; and men's response to the violence 22 they experience from women is on occasion expressed by turning the violence that women train men to use to protect women back against the women themselves.

So, finally, I think we can add another fact: Women, as a class, by 23 their socially conditioned manipulative sexual behavior and their attitude of moral superiority, create the conditions that cause rape; but it is an individual woman, often no more responsible than any other woman, who gets raped.

Of course, women welcome the power that sexual manipulation 24 and tantalizing of men gives them. As one woman put it: "You've got to use your body. It's the only asset you've got . . ." But obviously women do not normally welcome the undesirable consequences of their behavior, the violence of rape and assault. So we can add another fact: Most, if not all, women do not want to be raped.

Another consequence of the sexist perception that women are 25 morally superior to men is the reality that we men are assaulted from birth (primarily by women, for example, mothers, teachers, and so on) with the perception that we should be morally ashamed of ourselves because we are men. The result of this is that men seem unable to look at their exploited situation and cannot demand an end to this exploitation and oppression. Instead, ironically, men have been socially conditioned to protect and defend their oppressors—"morally superior" women. But I am no longer willing to accept this sexist attitude of moral inferiority for men. In fact, I confess to being rather proud that we men control our rage at women so well that so few of us express it violently.

It shouldn't be necessary for me to say this, but this does not mean 26 I think rape is acceptable behavior. I do not approve of rape, and I do not consider it or other forms of violence as acceptable behavior. But I also do not think the manipulative, teasing behavior and the attitude of moral superiority held by many women to be acceptable behavior either; they are merely other forms of violence. It needs to be recognized that as long as women persist in these latter forms of violent behavior, rapes and other violence will also continue. Women who demand that men change their behavior, while refusing to examine and change their own violent behavior toward men, are just plain sexists.

So what of the future? Is there a possibility to eliminate sexual 27 assaults? If there is, it will surely come, not by legislating greater penalties and attempting to generate even greater guilt-feelings in men, but by removing the basic causes of rape—the manipulation, the teasing, and the dangling of sex by women, the unavailability of sex for men, and the chauvinist attitude that women are morally superior to men.

This is a challenge for mothers, and for the increasing numbers of 28 fathers who are succeeding in the struggle to have more involvement with their children. And this will not be an easy struggle, because quite a lot of women appear to like the advantages of their current roles. The control over men and the feelings of self-righteous indignation and moral superiority may simply be too much to give up for mere equality. A great many women may choose to maintain their female chauvinistic attitudes and other sexist behavior, in which case men will continue to respond to this violence by violence of their own, and rape and assault will continue to be an ongoing threat to all women.

Since we men stand to benefit greatly by the elimination of both 29 male and female chauvinism, through a better self-image, greater availability of sex, prolonged lifespan, and the elimination of other special privileges of women, I hope the choice will be to eliminate the violence by both sexes—though whether this is possible in a highly competitive society such as ours remains to be seen.

Study Questions

1. In an argumentative essay the author may first present the conclusions and then the reasons, or may lead into the conclusions after presenting the reasons. What method does the author use in this essay? What effect does he gain by this method?
2. What is the effect of the author's failure to cite the source of the study he refers to in paragraph 6?
3. Is the author's method primarily inductive or deductive? Explain.
4. In paragraphs 10 and 11 the author uses an analogy. Is it appropriate to his purpose? Explain.
5. What type of development is used in paragraphs 5, 14, and 18?
6. How does the author attempt to validate his position on female chauvinism as a cause of rape?

A Reply to Roy Schenk

GINA ALLEN

Gina Allen (1918–   ) was born in Trenton, Nebraska, attended the University of Nebraska, and graduated from Northwestern in 1948. An involved citizen, she works for youth commissions, the Democratic Party, the PTA, and the Authors League. As a free-lance writer, she has published short stories, articles, and novelettes in numerous magazines. Allen's books include *Prairie Children* (1941), *Tepee Days* (1941), *On the Oregon Trail* (1942), *Rustics for Keep* (1948), *The Forbidden Man* (1961), and *Gold!* (1964). Many of her writings are for young people.

Dr. Schenk proposes that rape is a violent response by some 1 men to the nonphysical violence committed by all women against all men. The violence of which he accuses women consists of sexual deprivation, cockteasing (to borrow a word from my high-school days), and moral superiority.

I would suggest that women aren't to blame for any of these. 2 Everybody, including women, is sexually deprived in our Puritanical society. Sex education is nil or inadequate in our schools. Young people legally under age but sexually mature and active are denied birth-control information and contraception. As a result, teenage out-of-wedlock pregnancy is higher than it has ever been. Young people, particularly young women, pay a high price for sexual activity.

The sex titillation to which men are subjected comes less from 3 women than from advertisers who exploit them as sex objects to sell everything from cars to soft drinks to magazines to pornography. Women are subjected to the same propaganda. They feel they must dress and act as sex objects to attract a man, while trying to remain virgins to deserve respect and merit marriage. This is sex deprivation, not moral superiority. Nor did women invent the double standard that demands a virgin bride. Mostly, they envy the young men out sowing their wild oats.

Because of the nonphysical violence visited on men by women, Dr. 4 Schenk tells us, men are in a rage against women. And in about 70 percent of all rapes, rage is the primary motivating emotion. I have no doubt that this is true. What I doubt is that the rage is directed solely

This article first appeared in the *Humanist* Mar./Apr. 1979 and is reprinted by permission.

99

against women. I think it's much more general and that women become the targets in part because they are usually smaller, weaker, and less able to defend themselves than men are.

According to sociological researchers (notably Menachem Amir, in 5 Philadelphia) and the FBI's annual Uniform Crime Reports, 90 percent of all the apprehended rapists come from the bottom of the economic ladder. They live in our slums and our ghettos. It's not just sex they're deprived of. It's everything.

Whatever they learn in the home, or on the streets, they learn that 6 they must live by violence. It's a matter of survival. Violently they take what they can from an affluent society that dangles its goodies before them—on billboards and television—and denies them even the basic essentials of a civilized life. Among the goodies are beautiful female sex objects.

But it's not just women they want, and it's not just women they 7 attack. Their median age is twenty-three, but most are from fifteen to nineteen years old when they first rape a victim—often in pairs and groups, to prove their manhood to each other. Despite their youth, 70 percent have prior records from crimes ranging from burglary to robbery to assault. Eighty-five percent go on to commit other crimes. Obviously, raping women is not the only thing on their minds. And women are not the only objects of their rage.

I agree with Dr. Schenk that it would be helpful if we could change 8 the training children get from parents. Let's erase sex roles. Let's teach little girls that they don't have to be seductive and virginal, dependent and submissive, to be feminine. Let's teach little boys that they don't have to be aggressive little devils and macho tough guys to be masculine. Let's teach both boys and girls to respect and love each other as unique individuals and worthy human beings. That could greatly enrich the lives and relationships of the next generation.

But that alone won't do away with rape. We need to reorder 9 priorities so that underprivileged youth have options other than violence for getting their fair share of our abundance; so that women are treated as people, not denigrated as sex objects; so that people become more important than the Pentagon; so that violence, including war, is banished from the earth.

All these things must be done, but all will come too late to prevent 10 the quarter of a million rapes that will occur this year. We face an emergency. While overall crime decreases, rape increases at a rate of 62 percent every five years. I think of the young mother in the San Francisco Bay area, recently raped and slain while jogging. I think of the fifteen-year-old youngster in a California hospital, now trying to learn to live without her hands, chopped off by the man who raped her.

We can't wait. We must take rape seriously as the violent crime it 11 is. We must stop joking about it. ("Lie back and enjoy it". . . . "Rape is impossible since a woman can run faster with her skirt up than a man can with his pants down" . . . "Women ask for it" . . . "They won't admit it but they love it" . . . "At her age she should be flattered.")

In our courts we must stop trying the victim instead of the 12 perpetrator of the crime, or women will continue to report only one in five rapes, and rapists will continue to go free to rape again. We must immediately begin to prosecute rapists as vigorously as we prosecute burglars and arsonists. To do less is to admit that we value women less than property and to jeopardize the lives and well-being of over half our population.

Study Questions

1. What type of argument does Allen use to refute Schenk?
2. How does Allen develop the topics of paragraphs 10 and 11?
3. What are the major differences in the sentence structure used by Allen and Schenk?
4. What is Allen's strategy in the first sentence of paragraph 2?
5. Of the two arguments—Schenk's and Allen's—which is the more convincing? Explain.

Separating
JOHN UPDIKE

John Updike (1932–   ) was born in Shillington, Pennsylvania, and attended Harvard University, where he edited the *Lampoon* and graduated *summa cum laude*. Later he attended the Ruskin School of Drawing and Fine Art at Oxford. While still in his twenties, he became an established figure in American letters. He has been a recipient of the O. Henry Prize Story Award as well as a Guggenheim Fellowship, the Rosenthal Award of the National Institute of Arts and Letters, of which he is a member, and the National Book Award. In the 1950s he was on the staff of the *New Yorker* as a reporter for the "Talk of the Town" column. He continues to contribute verse, parodies, and humorous essays to this magazine. Updike has published verse, *Telephone Poles and Other Poems* (1963), and is well known for his short stories, many of which have appeared in collections such as *The Same Door* (1959) and *Pigeon Feathers* (1962). However, his fame rests on his best-selling novels: *The Poorhouse Fair* (1959), *Rabbit Run* (1960), *The Centaur* (1963), *Of the Farm* (1965), *Couples* (1968), *Bech: A Book* (1970), *Rabbit Redux* (1971), *A Month of Sundays* (1975), *Marry Me* (1976), *The Coup* (1978), and *Rabbit Is Rich* (1981). He says that if he weren't a writer, he would choose to be a turtle.

The day was fair. Brilliant. All that June the weather had   1
mocked the Maples' internal misery with solid sunlight—golden shafts
and cascades of green in which their conversations had wormed
unseeing, their sad murmuring selves the only stain in Nature.
Usually by this time of the year they had acquired tans; but when they
met their elder daughter's plane on her return from a year in England
they were almost as pale as she, though Judith was too dazzled by the
sunny opulent jumble of her native land to notice. They did not spoil
her homecoming by telling her immediately. Wait a few days, let her
recover from jet lag, had been one of their formulations, in that string
of gray dialogues—over coffee, over cocktails, over Cointreau—that
had shaped the strategy of their dissolution, while the earth performed
its annual stunt of renewal unnoticed beyond their closed windows.
Richard had thought to leave at Easter; Joan had insisted they wait
until the four children were at last assembled, with all exams passed
and ceremonies attended, and the bauble of summer to console them.
So he had drudged away, in love, in dread, repairing screens, getting
the mowers sharpened, rolling and patching their new tennis court.

The court, clay, had come through its first winter pitted and   2
windswept bare of redcoat. Years ago the Maples had observed how
often, among their friends, divorce followed a dramatic home improvement, as if the marriage were making one last effort to live; their
own worst crisis had come amid the plaster dust and exposed plumbing
of a kitchen renovation. Yet, a summer ago, as canary-yellow bulldozers gaily churned a grassy, daisy-dotted knoll into a muddy plateau,
and a crew of pigtailed young men raked and tamped clay into a plane,
this transformation did not strike them as ominous, but festive in its
impudence; their marriage could rend the earth for fun. The next
spring, waking each day at dawn to a sliding sensation as if the bed
were being tipped, Richard found the barren tennis court—its net and
tapes still rolled in the barn—an environment congruous with his
mood of purposeful desolation, and the crumbling of handfuls of clay
into cracks and holes (dogs had frolicked on the court in a thaw;
rivulets had eroded trenches) an activity suitably elemental and
interminable. In his sealed heart he hoped the day would never come.

Now it was here. A Friday, Judith was re-acclimated; all four   3
children were assembled, before jobs and camps and visits again
scattered them. Joan thought they should be told one by one. Richard
was for making an announcement at the table. She said, "I think just
making an announcement is a cop-out. They'll start quarreling and
playing to each other instead of focusing. They're each individuals, you
know, not just some corporate obstacle to your freedom."

"O.K., O.K. I agree." Joan's plan was exact. That evening, they   4
were giving Judith a belated welcome-home dinner, of lobster and
champagne. Then, the party over, they, the two of them, who nineteen
years before would push her in a baby carriage along Fifth Avenue to
Washington Square, were to walk her out of the house, to the bridge
across the salt creek, and tell her, swearing her to secrecy. Then
Richard Jr., who was going directly from work to a rock concert in

Boston, would be told, either late when he returned on the train or early Saturday morning before he went off to his job; he was seventeen and employed as one of a golf-course maintenance crew. Then the two younger children, John and Margaret, could, as the morning wore on, be informed.

"Mopped up, as it were," Richard said.   5

"Do you have any better plan? That leaves you the rest of Saturday   6
to answer any questions, pack, and make your wonderful departure."

"No," he said, meaning he had no better plan, and agreed to hers,   7
though to him it showed an edge of false order, a hidden plea for control, like Joan's long chore lists and financial accountings and, in the days when he first knew her, her too-copious lecture notes. Her plan turned one hurdle for him into four—four knife-sharp walls, each with a sheer blind drop on the other side.

All spring he had moved through a world of insides and outsides, of   8
barriers and partitions. He and Joan stood as a thin barrier between the children and the truth. Each moment was a partition, with the past on one side and the future on the other, a future containing this unthinkable *now*. Beyond four knifelike walls a new life for him waited vaguely. His skull cupped a secret, a white face, a face both frightened and soothing, both strange and known, that he wanted to shield from tears, which he felt all about him, solid as the sunlight. So haunted, he had become obsessed with battening down the house against his absence, replacing screens and sash cords, hinges and latches—a Houdini making things snug before his escape.

The lock. He had still to replace a lock on one of the doors of the   9
screened porch. The task, like most such, proved more difficult than he had imagined. The old lock, aluminum frozen by corrosion, had been deliberately rendered obsolete by manufacturers. Three hardware stores had nothing that even approximately matched the mortised hole its removal (surprisingly easy) left. Another hole had to be gouged, with bits too small and saws too big, and the old hole fitted with a block of wood—the chisels dull, the saw rusty, his fingers thick with lack of sleep. The sun poured down, beyond the porch, on a world of neglect. The bushes already needed pruning, the windward side of the house was shedding flakes of paint, rain would get in when he was gone, insects, rot, death. His family, all those he would lose, filtered through the edges of his awareness as he struggled with screw holes, splinters, opaque instructions, minutiae of metal.

Judith sat on the porch, a princess returned from exile. She regaled 10
them with stories of fuel shortages, of bomb scares in the Underground, of Pakistani workmen loudly lusting after her as she walked past on her way to dance school. Joan came and went, in and out of the house, calmer than she should have been, praising his struggles with the lock as if this were one more and not the last of their long succession of shared chores. The younger of his sons for a few minutes held the rickety screen door while his father clumsily hammered and chiseled, each blow a kind of sob in Richard's ears. His younger daughter,

having been at a slumber party, slept on the porch hammock through all the noise—heavy and pink, trusting and forsaken. Time, like the sunlight, continued relentlessly; the sunlight slowly slanted. Today was one of the longest days. The lock clicked, worked. He was through. He had a drink; he drank it on the proch, listening to his daughter. "It was so sweet," she was saying, "during the worst of it, how all the butchers and bakery shops kept open by candlelight. They're all so plucky and cute. From the papers, things sounded so much worse here—people shooting people in gas lines, and everybody freezing."

Richard asked her, "Do you still want to live in England forever?" 11 *Forever:* the concept, now a reality upon him, pressed and scratched at the back of his throat.

"No," Judith confessed, turning her oval face to him, its eyes still 12 childishly far apart, but the lips set as over something succulent and satisfactory. "I was anxious to come home. I'm an American." She was a woman. They had raised her; he and Joan had endured together to raise her, alone of the four. The others had still some raising left in them. Yet it was the thought of telling Judith—the image of her, their first baby, walking between them arm in arm to the bridge—that broke him. The partition between his face and the tears broke. Richard sat down to the celebratory meal with the back of his throat aching; the champagne, the lobster seemed phases of sunshine; he saw them and tasted them through tears. He blinked, swallowed, croakily joked about hay fever. The tears would not stop leaking through; they came not through a hole that could be plugged but through a permeable spot in a membrane, steadily, purely, endlessly, fruitfully. They became, his tears, a shield for himself against these others—their faces, the fact of their assembly, a last time as innocents, at a table where he sat the last time as head. Tears dropped from his nose as he broke the lobster's back; salt flavored his champagne as he sipped it; the raw clench at the back of his throat was delicious. He could not help himself.

His children tried to ignore his tears. Judith, on his right, lit a 13 cigarette, gazed upward in the direction of her too energetic, too sophisticated exhalation; on her other side, John earnestly bent his face to the extraction of the last morsels—legs, tail segments—from the scarlet corpse. Joan, at the opposite end of the table, glanced at him surprised, her reproach displaced by a quick grimace, of forgiveness, or of salute to his superior gift of strategy. Between them, Margaret, no longer called Bean, thirteen and large for her age, gazed from the other side of his pane of tears as if into a shopwindow at something she coveted—at her father, a crystalline heap of splinters and memories. It was not she, however, but John who, in the kitchen, as they cleared the plates and carapaces away, asked Joan the question: *"Why is Daddy crying?"*

Richard heard the question but not the murmured answer. Then he 14 heard Bean cry, "Oh, no-oh!"—the faintly dramatized exclamation of one who had long expected it.

John returned to the table carrying a bowl of salad. He nodded 15 tersely at his father and his lips shaped the conspiratorial words "She told."

"Told what?" Richard asked aloud, insanely. 16

The boy sat down as if to rebuke his father's distraction with the 17
example of his own good manners. He said quietly, "The separation."

Joan and Margaret returned; the child, in Richard's twisted vision, 18
seemed diminished in size, and relieved, relieved to have had the
bogieman at last proved real. He called out to her—the distances at the
table had grown immense—"You knew, you always knew," but the
clenching at the back of his throat prevented him from making sense of
it. From afar he heard Joan talking, levelly, sensibly, reciting what
they had prepared: it was a separation for the summer, an experiment.
She and Daddy both agreed it would be good for them; they needed
space and time to think; they liked each other but did not make each
other happy enough, somehow.

Judith, imitating her mother's factual tone, but in her youth 19
off-key, too cool, said, "I think it's silly. You should either live together
or get divorced."

Richard's crying, like a wave that has crested and crashed, had 20
become tumultuous; but it was overtopped by another tumult, for John,
who had been so reserved, now grew larger and larger at the table.
Perhaps his younger sister's being credited with knowing set him off.
"Why didn't you *tell* us?" he asked, in a large round voice quite unlike
his own. "You should have *told* us you weren't getting along."

Richard was startled into attempting to force words through his 21
tears. "We *do* get along, that's the trouble, so it doesn't show even to
us—" *That we do not love each other* was the rest of the sentence; he
couldn't finish it.

Joan finished for him, in her style. "And we've always, *especially,* 22
loved our children."

John was not mollified. "What do you care about *us?*" he boomed. 23
"We're just little things you *had.*" His sisters' laughing forced a laugh
from him, which he turned hard and parodistic: "Ha ha *ha.*" Richard
and Joan realized simultaneously that the child was drunk, on Judith's
home-coming champagne. Feeling bound to keep the center of the
stage, John took a cigarette from Judith's pack, poked it into his
mouth, let it hang from his lower lip, and squinted like a gangster.

"You're not little things we had," Richard called to him. "You're 24
the whole point. But you're grown. Or almost."

The boy was lighting matches. Instead of holding them to his 25
cigarette (for they had never seen him smoke; being "good" had been
his way of setting himself apart), he held them to his mother's face,
closer and closer, for her to blow out. Then he lit the whole folder—a
hiss and then a torch, held against his mother's face. Prismed by tears,
the flame filled Richard's vision; he didn't know how it was extinguished. He heard Margaret say, "Oh stop showing off," and saw John,
in response, break the cigarette in two and put the halves entirely into
his mouth and chew, sticking out his tongue to display the shreds to his
sister.

Joan talked to him, reasoning—a fountain of reason, unintelligi- 26
ble. "Talked about it for years . . . our children must help us . . . Daddy
and I both want . . ." As the boy listened, he carefully wadded a paper

napkin into the leaves of his salad, fashioned a ball of paper and lettuce, and popped it into his mouth, looking around the table for the expected laughter. None came. Judith said, "Be mature," and dismissed a plume of smoke.

Richard got up from this stifling table and led the boy outside. 27 Though the house was in twilight, the outdoors still brimmed with light, the lovely waste light of high summer. Both laughing, he supervised John's spitting out the lettuce and paper and tobacco into the pachysandra. He took him by the hand—a square gritty hand, but for its softness a man's. Yet, it held on. They ran together up into the field, past the tennis court. The raw banking left by the bulldozers was dotted with daisies. Past the court and a flat stretch where they used to play family baseball stood a soft green rise glorious in the sun, each weed and species of grass distinct as illumination on parchment. "I'm sorry, so sorry," Richard cried. "You were the only one who ever tried to help me with all the goddam jobs around this place."

Sobbing, safe within his tears and the champagne, John explained, 28 "It's not just the separation, it's the whole crummy year, I *hate* that school, you can't make any friends, the history teacher's a scud."

They sat on the crest of the rise, shaking and warm from their 29 tears but easier in their voices, and Richard tried to focus on the child's sad year—the weekdays long with homework, the weekends spent in his room with model airplanes, while his parents murmured down below, nursing their separation. How selfish, how blind, Richard thought; his eyes felt scoured. He told his son, "We'll think about getting you transferred. Life's too short to be miserable."

They had said what they could, but did not want the moment to 30 heal, and talked on, about the school, about the tennis court, whether it would ever again be as good as it had been that first summer. They walked to inspect it and pressed a few more tapes more firmly down. A little stiltedly, perhaps trying now to make too much of the moment, Richard led the boy to the spot in the field where the view was best, of the metallic blue river, the emerald marsh, the scattered islands velvety with shadow in the low light, the white bits of beach far away. "See," he said. "It goes on being beautiful. It'll be here tomorrow."

"I know," John answered, impatiently. The moment had closed.   31

Back in the house, the others had opened some white wine, the 32 champagne being drunk, and still sat at the table, the three females, gossiping. Where Joan sat had become the head. She turned, showing him a tearless face, and asked, "All right?"

"We're fine, he said, resenting it, though relieved, that the party 33 went on without him.

In bed she explained, "I couldn't cry I guess because I cried so much 34 all spring. It really wasn't fair. It's your idea, and you made it look as though I was kicking you out."

"I'm sorry," he said. "I couldn't stop. I wanted to but couldn't."   35

"You *didn't* want to. You loved it. You were having your way, 36 making a general announcement."

"I love having it over," he admitted. "God, those kids were great. So 37
brave and funny." John, returned to the house, had settled to a model
airplane in his room, and kept shouting down to them, "I'm O.K. No
sweat." "And the way," Richard went on, cozy in his relief, "they never
questioned the reasons we gave. No thought of a third person. Not even
Judith."

"That *was* touching," Joan said.   38

He gave her a hug. "You were great too. Very reassuring to 39
everybody. Thank you." Guiltily, he realized he did not feel separated.

"You still have Dickie to do," she told him. These words set before 40
him a black mountain in the darkness; its cold breath, its near weight
affected his chest. Of the four children, his elder son was most nearly
his conscience. Joan did not need to add, "That's one piece of your dirty
work I won't do for you."

"I know. I'll do it. You go to sleep."   41

Within minutes, her breathing slowed, became oblivious and 42
deep. It was quarter to midnight. Dickie's train from the concert would
come in at one-fourteen. Richard set the alarm for one. He had slept
atrociously for weeks. But whenever he closed his lids some glimpse of
the last hours scorched them—Judith exhaling toward the ceiling in a
kind of aversion, Bean's mute staring, the sunstruck growth in the
field where he and John had rested. The mountain before him moved
closer, moved within him; he was huge, momentous. The ache at the
back of his throat felt stale. His wife slept as if slain beside him. When,
exasperated by his hot lids, his crowded heart, he rose from bed and
dressed, she awoke enough to turn over. He told her then, "Joan, if I
could undo it all, I would."

"Where would you begin?" she asked. There was no place. Giving 43
him courage, she was always giving him courage. He put on shoes
without socks in the dark. The children were breathing in their rooms,
the downstairs was hollow. In their confusion they had left lights
burning. He turned off all but one, the kitchen overhead. The car
started. He had hoped it wouldn't. He met only moonlight on the road;
it seemed a diaphanous companion, flickering in the leaves along the
roadside, haunting his rearview mirror like a pursuer, melting under
his headlights. The center of town, not quite deserted, was eerie at this
hour. A young cop in uniform kept company with a gang of T-shirted
kids on the steps of the bank. Across from the railroad station, several
bars kept open. Customers, mostly young, passed in and out of the
warm night, savoring summer's novelty. Voices shouted from cars as
they passed; an immense conversation seemed in progress. Richard
parked and in his weariness put his head on the passenger seat, out of
the commotion and wheeling lights. It was as when, in the movies, an
assassin grimly carries his mission through the jostle of a carnival—
except the movies cannot show the precipitous, palpable slope you cling
to within. You cannot climb back down; you can only fall. The
synthetic fabric of the car seat, warmed by his cheek, confided to him
an ancient, distant scent of vanilla.

A train whistle caused him to lift his head. It was on time; he had 44

hoped it would be late. The slender drawgates descended. The bell of
approach tingled happily. The great metal body, horizontally fluted,
rocked to a stop, and sleepy teen-agers disembarked, his son among
them. Dickie did not show surprise that his father was meeting him at
this terrible hour. He sauntered to the car with two friends, both taller
than he. He said "Hi" to his father and took the passenger's seat with
an exhausted promptness that expressed gratitude. The friends got in
the back, and Richard was grateful; a few more minutes' postponement
would be won by driving them home.

He asked, "How was the concert?"   45

"Groovy," one boy said from the back seat.   46

"It bit," the other said.   47

"It was O.K.," Dickie said, moderate by nature, so reasonable that   48
in his childhood the unreason of the world had given him headaches,
stomach aches; nausea. When the second friend had been dropped off at
his dark house, the boy blurted, "Dad, my eyes are killing me with hay
fever! I'm out there cutting that mothering grass all day!"

"Do we still have those drops?"   49

"They didn't do any good last summer."   50

"They might this." Richard swung a U-turn on the empty street.   51
The drive home took a few minutes. The mountain was here, in his
throat. "Richard," he said, and felt the boy, slumped and rubbing his
eyes, go tense at his tone, "I didn't come to meet you just to make your
life easier. I came because your mother and I have some news for you,
and you're a hard man to get ahold of these days. It's sad news."

"That's O.K." The reassurance came out soft, but quick, as if   52
released from the tip of a spring.

Richard had feared that his tears would return and choke him, but   53
the boy's manliness set an example, and his voice issued forth steady
and dry. "It's sad news, but it needn't be tragic news, at least for you. It
should have no practical effect on your life, though it's bound to have
an emotional effect. You'll work at your job, and go back to school in
September. Your mother and I are really proud of what you're making
of your life; we don't want that to change at all."

"Yeah," the boy said lightly, on the intake of his breath, holding   54
himself up. They turned the corner; the church they went to loomed
like a gutted fort. The home of the woman Richard hoped to marry
stood across the green. Her bedroom light burned.

"Your mother and I," he said, "Have decided to separate. For the   55
summer. Nothing legal, no divorce yet. We want to see how it feels. For
some years now, we haven't been doing enough for each other, making
each other as happy as we should be. Have you sensed that?"

"No," the boy said. It was an honest, unemotional answer: true or   56
false in a quiz.

Glad for the factual basis, Richard pursued, even garrulously, the   57
details. His apartment across town, his utter accessibility, the split
vacation arrangements, the advantages to the children, the added
mobility and variety of the summer. Dickie listened, absorbing. "Do
the others know?"

"Yes."   58

"How did they take it?"   59

"The girls pretty calmly. John flipped out; he shouted and ate a 60 cigarette and made a salad out of his napkin and told us how much he hated school."

His brother chuckled. "He did?"   61

"Yeah. The school issue was more upsetting for him than Mom and 62 me. He seemed to feel better for having exploded."

"He did?" The repetition was the first sign that he was stunned.   63

"Yes. Dickie, I want to tell you something. This last hour, waiting 64 for your train to get in, has been about the worst of my life. I hate this. *Hate* it. My father would have died before doing it to me." He felt immensely lighter, saying this. He had dumped the mountain on the boy. They were home. Moving swiftly as a shadow, Dickie was out of the car, through the bright kitchen. Richard called after him, "Want a glass of milk or anything?"

"No thanks."   65

"Want us to call the course tomorrow and say you're too sick to 66 work?"

"No, that's all right." The answer was faint, delivered at the door to 67 his room; Richard listened for the slam that went with a tantrum. The door closed normally, gently. The sound was sickening.

Joan had sunk into that first deep trough of sleep and was slow to 68 awake. Richard had to repeat, "I told him."

"What did he say?"   69

"Nothing much. Could you go say goodnight to him? Please."   70

She left their room, without putting on a bathrobe. He sluggishly 71 changed back into his pajamas and walked down the hall. Dickie was already in bed, Joan was sitting beside him, and the boy's bedside clock radio was murmuring music. When she stood, an inexplicable light— the moon?—outlined her body through the nightie. Richard sat on the warm place she had indented on the child's narrow mattress. He asked him, "Do you want the radio on like that?"

"It always is."   72

"Doesn't it keep you awake? It would me."   73

"No."   74

"Are you sleepy?"   75

"Yeah."   76

"Good. Sure you want to get up and go to work? You've had a big 77 night."

"I want to."   78

Away at school this winter he had learned for the first time that 79 you can go short of sleep and live. As an infant he had slept with an immobile, sweating intensity that had alarmed his babysitters. In adolescence he had often been the first of the four children to go to bed. Even now, he would go slack in the middle of a television show, his sprawled legs hairy and brown. "O.K. Good boy. Dickie, listen. I love you so much, I never knew how much until now. No matter how this works out, I'll always be with you. Really."

Richard bent to kiss an averted face but his son, sinewy, turned 80 and with wet cheeks embraced him and gave him a kiss, on the lips, passionate as a woman's. In his father's ear he moaned one word, the crucial, intelligent word: *"Why?"*

Why. It was a whistle of a wind in a crack, a knife thrust, a window 81 thrown open on emptiness. The white face was gone, the darkness was featureless. Richard had forgotten why.

Study Questions

1. How does Updike use indirection in the first paragraphs to tell us about Richard's and Joan's relationship?
2. What is the purpose of the account about the tennis court?
3. What is the author's attitude toward each of the characters? How does he reveal his attitude in each case?
4. Are we supposed to sympathize more with Joan than with Richard? Explain.
5. What is the significance of the last sentence in the story?
6. Summarize in one sentence the central idea of the story.

Violent America

RESTLESS VIOLENCE ROUND ABOUT

3

Violent America is the newest section in *Strategies in Prose*. No other issue has become more prominent since the earliest editions of the text saw print. Hardly a day passes without some headline screaming the details of the latest violent crime. We are still outraged but no longer surprised when a political figure is assassinated. The media, particularly film and television, are under fire from critics and psychologists who claim that violence for entertainment breeds the real thing. We even hear of the violence of noise and the violence of language.

Albert Schweitzer opens this section with a finely modulated plea for reverence for life. Although he is discussing an abstract idea, Schweitzer's particularity brings his ideas within grasp. Martin Luther King, Jr. then approaches the issue head-on as he tells of his own increasing involvement in a nonviolence movement. Brooks Atkinson examines the so-called civilized life and life in the forest, and finds civilized man lacking. William Carlos Williams, doctor and artist, uses the short story to demonstrate that the use of force debases the user, and historian Arthur Schlesinger, Jr. examines the causes of violence in American society.

Larry Woiwode, Lance Morrow, and Martin Gansberg provide a variety of styles for examination. Woiwode uses the informal essay—at times he verges on the short story— to reveal his concern with the effect of guns on children. Morrow's essay—for all its use of statistics—is no less emotional in its cry for the banning of handguns. And still another writing style is introduced with Martin J. Gansberg's now famous *New York Times* article on the murder of Kitty Genovese. Especially worthy of note is Gansberg's use of diction, which helps form the reader's opinion. If Gansberg does not use a traditional journalistic style, it is nevertheless a style seen more and more in contemporary reporting.

Jacques Barzun and Abe Fortas provide the pro and con in this section. The issue is capital punishment; the discussants are educated and articulate. This grouping concludes with George Orwell's moving narrative about a hanging. When Orwell's essay is played against Barzun's and Fortas's, the dimensions of the issue grow.

We had hoped, when we introduced **Violent America** to the fourth edition, that it would not be of great import in a fifth and succeeding editions. Alas! Even articulate writers such as those represented here have seemingly gone unheeded. The issues are clearly before us. We continue to hope.

Reverence for Life
ALBERT SCHWEITZER

Albert Schweitzer (1875–1965) remains one of the most universally respected men of the century. Born in Kaysensberg, Upper Alsace, his university education prepared him in literature, medicine, and theology. Schweitzer was awarded almost numberless honorary degrees and in 1952, the Nobel Peace Prize. His books include *Kulturphilosophie* (1923), *Memoirs of Childhood and Youth* (1924), *Out of My Life and Thought* (1931), *The Problem of Peace in the World Today* (1954), *A Declaration of Conscience* (1957), and *Peace or Atomic War?* (1958). He founded the hospital at Lambaréné, French Equatorial Africa, and was an expert on the construction of pipe organs.

Explore around you, penetrate to the furthest limits of 1 human knowledge, and always you will come up against something inexplicable in the end. It is called life. It is a mystery so inexplicable that the knowledge of the educated and the ignorant is purely relative when contemplating it.

But what is the difference between the scientist who observes in 2 his microscope the most minute and unexpected signs of life; and the old farmer who by contrast can barely read or write, who stands in springtime in his garden and contemplates the buds opening on the branches of his trees? Both are confronted with the riddle of life. One may be able to describe life in greater detail, but for both it remains equally inscrutable. All knowledge is, in the final analysis, the knowledge of life. All realization is amazement at this riddle of life—a reverence for life in its infinite and yet ever-fresh manifestations. How amazing this coming into being, living, and dying! How fantastic that in other existences something comes into being, passes away again, comes into being once more, and so forth from eternity to eternity! How can it be? We can do all things, and we can do nothing. For in all our wisdom we cannot create life. What we create is dead.

Life means strength, will, arising from the abyss, dissolving into 3 the abyss again. Life is feeling, experience, suffering. If you study life deeply, looking with perceptive eyes into the vast animated chaos of this creation, its profundity will seize you suddenly with dizziness. In everything you recognize yourself. The tiny beetle that lies dead in your path—it was a living creature, struggling for existence like yourself, rejoicing in the sun like you, knowing fear and pain like you.

And now it is no more than decaying matter—which is what you will be sooner or later, too. . . .

What is this recognition, this knowledge within the reach of the 4 most scientific and the most childlike? It is reverence for life, reverence for the unfathomable mystery we confront in our universe, an existence different in its outward appearance and yet inwardly of the same character as our own, terribly similar, awesomely related. The strangeness between us and other creatures is here removed.

Reverence for the infinity of life means removal of the alienation, 5 restoration of empathy, compassion, sympathy. And so by the final result of knowledge is the same as that required of us by the commandment of love. Heart and reason agree together when we desire and dare to be men who seek to fathom the depths of the universe.

Reason discovers the bridge between love for God and love for 6 men—love for all creatures, reverence for all being, compassion with all life, however dissimilar to our own.

I cannot but have reverence for all that is called life. I cannot avoid 7 compassion for everything that is called life. That is the beginning and foundation of morality. Once a man has experienced it and continues to do so—and he who has once experienced it will continue to do so—he is ethical. He carries his morality within him and can never lose it, for it continues to develop within him. He who has never experienced this has only a set of superficial principles. These theories have no root in him, they do not belong to him, and they fall off him. The worst is that the whole of our generation had only such a set of superficial principles. Then the time came to put the ethical code to the test, and it evaporated. For centuries the human race had been educated with only a set of superficial principles. We were brutal, ignorant, and heartless without being aware of it. We had no scale of values, for we had no reverence for life.

It is our duty to share and maintain life. Reverence concerning all 8 life is the greatest commandment in its most elementary form. Or expressed in negative terms: "Thou shalt not kill." We take this prohibition so lightly, thoughtlessly plucking a flower, thoughtlessly stepping on a poor insect, thoughtlessly, in terrible blindness because everything takes its revenge, disregarding the suffering and lives of our fellow men, sacrificing them to trivial earthly goals.

Much talk is heard in our times about building a new human race. 9 How are we to build a new humanity? Only by leading men toward a true, inalienable ethic of our own, which is capable of further development. But this goal cannot be reached unless countless individuals will transform themselves from blind men into seeing ones and begin to spell out the great commandment which is: Reverence for Life. Existence depends more on reverence for life than the law and the prophets. Reverence for life comprises the whole ethic of love in its deepest and highest sense. It is the source of constant renewal for the individual and for mankind.

Study Questions

1. By what means does Schweitzer make something concrete out of abstract concepts?
2. Why are particular examples of details used in this essay, i.e., the insect, the flower, the beetle?
3. Where and why is parallelism used?
4. What is the difference between *sentiment* and *sentimental?* Would either word be appropriate in discussing this essay?
5. We know Schweitzer was a Christian. Can you find internal evidence in "Reverence for Life" to prove or disprove this?
6. Schweitzer says that reverence for the infinity of life will bring the "restoration of empathy, compassion, sympathy." How do empathy, compassion, and sympathy differ?

Pilgrimage to Nonviolence
MARTIN LUTHER KING, JR.

Born in Atlanta, Georgia, the son of a Baptist minister, Martin Luther King, Jr. (1929–1968), received his B.A. from Morehouse College, his B.D. from Crozier Theological Seminary, and his Ph.D. in systematic theology from Boston University. President of the Southern Christian Leadership Conference from its formation in 1957, Dr. King received the Nobel Peace Prize in 1964. The quest for justice and equality for his people that began with the Montgomery bus boycott in 1955 ended for Martin Luther King, Jr. when he was assassinated in Nashville, Tennessee, 13 years later. He reached his summit as a charismatic figure in 1963, when he delivered his address—"I Have a Dream"—to 250,000 persons assembled at the Lincoln Memorial during the mammoth March on Washington. His writings inclue *Stride Toward Freedom* (1958) and *Why We Can't Wait* (1964), accounts of the civil rights movement, and *Strength to Love* (1963), a collection of sermons.

When I went to Montgomery as a pastor, I had not the 1
slightest idea that I would later become involved in a crisis in which
nonviolent resistance would be applicable. I neither started the protest
nor suggested it. I simply responded to the call of the people for a
spokesman. When the protest began, my mind, consciously or unconsciously, was driven back to the Sermon on the Mount, with its sublime
teachings on love, and the Gandhian method of nonviolent resistance.
As the days unfolded, I came to see the power of nonviolence more and
more. Living through the actual experience of the protest, nonviolence
became more than a method to which I gave intellectual assent; it
became a commitment to a way of life. Many of the things that I had
not cleared up intellectually concerning nonviolence were now solved
in the sphere of practical action.

Since the philosophy of nonviolence played such a positive role in 2
the Montgomery Movement, it may be wise to turn to a brief discussion
of some basic aspects of this philosophy.

First, it must be emphasized that nonviolent resistance is not a 3
method for cowards; it does resist. If one uses this method because he is
afraid or merely because he lacks the instruments of violence, he is not
truly nonviolent. This is why Gandhi often said that if cowardice is the
only alternative to violence, it is better to fight. He made this
statement conscious of the fact that there is always another alternative: no individual or group need submit to any wrong, nor need they
use violence to right the wrong; there is the way of nonviolent
resistance. This is ultimately the way of the strong man. It is not a
method of stagnant passivity. The phrase "passive resistance" often
gives the false impression that this is a sort of "do-nothing method" in
which the resister quietly and passively accepts evil. But nothing is
further from the truth. For while the nonviolent resister is passive in
the sense that he is not physically aggressive toward his opponent, his
mind and emotions are always active, constantly seeking to persuade
his opponent that he is wrong. The method is passive physically, but
strongly active spiritually. It is not passive nonresistance to evil, it is
active nonviolent resistance to evil.

A second basic fact that characterizes nonviolence is that it does 4
not seek to defeat or humiliate the opponent, but to win his friendship
and understanding. The nonviolent resister must often express his
protest through noncooperation or boycotts, but he realizes that these
are not ends themselves; they are merely means to awaken a sense of
moral shame in the opponent. The end is redemption and reconciliation. The aftermath of nonviolence is the creation of the beloved
community, while the aftermath of violence is tragic bitterness.

A third characteristic of this method is that the attack is directed 5
against forces of evil rather than against persons who happen to be
doing the evil. It is evil that the nonviolent resister seeks to defeat, not
the persons victimized by evil. If he is opposing racial injustice, the
nonviolent resister has the vision to say that the basic tension is not
between races. As I like to say to the people in Montgomery: "The
tension in this city is not between white people and Negro people. The

tension is, at bottom, between justice and injustice, between the forces of light and the forces of darkness. And if there is a victory, it will be a victory not merely for fifty thousand Negroes, but a victory for justice and the forces of light. We are out to defeat injustice and not white persons who may be unjust."

A fourth point that characterizes nonviolent resistance is a willingness to accept suffering without retaliation, to accept blows from the opponent without striking back. "Rivers of blood may have to flow before we gain our freedom, but it must be our blood," Gandhi said to his countrymen. The nonviolent resister is willing to accept violence if necessary, but never to inflict it. He does not seek to dodge jail. If going to jail is necessary, he enters it "as a bridegroom enters the bride's chamber." 6

One may well ask: "What is the nonviolent resister's justification for this ordeal to which he invites men, for this mass political application of the ancient doctrine of turning the other cheek?" The answer is found in the realization that unearned suffering is redemptive. Suffering, the nonviolent resister realizes, has tremendous educational and transforming possibilities. "Things of fundamental importance to people are not secured by reason alone, but have to be purchased with their suffering," said Gandhi. He continues: "Suffering is infinitely more powerful than the law of the jungle for converting the opponent and opening his ears which are otherwise shut to the voice of reason." 7

A fifth point concerning nonviolent resistance is that it avoids not only external physical violence but also internal violence of spirit. The nonviolent resister not only refuses to shoot his opponent but he also refuses to hate him. At the center of nonviolence stands the principle of love. The nonviolent resister would contend that in the struggle for human dignity, the oppressed people of the world must not succumb to the temptation of becoming bitter or indulging in hate campaigns. To retaliate in kind would do nothing but intensify the existence of hate in the universe. Along the way of life, someone must have sense enough and morality enough to cut off the chain of hate. This can only be done by projecting the ethic of love to the center of our lives. 8

In speaking of love at this point, we are not referring to some sentimental or affectionate emotion. It would be nonsense to urge men to love their oppressors in an affectionate sense. Love in this connection means understanding, redemptive good will. Here the Greek language comes to our aid. There are three words for love in the Greek New Testament. First, there is *eros*. In Platonic philosophy *eros* meant the yearning of the soul for the realm of the divine. It has come now to mean a sort of aesthetic or romantic love. Second, there is *philia*, which means intimate affection between personal friends. *Philia* denotes a sort of reciprocal love; the person loves because he is loved. When we speak of loving those who oppose us, we refer to neither *eros* nor *philia;* we speak of a love which is expressed in the Greek word *agape*. *Agape* means understanding, redeeming good will for all men. It is an overflowing love which is purely spontaneous, unmotivated, ground- 9 less, and creative. It is not set in motion by any quality or function of its object. It is the love of God operating in the human heart.

Agape is disinterested love. It is a love in which the individual 10 seeks not his own good, but the good of his neighbor (I Cor. 10:24). *Agape* does not begin by discriminating between worthy and unworthy people, or any qualities people possess. It begins by loving others *for their sakes.* It is entirely "neighbor-regarding concern for others," which discovers the neighbor in every man it meets. There, *agape* makes no distinction between friend and enemy; it is directed toward both. If one loves an individual merely on account of friendliness, he loves him for the sake of the benefits to be gained from the friendship, rather than for the friend's own sake. Consequently, the best way to assure oneself that Love is disinterested is to have love for the enemy-neighbor from whom you can expect no good in return, but only hostility and persecution.

Another basic point about *agape* is that it springs from the *need* of 11 the other person—his need for belonging to the best in the human family. The Samaritan who helped the Jew on the Jericho Road was "good" because he responded to the human need that he was presented with. God's love is eternal and fails not because man needs his love. St. Paul assures us that the loving act of redemption was done "while we were yet sinners"—that is, at the point of our greatest need for love. Since the white man's personality is greatly distorted by segregation, and his soul is greatly scarred, he needs the love of the Negro. The Negro must love the white man, because the white man needs his love to remove his tensions, insecurities, and fears.

Agape is not a weak, passive love. It is love in action. *Agape* is love 12 seeking to preserve and create community. It is insistence on community even when one seeks to break it. *Agape* is a willingness to sacrifice in the interest of mutuality. *Agape* is a willingness to go to any length to restore community. It doesn't stop at the first mile, but it goes the second mile to restore community. It is a willingness to forgive, not seven times, but seventy times seven to restore community. The cross is the eternal expression of the length to which God will go in order to restore broken community. The resurrection is a symbol of God's triumph over all the forces that seek to block community. The Holy Spirit˚ is the continuing community creating reality that moves through history. He who works against community is working against the whole of creation. Therefore, if I respond to hate with a reciprocal hate I do nothing but intensify cleavage in broken community. I can only close the gap in broken community by meeting hate with love. If I meet hate with hate, I become depersonalized, because creation is so designed that my personality can only be fulfilled in the context of community. Booker T. Washington was right: "Let no man pull you so low as to make you hate him." When he pulls you that low he brings you to the point of working against community; he drags you to the point of defying creation, and thereby becoming depersonalized.

In the final analysis, *agape* means a recognition of the fact that all 13 life is interrelated. All humanity is involved in a single process, and all men are brothers. To the degree that I harm my brother, no matter what he is doing to me, to that extent I am harming myself. For example, white men often refuse federal aid to education in order to avoid giving the Negro his rights; but because all men are brothers they cannot deny Negro children without harming their own. They end, all efforts to the contrary, by hurting themselves. Why is this? Because men are brothers. If you harm me, you harm yourself.

Love, *agape,* is the only cement that can hold this broken commu- 14 nity together. When I am commanded to love, I am commanded to restore community, to resist injustice, and to meet the needs of my brothers.

A sixth basic fact about nonviolent resistance is that it is based on 15 the conviction that the universe is on the side of justice. Consequently, the believer in nonviolence has deep faith in the future. This faith is another reason why the nonviolent resister can accept suffering without retaliation. For he knows that in his struggle for justice he has cosmic companionship. It is true that there are devout believers in nonviolence who find it difficult to believe in a personal God. But even these persons believe in the existence of some creative force that works for universal wholeness. Whether we call it an unconscious process, an impersonal Brahman, or a Personal Being of matchless power and infinite love, there is a creative force in this universe that works to bring the disconnected aspects of reality into a harmonious whole.

Study Questions

1. What is the thesis of this essay? Is it explicit or implicit?
2. How many "basic facts" about nonviolence are presented? Are they presented as being of equal importance?
3. Comment on the relevance, in terms of the structuring of this essay, of the disquisition on love.
4. Who or what are the sources of King's quotations? Are these sources appropriate to the topic? How do you feel about King's quoting himself (paragraph 5)?
5. Do you find the last paragraph serviceable as a conclusion? If not, supply an alternative of your own, drawn from the content of this essay.

The Dark Heart of American History

ARTHUR SCHLESINGER, JR.

Arthur M. Schlesinger, Jr. (1917–   ) was born in Columbus, Ohio. He graduated *summa cum laude* from Harvard University in 1938. During World War II he served in the Office of War Information and as deputy chief of the Office of Strategic Services. For a time he was film critic for *Saturday Review,* but he is now Albert Schweitzer Professor of Humanities at the City University of New York. He has received a National Book Award and two Pulitzer Prizes. Schlesinger's books include *The Age of Jackson* (1945), *The Coming of the New Deal* (1958), *A Thousand Days: John F. Kennedy in the White House* (1965), and *The Imperial Presidency* (1973).

1   The murders within five years of John F. Kennedy, Martin Luther King, Jr., and Robert F. Kennedy raise—or ought to raise—somber questions about the character of contemporary America. One such murder might be explained away as an isolated horror, unrelated to the inner life of our society. But the successive shootings, in a short time, of three men who greatly embodied the idealism of American life suggest not so much a fortuitous set of aberrations as an emerging pattern of response and action—a spreading and ominous belief in the efficacy of violence and the politics of the deed.

2   Yet, while each of these murders produced a genuine season of national mourning, none has produced a sustained season of national questioning. In every case, remorse has seemed to end, not as an incitement to self-examination, but as an escape from it. An orgy of sorrow and shame becomes an easy way of purging a bad conscience and returning as quickly as possible to business as usual.

3   "It would be ... self-deceptive," President Johnson said after the shooting of Robert Kennedy, "to conclude from this act that our country is sick, that it has lost its balance, that it has lost its sense of direction, even its common decency. Two hundred million Americans did not strike down Robert Kennedy last night any more than they struck down John F. Kennedy in 1963 or Dr. Martin Luther King in April of this year."

4   I do not quarrel with these words. Of course two hundred million

Americans did not strike down these men. Nor, in my judgment, is this a question of a "sick society" or of "collective guilt." I do not know what such phrases mean, but I am certain that they do not represent useful ways of thinking about our problem. Obviously most Americans are decent and God-fearing people. Obviously most Americans were deeply and honestly appalled by these atrocities. Obviously most Americans rightly resent being told that they were "guilty" of crimes they neither willed nor wished.

Still, it is not enough to dismiss the ideas of a sick society and of   5
collective guilt and suppose that such dismissal closes the question. For a problem remains—the problem of a contagion of political murder in the United States in the 1960s unparalleled in our own history and unequaled today anywhere in the world. If we minimize this problem, if we complacently say it is all the work of lunatics and foreigners, that nothing is wrong and that our society is beyond criticism, if we cry like Macbeth: "Thou canst not say I did it; never shake Thy gory locks at me," then we lose all hope of recovering control of the destructive impulse within. Then we will only continue the downward spiral of social decomposition and moral degradation.

Self-knowledge is the indispensable prelude to self-control; and   6
self-knowledge, for a nation as well as for an individual, begins with history. We like to think of ourselves as a peaceful, tolerant, benign people who have always lived under a government of laws and not of men. And, indeed, respect for persons and for law has been one characteristic strain in the American tradition. Most Americans probably pay this respect most of their lives. Yet this is by no means the only strain in our tradition. For we also have been a violent people. When we refuse to acknowledge the existence of this other strain, we refuse to see our nation as it is.

We began, after all, as a people who killed red men and enslaved   7
black men. No doubt we often did this with a Bible and a prayer book. But no nation, however righteous its professions, could act as we did without burying deep in itself—in its customs, its institutions, and its psyche—a propensity toward violence. However much we pretended that Indians and Negroes were subhuman, we really knew that they were God's children too.

Nor did we confine our violence to red men and black men. We   8
gained our freedom, after all, through revolution. The first century after independence were years of incessant violence—wars, slave insurrections, Indian fighting, urban riots, murders, duels, beatings. Members of Congress went armed to the Senate and House. In his first notable speech, in January 1838, before the Young Men's Lyceum of Springfield, Illinois, Abraham Lincoln named internal violence as the supreme threat to American political institutions. He spoke of "the increasing disregard for law which pervades the country; the growing disposition to substitute the wild and furious passions, in lieu of the sober judgment of Courts; and the worse than savage mobs, for the executive ministers of justice." The danger to the American republic, he said, was not from foreign invasion:

At what point then is the approach of danger to be expected? I answer, if it ever reach us, it must spring up amongst us. It cannot come from abroad. If destruction be our lot, we must ourselves be its author and finisher. As a nation of freemen, we must live through all time, or die by suicide.

So the young Lincoln named the American peril—a peril he did not 9 fear to locate within the American breast. Indeed, the sadness of America has been that our worst qualities have so often been the other face of our best. Our commitment to morality, our faith in experiment: these have been sources of America's greatness, but they have also led Americans into our error. For our moralists have sometimes condoned murder if the cause is deemed good; so Emerson and Thoreau applauded John Brown of Osawatomie. And our pragmatists have sometimes ignored the means if the result is what they want. Moralism and pragmatism have not provided infallible restraints on the destructive instinct.

America, Martin Luther King correctly said, has been "a schizo- 10 phrenic personality, tragically divided against herself." The impulses of violence and civility continued after Lincoln to war within the American breast. The insensate bloodshed of the Civil War exhausted the national capacity for violence and left the nation emotionally and psychologically spent. For nearly a century after Appomattox, we appeared on the surface the tranquil and friendly people we still like to imagine ourselves to be. The amiability of that society no doubt exerted a restraining influence. There were still crazy individuals, filled with grievance, bitterness, and a potential for violence. But most of the people expended their sickness in fantasy; the Guiteaus and Czolgoszs were the exception. These years of stability, a stability fitfully recaptured after the First World War, created the older generation's image of a "normal" America.

Yet even in the kindly years we did not wholly eradicate the 11 propensity toward violence which history had hidden in the national unconscious. In certain moods, indeed, we prided ourselves on our violence; we almost considered it evidence of our virility. "Above all," cried Theodore Roosevelt, "let us shrink from no strife, moral or physical, within or without the nation, provided we are certain that the strife is justified." That fatal susceptibility always lurked under the surface, breaking out in Indian wars and vigilantism in the West, lynchings in the South, in labor riots and race riots and gang wars in the cities.

It is important to distinguish collective from individual violence— 12 the work of mobs from the work of murderers; for the motive and the effect can be very different. There can, of course, be murder by a mob. But not all mobs aim at murder. Collective violence—rioting against what were considered illegal British taxes in Boston in 1773, or dangerous Papist influence sixty years later, or inequitable draft laws in New York in 1863, or unfair labor practices in Chicago in 1937—is more characteristically directed at conditions than at individuals. In many cases (though by no means all), the aim has been to protest rather than protect the status quo; and the historian is obliged to concede that collective violence, including the recent riots in black ghettos, has often quickened the disposition of those in power to redress just grievances. Extralegal group action, for better or worse, has been part of the process of American democracy. Violence, for better or worse, *does* settle some questions, and for the better. Violence secured American independence, freed the slaves, and stopped Hitler.

But this has ordinarily been the violence of a society. The indi- 13 vidual who plans violence is less likely to be concerned with reforming conditions than with punishing persons. On occasion the purpose is to protect the status quo by destroying men who symbolize or threaten social change (a tactic which the anarchists soon began to employ in reverse). A difference exists in psychic color and content between spontaneous mass convulsions and the premeditated killing of individuals. The first signifies an unstable society, the second, a murderous society. America has exhibited both forms of violence.

Now in the third quarter of the twentieth century, violence has 14 broken out with new ferocity in our country. What has given our old propensity new life? Why does the fabric of American civility no longer exert restraint? What now incites crazy individuals to act out their murderous dreams? What is it about the climate of this decade that suddenly encourages—that for some evidently legitimatizes—the relish for hate and the resort to violence? Why, according to the Federal Bureau of Investigation, have assaults with a gun increased 77 per cent in the four years from 1964 through 1967?

We talk about the legacy of the frontier. No doubt, the frontier has 15 bequeathed us a set of romantic obsessions about six-shooters and gun fighters. But why should this legacy suddenly reassert itself in the 1960s?

We talk about the tensions of industrial society. No doubt the 16 ever-quickening pace of social change depletes and destroys the institutions which make for social stability. But this does not explain why Americans shoot and kill so many more Americans than Englishmen kill Englishmen or Japanese kill Japanese. England, Japan, and West Germany are, next to the United States, the most heavily industrialized countries in the world. Together they have a population of 214 million people. Among these 214 million, there are 135 gun murders a year. Among the 200 million people of the United States there are 6,500 gun murders a year—about *forty-eight times* as many.

We talk about the fears and antagonisms generated by racial 17 conflict. Unquestionably this has contributed to the recent increase in violence. The murders of Dr. King and Senator Kennedy seem directly traceable to ethnic hatreds. Whites and blacks alike are laying in arms, both sides invoking the needs of self-defense. Yet this explanation still does not tell us why in America today we are tending to convert political problems into military problems—problems of adjustment into problems of force.

The New Left tells us that we are a violent society because we are a 18 capitalist society—that capitalism is itself institutionalized violence; and that life under capitalism inevitably deforms relations among men. This view would be more impressive if the greatest violence of man against man in this century had not taken place in noncapitalist societies—in Nazi Germany, in Stalinist Russia, in precapitalist Indonesia. The fact is that every form of society is in some sense institutionalized violence; man in society always gives up a measure of "liberty" and accepts a measure of authority.

We cannot escape that easily. It is not just that we were a frontier 19 society or have become an industrial society or are a racist or a capitalist society; it is something more specific than that. Nor can we blame the situation on our gun laws, or the lack of them; though here possibly we are getting closer. There is no question, of course, that we need adequate federal gun laws. Statistics make it evident that gun controls have some effect. Sixty per cent of all murders in the United States are by firearms; and states with adequate laws—New Jersey, New York, Massachusetts, Rhode Island—have much lower rates of gun murder than states with no laws or weak ones—Texas, Mississippi, Louisiana, Nevada.

Still, however useful in making it harder for potential murderers 20 to get guns, federal gun legislation deals with the symptoms and not with the causes of our trouble. We must go further to account for the resurgence in recent years of our historical propensity toward violence.

One reason surely for the enormous tolerance of violence in 21 contemporary America is the fact that our country has now been more or less continuously at war for a generation. The experience of war over a long period devalues human life and habituates people to killing. And the war in which we are presently engaged is far more brutalizing than was the Second World War or the Korean War. It is more brutalizing because the destruction we have wrought in Vietnam is so wildly out of proportion to any demonstrated involvement of our national security or any rational assessment of our national interest. In the other wars we killed for need. In this war we are killing beyond need, and, as we do so, we corrupt our national life. When violence is legally sanctioned for a cause in which people see no moral purpose, this is an obvious stimulus to individuals to use violence for what they may maniacally consider moral purposes of their own.

A second reason for the climate of violence in the United States is 22 surely the zest with which the mass media, and especially television and film, dwell on violence. One must be clear about this. The mass media do *not* create violence. But they *reinforce* aggressive and destructive impulses, and they may well *teach* the morality as well as the methods of violence.

In recent years the movies and television have developed a 23 pornography of violence far more demoralizing than the pornography of sex, which still seizes the primary attention of the guardians of civic virtue. Popular films of our day like *Rosemary's Baby* and *Bonnie and Clyde* imply a whole culture of human violation, psychological in one case, physical in the other. *Bonnie and Clyde,* indeed, was greatly admired for its blithe acceptance of the world of violence—an acceptance which almost became a celebration. Thus a student in a film course in San Francisco noted:

> There is a certain spirit that belongs to us. We the American people. It is pragmatic, rebellious, violent, joyous. It can create or kill. Everything about *Bonnie and Clyde* captures this spirit.

> John Brown was motivated by this spirit and it has scared the hell out of historians ever since. The Black Panthers have it. Cab drivers, musicians, used car salesmen and bus drivers understand it, but doctors, dentists and real estate salesmen don't.

Television is the most pervasive influence of all. The children of 24 the electronic age sit hypnotized by the parade of killings, beatings, gunfights, knifings, maimings, brawls which flash incessantly across the tiny screen, and now in "living" color.

For a time, the television industry comforted itself with the theory 25 that children listened to children's programs and that, if by any chance they saw programs for adults, violence would serve as a safety valve, offering a harmless outlet for pent-up aggressions: the more violence on the screen, the less in life. Alas, this turns out not to be necessarily so. As Dr. Wilbur Schramm, director of the Institute of Communication Research at Stanford has reported, children, even in the early elementary school years, view more programs designed for adults than for themselves; "above all, they prefer the more violent type of adult program including the Western, the adventure program, and the crime drama." Experiments show that such programs, far from serving as safety valves for aggression, attract children with high levels of aggression and stimulate them to seek overt means of acting out their aggressions. Evidence suggests that these programs work the same incitement on adults. And televiolence does more than condition emotion and behavior. It also may attenuate people's sense of reality. Men murdered on the television screen ordinarily spring to life after the episode is over: all death is therefore diminished. A child asked a man last June where he was headed in his car. "To Washington," he said. "Why?" he asked. "To attend the funeral of Senator Kennedy." The child said, "Oh yeah—they shot him again." And such shooting may well condition the manner in which people approach the perplexities of existence. On television the hero too glibly resolves his problems by shooting somebody. The *Gunsmoke* ethos, however, is not necessarily the best way to deal with human or social complexity. It is hardly compatible with any kind of humane or libertarian democracy.

The problem of electronic violence raises difficult questions of 26 prescription as well as of analysis. It would be fatal to restrain artistic exploration and portrayal, even of the most extreme and bitter aspects of human experience. No rational person wants to re-establish a reign of censorship or mobilize new Legions of Decency. Nor is there great gain in making the electronic media scapegoats for propensities which they reflect rather than create—propensities which spring from our history and our hearts.

Yet society retains a certain right of self-defense. Is it inconceiv- 27
able that the television industry might work out forms of self-
restraint? Beyond this, it should be noted that the networks and the
stations do *not* own the airwaves; the nation does; and, if the industry
cannot restrain itself, the Communications Act offers means, as yet
unused, of democratic control.

We have a bad inheritance as far as violence is concerned; and in 28
recent years war and television have given new vitality to the darkest
strains in our national psyche. How can we master this horror in our
souls before it rushes us on to ultimate disintegration?

There is not a problem of collective guilt, but there is a problem of 29
collective responsibility. Certainly two hundred million Americans did
not strike down John Kennedy or Martin Luther King or Robert
Kennedy. But two hundred million Americans are plainly responsible
for the character of a society that works on deranged men and incites
them to depraved acts. There were Lee Harvey Oswalds and James
Earl Rays and Sirhan Bishara Sirhans in America in the Thirties—
angry, frustrated, alienated, resentful, marginal men in rootless,
unstable cities like Dallas and Memphis and Los Angeles. But our
society in the Thirties did not stimulate such men to compensate for
their own failure by killing leaders the people loved.

Some of the young in their despair have come to feel that the 30
answer to reason is unreason, the answer to violence, more violence;
but these only hasten the plunge toward the abyss. The more intelligent disagree. They do not want America to beat its breast and go back
to the golf course. *They do want America to recognize its responsibility.*
They want us to tell it like it is—to confront the darkness in our past
and the darkness in our present. They want us to realize that life is not
solid and predictable but infinitely chancy, that violence is not the
deviation but the ever-present possibility, that we can therefore never
rest in the effort to prevent unreason from rending the skin of civility.
They want our leaders to *talk* less about law and order and *do* more
about justice.

Perhaps the old in American society might now learn that 31
sanctimony is not a persuasive answer to anguish, and that we never
cure ourselves if we deny the existence of a disease. If they learn this, if
they face up to the schism in our national tradition, we all will have a
better chance of subduing the impulse of destruction and of fulfilling
the vision of Lincoln—that noble vision of a serene and decent society,
united by bonds of affection and mystic chords of memory, dedicated at
last to our highest ideals.

Study Questions

1. How many paragraphs constitute Schlesinger's introduction? How does the length of the introduction help
   Schlesinger set up his case?

2. *And, or, nor, for, but, so yet* are generally used to connect the independent clauses in compound sentences. Schlesinger often uses them to begin sentences. Why?
3. Why does Schlesinger use quotations? Does he use them effectively? Comment also on his use of statistics and dates.
4. Find and discuss examples of parallelism to begin paragraphs.
5. Would you say that Schlesinger offers a solution to the problem he discusses? Does he effectively and convincingly discuss the causes?

Guns
LARRY WOIWODE

Larry Woiwode (1941–   ) was born in Carrington, North Dakota. His first novel, *What I'm Going to Do, I Think* (1969), resulted in national recognition. In 1971 he held a Guggenheim fellowship, and in 1972 he served on the executive board of P.E.N. He has been a judge in the National Book Awards and Writer in Residence at the University of Wisconsin. His essays and stories have appeared in the *New Yorker, The New York Times, Audience, Atlantic Monthly, Esquire, Mademoiselle,* the *New American Review,* and the *Partisan Review.* His other works include *Beyond the Bedroom Wall: A Family Album* (1975) and *Even Tide* (1975).

1   **O**nce in the middle of a Wisconsin winter I shot a deer, my only one, while my wife and daughter watched. It had been hit by a delivery truck along a country road a few miles from where we lived and one of its rear legs was torn off at the hock; a shattered shin and hoof lay steaming in the red-beaded snow. The driver of the truck and I stood and watched as it tried to leap a fence, kicked a while at the top wire it was entangled in, flailing the area with fresh ropes of blood, and then went hobbling across a pasture toward a wooded hill. Placid cows followed it with a curious awe. "Do you have a rifle with you?" the driver asked. "No, not with me. At home." He looked once more at the deer, then got in his truck and drove off.

2   I went back to our Jeep where my wife and daughter were waiting, pale and withdrawn, and told them what I was about to do, and

Originally appeared in *Esquire,* December 1975. Reprinted by permission of Candida Donadio. Copyright © 1975 by Larry Woiwode.

suggested that they'd better stay at home. No, they wanted to be with me, they said; they wanted to watch. My daughter was three and a half at the time. I got my rifle, a .22, a foolishly puny weapon to use on a deer but the only one I had, and we came back and saw that the deer was lying in some low brush near the base of the hill; no need to trail its blatant spoor. When I got about a hundred yards off, marveling at how it could have made it so far in its condition through snow that came over my boot tops, the deer tried to push itself up with its front legs, then collapsed. I aimed at the center of its skull, thinking, *This will be the quickest,* and heard the bullet ricochet off and go singing through the woods.

The deer was on its feet, shaking its head as though stung, and I   3
fired again at the same spot, quickly, and apparently missed. It was now moving at its fastest hobble up the hill, broadside to me, and I took my time to sight a heart shot. Before the report even registered in my mind, the deer went down in an explosion of snow and lay struggling there, spouting blood from its stump and a chest wound. I was shaking by now. Deer are color-blind as far as science can say, and as I went toward its quieting body to deliver the coup de grace, I realized I was being seen in black and white, and then the deer's eye seemed to home in on me, and I was struck with the understanding that I was its vision of approaching death. And then I seemed to enter its realm through its eye and saw the countryside and myself in shades of white and grey. *But I see the deer in color,* I thought.

A few yards away, I aimed at its head once more, and there was the   4
crack of a shot, the next-to-last round left in the magazine. The deer's head came up, and I could see its eye clearly now, dark, placid, filled with an appeal, it seemed, and then felt the surge of black and white surround and subsume me again. The second shot, or one of them, had pierced its neck; a grey-blue tongue hung out over its jaw; urine was trickling from below its tail; a doe. I held the rifle barrel inches from its forehead, conscious of my wife's and daughter's eyes on me from behind, and as I fired off the final and fatal shot, felt myself drawn by them back into my multicolored, many-faceted world again.

I don't remember my first gun, the heritage is so ingrained in me,   5
but know I've used a variety of them to kill birds, reptiles, mammals, amphibians, plant life, insects (bees and butterflies with a shotgun), fish that came too close to shore—never a human being, I'm quick to interject, although the accumulated carnage I've put away with bullets since boyhood is probably enough to add up to a couple of cows, not counting the deer; and have fired, at other targets living and fairly inert, an old ten gauge with double hammers that left a welt on my shoulder that lasted a week, a Mauser, a twelve-gauge sawed-off shotgun, an M-16, at least a dozen variations on the .22—pump, bolt action, lever action, target pistols, special scopes and sights and stocks—a .410 over-and-under, a zip gun that blew up and scattered shrapnel that's still imbedded in my arm, an Italian carbine, a Luger, and, among others, a fancily engraved, single-trigger, double-barreled twenty gauge at snowballs thrown from behind my shoulder out over a

bluff; and on that same bluff on the first day of this year, after some wine and prodding, I found myself at the jittering rim of stutters from a paratrooper's lightweight machine gun with a collapsible, geometrically reinforced metal stock, watched the spout of its trajectory of tangible tracers go off across the night toward the already-set sun, and realized that this was perhaps the hundredth weapon I'd had performing in my hands.

I was raised in North Dakota, near the edge of the West, during the **6** turbulence and then the aftermath of the Second World War, which our country ended in such an unequivocal way there was a sense of vindication about our long-standing fetish for guns, not to say pride in it, too. "Bang! Bang! You're dead" returns to me from that time without the least speck of friction or reflection. When we weren't playing War, or Cowboys and Indians, or Cops and Robbers, we were reading War Comics (from which you could order for less than a dollar little cardboard chests of plastic weaponry and soldiers to stage your own debacles), or Westerns, or listening to *The Lone Ranger* and *Richard Diamond, Private Detective* and other radio shows—all of which openly glorified guns, and the more powerful the better.

My fantasies, when I was frustrated, angry, or depressed, were rife **7** with firearms of the most lethal sort, flying shot, endless rounds of shattering ammunition; the enemy bodies blown away and left in bloody tableaux. And any gun was an engineered instrument—much more far-ranging and accurate than bows and arrows or slingshots— that detached you from your destructiveness or crime or sometimes even from being a source of death.

I've only owned three firearms in my life as an adult. Two I **8** brought back to the shops within a week after I'd bought them, realizing I was trying to reach out in some archaic way, and the limits to my maturity and imagination that that implied, plus the bother to my daughter of their powing sounds; and the third, the .22, after trembling over it a few years and using it to shoot holes in the floor to enact a between-the-legs suicide, I gave away. To my younger brother. Who was initiated into the buck-fever fraternity in the forests of northern Wisconsin when he was an adolescent by a seasoned local who said to him, "If you see anything moving out there tomorrow, boy, *shoot it*. You can check out later what it is. Nobody gives a shit up here." And on a hunting trip years later, an acquaintance from the village my brother lived in then, a lawyer, was shot in the head with a deer rifle, but somehow survived. And even went back to practicing law. It was thought to be an accident at first, what with all the bullets embroidering the air that day, and then rumor had it that another member of the party hunting on adjoining land, an old friend of the lawyer's, had found out a week before the season that the lawyer had been having his wife for a while. The two men were polite enough to one another in the village after that, my brother said, but not such good friends, of course. Just balanced, justice-balanced males.

For months and seasons after I'd shot the crippled doe, every time **9** we passed the field in our Jeep, my daughter would say, "Here's where

Daddy shooted the deer." In exactly that manner, using the tone and detachment of a storyteller or tourist guide. And I'd glance into the rearview mirror and see her in her car seat, studying the hill with troubled and sympathetic eyes. One day I stopped. "Does it bother you so much that I shot it?" I asked. There was no answer, and then I saw that she was nodding her head, her gaze still fixed on the hill.

"Well, if I wouldn't have, it could have suffered a long time. You 10 say how badly hurt it was. It couldn't have lived that way. I didn't like doing it, either, but it was best for the deer. When I told the game warden about it, he even thanked me and said, 'Leave it for the foxes and crows.' They have to eat, too, you know, and maybe the deer made the winter easier for them." And I thought, Oh, what a self-justifying fool and ass and pig you are. Why didn't you leave her at home? Why didn't you go to the farmer whose land the deer was on, which would have been as quick or quicker than going back for the .22—a man who would have had a deer rifle, or at least a shotgun with rifled slugs, and would have put the deer away with dispatch in one shot and might have even salvaged the hide and venison? And who could say it wouldn't have lived, the way some animals do after tearing or chewing off a limb caught in a trap? Who was to presume it wouldn't have preferred to die a slow death in the brush, looking out over the pasture, as the crimson stain widening in the snow drew away and dimmed its colorless world until all went black? Why not admit that I was a common backcountry American and, like most men of my mold, had used an arsenal of firearms to kill and was as excited about putting away a deer as moved by compassion for its suffering? Then again, given my daughter's understanding and the person I am, perhaps she sensed this, and more.

I once choked a chicken to death. It was my only barefaced, not to 11 say barehanded, confrontation with death and the killer in me and happened on my grandparents' farm. I couldn't have been more than nine or ten and no firearms were included or necessary. I was on my knees and the chicken fluttered its outstretched wings with the last of the outraged protest. I gripped, beyond release, above its swollen crop, its beak gaping, translucent eyelids sliding up and down. An old molting specimen. A hen, most likely; a worse loss, because of eggs, than a capon or cock. My grandfather, who was widely traveled and world-wise, in his eighties then, and had just started using a cane from earlier times, came tapping at that moment around the corner of the chicken coop and saw what I was doing and started gagging at the hideousness of it, did a quick assisted spin away and never again, hours later nor for the rest of his life, for that matter, ever mentioned the homicidal incident to me. Keeping his silence, he seemed to understand; and yet whenever I'm invaded by the incident, the point of it seems to be his turning away from me.

My wife once said she felt I wanted to kill her. A common enough 12 feeling among long-married couples, I'm sure, and not restricted to either sex (I know, for instance, that there were times when she wanted to kill me), but perhaps with firsthand experience infusing the feeling, it became too much to endure. I now live in New York City, where the clock keeps moving toward my suitcase, alone, and she and my daughter in the Midwest. The city has changed in the seven years since the three of us lived here together. There are more frivolous and not-so-frivolous wares—silk kerchiefs, necklaces and rings, roach clips, rolling papers, socks, a display of Florida coral across a convertible top, books of every kind—being sold in the streets than anybody can remember seeing in recent years. People openly saying that soon it will be like the Thirties once were, with us *all* in the streets selling our apples, or whatever, or engaged in a tacit and friendly sort of gangsterism to survive. Outside my window, a spindly deciduous species has a sign strung on supporting posts on either side of it, in careful hand-lettering, that reads, THIS TREE GIVES OXYGEN. GIVE IT LOVE. More dogs in the streets and parks than they'd remembered, and more canine offal sending up its open-ended odor; at least half the population giving up cigarette smoking, at last, for good, they say, and many actually are. The mazed feeling of most everywhere now of being in the midst of a slowly forging and forgiving reciprocity. An air of bravura about most everybody in maintaining one's best face, with a few changes of costumish clothing to reflect it, perhaps, no matter what might yet evolve. A unisex barbershop or boutique on nearly every other block, it seems.

Sometimes I think this is where I really belong. Then a man is **13** gunned down in a neighborhood bar I used to drop into and the next day a mob leader assassinated, supposedly by members of his own mob. *Perhaps this is where I'm most at home*, I equivocate again and have an image of myself in a Stetson traveling down a crosstown street at a fast-paced and pigeon-toed shamble toward the setting sun (setting this far east, but not over my wife and daughter yet), my eyes cast down and shoulders forward, hands deep in my empty Levi pockets, a suspect closet-faggot-cowboy occasionally whistled at by queens.

I won't (and can't) refute my heritage, but I doubt that I'll use a **14** firearm again, or, if I do, only in the direst sort of emergency. Which I say to protect my flanks. The bloody, gun-filled fantasies seldom return now, and when they do they're reversed: I'm the one being shot, or shot at, or think I am.

Study Questions

1. The description of the shooting of the deer in paragraphs 3–4 is terribly specific. Why?
2. Which uses of italics in this essay are traditional? Explain the other occasions when they occur.
3. Woiwode moves easily back and forth between the present and the past. How does he make the transition in each instance?

4. Are there any paragraphs that occur for strictly narrative purposes rather than, for instance, persuasion or exposition?
5. How does Woiwode use the presence of his daughter to advance his case?

It's Time to Ban Handguns
LANCE MORROW

Lance Morrow (1939–   ) was born in Philadelphia and grew up in Washington, D.C. He graduated *magna cum laude* from Harvard in 1963. He worked as a reporter for the *Washington Star* before joining the staff of *Time* as a contributing editor in 1965. At *Time*, he wrote first for the "People" section, then the "Nation" section, and currently writes for the "Essay" section. He has written nearly 60 cover stories, including six "Man of the Year" covers. His first book is scheduled for publication in 1983.

By a curiosity of evolution, every human skull harbors a 1 prehistoric vestige: a reptilian brain. This atavism, like a hand grenade cushioned in the more civilized surrounding cortex, is the dark hive where many of mankind's primitive impulses originate. To go partners with that throwback, Americans have carried out of their own history another curiosity that evolution forgot to discard as the country changed from a sparsely populated, underpoliced agrarian society to a modern industrial civilization. That vestige is the gun—most notoriously the handgun, an anachronistic tool still much in use. Since 1963 guns have finished off more Americans (400,000) than World War II did.

After one more handgun made it into American history last week 2 (another nastily poignant little "Saturday night" .22 that lay like an orphan in a Dallas pawnshop until another of those clammy losers took it back to his rented room to dream on), a lot of Americans said to themselves, "Well, maybe *this* will finally persuade them to do something about those damned guns." Nobody would lay a dime on it. The National Rifle Association battened down its hatches for a siege of rough editorial weather, but calculated that the antigun indignation would presently subside, just as it always does. After Kennedy. After

King. After Kennedy. After Wallace. After Lennon. After Reagan.
After . . . the nation will be left twitching and flinching as before to the
pops of its 55 million pistols and the highest rate of murder by guns in
the world.

The rest of the planet is both appalled and puzzled by the spectacle   3
of a superpower so politically stable and internally violent. Countries
like Britain and Japan, which have low murder rates and virtual
prohibitions on handguns, are astonished by the over-the-counter ease
with which Americans can buy firearms.

Americans themselves are profoundly discouraged by the hand-   4
guns that seem to breed uncontrollably among them like roaches. For
years the majority of them have favored restrictions on handguns. In
1938 a Gallup poll discovered that 84% wanted gun controls. The latest
Gallup finds that 62% want stricter laws governing handgun sales. Yet
Americans go on buying handguns at the rate of one every 13 seconds.
The murder rate keeps rising. It is both a cause and an effect of gun
sales. And every few years—or months—some charismatic public
character takes a slug from an itinerant mental case caressing a
bizarre fantasy in his brain and the sick, secret weight of a pistol in his
pocket.

Why do the bloody years keep rolling by without guns becoming   5
subject to the kind of regulation we calmly apply to drugs, cars, boat
trailers, CB radios and dogs? The answer is only partly that the
National Rifle Association is, by some Senators' estimate, the most
effective lobbying organization in Washington and the deadliest at
targeting its congressional enemies at election time. The nation now
has laws, all right—a patchwork of some 25,000 gun regulations,
federal, state and local, that are so scattered and inconsistent as to be
preposterously ineffectual.

Firearms have achieved in the U.S. a strange sort of inevitabil-   6
ity—the nation's gun-ridden frontier heritage getting smokily mingled
now with a terror of accelerating criminal violence and a sense that as
the social contract tatters, the good guys must have their guns to
defend themselves against the rising tribes of bad guys. It is very hard
to persuade the good guys that all those guns in their hands wind up
doing more lethal harm to their own kind than to the animals they
fear; that good guys sometimes get drunk and shoot other good guys in
a rage, or blow their own heads off (by design or accident) or hit their
own children by mistake. Most murders are done on impulse, and
handguns are perfectly responsive to the purpose: a blind red rage
flashes in the brain and fires a signal through the nerves to the trigger
finger—BLAM! Guns do not require much work. You do not have to get
your hands bloody, as you would with a knife, or make the strenuous
and intimately dangerous effort required to kill with bare hands. The
space between gun and victim somehow purifies the relationship—at
least for the person at the trigger—and makes it so much easier to
perform the deed. The bullet goes invisibly across space to flesh. An
essential disconnection, almost an abstraction, is maintained. That's
why it is so easy—convenient, really—to kill with one of the things.

The post-assassination sermon, an earnest lamentation about the 7 "sickness of American society," has become a notably fatuous genre that blames everyone and then, after 15 minutes of earnestly empty regret, absolves everyone. It is true that there is a good deal of evil in the American air; television and the sheer repetitiousness of violence have made a lot of the country morally weary and dull and difficult to shock. Much of the violence, however, results not from the sickness of the society but the stupidity and inadequacy of its laws. The nation needs new laws to put at least some guns out of business. Mandatory additional punishments for anyone using a gun in a crime—the approach that Ronald Reagan favors—would help. But a great deal more is necessary. Because of the mobility of guns, only federal laws can have any effect upon them. Rifles and shotguns—long guns—are not the problem; they make the best weapons for defending the house anyway, and they are hard for criminals to conceal. Most handguns are made to fire at people, not at targets or game. Such guns should be banned. The freedoms of an American individualism bristling with small arms must yield to the larger communal claim to sanity and safety—the "pursuit of happiness."

That would, of course, still leave millions of handguns illegally in 8 circulation; the penalties for possessing such weapons, and especially for using them in crime, would have to be severe. Even at that, it would take years to start cleansing the nation of handguns. Whatever its content, no substantive program for controlling guns probably stands any chance of getting through Congress unless Ronald Reagan supports it. He ought to do so, not because he has been shot in the chest but because it should be done.

The indiscriminate mass consumption of guns has finally come to 9 disgrace Americans abroad and depress them at home. It has been almost 90 years since the historian Frederick Jackson Turner propounded his famous thesis about the end of the American frontier. But the worst part of the frontier never did vanish. Its violence, once tolerable in the vast spaces, has simply backed up into modern America, where it goes on blazing away.

Study Questions

1. To what causes does Morrow attribute contemporary violence? To what extent does he present this as metaphorical?
2. Find examples of unsupported generalizations. Are you willing to accept them? Why or why not?
3. Examine Morrow's use of statistics. Would fewer or more, older or more recent statistics be helpful in his argument?
4. What other means does Morrow use to persuade the reader that his cause is right, to move the reader to action?

38 Who Saw Murder Didn't Call the Police

MARTIN J. GANSBERG

Martin J. Gansberg (1920–   ) was born in Brooklyn. He received a Bachelor of Science degree from St. John's University. The article reprinted here is one of many in a distinguished career as an editor and reporter for *The New York Times,* which he joined in 1942, and for three years served as editor of the Paris international edition. "38 Who Saw Murder...." earned him the Page One Award for local reporting, given by the Newspaper Guild of New York; the Newspaper Reporters Association of New York City Award for excellent feature treatment; and the Silurian Society Award for the best news story of the year. Gansberg also taught for fifteen years at Fairleigh Dickinson University. His byline appears in numerous periodicals.

For more than half an hour 38 respectable, law-abiding 1 citizens in Queens watched a killer stalk and stab a woman in three separate attacks in Kew Gardens.

Twice their chatter and the sudden glow of their bedroom lights 2 interrupted him and frightened him off. Each time he returned, sought her out, and stabbed her again. Not one person telephoned the police during the assault; one witness called after the woman was dead.

That was two weeks ago today. 3

Still shocked is Assistant Chief Inspector Frederick M. Lussen, in 4 charge of the borough's detectives and a veteran of 25 years of homicide investigations. He can give a matter-of-fact recitation on many murders. But the Kew Gardens slaying baffles him—not because it is a murder, but because the "good people" failed to call the police.

"As we have reconstructed the crime," he said, "the assailant had 5 three chances to kill this woman during a 35-minute period. He returned twice to complete the job. If we had been called when he first attacked, the woman might not be dead now."

This is what the police say happened beginning at 3:20 A.M. in the 6 staid, middle-class, tree-lined Austin Street area:

Twenty-eight-year-old Catherine Genovese, who was called Kitty 7 by almost everyone in the neighborhood, was returning home from her job as manager of a bar in Hollis. She parked her red Fiat in a lot adjacent to the Kew Gardens Long Island Rail Road Station, facing Mowbray Place. Like many residents of the neighborhood, she had parked there day after day since her arrival from Connecticut a year ago, although the railroad frowns on the practice.

She turned off the lights of her car, locked the door, and started to 8 walk the 100 feet to the entrance of her apartment at 82-70 Austin Street, which is in a Tudor building, with stores in the first floor and apartments on the second.

The entrance to the apartment is in the rear of the building 9 because the front is rented to retail stores. At night the quiet neighborhood is shrouded in the slumbering darkness that marks most residential areas.

Miss Genovese noticed a man at the far end of the lot, near a 10 seven-story apartment house at 82-40 Austin Street. She halted. Then, nervously, she headed up Austin Street toward Lefferts Boulevard, where there is a call box to the 102nd Police Precinct in nearby Richmond Hill.

She got as far as a street light in front of a bookstore before the 11 man grabbed her. She screamed. Lights went on in the 10-story apartment house at 82-67 Austin Street, which faces the bookstore. Windows slid open and voices punctuated the early-morning stillness.

Miss Genovese screamed: "Oh, my God, he stabbed me! Please help 12 me! Please help me!"

From one of the upper windows in the apartment house, a man 13 called down: "Let that girl alone!"

The assailant looked up at him, shrugged and walked down Austin 14 Street toward a white sedan parked a short distance away. Miss Genovese struggled to her feet.

Lights went out. The killer returned to Miss Genovese, now trying 15 to make her way around the side of the building by the parking lot to get to her apartment. The assailant stabbed her again.

"I'm dying!" she shrieked. "I'm dying!"   16

Windows were opened again, and lights went on in many apart- 17 ments. The assailant got into his car and drove away. Miss Genovese staggered to her feet. A city bus, O-10, the Lefferts Boulevard line to Kennedy International Airport, passed. It was 3:35 A.M.

The assailant returned. By then, Miss Genovese had crawled to the 18 back of the building, where the freshly painted brown doors to the apartment house held out hope for safety. The killer tried the first door; she wasn't there. At the second door, 82-62 Austin Street, he saw her slumped on the floor at the foot of the stairs. He stabbed her a third time—fatally.

It was 3:50 by the time the police received their first call, from a 19 man who was a neighbor of Miss Genovese. In two minutes they were at the scene. The neighbor, a 70-year-old woman, and another woman were the only persons on the street. Nobody else came forward.

The man explained that he had called the police after much 20 deliberation. He had phoned a friend in Nassau County for advice and then he had crossed the roof of the building to the apartment of the elderly woman to get her to make the call.

"I didn't want to get involved," he sheepishly told the police.   21

Six days later, the police arrested Winston Moseley, a 29-year-old 22
business-machine operator, and charged him with homicide. Moseley
had no previous record. He is married, has two children and owns a
home at 133-19 Sutter Avenue, South Ozone Park, Queens. On
Wednesday, a court committed him to Kings County Hospital for
psychiatric observation.

When questioned by the police, Moseley also said that he had slain 23
Mrs. Annie May Johnson, 24, of 146-12 133rd Avenue, Jamaica, on
Feb. 29 and Barbara Kralik, 15, of 174-17 140th Avenue, Springfield
Gardens, last July. In the Kralik case, the police are holding Alvin L.
Mitchell, who is said to have confessed that slaying.

The police stressed how simple it would have been to have gotten   24
in touch with them. "A phone call," said one of the detectives, "would
have done it." The police may be reached by dialing "0" for operator or
SPring 7-3100.

Today witnesses from the neighborhood, which is made up of   25
one-family homes in the $35,000 to $60,000 range with the exception of
the two apartment houses near the railroad station, find it difficult to
explain why they didn't call the police.

A housewife, knowingly if quite casually, said, "We thought it was 26
a lover's quarrel." A husband and wife both said, "Frankly, we were
afraid." They seemed aware of the fact that events might have been
different. A distraught woman, wiping her hands in her apron, said, "I
didn't want my husband to get involved."

One couple, now willing to talk about that night, said they heard 27
the first screams. The husband looked thoughtfully at the bookstore
where the killer first grabbed Miss Genovese.

"We went to the window to see what was happening," he said, "but 28
the light from our bedroom made it difficult to see the street." The wife,
still apprehensive, added: "I put out the light and we were able to see
better."

Asked why they hadn't called the police, she shrugged and replied: 29
"I don't know."

A man peeked out from a slight opening in the doorway to his   30
apartment and rattled off an account of the killer's second attack. Why
hadn't he called the police at the time? "I was tired," he said without
emotion. "I went back to bed."

It was 4:25 A.M. when the ambulance arrived to take the body of   31
Miss Genovese. It drove off. "Then," a solemn police detective said, "the
people came out."

Study Questions

1. This article was written for *The New York Times*. How
   does the journalistic style differ from the styles of the
   more traditional essayists in this book?

2. The police account of what happened begins with the sixth paragraph. Where does the account end? What transition does the author make at that point?
3. What is the implication of the first sentence? In what sense are *respectable* and *law-abiding* redefined?
4. Cite specific words that indicate Gansberg has a definite attitude about his subject. What parts of speech are these words?
5. Gansberg undoubtedly chose certain quotations and eliminated others. Posit reasons for his selections.
6. Comment on the meaning and effectiveness of the concluding paragraph.

In Favor of Capital Punishment

JACQUES BARZUN

Jacques Barzun (1907–   ) was born in France and became a United States citizen in 1933. At Columbia University he earned an A.B. (1927), M.A. (1928), and Ph.D. (1932). His career on the faculty at Columbia has included positions as Professor of History, Dean of the Faculties and Provost, and University Professor of History. He is a member of the editorial board of the *American Scholar,* and has been president of the Institute of Arts and Letters. Barzun's many books include *The House of Intellect* (1959), *Classic, Romantic, and Modern* (1961), *Berlioz and the Romantic Century* (1969), and *The Use and Abuse of Art* (1974).

A passing remark of mine in the *Mid-Century* magazine 1 has brought me a number of letters and a sheaf of pamphlets against capital punishment. The letters, sad and reproachful, offer me the choice of pleading ignorance or being proved insensitive. I am asked whether I know that there exists a worldwide movement for the abolition of capital punishment which has everywhere enlisted able men of every profession, including the law. I am told that the death penalty is not only inhuman but also unscientific, for rapists and murderers are really sick people who should be cured, not killed. I am

Reprinted from *The American Scholar,* Volume 31, Number 2, Spring 1962. Copyright © 1962 by the United Chapters of Phi Beta Kappa. By permission of the publishers.

invited to use my imagination and acknowledge the unbearable horror
of every form of execution.

I am indeed aware that the movement for abolition is widespread   2
and articulate, especially in England. It is headed there by my old
friend and publisher, Mr. Victor Gollancz, and it numbers such
well-known writers as Arthur Koestler, C. H. Rolph, James Avery
Joyce and Sir John Barry. Abroad as at home the profession of
psychiatry tends to support the cure principle, and many liberal
newspapers, such as the *Observer,* are committed to abolition. In the
United States there are at least twenty-five state leagues working to
the same end, plus a national league and several church councils,
notably the Quaker and the Episcopal.

The assemblage of so much talent and enlightened goodwill behind   3
a single proposal must give pause to anyone who supports the other
side, and in the attempt to make clear my views, which are now close to
unpopular, I start out by granting that my conclusion is arguable; that
is, I am still open to conviction, *provided* some fallacies and frivolities
in the abolitionist argument are first disposed of and the difficulties
not ignored but overcome. I should be glad to see this happen, not only
because there is pleasure in the spectacle of an airtight case, but also
because I am not more sanguinary than my neighbor and I should
welcome the discovery of safeguards—for society *and* the criminal—
other than killing. But I say it again, these safeguards must really
meet, not evade or postpone, the difficulties I am about to describe. Let
me add before I begin that I shall probably not answer any more letters
on this arousing subject. If this printed exposition does not do justice to
my cause, it is not likely that I can do better in the hurry of private
correspondence.

I readily concede at the outset that present ways of dealing out   4
capital punishment are as revolting as Mr. Koestler says in his
harrowing volume, *Hanged by the Neck.* Like many of our prisons, our
modes of execution should change. But this objection to barbarity does
not mean that capital punishment—or rather, judicial homicide—
should not go on. The illicit jump we find here, on the threshold of the
inquiry, is characteristic of the abolitionist and must be disallowed at
every point. Let us bear in mind the possibility of devising a painless,
sudden and dignified death, and see whether its administration is
justifiable.

The four main arguments advanced against the death penalty are: 5
1. punishment for crime is a primitive idea rooted in revenge; *2.* capital
punishment does not deter; *3.* judicial error being possible, taking life
is an appalling risk; *4.* a civilized state, to deserve its name, must
uphold, not violate, the sanctity of human life.

I entirely agree with the first pair of propositions, which is why, a   6
moment ago, I replaced the term capital punishment with "judicial
homicide." The uncontrollable brute whom I want put out of the way is
not to be punished for his misdeeds, nor used as an example or a
warning; he is to be killed for the protection of others, like the wolf that

escaped not long ago in a Connecticut suburb. No anger, vindictiveness or moral conceit need preside over the removal of such dangers. But a man's inability to control his violent impulses or to imagine the fatal consequences of his acts should be a presumptive reason for his elimination from society. This generality covers drunken driving and teen-age racing on public highways, as well as incurable obsessive violence; it might be extended (as I shall suggest later) to other acts that destroy, precisely, the moral basis of civilization.

But why kill? I am ready to believe the statistics tending to show   7
that the prospect of his own death does not stop the murderer. For one thing he is often a blind egotist, who cannot conceive the possibility of his own death. For another, detection would have to be infallible to deter the more imaginative who, although afraid, think they can escape discovery. Lastly, as Shaw long ago pointed out, hanging the wrong man will deter as effectively as hanging the right one. So, once again, why kill? If I agree that moral progress means an increasing respect for human life, how can I oppose abolition?

I do so because on this subject of human life, which is to me the   8
heart of the controversy, I find the abolitionist inconsistent, narrow or blind. The propaganda for abolition speaks in hushed tones of the sanctity of human life, as if the mere statement of it as an absolute should silence all opponents who have any moral sense. But most of the abolitionists belong to nations that spend half their annual income on weapons of war and that honor research to perfect means of killing. These good people vote without a qualm for the political parties that quite sensibly arm their country to the teeth. The West today does not seem to be the time or place to invoke the absolute sanctity of human life. As for the clergymen in the movement, we may be sure from the experience of two previous world wars that they will bless our arms and pray for victory when called upon, the sixth commandment notwithstanding.

"Oh, but we mean the sanctity of life *within* the nation!" Very well: 9
is the movement then campaigning also against the principle of self-defense? Absolute sanctity means letting the cutthroat have his sweet will of you, even if you have a poker handy to bash him with, for you might kill. And again, do we hear any protest against the police firing at criminals on the street—mere bank robbers usually—and doing this, often enough, with an excited marksmanship that misses the artist and hits the bystander? The absolute sanctity of human life is, for the abolitionist, a slogan rather than a considered proposition.

Yet it deserves examination, for upon our acceptance or rejection of   10
it depend such other highly civilized possibilities as euthanasia and seemly suicide. The inquiring mind also wants to know, why the sanctity of *human* life alone? My tastes do not run to household pets, but I find something less than admirable in the uses to which we put animals—in zoos, laboratories, and space machines—without the excuse of the ancient law, "Eat or be eaten."

It should moreover be borne in mind that this argument about   11
sanctity applies—or would apply—to about ten persons a year in Great

Britain and to between fifty and seventy-five in the United States. These are the average numbers of those executed in recent years. The count by itself should not, of course, affect our judgment of the principle: one life spared or forfeited is as important, morally, as a hundred thousand. But it should inspire a comparative judgment: there are hundreds and indeed thousands whom, in our concern with the horrors of execution, we forget: on the one hand, the victims of violence; on the other, the prisoners in our jails.

The victims are easy to forget. Social science tends steadily to **12** mark a preference for the troubled, the abnormal, the problem case. Whether it is poverty, mental disorder, delinquency or crime, the "patient material" monopolizes the interest of increasing groups of people among the most generous and learned. Psychiatry and moral liberalism go together; the application of law as we have known it is thus coming to be regarded as an historic prelude to social work, which may replace it entirely. Modern literature makes the most of this same outlook, caring only for the disturbed spirit, scorning as bourgeois those who pay their way and do *not* stab their friends. All the while the determinism of natural science reinforces the assumption that society causes its own evils. A French jurist, for example, says that in order to understand crime we must first brush aside all ideas of Responsibility. He means the criminal's and takes for granted that of society. The murderer kills because reared in a broken home or, conversely, because at an early age he witnessed his parents making love. Out of such cases, which make pathetic reading in the literature of modern criminology, is born the abolitionist's state of mind: we dare not kill those we are beginning to understand so well.

If, moreover, we turn to the accounts of the crimes committed by **13** these unfortunates, who are the victims? Only dull ordinary people going about their business. We are sorry, of course, but they do not interest science on its march. Balancing, for example, the sixty to seventy criminals executed annually in the United States, there were the seventy to eighty housewives whom George Cvek robbed, raped and usually killed during the months of a career devoted to proving his virility. "It is too bad." Cvek alone seems instructive, even though one of the law officers who helped track him down quietly remarks: "As to the extent that his villainies disturbed family relationships, or how many women are still haunted by the specter of an experience they have never disclosed to another living soul, those questions can only lead themselves to sterile conjecture."

The remote results are beyond our ken, but it is not idle to **14** speculate about those whose death by violence fills the daily two inches at the back of respectable newspapers—the old man sunning himself on a park bench and beaten to death by four hoodlums, the small children abused and strangled, the middle-aged ladies on a hike assaulted and killed, the family terrorized by a released or escaped lunatic, the half-dozen working people massacred by the sudden maniac, the boatload of persons dispatched by the skipper, the mindless assaults upon schoolteachers and shopkeepers by the increasing

horde of dedicated killers in our great cities. Where does the sanctity of
life begin?

It is all very well to say that many of these killers are themselves 15
"children," that is, minors. Doubtless a nine-year-old mind is housed in
that 150 pounds of unguided muscle. Grant, for argument's sake, that
the misdeed is "the fault of society," trot out the broken home and the
slum environment. The question then is, What shall we do, not in the
Utopian city of tomorrow, but here and now? The "scientific" means of
cure are more than uncertain. The apparatus of detention only increases the killer's antisocial animus. Reformatories and mental
hospitals are full and have an understandable bias toward discharging
their inmates. Some of these are indeed "cured"—so long as they stay
under a rule. The stress of the social free-for-all throws them back on
their violent modes of self-expression. At that point I agree that society
has failed—twice; it has twice failed the victims, whatever may be its
guilt toward the killer.

As in all great questions, the moralist must choose, and choosing 16
has a price. I happen to think that if a person of adult body has not been
endowed with adequate controls against irrationally taking the life of
another, that person must be judicially, painlessly, regretfully killed
before that mindless body's horrible automation repeats.

I say "irrationally" taking life, because it is often possible to feel 17
great sympathy with a murderer. Certain *crimes passionnels* can be
forgiven without being condoned. Blackmailers invite direct retribution. Long provocation can be an excuse, as in that engaging case of
some years ago, in which a respectable carpenter of seventy found he
could no longer stand the incessant nagging of his wife. While she
excoriated him from her throne in the kitchen—a daily exercise for
fifty years—the husband went to his bench and came back with a
hammer in each hand to settle the score. The testimony to his
character, coupled with the sincerity implied by the two hammers, was
enough to have him sent into quiet and brief seclusion.

But what are we to say of the type of motive disclosed in a journal 18
published by the inmates of one of our Federal penitentiaries? The
author is a bank robber who confesses that money is not his object:

> My mania for power, socially, sexually, and otherwise can feel no degree of
> satisfaction until I feel sure I have struck the ultimate of submission and
> terror in the minds and bodies of my victims. ... It's very difficult to
> explain all the queer fascinating sensations pounding and surging
> through me while I'm holding a gun on a victim, watching his body
> tremble and sweat. ... This is the moment when all the rationalized
> hypocrisies of civilization are suddenly swept away and two men stand
> there facing each other morally and ethically naked, and right and wrong
> are the absolute commands of the man behind the gun.

This confused echo of modern literature and modern science 19
defines the choice before us. Anything deserving the name of cure for
such a man presupposes not only a laborious individual psycho-
analysis, with the means to conduct and to sustain it, socially
and economically, but also a re-education of the mind, so as to throw

into correct perspective the garbled ideas of Freud and Nietzsche, Gide and Dostoevski, which this power-seeker and his fellows have derived from the culture and temper of our times. Ideas are tenacious and give continuity to emotion. Failing a second birth of heart and mind, we must ask: How soon will this sufferer sacrifice a bank clerk in the interests of making civilization less hypocritical? And we must certainly question the wisdom of affording him more than one chance. The abolitionists' advocacy of an unconditional "let live" is in truth part of the same cultural tendency that animates the killer. The Western peoples' revulsion from power in domestic and foreign policy has made of the state a sort of counterpart of the bank robber: both having power and neither knowing how to use it. Both waste lives because hypnotized by irrelevant ideas and crippled by contradictory emotions. If psychiatry were sure of its ground in diagnosing the individual case, a philosopher might consider whether such dangerous obsessions should not be guarded against by judicial homicide *before* the shooting starts.

I raise the question not indeed to recommend the prophylactic **20** execution of potential murderers, but to introduce the last two perplexities that the abolitionists dwarf or obscure by their concentration on changing an isolated penalty. One of these is the scale by which to judge the offenses society wants to repress. I can for example imagine a truly democratic state in which it would be deemed a form of treason punishable by death to create a disturbance in any court or deliberative assembly. The aim would be to recognize the sanctity of orderly discourse in arriving at justice, assessing criticism and defining policy. Under such a law, a natural selection would operate to remove permanently from the scene persons who, let us say, neglect argument in favor of banging on the desk with their shoe. Similarly, a bullying minority in a diet, parliament or skupshtina would be prosecuted for treason to the most sacred institutions when fists or flying inkwells replace rhetoric. That the mere suggestion of such a law sounds ludicrous shows how remote we are from civilized institutions, and hence how gradual should be our departure from the severity of judicial homicide.

I say gradual and I do not mean standing still. For there is one **21** form of barbarity in our law that I want to see mitigated before any other. I mean imprisonment. The enemies of capital punishment—and liberals generally—seem to be satisfied with any legal outcome so long as they themselves avoid the vicarious guilt of shedding blood. They speak of the sanctity of life, but have no concern with its quality. They give no impression of ever having read what it is certain they have read, from Wilde's *De Profundis* to the latest account of prison life by a convicted homosexual. Despite the infamy of concentration camps, despite Mr. Charles Burney's remarkable work, *Solitary Confinement,* despite riots in prisons, despite the round of escape, recapture and return in chains, the abolitionists' imagination tells them nothing about the reality of being caged. They read without a qualm, indeed they read with rejoicing, the hideous irony of "Killer Gets Life"; they sigh with relief instead of horror. They do not see and suffer the cell, the drill, the clothes, the stench, the food; they do not feel the sexual racking of young and old bodies, the hateful promiscuity, the insane monotony, the mass degradation, the impotent hatred. They do not remember from Silvio Pellico that only a strong political faith, with a hope of final victory, can steel a man to endure long detention. They forget that Joan of Arc, when offered "life," preferred burning at the stake. Quite of another mind, the abolitionists point with pride to the "model prisoners" that murderers often turn out to be. As if a model prisoner were not, first, a contradiction in terms, and second, an exemplar of what a free society should not want.

I said a moment ago that the happy advocates of the life sentence 22 appear not to have understood what we know they have read. No more do they appear to read what they themselves write. In the preface to his useful volume of cases, *Hanged in Error,* Mr. Leslie Hale, M.P., refers to the tardy recognition of a minor miscarriage of justice—one year in jail: "The prisoner emerged to find that his wife had died and that his children and his aged parents had been removed to the workhouse. By the time a small payment had been assessed as 'compensation' the victim was incurably insane." So far we are as indignant with the law as Mr. Hale. But what comes next? He cites the famous Evans case, in which it is very probable that the wrong man was hanged, and he exclaims: "While such mistakes are possible, should society impose an irrevocable sentence?" Does Mr. Hale really ask us to believe that the sentence passed on the first man, whose wife died and who went insane, was in any sense *revocable?* Would not any man rather be Evans dead than that other wretch "emerging" with his small compensation and his reasons for living gone?

Nothing is revocable here below, imprisonment least of all. The 23 agony of a trial itself is punishment, and acquittal wipes out nothing. Read the heart-rending diary of William Wallace, accused quite implausibly of having murdered his wife and "saved" by the Court of Criminal Appeals—but saved for what? British ostracism by everyone and a few years of solitary despair. The cases of Adolf Beck, of Oscar Slater, of the unhappy Brooklyn bank teller who vaguely resembled a forger and spent eight years in Sing Sing only to "emerge" a broken, friendless, useless, "compensated" man—all these, if the dignity of the individual has any meaning, had better have been dead before the prison door ever opened for them. This is what counsel always says to the jury in the course of a murder trial and counsel is right: far better hang this man than "give him life." For my part, I would choose death without hesitation. If that option is abolished, a demand will one day be heard to claim it as a privilege in the name of human dignity. I shall believe in the abolitionist's present views only after he has emerged from twelve months in a convict cell.

The detached observer may want to interrupt here and say that the 24 argument has now passed from reasoning to emotional preference. Whereas the objector to capital punishment *feels* that death is the greatest of evils, I *feel* that imprisonment is worse than death. A moment's thought will show that feeling is the appropriate arbiter. All reasoning about what is right, civilized and moral rests upon sentiment, like mathematics. Only, in trying to persuade others, it is important to single out the fundamental feeling, the prime intuition, and from it to reason justly. In my view, to profess respect for human life and be willing to see it spent in a penitentiary is to entertain liberal feelings frivolously. To oppose the death penalty because, unlike a prison term, it is irrevocable is to argue fallaciously.

In the propaganda for abolishing the death sentence the recital of 25 numerous miscarriages of justice commits the same error and implies the same callousness: what is at fault in our present system is not the sentence but the fallible procedure. Capital cases being one in a thousand or more, who can be cheerful at the thought of all the "revocable" errors? What the miscarriages point to is the need for reforming the jury system, the rules of evidence, the customs of prosecution, the machinery of appeal. The failure to see that this is the great task reflects the sentimentality I spoke of earlier, that which responds chiefly to the excitement of the unusual. A writer on Death and the Supreme Court is at pains to point out that when the tribunal reviews a capital case, the judges are particularly anxious and careful. What a left-handed compliment to the highest judicial conscience of the country! Fortunately, some of the champions of the misjudged see the issue more clearly. Many of those who are thought wrongly convicted now languish in jail because the jury was uncertain or because a doubting governor commuted the death sentence. Thus Dr. Samuel H. Sheppard, Jr., convicted of his wife's murder in the second degree, is serving a sentence that is supposed to run for the term of his natural life. The story of his numerous trials, as told by Mr. Paul Holmes, suggests that police incompetence, newspaper demagogy, public envy of affluence and the mischances of legal procedure fashioned the result. But Dr. Sheppard's vindicator is under no illusion as to the conditions that this "lucky" evader of the electric chair will face if he is granted parole after ten years: "It will carry with it no right to resume his life as a physician. His privilege to practice medicine was blotted out with his conviction. He must all his life bear the stigma of a parolee, subject to unceremonious return to confinement for life for the slightest misstep. More than this, he must live out his life as a convicted murderer."

What does the moral conscience of today think it is doing? If such a 26 man is a dangerous repeater of violent acts, what right has the state to let him loose after ten years? What is, in fact, the meaning of a "life sentence" that peters out long before life? Paroling looks suspiciously like an expression of social remorse for the pain of incarceration, coupled with a wish to avoid "unfavorable publicity" by freeing a suspect. The man is let out when the fuss has died down; which would mean that he was not under lock and key for our protection at all. He *was* being punished, just a little—for so prison seems in the abolitionist's distorted view, and in the jury's and the prosecutor's, whose "second-degree" murder suggests killing someone "just a little."*

If, on the other hand, execution and life imprisonment are judged 27 to serve and the accused is expected to be harmless hereafter—punishment being ruled out as illiberal—what has society gained by wrecking his life and damaging that of his family?

What we accept, and what the abolitionist will clamp upon us all 28 the more firmly if he succeeds, is an incoherence which is not remedied by the belief that second-degree murder merits a kind of second-degree death; that a doubt as to the identity of a killer is resolved by commuting real death into intolerable life; and that our ignorance whether a maniac will strike again can be hedged against by measuring "good behavior" within the gates and then releasing the subject upon the public in the true spirit of experimentation.

These are some of the thoughts I find I cannot escape when I read 29 and reflect upon this grave subject. If, as I think, they are relevant to any discussion of change and reform, resting as they do on the direct and concrete perception of what happens, then the simple meliorists who expect to breathe a purer air by abolishing the death penalty are deceiving themselves and us. The issue is for the public to judge; but I for one shall not sleep easier for knowing that in England and America and the West generally a hundred more human beings are kept alive in degrading conditions to face a hopeless future; while others—possibly less conscious, certainly less controlled—benefit from a premature freedom dangerous alike to themselves and society. In short, I derive no comfort from the illusion that in giving up one manifest protection of the law-abiding, we who might well be in any of these three roles—victim, prisoner, licensed killer—have struck a blow for the sanctity of human life.

Study Questions

1. How are the introduction and conclusion related?
2. What specific purpose is served by the italics in this essay?
3. Analyze the argument in paragraph 15.
4. Where are the major turning points in Barzun's arguments?
5. To what extent do you feel the author's style and diction are literary rather than colloquial? Cite examples to show what you mean.

---

*The British Homicide Act of 1957, Section 2, implies the same reasoning in its definition of "diminished responsibility" for certain forms of mental abnormality. The whole question of irrationality and crime is in utter confusion, on both sides of the Atlantic.

The Case Against Capital Punishment

ABE FORTAS

Abe Fortas (1910–1982) was born in Memphis, Tennessee. He received an A.B. from Southwestern College in Memphis in 1930, and an LL.B. from Yale in 1933. Throughout his distinguished legal and public career Fortas contributed regularly to legal periodicals and to others of a more general nature. He served the federal government as Under Secretary of the Interior, acting counsel to the National Power Policy Commission, advisor to the U.S. delegation to the United Nations, and Associate Justice of the Supreme Court, among other such positions. Fortas left the Supreme Court under threat of impeachment—the first justice in history forced to do so—because of certain financial arrangements between Fortas and a family foundation later involved in a fraud case. His commitment to civil liberties and the rights of the individual and the poor made him the confidant of presidents. Fortas served also as chairman of the board of the Kennedy Center for the Performing Arts.

I believe that most Americans, even those who feel it is necessary, are repelled by capital punishment; the attitude is deeply rooted in our moral reverence for life, the Judeo-Christian belief that man is created in the image of God. Many Americans were pleased when on June 29, 1972, the Supreme Court of the United States set aside death sentences for the first time in its history. On that day the Court handed down its decision in *Furman v. Georgia,* holding that the capital-punishment statutes of three states were unconstitutional because they gave the jury complete discretion to decide whether to impose the death penalty or a lesser punishment in capital cases. For this reason, a bare majority of five Justices agreed that the statutes violated the "cruel and unusual punishment" clause of the Eighth Amendment.

The result of this decision was paradoxical. Thirty-six states proceeded to adopt new death-penalty statutes designed to meet the Supreme Court's objection, and beginning in 1974, the number of persons sentenced to death soared. In 1975 alone, 285 defendants were condemned—more than double the number sentenced to death in any previously reported year. Of those condemned in 1975, 93 percent had

1

2

been convicted of murder; the balance had been convicted of rape or kidnapping.

The constitutionality of these death sentences and of the new 3 statutes, however, was quickly challenged, and on July 2, 1976, the Supreme Court announced its rulings in five test cases. It rejected "mandatory" statutes that automatically imposed death sentences for defined capital offenses, but it approved statutes that set out "standards" to guide the jury in deciding whether to impose the death penalty. These laws, the court ruled, struck a reasonable balance between giving the jury some guidance and allowing it to take into account the background and character of the defendant and the circumstances of the crime.

The decisions may settle the basic constitutional issue until there 4 is a change in the composition of the Court, but many questions remain. Some of these are questions of considerable constitutional importance, such as those relating to appellate review. Others have to do with the sensational issues that accompany capital punishment in our society. Gary Gilmore generated an enormous national debate by insisting on an inalienable right to force the people of Utah to kill him. So did a district judge who ruled that television may present to the American people the spectacle of a man being electrocuted by the state of Texas.

The recent turns of the legislative and judicial process have done 5 nothing to dispose of the matter of conscience and judgment for the individual citizen. The debate over it will not go away; indeed, it has gone on for centuries.

Through the years, the number of offenses for which the state can 6 kill the offender has declined. Once, hundreds of capital crimes, including stealing more than a shilling from a person and such religious misdeeds as blasphemy and witchcraft, were punishable by death. But in the United States today, only two principal categories remain—major assaults upon persons, such as murder, kidnapping, rape, bombing and arson, and the major political crimes of espionage and treason. In addition, there are more than 20 special capital crimes in some of our jurisdictions, including train robbery and aircraft piracy. In fact, however, in recent years murder has accounted for about 90 percent of the death sentences and rape for most of the others, and the number of states prescribing the death penalty for rape is declining.

At least 45 nations, including most of the Western democracies, 7 have abolished or abandoned capital punishment. Ten U.S. states have no provision for the death penalty. In four, the statutes authorizing it have recently been declared unconstitutional under state law. The Federal Criminal Code authorizes capital punishment for various offenses, but there have been no executions under Federal civil law (excluding military jurisdiction) since the early 1960's.

Public-opinion polls in our nation have seesawed, with some 8 indication that they are affected by the relative stability or unrest in our society at the time of polling. In 1966, a public-opinion poll reported that 42 percent of the American public favored capital punishment, 47 percent opposed it and 11 percent were undecided. In 1972–1973, both the Gallup and Harris polls showed that 57 percent to 59 percent of the people favored capital punishment, and a recent Gallup poll asserts that 65 percent favor it.

Practically all scholars and experts agree that capital punishment 9 cannot be justified as a significantly useful instrument of law enforcement or of penology. There is no evidence that it reduces the serious crimes to which it is addressed. Professor William Bowers, for example, concludes in his excellent study, "Executions in America" that statutory or judicial developments that change the risk of execution are not paralleled by variations in homicide rates. He points out that over the last 30 years, homicide rates have remained relatively constant while the number of executions has steadily declined. He concludes that the "death penalty, as we use it, exerts no influence on the extent or rate of capital offenses."

I doubt that fear of the possible penalty affects potential capital 10 offenders. The vast majority of capital offenses are murders committed in the course of armed robbery that result from fear, tension or anger of the moment, and murders that are the result from fear, tension or anger of the moment, and murders that are the result of passion or mental disorder. The only deterrence derived from the criminal process probably results from the fear of apprehension and arrest, and possibly from the fear of significant punishment. There is little, if any, difference between the possible deterrent effect of life imprisonment and that of the death penalty.

In fact, the statistical possibility of execution for a capital offense is 11 extremely slight. We have not exceeded 100 executions a year since 1951, although the number of homicides in death-sentence jurisdictions alone has ranged from 7,500 to 10,000. In 1960, there were only 56 executions in the United States, and the number declined each year thereafter. There have been no executions since 1967. In the peak year of 1933, there were only 199 executions in the United States, while the average number of homicides in all of the states authorizing capital punishment for 1932–33 was 11,579.

A potential murderer who rationally weighed the possibility of 12 punishment by death (if there is such a person), would figure that he has considerably better than a 98 percent chance of avoiding execution in the average capital-punishment state. In the years from 1960 to 1967, his chances of escaping execution were better than 99.5 percent. The professional or calculating murderer is not apt to be deterred by such odds.

An examination of the reason for the infrequency of execution is 13 illuminating:

(1) Juries are reluctant to condemn a human being to death. The 14 evidence is that they are often prone to bring in a verdict of a lesser offense, or even to acquit, if the alternative is to impose the death

penalty. The reluctance is, of course, diminished when powerful
emotions come into play—as in the case of a black defendant charged
with the rape of a white woman.

(2) Prosecutors do not ask for the death penalty in the case of 15
many, perhaps a majority, of those who are arrested for participation
in murder or other capital offenses. In part, this is due to the difficulty
of persuading juries to impose death sentences; in part, it is due to plea
bargaining. In capital cases involving more than one participant, the
prosecutor seldom asks for the death penalty for more than one of
them. Frequently, in order to obtain the powerful evidence necessary
to win a death sentence, he will make a deal with all participants
except one. The defendants who successfully "plea bargain" testify
against the defendant chosen for the gallows and in return receive
sentences of imprisonment.

This system may be defensible in noncapital cases because of 16
practical exigencies, but it is exceedingly disturbing where the result
is to save the witness's life at the hazard of the life of another person.
The possibility is obvious that the defendant chosen for death will be
selected on a basis that has nothing to do with comparative guilt, and
the danger is inescapable that the beneficiary of the plea-bargain, in
order to save his life, will lie or give distorted testimony. To borrow a
phrase from Justice Byron R. White: "This is a grisly trade. . . ." A
civilized nation should not kill A on the basis of testimony obtained
from B in exchange for B's life.

(3) As a result of our doubts about capital punishment, and our 17
basic aversion to it, we have provided many escape hatches. Every
latitude is allowed the defendant and his counsel in the trial; most
lawyers representing a capital offender quite properly feel that they
must exhaust every possible defense, however technical or unlikely;
appeals are generally a matter of right; slight legal errors, which
would be disregarded in other types of cases, are grounds for reversal;
governors have, and liberally exercise, the power to commute death
sentences. Only the rare, unlucky defendant is likely to be executed
when the process is all over.

In 1975, 65 prisoners on death row had their death penalty status 18
changed as a result of appeals, court actions, commutation, resentenc-
ing, etc. This was more than 20 percent of the new deathrow prisoners
admitted during that peak year.

It is clear that American prosecutors, judges and juries are not 19
likely to cause the execution of enough capital offenders to increase the
claimed deterrent effect of capital-punishment laws or to reduce the
"lottery" effect of freakish selection. People generally may favor
capital punishment in the abstract but pronouncing that a living
person shall be killed is quite another matter. Experience shows that
juries are reluctant to order that a person be killed. Where juries have
been commanded by law to impose the death penalty, they have often
chosen to acquit or, in modern times, to convict of a lesser offense
rather than to return a verdict that would result in execution.

The law is a human instrument administered by a vast number of 20 different people in different circumstances, and we are inured to its many inequalities. Tweedledee may be imprisoned for five years for a given offense, while Tweedledum, convicted of a similar crime, may be back on the streets in a few months. We accept the inevitability of such discriminations although we don't approve of them, and we constantly seek to reduce their frequency and severity. But the taking of a life is different from any other punishment. It is final; it is ultimate; if it is erroneous, it is irreversible and beyond correction. It is an act in which the state is presuming to function, so to speak, as the Lord's surrogate.

We have gone a long way toward recognition of the unique 21 character of capital punishment. We insist that it be imposed for relatively few crimes of the most serious nature and that it be imposed only after elaborate precautions to reduce the possibility of error. We also inflict it in a fashion that avoids the extreme cruelty of such methods as drawing and quartering, though it still involves the barbaric rituals attendant upon electrocution, the gallows or the firing squad.

But fortunately, the death penalty is and will continue to be sought 22 in only a handful of cases and rarely carried out. So long as the death penalty is a highly exceptional punishment, it will serve no deterrent or penological function; it will fulfill no pragmatic purpose of the state; and inevitably, its selective imposition will continue to be influenced by racial and class prejudice.

All of the standards that can be written, all of the word magic and 23 the procedural safeguards that can be devised to compel juries to impose the death penalty on capital offenders without exception or discrimination will be of no avail. In a 1971 capital-punishment case, Justice John Harlan wrote on the subject of standards. "They do no more," he said, "than suggest some subjects for the jury to consider during its deliberations, and [the criteria] bear witness to the intractable nature of the problem of 'standards' which the history of capital punishment has from the beginning reflected."

Form and substance are important to the life of the law, but when 24 the law deals with a fundamental moral and constitutional issue—the disposition of human life—the use of such formulas is not an acceptable substitute for a correct decision on the substance of the matter.

The discrimination that is inescapable in the selection of the few to 25 be killed under our capital-punishment laws is unfortunately of the most invidious and unacceptable sort. Most of those who are chosen for extinction are black (53.5 percent in the years 1930 to 1975). The wheels of chance and prejudice begin to spin in the police station; they continue through the prosecutor's choice of defendants for whom he will ask the death penalty and those he will choose to spare; they continue through the trial and in the jury room, and finally they appear in the Governor's office. Solemn "presumptions of law" that the selection will be made rationally and uniformly violate human experience and the evidence of the facts. Efforts to bring about equality of sentence by writing "standards" or verbal formulas may comfort the heart of the legislator or jurist, but they can hardly satisfy his intelligence.

If deterrence is not a sufficient reason to justify capital- 26 punishment laws and if their selective application raises such disturbing questions, what possible reason is there for their retention? One other substantive reason, advanced by eminent authorities, is that the execution of criminals is justifiable as "retribution." This is the argument that society should have the right to vent its anger or abhorrence against the offender, that it may justifiably impose a punishment people believe the criminal "deserves." Albert Camus, in a famous essay, says of capital punishment:

"Let us call it by the name which, for lack of any other nobility, 27 will at least give the nobility of truth, and let us recognize it for what it is essentially: a revenge."

We may realize that deep-seated emotions underlie our capital- 28 punishment laws, but there is a difference between our understanding of the motivation for capital punishment and our acceptance of it as an instrument of our society. We may appreciate that the *lex talionis,* the law of revenge, has it roots in the deep recesses of the human spirit, but that awareness is not a permissible reason for retaining capital punishment.

It is also argued that capital punishment is an ancient sanction 29 that has been adopted by most of our legislatures after prolonged consideration and reconsideration, and that we should not override this history.

But the argument is not persuasive. If we were to restrict the 30 implementation of our Bill of Rights, by either constitutional decisions or legislative judgments, to those practices that its provisions contemplated in 1791, we would indeed be a retarded society. In 1816, Thomas Jefferson wrote a letter in which he spoke of the need for constitutions as well as other laws and institutions to move forward "hand in hand with the progress of the human mind." He said, "We might as well require a man to wear still the coat which fitted him when a boy, as civilized society to remain ever under the regimen of their barbarous ancestors."

As early as 1910, the Supreme Court, in the case of *Weems v.* 31 *United States,* applied this principle to a case in which the defendant had been sentenced to 15 years in prison for the crime of falsifying a public document as part of an embezzlement scheme. The Court held that the sentence was excessive and constituted "cruel and unusual punishment" in violation of the Eighth Amendment. In a remarkable opinion, Justice Joseph McKenna eloquently rejected the idea that prohibitions of the Bill of Rights, including the Eighth Amendment, must be limited to the practices to which they were addressed in 1791, when the great amendments were ratified. He said, "Time works changes, brings into existence new conditions and purposes. Therefore a principle, to be vital, must be capable of wider application than the mischief which gave it birth. This is peculiarly true of constitutions. They are not ephemeral enactments, designed to meet passing occasions." As to the "cruel and unusual punishment" clause of the Constitution, he said that it "is not fastened to the obsolete, but may acquire meaning as public opinion becomes enlightened by a humane justice."

We have also long recognized that the progressive implementation 32 of the Bill of Rights does not depend upon first obtaining a majority vote or a favorable Gallup or Harris poll. As the Supreme Court stated in the famous 1943 flag-salute case, "The very purpose of a Bill of Rights was to place [certain subjects] beyond the reach of majorities and officials. . . ."

Indeed, despite our polls, public opinion is unfathomable; in the 33 words of Judge Jerome Frank, it is a "slithery shadow"; and if known, no one can predict how profound or shallow it is as of the moment, and how long it will persist. Basically, however, the obligation of legislators and judges who question whether a law or practice is or is not consonant with our Constitution is inescapable; it cannot be delegated to the Gallup poll, or to the ephemeral evidence of public opinion.

We will not eliminate the objections to capital punishment by legal 34 legerdemain, by "standards," by procedures or by word formulas. The issue is fundamental. It is wrong for the state to kill offenders; it is a wrong far exceeding the numbers involved. In exchange for the pointless exercise of killing a few people each year, we expose our society to brutalization; lower the essential value that is the basis of our civilization; a pervasive, unqualified respect for life. And we subject ourselves and our legal institutions to the gross spectacle of a pageant in which death provides degrading, distorting excitement. Justice Felix Frankfurter once pointed out: "I am strongly against capital punishment. . . . When life is at hazard in a trial, it sensationalizes the whole thing almost unwittingly; the effect on juries, the bar, the public, the judiciary, I regard as very bad. I think scientifically the claim of deterrence is not worth much. Whatever proof there may be in my judgment does not outweigh the social loss due to the inherent sensationalism of a trial for life."

Beyond all of these factors is the fundamental consideration: In the 35 name of all that we believe in and hope for, why must we reserve to ourselves the right to kill 100 or 200 people? Why, when we can point to no tangible benefit; why, when in all honesty we must admit that we are not certain that we are accomplishing anything except serving the cause of "revenge" or retribution? Why, when we have bravely and nobly progressed so far in the recent past to create a decent, humane society, must we perpetuate the senseless barbarism of official murder?

In 1971, speaking of the death penalty, Justice William O. Douglas 36 wrote: "We need not read procedural due process as designed to satisfy man's deep-seated sadistic instincts. We need not in deference to those sadistic instincts say we are bound by history from defining procedural due process so as to deny men fair trials."

I hope to believe we will conclude that the time has come for us to 37
join the company of those nations that have repudiated killing as an
instrument of criminal law enforcement.

Study Questions

1. To what extent is the paradox discussed in the second paragraph tied to the belief stated in the first?
2. What are the major points in Fortas's case?
3. Comment on the use of statistics in this essay.
4. Barzun and Fortas are not writing directly for one another, but does either of them clearly seem to have bettered the other at any point in his essay?
5. Whose essay—Fortas's or Barzun's—seems the more reasoned? Is one of them more logical than the other? Which uses emotionally charged language to a greater extent?

A Hanging
GEORGE ORWELL

George Orwell (1903–1950) was the pen name of Eric Blair, who was born in Bengal, India. He graduated from Eton, served with the Indian Imperial Police in Burma from 1922 to 1927, and then returned to England to begin his career (1938) as a writer. His works include *Burmese Days* (1934), *Homage to Catalonia* (1938), *Dickens, Dali, and Others* (1946), and *Shooting an Elephant* (1950). His fame, however, is primarily the result of *Animal Farm* (1945) and *1984* (1949), the former one of the most famous modern satires and the latter a classic novel of social protest. His *Collected Essays* was published in 1969.

It was in Burma, a sodden morning of the rains. A sickly 1
light, like yellow tinfoil, was slanting over the high walls into the jail
yard. We were waiting outside the condemned cells, a row of sheds
fronted with double bars, like small animal cages. Each cell measured
about ten feet by ten and was quite bare within except for a plank bed
and a pot for drinking water. In some of them brown, silent men, were
squatting at the inner bars, with their blankets draped round them.

These were the condemned men, due to be hanged within the next week or two.

One prisoner had been brought out of his cell. He was a Hindu, a **2** puny wisp of a man, with a shaven head and vague liquid eyes. He had a thick, sprouting moustache, absurdly too big for his body, rather like the moustache of a comic man in the films. Six tall Indian warders were guarding him and getting him ready for the gallows. Two of them stood by with rifles and fixed bayonets, while the others handcuffed him, passed a chain through his handcuffs and fixed it to their belts, and lashed his arms tight to his sides. They crowded very close about him, with their hands always on him in a careful, caressing grip, as though all the while feeling him to make sure he was there. It was like men handling a fish which is still alive and may jump back into the water. But he stood quite unresisting, yielding his arms limply to the ropes, as though he hardly noticed what was happening.

Eight o'clock struck and a bugle call, desolately thin in the wet air, **3** floated from the distant barracks. The superintendent of the jail, who was standing apart from the rest of us, moodily prodding the gravel with his stick, raised his head at the sound. He was an army doctor, with a grey toothbrush moustache and a gruff voice. "For God's sake hurry up, Francis," he said irritably. "The man ought to have been dead by this time. Aren't you ready yet?"

Francis, the head jailer, a fat Dravidian in a white drill suit and **4** gold spectacles, waved his black hand. "Yes sir, yes sir," he bubbled. "All iss satisfactorily prepared. The hangman iss waiting. We shall proceed."

"Well, quick march, then. The prisoners can't get their breakfast **5** till this job's over."

We set out for the gallows. Two warders marched on either side of **6** the prisoner, with their rifles at the slope; two others marched close against him, gripping him by arm and shoulder, as though at once pushing and supporting him. The rest of us, magistrates and the like, followed behind. Suddenly, when we had gone ten yards, the procession stopped short without any order or warning. A dreadful thing had happened—a dog, come goodness knows whence, had appeared in the yard. It came bounding among us with a loud volley of barks and leapt round us wagging its whole body, wild with glee at finding so many human beings together. It was a large woolly dog, half Airedale, half pariah. For a moment it pranced round us, and then, before anyone could stop it, it had made a dash for the prisoner, and jumping up tried to lick his face. Everybody stood aghast, too taken aback even to grab the dog.

"Who let that bloody brute in here?" said the superintendent **7** angrily. "Catch it, someone!"

A warder detached from the escort, charged clumsily after the dog, **8** but it danced and gambolled just out of his reach, taking everything as part of the game. A young Eurasian jailer picked up a handful of gravel and tried to stone the dog away, but it dodged the stones and came after us again. Its yaps echoed from the jail walls. The prisoner, in the grasp

of the two wardens looked on incuriously, as though this was another
formality of the hanging. It was several minutes before someone
managed to catch the dog. Then we put my handkerchief through its
collar and moved off once more, with the dog still straining and
whimpering.

It was about forty yards to the gallows. I watched the bare brown 9
back of the prisoner marching in front of me. He walked clumsily with
his bound arms, but quite steadily, with that bobbing gait of the Indian
who never straightens his knees. At each step his muscles slid neatly
into place, the lock of hair on his scalp danced up and down, his feet
printed themselves on the wet gravel. And once, in spite of the men
who gripped him by each shoulder, he stepped lightly aside to avoid a
puddle on the path.

It is curious, but till that moment I had never realized what it 10
means to destroy a healthy, conscious man. When I saw the prisoner
step aside to avoid the puddle I saw the mystery, the unspeakable
wrongness, of cutting a life short when it is in full tide. This man was
not dying, he was alive just as we are alive. All the organs of his body
were working—bowels digesting food, skin renewing itself, nails
growing, tissues forming—all toiling away in solemn foolery. His nails
would still be growing when he stood on the drop, when he was falling
through the air with a tenth-of-a-second to live. His eyes saw the
yellow gravel and the grey walls, and his brain still remembered,
foresaw, reasoned—even about puddles. He and we were a party of men
walking together, seeing, hearing, feeling, understanding the same
world; and in two minutes, with a sudden snap, one of us would be
gone—one mind less, one world less.

The gallows stood in a small yard, separate from the main grounds 11
of the prison, and overgrown with tall prickly weeds. It was a brick
erection like three sides of a shed, with planking on top, and above that
two beams and a crossbar with the rope dangling. The hangman, a
grey-haired convict in the white uniform of the prison, was waiting
beside his machine. He greeted us with a servile crouch as we entered.
At a word from Francis the two warders, gripping the prisoner more
closely than ever, half led, half pushed him to the gallows and helped
him clumsily up the ladder. Then the hangman climbed up and fixed
the rope round the prisoner's neck.

We stood waiting, five yards away. The warders had formed in a 12
rough circle round the gallows. And then, when the noose was fixed,
the prisoner began crying to his god. It was a high, reiterated cry of
"Ram! Ram! Ram! Ram!" not urgent and fearful like a prayer or cry for
help, but steady, rhythmical, almost like the tolling of a bell. The dog
answered the sound with a whine. The hangman, still standing on the
gallows, produced a small cotton bag like a flour bag and drew it down
over the prisoner's face. But the sound, muffled by the cloth, still
persisted, over and over again: "Ram! Ram! Ram! Ram! Ram!"

The hangman climbed down and stood ready, holding the lever. 13
Minutes seemed to pass. The steady, muffled crying from the prisoner
went on and on, "Ram! Ram! Ram!" never faltering for an instant. The

superintendent, his head on his chest, was slowly poking the ground with his stick; perhaps he was counting the cries, allowing the prisoner a fixed number—fifty, perhaps, or a hundred. Everyone had changed colour. The Indians had gone grey like bad coffee, and one or two of the bayonets were wavering. We looked at the lashed, hooded man on the drop, and listened to his cries—each cry another second of life; the same thought was in all our minds: oh, kill him quickly, get it over, stop that abominable noise!

Suddenly the superintendent made up his mind. Throwing up his **14** head he made a swift motion with his stick. "Chalo!" he shouted almost fiercely.

There was a clanking noise, and then dead silence. The prisoner **15** had vanished, and the rope was twisting on itself. I let go of the dog, and it galloped immediately to the back of the gallows; but when it got there it stopped short, barked, and then retreated into a corner of the yard, where it stood among the weeds, looking timorously out at us. We went round the gallows to inspect the prisoner's body. He was dangling with his toes pointed straight downwards, very slowly revolving, as dead as a stone.

The superintendent reached out with his stick and poked the bare **16** brown body; it oscillated slightly. *"He's* all right," said the superintendent. He backed out from under the gallows, and blew out a deep breath. The moodly look had gone out of his face quite suddenly. He glanced at his wrist-watch. "Eight minutes past eight. Well, that's all for this morning, thank God."

The warders unfixed bayonets and marched away. The dog, so- **17** bered and conscious of having misbehaved itself, slipped after them. We walked out of the gallows yard, past the condemned cells with their waiting prisoners, into the big central yard of the prison. The convicts, under the command of warders armed with lathis, were already receiving their breakfast. They squatted in long rows, each man holding a tin pannikin, while two warders with buckets marched round ladling out rice; it seemed quite a homely, jolly scene, after the hanging An enormous relief had come upon us now that the job was done. One felt an impulse to sing, to break into a run, to snigger. All at once everyone began chattering gaily.

The Eurasian boy walking beside me nodded towards the way we **18** had come, with a knowing smile: "Do you know, sir, our friend (he meant the dead man) when he heard his appeal had been dismissed, he pissed on the floor of his cell. From fright. Kindly take one of my cigarettes, sir. Do you not admire my new silver case, sir? From the boxwallah, two rupees eight annas. Classy European style."

Several people laughed—at what, nobody seemed certain. **19**

Francis was walking by the superintendent talking garrulously: **20** "Well, sir, all hass passed off with the utmost satisfactoriness. It was all finished—flick! like that. It iss not always so—oah, no! I have known cases where the doctor was obliged to go beneath the gallows and pull the prisoner's legs to ensure decease. Most disagreeable!"

"Wriggling about, eh? That's bad," said the superintendent. **21**

"Ach, sir, it iss worse when they become refractory! One man, I 22 recall, clung to the bars of hiss cage when we went to take him out. You will scarcely credit, sir, that it took six warders to dislodge him, three pulling at each leg. We reasoned with him. 'My dear fellow,' we said, 'think of all the pain and trouble you are causing to us!' But no, he would not listen! Ach, he wass very troublesome!"

I found that I was laughing quite loudly. Everyone was laughing. 23 Even the superintendent grinned in a tolerant way. "You'd better all come out and have a drink," he said quite genially. "I've got a bottle of whisky in the car. We could do with it."

We went through the big double gates of the prison into the road. 24 "Pulling at his legs!" exclaimed a Burmese magistrate suddenly, and burst into a loud chuckling. We all began laughing again. At the moment Francis' anecdote seemed extraordinarily funny. We all had a drink together, native and European alike, quite amicably. The dead man was a hundred yards away.

Study Questions

1. What is the *tone* of the essay? How does the narrator's attitude toward the hanging help determine the response elicited from the reader?
2. Why is the superintendent irritated by the delay in the hanging?
3. How does the incident with the dog contribute to the effectiveness of "A Hanging"?
4. Why does the prisoner's stepping aside to avoid a puddle bring the narrator to a full realization of the scene before him?
5. Why do the men feel "an impulse to sing, to break into a run, to snigger" after the hanging? Why does Orwell end his essay with "The dead man was a hundred yards away"?

The Use of Force
WILLIAM CARLOS WILLIAMS

William Carlos Williams (1883–1963) was born in Rutherford, New Jersey. A graduate of the University of Pennsylvania Medical School, Williams became a pediatrician in his hometown, where he remained throughout his life. Williams published his first collection, *Poems,* in 1909. Other volumes include *The Tempers* (1913), *Sour Grapes* (1921), *Collected Poems* (1934), *Complete Collected Poems* (1938), *The Broken Span* (1941), *Journey to Love* (1955), and the 1964 Pulitzer Prize-winning *Pictures from Bruegel.* Williams also wrote essays, published in several volumes including *Selected Essays* (1954); and plays collected in, among others, *Many Loves* (1961); novels, *A Voyage to Pagany* (1928), *White Mule* (1937), *The Build-Up* (1952); and even the libretto for a three-act opera. His collected stories and his autobiography were both published in 1961.

They were new patients to me, all I had was the name, 1 Olson. Please come down as soon as you can, my daughter is very sick.

When I arrived I was met by the mother, a big startled-looking 2 woman, very clean and apologetic who merely said, Is this the doctor? and let me in. In the back, she added. You must excuse us, doctor, we have her in the kitchen where it is warm. It is very damp here sometimes.

The child was fully dressed and sitting on her father's lap near the 3 kitchen table. He tried to get up, but I motioned for him not to bother, took off my overcoat and started to look things over. I could see that they were all very nervous, eyeing me up and down distrustfully. As often, in such cases, they weren't telling me more than they had to, it was up to me to tell them; that's why they were spending three dollars on me.

The child was fairly eating me up with her cold, steady eyes, and 4 no expression to her face whatever. She did not move and seemed, inwardly, quiet; an unusually attractive little thing, and as strong as a heifer in appearance. But her face was flushed, she was breathing rapidly, and I realized that she had a high fever. She had magnificent blonde hair, in profusion. One of those picture children often reproduced in advertising leaflets and the photogravure sections of the Sunday papers.

She's had a fever for three days, began the father and we don't 5 know what it comes from. My wife has given her things, you know, like people do, but it don't do no good. And there's been a lot of sickness around. So we tho't you'd better look her over and tell us what is the matter.

As doctors often do I took a trial shot at it as a point of departure. **6** Has she had a sore throat?

Both parents answered me together, No . . . No, she says her throat **7** don't hurt her.

Does your throat hurt you? added the mother to the child. But the **8** little girl's expression didn't change nor did she move her eyes from my face.

Have you looked? **9**

I tried to, said the mother, but I couldn't see. **10**

As it happens we had been having a number of cases of diphtheria **11** in the school to which this child went during that month and we were all, quite apparently, thinking of that, though no one had as yet spoken of the thing.

Well, I said, suppose we take a look at the throat first. I smiled in **12** my best professional manner and asking for the child's first name I said, come on, Mathilda, open your mouth and let's take a look at your throat.

Nothing doing. **13**

Aw, come on, I coaxed, just open your mouth wide and let me take a **14** look. Look, I said opening both hands wide, I haven't anything in my hands. Just open up and let me see.

Such a nice man, put in the mother. Look how kind he is to you. **15** Come on, do what he tells you to. He won't hurt you.

At that I ground my teeth in disgust. If only they wouldn't use the **16** word "hurt" I might be able to get somewhere. But I did not allow myself to be hurried or disturbed but speaking quietly and slowly I approached the child again.

As I moved my chair a little nearer suddenly with one catlike **17** movement both her hands clawed instinctively for my eyes and she almost reached them too. In fact she knocked my glasses flying and they fell, though unbroken, several feet away from me on the kitchen floor.

Both the mother and father almost turned themselves inside out in **18** embarrassment and apology. You bad girl, said the mother, taking her and shaking her by one arm. Look what you've done. The nice man . . .

For heaven's sake, I broke in. Don't call me a nice man to her. I'm **19** here to look at her throat on the chance that she might have diphtheria and possibly die of it. But that's nothing to her. Look here, I said to the child, we're going to look at your throat. You're old enough to understand what I'm saying. Will you open it now by yourself or shall we have to open it for you?

Not a move. Even her expression hadn't changed. Her breaths **20** however were coming faster and faster. Then the battle began. I had to do it. I had to have a throat culture for her own protection. But first I told the parents that it was entirely up to them. I explained the danger but said that I would not insist on a throat examination so long as they would take the responsibility.

If you don't do what the doctor says you'll have to go the hospital, **21** the mother admonished her severely.

Oh yeah? I had to smile to myself. After all, I had already fallen in 22 love with the savage brat, the parents were contemptible to me. In the ensuing struggle they grew more and more abject, crushed, exhausted while she surely rose to magnificent heights of insane fury of effort bred of her terror of me.

The father tried his best, and he was a big man but the fact that 23 she was his daughter, his shame at her behavior and his dread of hurting her made him release her just at the critical moment several times when I had almost achieved success, till I wanted to kill him. But his dread also that she might have diphtheria made him tell me to go on, go on though he himself was almost fainting, while the mother moved back and forth behind us raising and lowering her hands in an agony of apprehension.

Put her in front of you on your lap, I ordered, and hold both her 24 wrists.

But as soon as he did the child let out a scream. Don't, you're 25 hurting me. Let go of my hands. Let them go I tell you. Then she shrieked terrifyingly, hysterically. Stop it! Stop it! You're killing me!

Do you think she can stand it, doctor! said the mother.   26

You get out, said the husband to his wife. Do you want her to die of 27 diphtheria?

Come on now, hold her, I said.   28

Then I grasped the child's head with my left hand and tried to get 29 the wooden tongue depressor between her teeth. She fought, with clenched teeth, desperately! But now I also had grown furious—at a child. I tried to hold myself down but I couldn't. I know how to expose a throat for inspection. And I did my best. When finally I got the wooden spatula behind the last teeth and just the point of it into the mouth cavity, she opened up for an instant but before I could see anything she came down again and gripping the wooden blade between her molars she reduced it to splinters before I could get it out again.

Aren't you ashamed, the mother yelled at her. Aren't you ashamed 30 to act like that in front of the doctor?

Get me a smooth-handled spoon of some sort, I told the mother. 31 We're going through with this. The child's mouth was already bleeding. Her tongue was cut and she was screaming in wild hysterical shrieks. Perhaps I should have desisted and come back in an hour or more. No doubt it would have been better. But I have seen at least two children lying dead in bed of neglect in such cases, and feeling that I must get a diagnosis now or never I went at it again. But the worst of it was that I too had got beyond reason. I could have torn the child apart in my own fury and enjoyed it. It was a pleasure to attack her. My face was burning with it.

The damned little brat must be protected against her own idiocy, 32 one says to one's self at such times. Others must be protected against her. It is social necessity. And all these things are true. But a blind fury, a feeling of adult shame, bred of a longing for muscular release are the operatives. One goes on to the end.

In a final unreasoning assault I overpowered the child's neck and 33 jaws. I forced the heavy silver spoon back of her teeth and down her throat till she gagged. And there it was—both tonsils covered with membrane. She had fought valiantly to keep me from knowing her secret. She had been hiding that sore throat for three days at least and lying to her parents in order to escape just such an outcome as this.

Now truly she *was* furious. She had been on the defensive before **34** but now she attacked. Tried to get off her father's lap and fly at me while tears of defeat blinded her eyes.

Study Questions

1. What is Williams telling us about the *use* of force? What is the theme of the story?
2. The doctor loses self-control. Why? Does he enjoy the battle?
3. Some critics have found sexual conflict in this story. Do you? Is there any evidence to support this common critical view?
4. Why does Williams choose not to use quotation marks?
5. If the point of view were changed from first to third person, how might this affect your reaction to the doctor's behavior?
6. Why does Williams italicize *was* in the last paragraph? How would the meaning of the sentence in which *was* appears be changed if any other word were italicized?

The Warfare in the Forest Is Not Wanton
BROOKS ATKINSON

Brooks Atkinson (1894–   ) was born in Melrose, Massachusetts, and was graduated from Harvard University. Although he taught English at Dartmouth, he is primarily known for his work on various newspapers, including *The New York Times,* as reporter, editor, book reviewer, war correspondent, and preeminently drama critic. He was the first president of the New York Drama Critics Circle, won the Pulitzer Prize in journalism in 1947, and has been awarded numerous honorary degrees. The Mansfield Theatre was renamed in his honor in 1960, probably as a result of his devoted attention to off-Broadway productions. Included in his writings are *Skyline Promenade* (1925), *Broadway Scrapbook* (1947), *Brief Chronicles* (1966), *This Bright Land* (1972), and *The Lively Years* (1973).

After thirty-five years the forest in Spruce Notch is tall and   1
sturdy. It began during the Depression when work gangs planted
thousands of tiny seedlings in abandoned pastures on Richmond Peak
in the northern Catskills. Nothing spectacular has happened there
since; the forest has been left undisturbed.

But now we have a large spread of Norway spruces a foot thick the   2
butt and 40 or 50 feet high. Their crowns look like thousands of dark
crosses reaching into the sky.

The forest is a good place in which to prowl in search of wildlife.   3
But also in search of ideas. For the inescapable fact is that the world of
civilized America does not have such a clean record. Since the seedlings were planted the nation has fought three catastrophic wars in one
of which the killing of combatants and the innocent continues. During
the lifetime of the forest 350,000 Americans have died on foreign
battlefields.

Inside America civilized life is no finer. A President, a Senator, a   4
man of God have been assassinated. Citizens are murdered in the
streets. Riots, armed assaults, looting, burning, outbursts of hatred
have increased to the point where they have become commonplace.

Life in civilized America is out of control. Nothing is out of control   5
in the forest. Everything complies with the instinct for survival—
which is the law and order of the woods.

Although the forest looks peaceful it supports incessant warfare,   6
most of which is hidden and silent. For thirty-five years the strong
have been subduing the weak. The blueberries that once flourished on
the mountain have been destroyed. All the trees are individuals, as all
human beings are individuals; and every tree poses a threat to every
other tree. The competition is so fierce that you can hardly penetrate
some of the thickets where the lower branches of neighboring trees are
interlocked in a blind competition for survival.

Nor is the wildlife benign. A red-tailed hawk lived there last   7
summer—slowly circling in the sky and occasionally drawing attention to himself by screaming. He survived on mice, squirrels, chip-
munks and small birds. A barred owl lives somewhere in the depth of
the woods. He hoots in midmorning as well as at sunrise to register his
authority. He also is a killer. Killing is a fundamental part of the
process. The nuthatches kill insects in the bark. The woodpeckers dig
insects out. The thrushes eat beetles and caterpillars.

But in the forest, killing is not wanton or malicious. It is for   8
survival. Among birds of equal size most of the warfare consists of
sham battles in which they go through the motions of warfare until one
withdraws. Usually neither bird gets hurt.

Nor is the warfare between trees vindictive. Although the spruces   9
predominate they do not practice segregation. On both sides of Lost
Lane, which used to be a dirt road, maples, beeches, ashes, aspens and
a few red oaks live, and green curtains of wild grapes cover the wild
cherry trees. In the depths of the forest there are a few glades where
the spruces stand aside and birches stretch and grow. The forest is a
web of intangible tensions. But they are never out of control. Although
they are wild they are not savage as they are in civilized life.

For the tensions are absorbed in the process of growth, and the 10
clusters of large cones on the Norway spruces are certificates to a good
future. The forest gives an external impression of discipline and
pleasure. Occasionally the pleasure is rapturously stated. Soon after
sunrise one morning last summer when the period of bird song was
nearly over, a solitary rose-breasted grosbeak sat on the top of a tall
spruce and sang with great resonance and beauty. He flew a few rods to
another tree and continued singing: then to another tree where he
poured out his matin again, and so on for a half hour. There was no
practical motive that I was aware of.

After thirty-five uneventful years the spruces have created an 11
environment in which a grosbeak is content, and this one said so
gloriously. It was a better sound than the explosion of bombs, the
scream of the wounded, the crash of broken glass, the crackle of
burning buildings, the shriek of the police siren.

The forest conducts its affairs with less rancor and malevolence 12
than civilized America.

Study Questions

1. Can you suggest a reason for paragraphs 1 and 2 being
   separated? Would you combine them? Why or why not?
2. Without using the rest of Atkinson's essay to answer this
   question, explain what he means by "such a clean record"
   in paragraph 2. He is beginning his analogy. Has he
   begun too soon?
3. Find examples of Atkinson's using parallelism as a
   persuasive device.
4. Is Atkinson's argument emotional or reasoned? How does
   he use the grosbeak?
5. Is Atkinson's analogy ultimately convincing? How do
   civilized life and life in the forest compare and contrast?

Earth and the Unearthly
BRAVE NEW WORLD

4

This section brings together a number of selections concerned with the natural world, or with objectivity and truth in our approach to that world. Although it is tightly knit thematically, the section offers a tremendous variety of approaches to the material.

Thomas Henry Huxley first explains the scientific method; his remarks were originally addressed to a group of English workingmen, but they work equally well for a contemporary lay audience. The two selections that follow—by Sir James Jeans and Roy C. Selby, Jr.—present complicated processes or theoretical knowledge in simple but accurate language.

Isaac Asimov's article on science fiction tells us where such fiction goes astray. Asimov's style is as informal as Huxley's, for instance, is formal, but is nonetheless a factual, objective approach to the material. Asimov himself is the subject of James Lincoln Collier's essay; Collier presents the scientist as a quirky, volatile personality. As a cautionary note, we also present Shirley Jackson's short story about the perils of dehumanization: the approach is humorous, the subject is not.

Rhetorically, the selections on stars and hawks offer the widest opportunity for comparison of types and styles. George Santayana's literary style provides a contrast to Clark's more matter-of-fact examination; the two men are not using the same lens in their scanning of the heavens. Then John James Audubon opens the subsection on hawks with a nearly purely objective description of the sparrow hawk. Loren C. Eiseley and Walter Van Tilburg Clark use still different forms in writing about hawks. Eiseley's prose is lyrical, almost poetic. Clark demonstrates his skill with point of view and paragraph structure within the form of the short story. Richard Allen trains his student's eye on Clark's prose and finds mastery of style. The six selections in these two clusters vividly reveal the effectiveness of suiting style and form to content.

We hasten to add that our clusters need not be read as clusters. We have been careful to make selections that stand independently as models of basic rhetorical modes for the student writer to emulate.

The Method of Scientific Investigation
THOMAS HENRY HUXLEY

Thomas Henry Huxley (1825–1895) was born in Ealing, near London. He attended schools at Ealing and Coventry, entered London University to study medicine in 1842, and graduated with an M.B. in 1845. He spent four years at sea as assistant surgeon on H.M.S. *Rattlesnake*. After leaving the Navy, he lectured at the Royal School of Mines in London and became a naturalist for the Government Geological Survey. For over twenty years Huxley was the chief opponent of the orthodox point of view on the origin of man, winning an ongoing debate against such famous antagonists as the Bishop of Oxford and Gladstone. His labors won him honorary degrees from the universities of Edinburgh, Dublin, Oxford, and Cambridge. He received the Darwin Medal in 1894. His works include *Man's Place in Nature* (1863), *Lay Sermons, Addresses and Reviews* (1877), *Hume* (1878), and *Essays on Some Controverted Questions* (1892).

The method of scientific investigation is nothing but the expression of the necessary mode of working of the human mind. It is simply the mode at which all phenomena are reasoned about, rendered precise and exact. There is no more difference, but there is just the same kind of difference, between the mental operations of a man of science and those of an ordinary person, as there is between the operations and methods of a baker or of a butcher weighing out his goods in common scales, and the operations of a chemist in performing a difficult and complex analysis by means of his balance and finely-graduated weights. It is not that the action of the scales in the one case, and the balance in the other, differ in the principles of their construction or manner of working; but the beam of one is set on an infinitely finer axis than the other, and of course turns by the addition of a much smaller weight. 1

You will understand this better, perhaps, if I give you some familiar example. You have all heard it repeated, I dare say, that men of science work by means of Induction and Deduction, and that by the help of these operations, they, in a sort of sense, wring from Nature certain other things, which are called Natural Laws, and Causes, and that out of these, by some cunning skill of their own, they build up Hypotheses and Theories. And it is imagined by many, that the 2 operations of the common mind can be by no means compared with these processes, and that they have to be acquired by a sort of special apprenticeship to the craft. To hear all these large words, you would think that the mind of a man of science must be constituted differently from that of his fellow men; but if you will not be frightened by terms, you will discover that you are quite wrong, and that all these terrible apparatus are being used by yourselves every day and every hour of your lives.

There is a well-known incident in one of Molière's plays, where the author makes the hero express unbounded delight on being told that he had been talking prose during the whole of his life. In the same way, I trust, that you will take comfort, and be delighted with yourselves, on the discovery that you have been acting on the principles of inductive and deductive philosophy during the same period. Probably there is not one here who has not in the course of the day had occasion to set in motion a complex train of reasoning, of the very same kind, though differing of course in degree, as that which a scientific man goes through in tracing the causes of natural phenomena.

A very trivial circumstance will serve to exemplify this. Suppose you go into a fruiterer's shop, wanting an apple,—you take up one, and, on biting it, you find it is sour; you look at it, and see that it is hard and green. You take up another one, and that too is hard, green, and sour. The shopman offers you a third; but, before biting it, you examine it, and find that it is hard and green, and you immediately say that you will not have it, as it must be sour, like those that you have already tried.

Nothing can be more simple than that, you think; but if you will take the trouble to analyze and trace out into its logical elements what has been done by the mind, you will be greatly surprised. In the first place, you have performed the operation of Induction. You found that, in two experiences, hardness and greenness in apples go together with sourness. It was so in the first case, and it was confirmed by the second. True, it is a very small basis, but still it is enough to make an induction from; you generalize the facts, and you expect to find sourness in apples where you get hardness and greenness. You found upon that a general law, that all hard and green apples are sour; and that, so far as it goes, is a perfect induction. Well, having got your natural law in this way, when you are offered another apple which you find is hard and green, you say, "All hard and green apples are sour; this apple is hard and green, therefore this apple is sour." That train of reasoning is what logicians call a syllogism, and has all its various parts and terms,—its major premiss, its minor premiss, and its conclusion. And, by the help of further reasoning, which, if drawn out, would have to be exhibited in two or three other syllogisms, you arrive at your final determination, "I will not have that apple." So that, you see, you have, in the first place, established a law by Induction, and upon that you have founded a Deduction, and reasoned out the special conclusion of the particular case. Well now, suppose, having got your law, that at some time afterwards, you are discussing the qualities of apples with a friend: you will say to him, "It is a very curious thing,—but I find that all hard and green apples are sour!" Your friend says to you, "But how do you know that?" You at once reply, "Oh, because I have tried it over and over again, and have always found them to be so." Well, if we were talking science instead of common sense, we should call that an Experimental Verification. And, if still opposed, you go further, and say, "I have heard from the people in Somersetshire and Devonshire, where a large number of apples are grown, that they have observed the same thing. It is also found to be the case in Normandy, and in North America. In short, I find it to be the universal experience of mankind wherever attention has been directed to the subject." Whereupon, your friend, unless he is a very unreasonable man, agrees with you, and is convinced that you are quite right in the conclusion you have drawn. He believes, although perhaps he does not know he believes it, that the more extensive Verifications are,—that the more frequently experiments have been made, and results of the same kind arrived at,—that the more varied the conditions under which the same results have been attained, the more certain is the ultimate conclusion, and he disputes the question no further. He sees that the experiment has been tried under all sorts of conditions, as to time, place, and people, with the same result; and he says with you, therefore, that the law you have laid down must be a good one, and he must believe it.

In science we do the same thing;—the philosopher exercises 6
precisely the same faculties, though in a much more delicate manner. In scientific inquiry it becomes a matter of duty to expose a supposed law to every possible kind of verification, and to take care, moreover, that this is done intentionally, and not left to a mere accident, as in the case of the apples. And in science, as in common life, our confidence in a law is in exact proportion to the absence of variation in the result of our experimental verifications. For instance, if you let go your grasp of an article you may have in your hand, it will immediately fall to the ground. That is a very common verification of one of the best established laws of nature—that of gravitation. The method by which men of science establish the existence of that law is exactly the same as that by which we have established the trivial proposition about the sourness of hard and green apples. But we believe it in such an extensive, thorough, and unhesitating manner because the universal experience of mankind verifies it, and we can verify it ourselves at any time; and that is the strongest possible foundation on which any natural law can rest.

So much by way of proof that the method of establishing laws in 7
science is exactly the same as that pursued in common life. Let us now turn to another matter (though really it is but another phase of the same question), and that is, the method by which, from the relations of certain phenomena, we prove that some stand in the position of causes towards the others.

I want to put the case clearly before you, and I will therefore show 8
you what I mean by another familiar example. I will suppose that one of you, on coming down in the morning to the parlour of your house,

finds that a tea-pot and some spoons which had been left in the room on the previous evening are gone,—the window is open, and you observe the mark of a dirty hand on the window-frame, and perhaps, in addition to that, you notice the impress of a hob-nailed shoe on the gravel outside. All these phenomena have struck your attention instantly, and before two minutes have passed you say, "Oh, somebody has broken open the window, entered the room, and run off with the spoons and the tea-pot!" That speech is out of your mouth in a moment. And you will probably add, "I know there has; I am quite sure of it!" You mean to say exactly what you know; but in reality what you have said has been the expression of what is, in all essential particulars, an Hypothesis. You do not *know* it at all; it is nothing but an hypothesis rapidly framed in your own mind! And it is an hypothesis founded on a long train of inductions and deductions.

What are those inductions and deductions, and how have you got at   9 this hypothesis? You have observed, in the first place, that the window is open; but by a train of reasoning involving many Inductions and Deductions, you have probably arrived long before at the General Law—and a very good one it is—that windows do not open of themselves; and you therefore conclude that something has opened the window. A second general law that you have arrived at in the same way is, that tea-pots and spoons do not go out of a window spontaneously, and you are satisfied that, as they are not now where you left them, they have been removed. In the third place, you look at the marks on the windowsill, and the shoe-marks outside, and you say that in all previous experience the former kind of mark has never been produced by anything else but the hand of a human being; and the same experience shows that no other animal but man at present wears shoes with hob-nails on them such as would produce the marks in the gravel. I do not know, even if we could discover any of those "missing links" that are talked about, that they would help us to any other conclusion! At any rate the law which states our present experience is strong enough for my present purpose. You next reach the conclusion, that as these kinds of marks have not been left by any other animals than men, or are liable to be formed in any other way than by a man's hand and shoe, the marks in question have been formed by a man in that way. You have, further, a general law, founded on observation and experience, and that, too, is, I am sorry to say, a very universal and unimpeachable one,—that some men are thieves; and you assume at once from all these premises—and that is what constitutes your hypothesis—that the man who made the marks outside and on the windowsill, opened the window, got into the room, and stole your tea-pot and spoons. You have now arrived at a *Vera Causa;*—you have assumed a Cause which it is plain is competent to produce all the phenomena you have observed. You can explain all these phenomena only by the hypothesis of a thief. But that is a hypothetical conclusion, of the justice of which you have no absolute proof at all; it is only rendered highly probable by a series of inductive and deductive reasonings.

I suppose your first action, assuming you are a man of ordinary 10
common sense, and that you have established this hypothesis to your
own satisfaction, will very likely be to go off for the police, and set them
on the track of the burglar, with the view to the recovery of your
property. But just as you are starting with this object, some person
comes in, and on learning what you are about, says, "My good friend,
you are going on a great deal too fast. How do you know that the man
who really made the marks took the spoons? It might have been a
monkey that took them, and the man may have merely looked in
afterwards." You would probably reply, "Well, that is all very well, but
you see it is contrary to all experience of the way tea-pots and spoons
are abstracted; so that, at any rate, your hypothesis is less probable
than mine." While you are talking the thing over in this way, another
friend arrives, one of that good kind of people that I was talking of a
little while ago. And he might say, "Oh, my dear sir, you are certainly
going on a great deal too fast. You are most presumptuous. You admit
that all these occurrences took place when you were fast asleep, at a
time when you could not possibly have known anything about what
was taking place. How do you know that the laws of Nature are not
suspended during the night? It may be that there has been some kind
of supernatural interference in this case." In point of fact, he declares
that your hypothesis is one of which you cannot at all demonstrate the
truth, and that you are by no means sure that the laws of Nature are
the same when you are asleep as when you are awake.

Well, now, you cannot at the moment answer that kind of reason- 11
ing. You feel that your worthy friend has you somewhat at a disadvan-
tage. You will feel perfectly convinced in your own mind, however, that
you are quite right, and you say to him, "My good friend, I can only be
guided by the natural probabilities of the case, and if you will be kind
enough to stand aside and permit me to pass, I will go and fetch the
police." Well, we will suppose that your journey is successful, and that
by good luck you meet with a policeman; that eventually the burglar is
found with your property on his person, and the marks correspond to
his hand and to his boots. Probably any jury would consider those facts
a very good experimental verification of your hypothesis, touching the
cause of the abnormal phenomena observed in your parlour, and would
act accordingly.

Now, in this suppositious case, I have taken phenomena of a very 12
common kind, in order that you might see what are the different steps
in an ordinary process of reasoning, if you will only take the trouble to
analyze it carefully. All the operations I have described, you will see,
are involved in the mind of any man of sense in leading him to a
conclusion as to the course he should take in order to make good a
robbery and punish the offender. I say that you are led, in that case, to
your conclusion by exactly the same train of reasoning as that which a
man of science pursues when he is endeavouring to discover the origin
and laws of the most occult phenomena. The process is, and always
must be, the same; and precisely the same mode of reasoning was
employed by Newton and Laplace in their endeavours to discover and

define the causes of the movements of the heavenly bodies, as you, with your own common sense, would employ to detect a burglar. The only difference is, that the nature of the inquiry being more abstruse, every step has to be most carefully watched, so that there may not be a single crack or flaw in your hypothesis. A fláw or crack in many of the hypotheses of daily life may be of little or no moment as affecting the general correctness of the conclusions at which we may arrive; but in a scientific inquiry a fallacy, great or small, is always of importance, and is sure to be constantly productive of mischievous, if not fatal, results in the long run.

Do not allow yourselves to be misled by the common notion that an 13 hypothesis is untrustworthy simply because it is an hypothesis. It is often urged, in respect to some scientific conclusion, that, after all, it is only an hypothesis. But what more have we to guide us in nine-tenths of the most important affairs of daily life than hypotheses, and often very ill-based ones? So that in science, where the evidence of an hypothesis is subjected to the most rigid examination, we may rightly pursue the same course. You may have hypotheses and hypotheses. A man may say, if he likes, that the moon is made of green cheese: that is an hypothesis. But another man, who has devoted a great deal of time and attention to the subject, and availed himself of the most powerful telescopes and the results of the observations of others, declares that in his opinion it is probably composed of materials very similar to those of which our own earth is made up: and that is also only an hypothesis. But I need not tell you that there is an enormous difference in the value of the two hypotheses. That one which is based on sound scientific knowledge is sure to have a corresponding value; and that which is a mere hasty random guess is likely to have but little value. Every great step in our progress in discovering causes has been made in exactly the same way as that which I have detailed to you. A person observing the occurrence of certain facts and phenomena asks, naturally enough, what process, what kind of operation known to occur in nature applied to the particular case, will unravel and explain the mystery? Hence you have the scientific hypothesis; and its value will be proportionate to the care and completeness with which its basis had been tested and verified. It is in these matters as in the commonest affairs of practical life: the guess of the fool will be folly, while the guess of the wise man will contain wisdom. In all cases, you see that the value of the result depends on the patience and faithfulness with which the investigator applies to his hypothesis every possible kind of verification.

Study Questions

1. This selection is from a lecture Huxley delivered in 1863 to a group of "workingmen." What indications are there that Huxley was aware of his audience? How would you describe his tone? Is he funny? Does he talk down to his

audience? What changes would you recommend he make for a contemporary audience of workingmen?

2. Is Huxley's first sentence objective or subjective? With what kinds of evidence does he support that sentence?

3. By what means does Huxley attempt to allay his audience's fear of "large words"?

4. In what sense are Huxley's examples judiciously chosen? Do any of his examples seem too literary?

5. Comment on the transitions between paragraphs. Does any paragraph serve as a transition between major divisions of the selection?

Why the Sky Is Blue
SIR JAMES JEANS

Sir James Jeans (1877–1946) was educated at the Merchant Taylor's School, London, and Trinity College, Cambridge. He taught at Princeton, lectured at Cambridge, and served as a research associate at the Mt. Wilson Observatory. Jeans was honored by the Royal Society, the New York Museum of Science and Industry, and *Scientific Monthly,* among others. In many of his publications he made mathematics intelligible to the non-mathematically oriented. His books include *Radiation and Quantum Theory* (1914), *Astronomy and Cosmogony* (1928), *The Mysterious Universe* (1930), *The Stars in Their Courses* (1931), *Science and Music* (1937), and *Introduction to the Kenetic Theory of Gases* (1940).

Imagine that we stand on any ordinary seaside pier, and 1 watch the waves rolling in and striking against the iron columns of the pier. Large waves pay very little attention to the columns—they divide right and left and re-unite after passing each column, much as a regiment of soldiers would if a tree stood in their road; it is almost as though the columns had not been there. But the short waves and ripples find the columns of the pier a much more formidable obstacle. When the short waves impinge on the columns, they are reflected back and spread as new ripples in all directions. To use the technical term, they are "scattered." The obstacle provided by the iron columns hardly affects the long waves at all, but scatters the short ripples.

We have been watching a sort of working model of the way in 2

Sir James Jeans, "Why the Sky Is Blue," from *The Stars in Their Courses.* Reprinted by permission of the Cambridge University Press.

which sunlight struggles through the earth's atmosphere. Between us on earth and outer space the atmosphere interposes innumerable obstacles in the form of molecules of air, tiny droplets of water, and small particles of dust. These are represented by the columns of the pier.

The waves of the sea represent the sunlight. We know that 3 sunlight is a blend of lights of many colours—as we can prove for ourselves by passing it through a prism, or even through a jug of water, or as Nature demonstrates to us when she passes it through the raindrops of a summer shower and produces a rainbow. We also know that light consists of waves, and that the different colours of light are produced by waves of different lengths, red light by long waves and blue light by short waves. The mixture of waves which constitutes sunlight has to struggle through the obstacles it meets in the atmosphere, just as the mixture of waves at the seaside has to struggle past the columns of the pier. And these obstacles treat the light-waves much as the columns of the pier treat the sea-waves. The long waves which constitute red light are hardly affected, but the short waves which constitute blue light are scattered in all directions.

Thus, the different constituents of sunlight are treated in different 4 ways as they struggle through the earth's atmosphere. A wave of blue light may be scattered by a dust particle, and turned out of its course. After a time a second dust particle again turns it out of its course, and so on, until finally it enters our eyes by a path as zigzag as that of a flash of lightning. Consequently the blue waves of the sunlight enter our eyes from all directions. And that is why the sky looks blue.

Study Questions

1. Set up the terms of the analogy Jeans makes. Does it work? Find an example of metaphorical language within the analogy. Does it work?
2. Comment on the tone of this selection. Does Jeans use formal diction? Does he use scientific jargon?
3. Without the biographical note, is there internal evidence to demonstrate that Jeans is English?
4. Discuss the effectiveness or appropriateness of *thus* and *consequently* as transitional words.
5. Is the conclusion abrupt?

A Delicate Operation

ROY C. SELBY, JR.

Roy C. Selby, Jr. (1930–   ) was born in Little Rock, Arkansas. He received a B.S. from Louisiana State University (1952) and an M.D. from the University of Arkansas (1956). He presently practices medicine, specializing in neurosurgery, in Wheaton, Illinois. Selby has been honored by numerous professional and medical organizations, and was named Commander Defender of the King's Government of Malaysia in 1970. His articles and editorials have appeared in national and international professional journals.

In the autumn of 1973 a woman in her early fifties noticed, upon closing one eye while reading, that she was unable to see clearly. Her eyesight grew slowly worse. Changing her eyeglasses did not help. She saw an ophthalmologist, who found that her vision was seriously impaired in both eyes. She then saw a neurologist, who confirmed the finding and obtained X rays of the skull and an EMI scan—a photograph of the patient's head. The latter revealed a tumor growing between the optic nerves at the base of the brain. The woman was admitted to the hospital by a neurosurgeon. 1

Further diagnosis, based on angiography, a detailed X-ray study of the circulatory system, showed the tumor to be about two inches in diameter and supplied by many small blood vessels. It rested beneath the brain, just above the pituitary gland, stretching the optic nerves to either side and intimately close to the major blood vessels supplying the brain. Removing it would pose many technical problems. Probably benign and slow-growing, it may have been present for several years. If left alone it would continue to grow and produce blindness and might become impossible to remove completely. Removing it, however, might not improve the patient's vision and could make it worse. A major blood vessel could be damaged, causing a stroke. Damage to the undersurface of the brain could cause impairment of memory and changes in mood and personality. The hypothalamus, a most important structure of the brain, could be injured, causing coma, high fever, bleeding from the stomach, and death. 2

The neurosurgeon met with the patient and her husband and discussed the various possibilities. The common decision was to operate. 3

The patient's hair was shampooed for two nights before surgery. 4

She was given a cortisonelike drug to reduce the risk of damage to the brain during surgery. Five units of blood were cross-matched, as a contingency against hemorrhage. At 1:00 P.M. the operation began. After the patient was anesthetized her hair was completely clipped and shaved from the scalp. Her head was prepped with an organic iodine solution for ten minutes. Drapes were placed over her, leaving exposed only the forehead and crown of the skull. All the routine instruments were brought up—the electrocautery used to coagulate areas of bleeding, bipolar coagulation forceps to arrest bleeding from individual blood vessels without damaging adjacent tissues, and small suction tubes to remove blood and cerebrospinal fluid from the head, thus giving the surgeon a better view of the tumor and surrounding areas.

A curved incision was made behind the hairline so it would be   5
concealed when the hair grew back. It extended almost from ear to ear. Plastic clips were applied to the cut edges of the scalp to arrest bleeding. The scalp was folded back to the level of the eyebrows. Incisions were made in the muscle of the right temple, and three sets of holes were drilled near the temple and the top of the head because the tumor had to be approached from directly in front. The drill, powered by nitrogen, was replaced with a fluted steel blade, and the holes were connected. The incised piece of skull was pried loose and held out of the way by a large sponge.

Beneath the bone is a yellowish leatherlike membrane, the dura,   6
that surrounds the brain. Down the middle of the head the dura carries a large vein, but in the area near the nose the vein is small. At that point the vein and dura were cut, and clips made of tantalum, a hard metal, were applied to arrest and prevent bleeding. Sutures were put into the dura and tied to the scalp to keep the dura open and retracted. A malleable silver retractor, resembling the blade of a butter knife, was inserted between the brain and skull. The anesthesiologist began to administer a drug to relax the brain by removing some of its water, making it easier for the surgeon to manipulate the retractor, hold the brain back, and see the tumor. The nerve tracts for smell were cut on both sides to provide additional room. The tumor was seen approximately two-and-one-half inches behind the base of the nose. It was pink in color. On touching it, it proved to be very fibrous and tough. A special retractor was attached to the skull, enabling the other retractor blades to be held automatically and freeing the surgeon's hands. With further displacement of the frontal lobes of the brain, the tumor could be seen better, but no normal structures—the carotid arteries, their branches, and the optic nerves—were visible. The tumor obscured them.

A surgical microscope was placed above the wound. The surgeon   7
had selected the lenses and focal length prior to the operation. Looking through the microscope, he could see some of the small vessels supplying the tumor and he coagulated them. He incised the tumor to attempt to remove its core and thus collapse it, but the substance of the tumor was too firm to be removed in this fashion. He then began to

slowly dissect the tumor from the adjacent brain tissue and from where he believed the normal structures to be.

Using small squares of cotton, he began to separate the tumor from 8 very loose fibrous bands connecting it to the brain and to the right side of the part of the skull where the pituitary gland lies. The right optic nerve and carotid artery came into view, both displaced considerably to the right. The optic nerve had a normal appearance. He protected these structures with cotton compresses placed between them and the tumor. He began to raise the tumor from the skull and slowly to reach the point of its origin and attachment—just in front of the pituitary gland and medial to the left optic nerve, which still could not be seen. The small blood vessels entering the tumor were cauterized. The upper portion of the tumor was gradually separated from the brain, and the branches of the carotid arteries and the branches to the tumor were coagulated. The tumor was slowly and gently lifted from its bed, and for the first time the left carotid artery and optic nerve could be seen. Part of the tumor adhered to this nerve. The bulk of the tumor was amputated, leaving a small bit attached to the nerve. Very slowly and carefully the tumor fragment was resected.

The tumor now removed, a most impressive sight came into 9 view—the pituitary gland and its stalk of attachment to the hypothalamus, the hypothalamus itself, and the brainstem, which conveys nerve impulses between the body and the brain. As far as could be determined, no damage had been done to these structures or other vital centers, but the left optic nerve, from chronic pressure of the tumor, appeared gray and thin. Probably it would not completely recover its function.

After making certain there was no bleeding, the surgeon closed the 10 wounds and placed wire mesh over the holes in the skull to prevent dimpling of the scalp over the points that had been drilled. A gauze dressing was applied to the patient's head. She was awakened and sent to the recovery room.

Even with the microscope, damage might still have occurred to the 11 cerebral cortex and hypothalamus. It would require at least a day to be reasonably certain there was none, and about seventy-two hours to monitor for the major postoperative dangers—swelling of the brain and blood clots forming over the surface of the brain. The surgeon explained this to the patient's husband, and both of them waited anxiously. The operation had required seven hours. A glass of orange juice had given the surgeon some additional energy during the closure of the wound. Though exhausted, he could not fall asleep until after two in the morning, momentarily expecting a call from the nurse in the intensive care unit announcing deterioration of the patient's condition.

At 8:00 A.M. the surgeon saw the patient in the intensive care unit. 12 She was alert, oriented, and showed no sign of additional damage to the optic nerves or the brain. She appeared to be in better shape than the surgeon or her husband.

Study Questions

1. Notice how carefully Selby defines any scientific or medical term. How does he work them into the text without interrupting the flow of thought?
2. Selby's essay has three major sections. Find the transitional paragraphs between the sections.
3. Why are so many of Selby's sentences simple in structure? Does he use traditional topic sentences within paragraphs?
4. Comment on the final sentence of the essay. Is it humorous?

If It's Good Science Fiction . . .

The Writers Know Some Science

ISAAC ASIMOV

Isaac Asimov (1920–   ) was born in Petrovich, Russia, and became a United States citizen in 1928. A biochemist, he received his B.S. (1939), M.A. (1941), and Ph.D. (1948) from Columbia University. His verbal skill earned him the American Chemical Society's James T. Grady Award for scientific writing. Asimov's books include *Pebble in the Sky* and *I, Robot* (1950), *The Intelligent Man's Guide to Science* (1960), *Of Time and Space and Other Things* (1965), *Earth: Our Crowded Spaceship* (1974), *By Jupiter and Other Stories* and *Lecherous Limericks* (1975), and *Poems Annotated* (1977). He has written, astonishingly, approximately 200 books.

The phenomenal success of "Star Wars" could not help but   **1** stimulate a new wave of science fiction in the movies and on TV, and the first drenchings have already washed over our television screens. It is inevitable that along with the good comes the bad, and in the case of science fiction, at least, the bad is horrible.

Why is that? What makes some science fiction bad?   **2**

In considering a piece of science fiction writing, the first rule is   **3**

Isaac Asimov, "If It's Good Science Fiction . . .," Dec. 24, 1977. Reprinted with permission from *TV Guide* ® Magazine. Copyright © 1977 by Triangle Publications, Inc., Radnor, PA 19088.

that *if it is bad fiction, it is bad science fiction.* There is no magic that can convert something bad into something good just because it is science fiction.

The reverse is not true, however. *A piece of science fiction writing* 4 *may be good fiction but bad science fiction.*

There is an extra ingredient required by science fiction that makes 5 literary and dramatic virtue not entirely sufficient. There must also be some indication that the writer knows science.

This does not mean that the science has to be detailed and 6 stultifying; there need only be casual references—but the references must be correct. Nor does it mean that the writer cannot take liberties—but he must know what liberties he can take, and how he can justify them without sounding like an ignoramus.

It may be that most of the audience knows so little science that 7 they wouldn't recognize ignorance if they saw or heard it, or care either. That doesn't matter. I am not trying to define what makes a science fiction show popular or successful, but what makes it good. It is perfectly possible for a dreadful science fiction show (or a dreadful *anything* show) to make a lot of money, but that doesn't make it one whit less dreadful; it simply tells us something about the audience.

Let's take some examples.   8

I enjoyed "Star Wars." It is deliberately campy and it is utterly 9 brainless, but the special effects are fun and it is restful sometimes to park one's brain outside. One can even forgive the kind of slip that makes "parsec" a unit of speed rather than of distance, and consider it the equivalent of a typographical error.

But. The most popular scene in the picture involves numerous 10 extraterrestrials gathered round a bar, drinking. It is the interplanetary equivalent of the ask-no-questions-and-no-holds-barred saloon in many Westerns. As a deliberate satire on these Western bars, it is funny, and we must admire the imagination of the makeup artists in creating the different beings.

However, are all these strange beings perfectly at home in a single 11 atmosphere, at a single temperature and pressure? Should some not find an environment insufferable that others find comfortable?

It might spoil the fun if such a complication had to be introduced 12 and it could, after all, be supposed that all these creatures just happened to find an Earth-type atmosphere endurable. That would violate no scientific law; only the rules of probability.

Yet one of these creatures might have had to wear a spacesuit, or 13 might have had to keep sniffing at a gas cylinder, or ducking its head into a bowl of water. It would have meant very little trouble and would have made the scene much better science fiction.

Consider, in contrast, the television science fiction show *Logan's* 14 *Run.* Some of the people working for it also worked for *Star Trek,* so it's not surprising that its attitude toward science shows promise.

In one episode, for instance, an extraterrestrial spaceship is 15 picking up samples of the dominant species from different worlds. They have just picked up our hero and heroine, and on the ship are also several pairs of extraterrestrials who have been picked up on their own planets. One pair is in a cage that is filled with an atmosphere they can breathe but is poisonous to human beings. This is good science fiction, and it is satisfactory to have it made pertinent to the plot.

Consider another point from the same show. In recent years, there 16 has arisen the illiterate fancy that the word "galaxy" refers to anything not in our own solar system. Everyone and everything "comes from a different galaxy." (This is like supposing that everything that does not come from our own town comes from a different continent.)

In *Logan's Run,* however, one of the characters referred to ex- 17 traterrestrials as being "from another solar system" and a great peace descended on me. At least the writer knows what a galaxy is and is not.

No such effort is made in *Man from Atlantis.* The core of the plot 18 involves a creature (manlike, but a nonhuman species) who can live underwater and who has webbed hands and feet. We can accept that as given.

In one episode, Victor Buono, as the unctuously comic villain, is 19 melting the Earth's icecaps by a microwave device in order to raise the sea level and "attract attention."

The energy required to melt the icecaps as rapidly as he is 20 described as doing it would be utterly prohibitive. It would take centuries to melt the icecaps under any rational human-made urgings and, once partial melting had taken place, it would take centuries to persuade the water to refreeze.

There is almost an understanding of this. The villain gets the hero 21 to cooperate by saying he has ceased the melting process and shows faked movies to indicate the sea level is receding. After a long time, the hero suddenly realizes that the sea level wouldn't recede once the process is stopped. The excess water must evaporate first, he says. (That's right, and it must refreeze in the polar regions, which would take a long, long time.) He therefore knows that Buono has faked the picture and in his anger he does what he should have done at the very start—he destroys the microwave equipment with his mental powers.

And the instant the equipment is destroyed, the sea level *does* 22 recede. Unbearably bad science fiction!

Even children's programs must not show scientific ignorance— 23 they least of all, in fact. On Saturday mornings, there is *Space Academy* and in one recent episode two ships pass through a black hole and later return.

There isn't a single sign, however, that anyone connected with the 24 show knows one single thing about black holes, what they are or what they do.

It would seem that the hard-working, but uneducated, people 25 behind the show think that a black hole is a gap among the stars, or perhaps a space whirlpool, through which one can scoot and return.

Actually, a black hole is a quantity of mass so great and so 26 compressed as to produce a gravitational field that will let nothing escape, not even light. Anything moving too close to a black hole will fall in and be forever unable to emerge.

There are, indeed, some theories (not universally accepted) that if 27 a black hole rotates, matter falling in may emerge in a far different part of the universe. Even then, any organized bit of matter, such as a ship or a human being or even an atom, is destroyed, and will emerge as energy only.

A black hole can give rise to a number of highly dramatic 2. situations—but you must understand it first.

And although children's shows need not necessarily be educa- 2 tional, it is surely not too much to ask that they not be mis-educational.

To the general public, science fiction may seem to include the : "superman" story and, in fact, this can almost be justified.

The *Bionic Woman,* for instance, traces the superpowers of its protagonist to the use of powered prostheses and of bionic organs with greater ranges of abilities than the living organs they replace.

One can imagine, without too much embarrassment, an artificial eye sensitive to a broader range of light waves and to dimmer illumination than a natural eye is; or nuclear-powered limbs of supernormal strength and capable of great bursts of speed or thrust. Given that, one needs only imaginative plots and good acting (a big "only," of course) to have decent science fiction.

The *New Adventures of Wonder Woman,* on the other hand, is hopeless, since the conversion of an ordinary woman to a superkangaroo in red-white-and-blue is achieved merely by spinning in place (Superman at least stepped into a phone booth).

Wonder Woman is mere fantasy, therefore, and can in no way b considered science fiction. To be sure, lest anyone think I failed t notice, Wonder Woman herself is a supernormal resting place for th eye, but that doesn't constitute science fiction—just terrific biology.

Wonder Woman might be saved if it took the attitude that the ol *Batman* show did. In *Batman* the science was laughable, but it wa used for that very purpose. *Batman* was deliberate farce, which mad effective fun of many of the trappings of popular literature and science fiction, too. And it becomes good science fiction to make fun science fiction *knowledgeably.*

A very faint echo of that laughter is still to be found in t Saturday-morning cartoon version of *Batman.* A little mouseli creature, Batmite, is added, and, true to the tradition that superm: cles mean microbrains and vice versa, little Batmite is the or character in the cartoon that shows any spark of intelligence—a that must be on purpose.

Study Questions

1. What is a *paradox,* and is the distinction Asimov ma between good fiction and good science fiction parad. cal?
2. What is the thesis of this essay?
3. Comment on Asimov's use of *but* as a complete sente in paragraph 10.

4. Does Asimov define all the terms he uses? Compare, for instance, his use of *galaxy, solar system,* and *black hole.*
5. To what extent is his paragraphing traditional?
6. What distinction does Asimov make between *science fiction* and *science fantasy?*
7. How effective are Asimov's examples? Why?

Asimov, the Human Writing Machine
JAMES LINCOLN COLLIER

James Lincoln Collier (1928–   ) was born in New York City and educated at Hamilton College. He is a professional writer who travels widely, and has lived in London and Paris. Among his many, many books are *Cheers* (1961), *Somebody Up There Hates Me* (1963), *The Teddy Bear Habit, or, How I Became a Winner* (1967), *Which Musical Instrument Shall I Play?* (1969), *Why Does Everybody Think I'm Nutty?* (1971), *The Hard Life of the Teenager* (1972), *Inside Jazz* (1973), and *My Brother Sam Is Dead* (1974), which was nominated for a National Book Award and named a Newberry Honor Book. Collier has contributed nearly 600 articles, many of them about music, to both popular and scholarly periodicals.

Most of us find writing a four-line thank-you note troublesome. Even professional writers often have to drag themselves to the typewriter to face that blank page. What then are we to say about a man who would rather write than do anything else? A man who usually starts to write at eight o'clock in the morning and often goes on until ten o'clock at night, typing steadily at the rate of 90 words a minute. 1

Isaac Asimov is such a writing machine. "Thinking is the activity I love best," he says, "and writing is simply thinking through my fingers." In his 40-year literary career, the first 20 years part-time, he has written 188 books and 1,000 magazine and newspaper articles, particularly in the fields of science, math, and science fiction. At present he is writing about 12 books and 40 magazine articles a year, in addition to speeches, introductions and prefaces. Asimov also answers all his fan mail himself, some 70 letters a week. 2

He uses an electric typewriter (keeping two other machines in 3
reserve), and is usually working simultaneously in his New York City
study on any number of partially completed manuscripts—a magazine
article on the newest wrinkle in sub-atomic particles, a book on the
universe's "black holes," a science-fiction novel. If he bogs down
temporarily on one, he switches to another manuscript as easily as
other men change shirts.

But his work is not just quantity. Science-fiction writer Theodore 4
Sturgeon said in *The New York Times Book Review,* "Asimov has
achieved a unique status, for not only is he admired and, by many,
loved for his work in science fiction, but he is equally respected by
professionals in some 20-odd scientific disciplines."

This may make Asimov sound as if he were some pinch-faced robot 5
with a dictionary for a brain but, in fact, he is outgoing and loves to
talk and spin stories for hours. He gives more than 30 lectures a year.
"He is," says one friend, "a born ham," and on occasion he has asked a
program chairman what sort of speech he is to give as he is walking up
to the stage.

Almost from the moment he was born in 1920 in Petrovichi, 6
Russia, a little town 200 miles west of Moscow, Asimov showed a drive
for knowledge. When he was three, his father moved the family to
Brooklyn, where he thought prospects for his children would be better,
and opened the first of a succession of candy stores. Isaac's life revolved
around the store and the public library.

He taught himself to read at the age of five, and entered the first 7
grade as the only reader in his class. Thereafter he read omnivorously,
began skipping grades, and was 2½ years ahead when he entered the
ninth grade. "I had some problems with the other kids and I probably
deserved them," Asimov says today. "I was always shooting my hand
up to give the teacher the answer. I used to boast about getting 100
percent on tests, and I was always correcting people, including grown-
ups. But I didn't have the brains not to be snotty.

"I got my first library card when I was six, but we were allowed to 8
take out only two books at a time. I would pick out the biggest books I
could find to make them last and, when we got our new textbooks at
the beginning of each school year, I would read them all the first week.
I could remember everything I read, and even today I don't have to
research most of my books. The stuff is in my head, and all I have to do
is check the facts after I've finished writing."

At about the age of nine, he discovered science fiction in a 9
magazine called *Science Wonder Stories.* Thus began his lifetime love
affair with that genre. At age 11, he started writing a series of long
stories, and at 15 entered Columbia University in a pre-med course.
Then, at 17, it occurred to him that he might try to write for
publication. He made a stab at a piece, which he left unfinished, and
that might have been that, except that a year later he went down to the
offices of *Astounding Science Fiction,* the leading magazine in the field,
to see why the June issue was late.

As a result of his visit, he went back to the story he had started. 10
When it was finished, he took it to the editor of *Astounding,* at his

father's suggestion. John Wood Campbell, Jr., who was to become one of the foremost science-fiction editors, was cordial, and interested. He told Asimov later, "I saw something in you. As long as you were willing to work hard at improving, I was willing to work with you. "Six stories and four months later, Asimov sold his first magazine piece.

At 19, he graduated from Columbia but was turned down by 11 medical schools, probably because he was immature. "I was very upset because I had failed," Asimov says, "but I was relieved, too. I had never really wanted to be a doctor."

He thereafter did graduate study in chemistry, married, did war 12 work in a laboratory in Philadelphia and, in 1949, became an instructor in biochemistry at Boston University. He also continued to write, spending more and more evenings and weekends in an attic room, his fingers flying over typewriter keys.

By 1950, he had written *Nightfall* and the first volume of his 13 "Robot" series, probably his best-known short pieces, and had completed the *Foundation* trilogy, published shortly thereafter, on which his main fame in the world of science fiction rests.

Asimov also began to turn to nonfiction: as a writer *and* a scientist 14 he made an ideal combination. Quickly it became apparent that he had a gift for explaining complex subjects in ways that a layman could understand, and by the mid-1950s his writing was on the way to making him rich and famous.

When, in 1958, he suggested to his wife, Gertrude, that he give up 15 teaching to write full time, she wailed, "But what will we live on?"

"The books," he replied.   16

"Don't count on the books," she protested. "That won't last."   17

But he did quit teaching that year, and took to his attic. The 18 outpouring of books and articles became a torrent. Besides his array of science and science-fiction books, he has annotated Shakespeare's plays, Milton's *Paradise Lost,* Byron's *Don Juan* and the Bible. He has written history books, murder mysteries, children's books, joke books and three collections of mildly "Lecherous Limericks." (He writes these last on trains going to and from lectures, simply because he cannot keep his mind from writing.) He has also introduced a new magazine called *Isaac Asimov's Science Fiction Magazine.* What drives him so?

The fact is that Isaac Asimov, a confirmed work junkie, is also a 19 chronic and relentless worrier about everything and anything. His worries about planes force him to take trains to distant lectures. If his wife, Janet, whom he married in 1973 after the breakup of his first marriage, is five minutes late to meet him, he worries that she has been mugged or struck by a car.

Asimov's brother Stanley, assistant publisher of *Newsday,* reveals: 20 "Isaac worries about not being successful, about being poor. But it worries him that he's rich, too. He feels that if you're happy, some horrible fate will befall you."

In 1972, he discovered that he had a cancerous lump on his thyroid 21 gland, and an operation was needed. What worried Asimov? He thought, "I'm only 52; if I die now I'll look foolish, I'll look like a jerk, because I won't have done a full life's work." As if to remedy that situation, while in the hospital before the operation, he wrote a short mystery. It was not his possible death that worried him but the fear of not measuring up. Underneath the famous author there is a small boy worried that he is about to get a bad report card.

Actually, Asimov is worrying less these days. His second marriage 22 is a happy one, and his position in the world of books is secure. Says Carl Sagan, one of America's leading astronomers, "In this technological century, we need an interface between science and the public, and nobody can do that job as well as Asimov. He's the great explainer of the age."

Study Questions

1. What two major divisions does Collier's article contain?
2. What indications are there that Collier interviewed Asimov? Do any of the conversations seem fictitious?
3. What sort of man is Asimov? Comment on his personality. How does Collier create this impression?
4. Which paragraph compresses the most time? Does it work?
5. Collier says that beneath the famous author there is a worried small boy (paragraph 21). Does he mean Asimov is immature?
6. What does the quotation from Sagan contribute to Collier's portrait of Asimov?
7. After all is said and done, do you understand what makes Asimov run?

My Life with R. H. Macy
SHIRLEY JACKSON

Shirley Jackson (1919–1965) was born in California. She received her education at Syracuse University and lived for most of her adult life in Vermont. Her writings are concerned with disturbed, somtimes psychopathic, people and weird events, generally presented in understated, realistic settings. Among her novels are *The Road Through the Wall* (1948), *Hangsman* (1951), *The Bird's Nest* (1954), *The Sundial* (1958), and *The Haunting of Hill House* (1959). A short-story collection, *The Lottery* (1949), contains the story of the same title and is possibly her most famous work.

And the first thing they did was segregate me. They 1
segregated me from the only person in the place I had even a speaking
acquaintance with; that was a girl I had met going down the hall who
said to me: "Are you as scared as I am?" And when I said, "Yes," she
said, "I'm in lingerie, what are you in?" and I thought for a while and
then said, "Spun glass," which was as good an answer as I could think
of, and she said, "Oh. Well, I'll meet you here in a sec." And she went
away and was segregated and I never saw her again.

Then they kept calling my name and I kept trotting over to 2
wherever they called it and they would say ("They" all this time being
startlingly beautiful young women in tailored suits and with short-
clipped hair), "Go with Miss Cooper, here. She'll tell you what to do."
All the women I met my first day were named Miss Cooper. And Miss
Cooper would say to me: "What are you in?" and I had learned by that
time to say, "Books," and she would say, "Oh, well, then, you belong
with Miss Cooper here," and then she would call "Miss Cooper?" and
another young woman would come and the first one would say,
"13-3138 here belongs with you," and Miss Cooper would say, "What is
she in?" and Miss Cooper would answer, "Books," and I would go away
and be segregated again.

Then they taught me. They finally got me segregated into a 3
classroom, and I sat there for a while all by myself (that's how far
segregated I was) and then a few other girls came in, all wearing
tailored suits (I was wearing a red velvet afternoon frock) and we sat
down and they taught us. They gave us each a big book with R. H.
Macy written on it, and inside this book were pads of little sheets
saying (from left to right): "Comp. keep for ref. cust. d.a. no. or c.t. no.
salesbook no. salescheck no. clerk no. dept. date M." After M there was
a long line for Mr. or Mrs. and the name, and then it began again with
"No. item. class. at price. total." And down at the bottom was written
ORIGINAL and then again, "Comp. keep for ref.," and "Paste yellow gift
stamp here." I read all this very carefully. Pretty soon a Miss Cooper
came, who talked for a little while on the advantages we had in
working at Macy's, and she talked about the salesbooks, which it seems
came apart into a sort of road map and carbons and things. I listened
for a while, and when Miss Cooper wanted us to write on the little
pieces of paper, I copied from the girl next to me. That was training.

Finally someone said we were going on the floor, and we descended 4
from the sixteenth floor to the first. We were in groups of six by then,
all following Miss Cooper doggedly and wearing little tags saying BOOK
INFORMATION. I never did find out what that meant. Miss Cooper said I
had to work on the special sale counter, and showed me a little book
called *The Stage-Struck Seal*, which it seemed I would be selling. I had
gotten about halfway through it before she came back to tell me I had
to stay with my unit.

I enjoyed meeting the time clock, and spent a pleasant half-hour 5
punching various cards standing around, and then someone came in
and said I couldn't punch the clock with my hat on. So I had to leave,
bowing timidly at the time clock and its prophet, and I went and found
out my locker number, which was 1773, and my time clock number,

which was 712, and my cash-box number, which was 1336, and my cash-register number, which was 253, and my cash-register-drawer number, which was K, and my cash-register-drawer-key number, which was 872, and my department number, which was 13. I wrote all these numbers down. And that was my first day.

My second day was better. I was officially on the floor. I stood in a **6** corner of a counter, with one hand possessively on *The Stage-Struck Seal,* waiting for customers. The counter head was named 13-2246, and she was very kind to me. She sent me to lunch three times, because she got me confused with 13-6454 and 13-3141. It was after lunch that a customer came. She came over and took one of my stage-struck seals, and said "How much is this?" I opened my mouth and the customer said "I have a D.A. and I will have this sent to my aunt in Ohio. Part of that D.A. I will pay for with a book dividend of 32 cents, and the rest of course will be on my account. Is this book price-fixed?" That's as near as I can remember what she said. I smiled confidently, and said "Certainly; will you wait just one moment?" I found a little piece of paper in a drawer under the counter: it had "Duplicate Triplicate" printed across the front in big letters. I took down the customer's name and address, her aunt's name and address, and wrote carefully across the front of the duplicate triplicate "1 Stg. Strk. Sl." Then I smiled at the customer again and said carelessly: "That will be seventy-five cents." She said "But I have a D.A." I told her that all D.A.'s were suspended for the Christmas rush, and she gave me seventy-five cents, which I kept. Then I rang up a "No Sale" on the cash register and I tore up the duplicate triplicate because I didn't know what else to do with it.

Later on another customer came and said "Where would I find a **7** copy of Ann Rutherford Gwynn's *He Came Like Thunder?*" and I said "In medical books, right across the way," but 13-2246 came and said "That's philosophy, isn't it?" and the customer said it was, and 13-2246 said "Right down this aisle, in dictionaries." The customer went away, and I said to 13-2246 that her guess was as good as mine, anyway, and she stared at me and explained that philosophy, social sciences and Bertrand Russell were all kept in dictionaries.

So far I haven't been back to Macy's for my third day, because that **8** night when I started to leave the store, I fell down the stairs and tore my stockings and the doorman said that if I went to my department head Macy's would give me a new pair of stockings and I went back and I found Miss Cooper and she said, "Go to the adjuster on the seventh floor and give him this," and she handed me a little slip of pink paper and on the bottom of it was printed "Comp. keep for ref. cust. d.a. no. or c.t. no. salesbook no. salescheck no. clerk no. dept. date M." And after M, instead of a name, she had written 13-3138. I took the little pink slip and threw it away and went up to the fourth floor and bought myself a pair of stockings for $.69 and then I came down and went out the customers' entrance.

I wrote Macy's a long letter, and I signed it with all my numbers **9** added together and divided by 11,700, which is the number of employees in Macy's. I wonder if they miss me.

Study Questions

1. What satirical devices are used to present the experience in the story?
2. How does point of view contribute to the tone of the story?
3. At what point in the story does efficiency fail? Why?
4. Why is *segregated* used so often? Why do so many sentences begin with *and,* and so many paragraphs begin with words indicating time (such as *then, finally* and *later*)?
5. Comment on the variations in sentence structure and length.

The Stars
GEORGE SANTAYANA

George Santayana (1863–1952) was born in Madrid, Spain, and moved with his family to Boston in 1872. Although he attended the University of Berlin, he earned his B.A. (1886), M.A., and Ph.D. (1889) all at Harvard. Santayana taught philosophy at Harvard from 1889 to 1912, and then left the United States to spend the rest of his life in Oxford and Rome. He is generally considered among the most eminent of modern philosophers. Among his numerous books are philosophical studies: *The Sense of Beauty* (1896), *Reason in Religion* (1905), and *Realms of Being* (1942); poetry: *Lucifer: A Theological Tragedy* (1898) and *The Hermit of Carmel and Other Poems* (1901); and a novel, *The Last Puritan* (1935). His autobiography was published in three volumes: *Persons and Places* (1944), *The Middle Span* (1945), and *My Host the World* (1953). In his classes at Harvard were many who later achieved eminence, including T. S. Eliot, Conrad Aiken, Walter Lippmann, Felix Frankfurter, and Robert Benchley.

To most people, I fancy, the stars are beautiful; but if you 1 ask why, they would be at a loss to reply, until they remembered what they had heard about astronomy, and the great size and distance and possible habitation of those orbs. The vague and illusive ideas thus aroused fall in so well with the dumb emotion we were already feeling, that we attribute this emotion to those ideas, and persuade ourselves

George Santayana, "The Stars," in *Little Essays Drawn from the Writings of George Santayana,* Edited by Logan Pearsall Smith. Reprinted with the permission of Charles Scribner's Sons.

that the power of the starry heavens lies in the suggestion of astronomical facts.

The idea of the insignificance of our earth and of the incomprehen- **2** sible multiplicity of worlds is indeed immensely impressive; it may even be intensely disagreeable. There is something baffling about infinity; in its presence the sense of finite humility can never wholly banish the rebellious suspicion that we are being deluded. Our mathematical imagination is put on the rack by our attempted conception that has all the anguish of a nightmare and probably, could we but awake, all its laughable absurdity. But the obsession of this dream is an intellectual puzzle, not an aesthetic delight. Before the days of Kepler the heavens declared the glory of the Lord; and we needed no calculation of stellar distances, no fancies about a plurality of worlds, no image of infinite spaces, to make the stars sublime.

Had we been taught to believe that the stars governed our **3** fortunes, and were we reminded of fate whenever we looked at them, we should similarly tend to imagine that this belief was the source of their sublimity; and if the superstition were dispelled, we should think the interest gone from the apparition. But experience would soon undeceive us, and prove that the sensuous character of the object was sublime in itself. For that reason the parable of the natal stars governing our lives is such a natural one to express our subjection to circumstances, and can be transformed by the stupidity of disciples into a literal tenet. In the same way, the kinship of the emotion produced by the stars with the emotion proper to certain religious moments makes the stars seem a religious object. They become, like impressive music, a stimulus to worship. But fortunately there are experiences which remain untouched by theory, and which maintain the mutual intelligence of men through the estrangements wrought by intellectual and religious systems. When the superstructures crumble, the common foundation of human sentience and imagination is exposed beneath. Did not the infinite, by this initial assault upon our senses, awe us, and overwhelm us, as solemn music might, the idea of it would be abstract and mental like that of the infinitesimal, and nothing but an amusing curiosity. The knowledge that the universe is a multitude of minute spheres circling, like specks of dust, in a dark and boundless void, might leave us cold and indifferent, if not bored and depressed, were it not that we identify this hypothetical scheme with the visible splendor, the poignant intensity, and the baffling number of the stars. So far is the object from giving value to the impression, that it is here, as it must always ultimately be, the impression that gives value to the object. For all worth leads us back to actual feeling somewhere, or else evaporates into nothing—into a word and a superstition.

Now, the starry heavens are very happily designed to intensify the **4** sensations on which their fascination must rest. The continuum of space is broken into points, numerous enough to give the utmost idea of multiplicity, and yet so distinct and vivid that it is impossible not to remain aware of their individuality. The sensuous contrast of the dark background—the blacker the clearer the night and the more stars we can see—with the palpitating fire of the stars themselves, could not be exceeded by any possible device.

Fancy a map of the heavens and every star plotted upon it, even **5** those invisible to the naked eye: why would this object, as full of scientific suggestions surely as the reality, leave us so comparatively cold? The sense of multiplicity is naturally in no way diminished by the representation; but the poignancy of the sensation, the life of the light, are gone; and with the dulled impression the keenness of the emotion disappears. Or imagine the stars, undiminished in number, without losing any of their astronomical significance and divine immutability, marshalled in geometrical patterns; say in a Latin cross, with the words *In hoc signo vinces* in a scroll around them. The beauty of the illumination would be perhaps increased, and its import, practical, religious, and cosmic, would surely be a little plainer; but where would be the sublimity of the spectacle? Irretrievably lost; and lost because the form of the object would no longer tantalize us with its sheer multiplicity, and with the consequent overpowering sense of suspense and awe. Accordingly things which have enough multiplicity, as the lights of a city seen across water, have an effect similar to that of the stars, if less intense; whereas a star, if alone, because the multiplicity is lacking, makes a wholly different impression. The single star is tender, beautiful, and mild; we can compare it to the humblest and sweetest of things:

> A violet by a mossy stone
> Half hidden from the eye,
> Fair as *a star when only one*
> *Is shining in the sky.*

It is, not only in fact but in nature, an attendant on the moon, **6** associated with the moon, if we may be so prosaic here, not only by contiguity but also by similarity.

> Fairer than Phoebe's sapphire-regioned star
> Or vesper, amorous glow-worm of the sky.

The same poet can say elsewhere of a passionate lover:　　**7**

> He arose
> Ethereal, flushed, and like a throbbing star,
> Amid the sapphire heaven's deep repose.

How opposite is all this from the cold glitter, the cruel and **8** mysterious sublimity of the stars when they are many! With these we have no tender associations; they make us think rather of Kant who could hit on nothing else to compare with his categorical imperative, perhaps because he found in both the same baffling incomprehensibility and the same fierce actuality. Such ultimate feelings are sensations of physical tension.

Study Questions

1. Santayana's argument advances by *dismissing* reasons given for people believing that stars are beautiful. How many of these explanations does he discard? Where does he provide the answer to the "why" of the first paragraph?
2. What is the function of the fourth paragraph? Comment on the use of *now* followed by a comma.
3. Cite examples of *periodic sentences* in this essay.
4. Santayana uses similes and metaphors sparingly. How effective and appropriate are those that he does use?
5. Kepler, Kant, poets—what disciplines do these represent? How is Santayana's argument aided by the accretion?

The Star of the Magi
ARTHUR C. CLARKE

Arthur C. Clarke (1917–   ) is a native of Somersetshire, England. He was educated at King's College, University of London, and served in the British Civil Service and the Royal Air Force. At home in both space and undersea explorations, Clarke's writings encompass both areas. He suggested the use of space satellites for communication as early as 1945. Honors awarded him include the International Fantasy Award (1952), the Kalinga Prize (1961), and the Franklin Institute Ballantine Medal (1963). Clarke is probably best known to the general public as the author of the screenplay for *2001: A Space Odyssey,* written with Stanley Kubrick. His nonfiction works include *Interplanetary Flight* (1950), *The Coast of Coral* (1956), *The Challenge of the Sea* (1960), *Profiles of the Future* (1962), and *The Coming of the Space Age* (1967). He has also written numerous novels, and over 300 articles and short stories. His most recent book, *The View from Serendip,* was published in 1978.

G̲o out of doors any morning this December and look up at   1
the eastern sky an hour or so before dawn. You will see there one of the most beautiful sights in all the heavens—a blazing, blue-white beacon,

Reprinted by permission of the author and the author's agents, Scott Meredith Literary Agency, Inc., 845 Third Avenue, New York, NY 10022.

many times brighter than Sirius, the most brilliant of the stars. Apart from the Moon itself, it will be the brightest object you will ever see in the night sky. It will still be visible even when the Sun rises; you will even be able to find it at midday if you know exactly where to look.

It is the planet Venus, our sister world, reflecting across the gulfs 2 of space the sunlight glancing from her unbroken cloud shield. Every nineteen months she appears in the morning sky, rising shortly before the Sun, and all who see this brilliant herald of the Christmas dawn will inevitably be reminded of the star that led the Magi to Bethlehem.

What was that star, assuming that it had some natural explana- 3 tion? Could it, in fact, have been Venus? At least one book has been written to prove this theory, but it will not stand up to serious examination. To all the people of the Eastern world, Venus was one of the most familiar objects in the sky. Even today, she serves as a kind of alarm clock to the Arab nomads. When she rises, it is time to start moving, to make as much progress as possible before the Sun begins to blast the desert with its heat. For thousands of years, shining more brilliantly than we ever see her in our cloudy northern skies, she has watched the camps struck and the caravans begin to move.

Even to the ordinary, uneducated Jews of Herod's kingdom, there 4 could have been nothing in the least remarkable about Venus. And the Magi were no ordinary men; they were certainly experts on astronomy, and must have known the movements of the planets better than do ninety-nine people out of a hundred today. To explain the Star of Bethlehem we must look elsewhere.

The Bible gives us very few clues; all that we can do is to consider 5 some possibilities which at this distance in time can be neither proved nor disproved. One of these possibilities—the most spectacular and awe-inspiring of all—has been discovered only in the last few years, but let us first look at some of the earliest theories.

In addition to Venus, there are four other planets visible to the 6 naked eye—Mercury, Mars, Jupiter, and Saturn. During their move- ments across the sky, two planets may sometimes appear to pass very close to one another—though in reality, of course, they are actually millions of miles apart.

Such occurrences are called "conjunctions"; on occasion they may 7 be so close that the planets cannot be separated by the naked eye. This happened for Mars and Venus on October 4, 1953, when for a short while the two planets appeared to be fused together to give a single star. Such a spectacle is rare enough to be very striking, and the great astronomer Johannes Kepler devoted much time to proving that the Star of Bethlehem was a special conjunction of Jupiter and Saturn. The planets passed very close together (once again, remember, this was purely from the Earth's point of view—in reality they were half a billion miles apart!) in May, 7 B.C. This is quite near the date of Christ's birth, which probably took place in the spring of 7 or 6 B.C. (This still surprises most people, but as Herod is known to have died early in 4 B.C., Christ must have been born before 5 B.C. We should add six years to the calendar for A.D. to mean what it says.)

Kepler's proposal, however, is as unconvincing as the Venus 8
theory. Better calculations than those he was able to make in the
seventeenth century have shown that this particular conjunction was
not a very close one, and the planets were always far enough apart to
be easily separated by the eye. Moreover, there was a closer conjunction in 66 B.C., which on Kepler's theory should have brought a
delegation of wise men to Bethlehem sixty years too soon!

In any case, the Magi could be expected to be as familiar with such 9
events as with all other planetary movements, and the Biblical account
also indicates that the Star of Bethlehem was visible over a period of
weeks (it must have taken the Magi a considerable time to reach
Judea, have their interview with Herod, and then go on to Bethlehem).
The conjunction of two planets lasts only a very few days, since they
soon separate in the sky and go once more upon their individual ways.

We can get over the difficulty if we assume that the Magi were 10
astrologers ("Magi" and "magician" have a common root) and had
somehow deduced the birth of the Messiah from a particular configuration of the planets, which to them, if to no one else, had a unique
significance. It is an interesting fact that the Jupiter-Saturn conjunction of 7 B.C. occurred in the constellation Pisces, the Fish. Now though
the ancient Jews were too sensible to believe in astrology, the constellation Pisces was supposed to be connected with them. Anything
peculiar happening in Pisces would, naturally, direct the attention of
Oriental astrologers toward Jerusalem.

This theory is simple and plausible, but a little disappointing. One 11
would like to think that the Star of Bethlehem was something more
dramatic and not anything to do with the familiar planets whose
behavior had been perfectly well known for thousands of years before
the birth of Christ. Of course, if one accepts as *literally* true the
statement that "the star, which they saw in the east, *went before them,
till it came and stood over where the young Child was,*" no natural
explanation is possible. Any heavenly body—star, planet, comet, or
whatever—must share in the normal movement of the sky, rising in
the east and setting some hours later in the west. Only the Pole Star,
because it lies on the invisible axis of the turning Earth, appears
unmoving in the sky and can act as a fixed and constant guide.

But the phrase, "went before them," like so much else in the Bible, 12
can be interpreted in many ways. It may be that the star—whatever it
might have been—was so close to the Sun that it could be seen only for
a short period near dawn, and so would never have been visible except
in the eastern sky. Like Venus when she is a morning star, it might
have risen shortly before the Sun, then been lost in the glare of the new
day before it could climb very far up the sky. The wise men would thus
have seen it ahead of them at the beginning of each day, and then lost
it in the dawn before it had veered around to the south. Many other
readings are also possible.

Very well, then, can we discover some astronomical phenomenon 13
sufficiently startling to surprise men completely familiar with the
movements of the stars and planets and which fits the Biblical text?

Let's see if a comet would answer the specification. There have **14** been no really spectacular comets in this century—though there were several in the 1800s—and most people do not know what they look like or how they behave. They even confuse them with meteors, which any observer is bound to see if he goes out on a clear night and watches the sky for half an hour.

No two classes of object could be more different. A meteor is a speck **15** of matter, usually smaller than a grain of sand, which burns itself up by friction as it tears through the outer layers of Earth's atmosphere. But a comet may be millions of times larger than the entire Earth, and may dominate the night sky for weeks on end. A really great comet may look like a searchlight shining across the stars, and it is not surprising that such a portentous object always caused alarm when it appeared in the heavens. As Calpurnia said to Caesar:

When beggars die, there are no comets seen;
The heavens themselves blaze forth the death of princes.

Most comets have a bright, starlike core, or nucleus, which is **16** completely dwarfed by their enormous tail—a luminous appendage which may be in the shape of a narrow beam or a broad, diffuse fan. At first sight it would seem very unlikely that anyone would call such an object a star, but as a matter of fact in old records comets are sometimes referred to, not inaptly, as "hairy stars."

Comets are unpredictable: the great ones appear without warning, **17** come racing in through the planets, bank sharply around the Sun, and then head out toward the stars, not to be seen again for hundreds or even millions of years. Only a few large comets—such as Halley's— have relatively short periods and have been observed on many occasions. Halley's comet, which takes seventy-five years to go around its orbit, has managed to put in an appearance at several historic events. It was visible just before the sack of Jerusalem in A.D. 66, and before the Norman invasion of England in A.D. 1066. Of course, in ancient times (or modern ones, for that matter) it was never very difficult to find a suitable disaster to attribute to any given comet. It is not surprising, therefore, that their reputation as portents of evil lasted for so long.

It is perfectly possible that a comet appeared just before the birth of **18** Christ. Attempts have been made, without success, to see if any of the known comets were visible around that date. (Halley's, as will be seen from the figures above, was just a few years too early on its last appearance before the fall of Jerusalem.) But the number of comets whose paths and periods we do know is very small compared with the colossal number that undoubtedly exists. If a comet did shine over Bethlehem, it may not be seen again from Earth for a hundred thousand years.

We can picture it in that Oriental dawn—a band of light streaming **19** up from the eastern horizon, perhaps stretching vertically toward the zenith. The tail of a comet always points away from the Sun; the comet would appear, therefore, like a great arrow, aimed at the east. As the

Sun rose, it would fade into invisibility; but the next morning, it would be in almost the same place, still directing the travelers to their goal. It might be visible for weeks before it disappeared once more into the depths of space.

The picture is a dramatic and attractive one. It may even be the 20 correct explanation; one day, perhaps, we shall know.

But there is yet another theory, and this is the one which most 21 astronomers would probably accept today. It makes the other explanations look very trivial and commonplace indeed, for it leads us to contemplate one of the most astonishing—and terrifying—events yet discovered in the whole realm of nature.

We will forget now about planets and comets and the other 22 denizens of our own tight little Solar System. Let us go out across *real* space, right out to the stars—those other suns, many far greater than our own, which sheer distance has dwarfed to dimensionless points of light.

Most of the stars shine with unwavering brilliance, century after 23 century. Sirius appears now exactly as it did to Moses, as it did to Neanderthal man, as it did to the dinosaurs—if they ever bothered to look at the night sky. Its brilliance has changed little during the entire history of our Earth and will be the same a billion years from now.

But there are some stars—the so-called "novae," or new stars— 24 which through internal causes suddenly become celestial atomic bombs. Such a star may explode so violently that it leaps a hundred-thousand-fold in brilliance within a few hours. One night it may be invisible to the naked eye; on the next, it may dominate the sky. If our Sun became such a nova, Earth would melt to slag and puff into vapor in a matter of minutes, and only the outermost of the planets would survive.

Novae are not uncommon; many are observed every year, though 25 few are near enough to be visible except through telescopes. They are the routine, everyday disasters of the Universe.

Two or three times in every thousand years, however, there occurs 26 something which makes a mere nova about as inconspicuous as a firefly at noon. When a star becomes a *super*nova, its brilliance may increase not by a hundred thousand but by a *billion* in the course of a few hours. The last time such an event was witnessed by human eyes was in A.D. 1604; there was another supernova in A.D. 1572 (so brilliant that it was visible in broad daylight); and the Chinese astronomers recorded one in A.D. 1054. It is quite possible that the Bethlehem star was such a supernova, and if so one can draw some very surprising conclusions.

We'll assume that Supernova Bethlehem was about as bright as 27 the supernova of A.D. 1572—often called "Tycho's star," after the great astronomer who observed it at the time. Since this star could have been seen by day, it must have been as brilliant as Venus. As we also know that a supernova is, in reality, at least a hundred million times more brilliant than our own Sun, a very simple calculation tells us how far away it must have been for its *apparent* brightness to equal that of Venus.

It turns out that Supernova Bethlehem was more than three 28
thousand light years—or, if you prefer, 18 quadrillion miles—away.
That means that its light had been traveling for at least three
thousand years before it reached Earth and Bethlehem, so that the
awesome catastrophe of which it was the symbol took place five
thousand years ago, when the Great Pyramid was still fresh from the
builders.

Let us, in imagination, cross the gulfs of space and time and go 29
back to the moment of the catastrophe. We might find ourselves
watching an ordinary star—a sun, perhaps, no different from our own.
There may have been planets circling it; we do not know how common
planets are in the scheme of the Universe, and how many suns have
these small companions. But there is no reason to think that they are
rare, and many novae must be the funeral pyres of worlds, and perhaps
races, greater than ours.

There is no warning at all—only a steadily rising intensity of the 30
sun's light. Within minutes the change is noticeable; within an hour,
the nearer worlds are burning. The star is expanding like a balloon,
blasting off shells of gas at a million miles an hour as it blows its outer
layers into space. Within a day, it is shining with such supernal
brilliance that it gives off more light than *all the other suns in the
Universe combined.* If it had planets, they are now no more than flecks
of flame in the still-expanding shells of fire. The conflagration will
burn for weeks before the dying star collapses back into quiescence.

But let us consider what happens to the light of the nova, which 31
moves a thousand times more swiftly than the blast wave of the
explosion. It will spread out into space, and after four or five years it
will reach the next star. If there are planets circling that star, they will
suddenly be illuminated by a second sun. It will give them no
appreciable heat, but will be bright enough to banish night completely,
for it will be more than a thousand times more luminous than our full
Moon. All that light will come from a single blazing point, since even
from its nearest neighbor Supernova Bethlehem would appear too
small to show a disk.

Century after century, the shell of light will continue to expand 32
around its source. It will flash past countless suns and flare briefly in
the skies of their planets. Indeed, on the most conservative estimate,
this great new star must have shone over thousands of worlds before its
light reached Earth—and to all those worlds it appeared far, far
brighter than it did to the men it led to Judea.

For as the shell of light expanded, it faded also. Remember, by the 33
time it reached Bethlehem it was spread over the surface of a sphere
six thousand light-years across. A thousand years earlier, when Homer
was singing the songs of Troy, the nova would have appeared twice as
brilliant to any watchers further upstream, as it were, to the time and
place of the explosion.

That is a strange thought; there is a stranger one to come. For the 34
light of Supernova Bethlehem is still flooding out through space; it has
left Earth far behind in the twenty centuries that have elapsed since

men saw it for the first and last time. Now that light is spread over a sphere ten thousand light-years across and must be correspondingly fainter. It is simple to calculate how bright the supernova must be to any beings who may be seeing it now as a new star in *their* skies. To them, it will still be far more brilliant than any other star in the entire heavens, for its brightness will have fallen only by 50 percent on its extra two thousand years of travel.

At this very moment, therefore, the Star of Bethlehem may still be **35** shining in the skies of countless worlds, circling far suns. Any watchers on those worlds will see its sudden appearance and its slow fading, just as the Magi did two thousand years ago when the expanding shell of light swept past the Earth. And for thousands of years to come, as its radiance ebbs out toward the frontiers of the Universe, Supernova Bethlehem will still have power to startle all who see it, wherever—and whatever—they may be.

Astronomy, as nothing else can do, teaches men humility. We **36** know now that our Sun is merely one undistinguished member of a vast family of stars, and no longer think of ourselves as being at the center of creation. Yet it is strange to think that before its light fades away below the limits of vision, we may have shared the Star of Bethlehem with the beings of perhaps a million worlds—and that to many of them, nearer to the source of the explosion, it must have been a far more wonderful sight than ever it was to any eyes on earth.

What did they make of it—and did it bring them good tidings, or **37** ill?

Study Questions

1. How does Clarke help the layman to understand the scientific information presented here?
2. Cite specific examples of words and phrases that create the colloquial tone of this essay.
3. A number of the paragraphs in this essay are short. Why?
4. How does Clarke use questions in presenting his evidence? Comment on the concluding question. Does it introduce new material? Is the real point of this essay embedded in it?
5. Why does Clarke use personal pronouns, such as *you, us, we?*

The American Sparrow-Hawk
JOHN JAMES AUDUBON

John James Audubon (1785–1851) was born in New Orleans and educated in France. In 1803 he inherited the Audubon estate near Philadelphia, where he performed the first bird-banding experiments in America. From 1808 to 1820 he lived in Henderson, Kentucky, continuing his ornithological studies. A curious combination of scientist and artist, Audubon went to Great Britain in 1826 to find a publisher for his drawings of birds. *The Birds of America* was published between 1827 and 1838; *Ornithological Biographies,* the accompanying text, followed between 1831 and 1839. The Audubon Society, dedicated to the preservation and study of wildlife in America, was named for him.

F*alco sparverius,* Linn.   1

We have few more beautiful hawks in the United States than this active little species, and I am sure, none half so abundant. It is found in every district from Louisiana to Maine, as well as from the Atlantic shores to the western regions. Everyone knows the Sparrow-Hawk, the very mention of its name never fails to bring to mind some anecdote connected with its habits, and, as it commits no depredations on poultry, few disturb it, so that the natural increase of the species experiences no check from man. During the winter months especially it may be seen in the Southern States about every old field, orchard, barn-yard, or kitchen-garden, but seldom indeed in the interior of the forest.

Beautifully erect, it stands on the highest fence-stake, the broken   2
top of a tree, the summit of a grain stack, or the corner of the barn, patiently and silently waiting until it spies a mole, a field-mouse, a cricket, or a grasshopper, on which to pounce. If disappointed in its expectation, it leaves its stand and removes to another, flying low and swiftly until within a few yards of the spot on which it wishes to alight, when all of a sudden, and in the most graceful manner, it rises towards it and settles with incomparable firmness of manner, merely suffering its beautiful tail to vibrate gently for a while, its wings being closed with the swiftness of thought. Its keen eye perceives something beneath, when down it darts, secures the object in its talons, returns to its stand, and devours its prey piece by piece. This done, the little hunter rises in the air, describes a few circles, moves on directly, balances itself steadily by a tremulous motion of its wings, darts towards the earth, but, as if disappointed, checks its course, reascends

and proceeds. Some unlucky finch crosses the field beneath it. The Hawk has marked it, and, anxious to secure its prize, sweeps after it; the chase is soon ended, for the poor affrighted and panting bird becomes the prey of the ruthless hunter, who, unconscious of wrong, carries it off to some elevated branch of a tall tree, plucks it neatly, tears the flesh asunder, and having eaten all that it can pick, allows the skeleton and wings to fall to the ground, where they may apprise the traveller that a murder has been committed.

Thus, reader, are the winter months spent by this little marauder. 3 When spring returns to enliven the earth, each male bird seeks for its mate, whose coyness is not less innocent than that of the gentle dove. Pursued from place to place, the female at length yields to the importunity of her dear tormenter, when side by side they sail, screaming aloud their love notes, which if not musical, are doubtless at least delightful to the parties concerned. With tremulous wings they search for a place in which to deposit their eggs secure from danger, and now they have found it.

On that tall mouldering headless trunk, the hawks have alighted 4 side by side. See how they caress each other! Mark! The female enters the deserted Woodpecker's hole, where she remains some time measuring its breadth and depth. Now she appears, exultingly calls her mate, and tells him there could not be a fitter place. Full of joy they gambol through the air, chase all intruders away, watch the Grakles and other birds to which the hole might be equally pleasing, and so pass the time, until the female has deposited her eggs, six, perhaps even seven in number, round, and beautifully spotted. The birds sit alternately, each feeding the other and watching with silent care. After a while the young appear, covered with white down. They grow apace, and now are ready to go abroad, when their parents entice them forth. Some launch into the air at once, others, not so strong, now and then fall to the ground; but all continue to be well provided with food, until they are able to shift for themselves. Together they search for grasshoppers, crickets, and such young birds as, less experienced than themselves, fall an easy prey. The family still resort to the same field, each bird making choice of a stand, the top of a tree, or that of the Great Mullein. At times they remove to the ground, then fly off in a body, separate, and again betake themselves to their stands. Their strength increases, their flight improves, and the field-mouse seldom gains her retreat before the little Falcon secures it for a meal.

The trees, of late so richly green, now disclose the fading tints of 5 autumn; the cricket becomes mute, the grasshopper withers on the fences, the mouse retreats to her winter quarters, dismal clouds obscure the eastern horizon, the sun assumes a sickly dimness, hoarfrosts cover the ground, and the long night encroaches on the domains of light. No longer are heard the feathered choristers of the woods, who throng towards more congenial climes, and in their rear rushes the Sparrow-Hawk.

Its flight is rather irregular, nor can it be called protracted. It flies 6 over a field, but seldom farther at a time; even in barren lands, a few hundred yards are all the extent it chooses to go before it alights. During the love season alone it may be seen sailing for half an hour, which is, I believe, the longest time I ever saw one on the wing. When chasing a bird, it passes along with considerable celerity, but never attains the speed of the Sharp-shinned Hawk or of other species. When teazing an Eagle or a Turkey Buzzard, its strength seems to fail in a few minutes, and if itself chased by a stronger hawk, it soon retires into some thicket for protection. Its migrations are pursued by day, and with much apparent nonchalance.

The cry of this bird so much resembles that of the European 7 Kestrel, to which it seems allied, that, were it rather stronger in intonation, it might be mistaken for it. At times it emits its notes while perched, but principally when on the wing, and more continually before and after the birth of its young, the weaker cries of which it imitates when they have left the nest and follow their parents.

The Sparrow-Hawk does not much regard the height of the place in 8 which it deposits its eggs, provided it be otherwise suitable, but I never saw it construct a nest for itself. It prefers the hole of a Woodpecker, but now and then is satisfied with an abandoned crow's nest. So prolific is it, that I do not recollect having ever found fewer than five eggs or young in the nest, and, as I have already said, the number sometimes amounts to seven. The eggs are nearly globular, of a deep buff-colour, blotched all over with dark brown and black. This Hawk sometimes raises two broods in the season, in the Southern States, where in fact it may be said to be a constant resident; but in the Middle and Eastern States, seldom if ever more than one. Nay, I have thought that in the South the eggs of a laying are more numerous than in the North, although of this I am not quite certain.

So much attached are they to their stand, that they will return to it 9 and sit there by preference for months in succession. My friend Bachman informed me that, through this circumstance, he has caught as many as seven in the same field, each from its favourite stump.

Although the greater number of these Hawks remove southward at 10 the approach of winter, some remain even in the State of New York during the severest weather of that season. These keep in the immediate neighbourhood of barns, where now and then they secure a rat or a mouse for their support. Sometimes this species is severely handled by the larger Hawks. One of them who had caught a Sparrow, and was flying off with it, was suddenly observed by a Red-tailed Hawk, which in a few minutes made it drop its prey: this contented the pursuer and enabled the pursued to escape.

Theodore Lincoln, Esq. of Dennisville, Maine, informed me that 11 the Sparrow-Hawk is in the habit of attacking the Republican Swallow, while sitting on its eggs, deliberately tearing the bottle-neck-like entrance of its curious nest, and seizing the occupant for its prey. This is as fit a place as any to inform you, that the father of that gentleman, who has resided at Dennisville upwards of forty years, found the swallow just mentioned abundant there, on his arrival in that then wild portion of the country.

In the Floridas the Sparrow-Hawk pairs as early as February, in 12 the Middle States about April, and in the northern parts of Maine seldom before June. Few are seen in Nova Scotia, and none in Newfoundland, or on the western coast of Labrador. Although abundant in the interior of East Florida, I did not observe one on any of the keys which border the coast of that singular peninsula. During one of my journeys down the Mississippi, I frequently observed some of these birds standing on low dead branches over the water, from which they would pick up the beetles that had accidentally fallen into the stream.

No bird can be more easily raised and kept than this beautiful 13 Hawk. I once found a young male that had dropped from the nest before it was able to fly. Its cries for food attracted my notice, and I discovered it lying near a log. It was large, and covered with soft white down, through which the young feathers protruded. Its little blue bill and yet grey eyes made it look not unlike an owl. I took it home, named it Nero, and provided it with small birds, at which it would scramble fiercely, although yet unable to tear their flesh, in which I assisted it. In a few weeks it grew very beautiful, and became so voracious, requiring a great number of birds daily, that I turned it out, to see how it would shift for itself. This proved a gratification to both of us: it soon hunted for grasshoppers and other insects, and on returning from my walks I now and then threw a dead bird high in the air, which it never failed to perceive from its stand, and towards which it launched with such quickness as sometimes to catch it before it fell to the ground. The little fellow attracted the notice of his brothers, brought up hard by, who, accompanied by their parents, at first gave it chase, and forced it to take refuge behind one of the window-shutters, where it usually passed the night, but soon became gentle towards it, as if forgiving its desertion. My bird was fastidious in the choice of food, would not touch a Woodpecker, however fresh, and as he grew older, refused to eat birds that were in the least tainted. To the last he continued kind to me, and never failed to return at night to his favourite roost behind the window-shutter. His courageous disposition often amused the family, as he would sail off from his stand, and fall on the back of a tame duck, which, setting up a loud quack, would waddle off in great alarm with the Hawk sticking to her. But, as has often happened to adventurers of similar spirit, his audacity cost him his life. A hen and her brood chanced to attact his notice, and he flew to secure one of the chickens, but met one whose parental affection inspired her with a courage greater than his own. The conflict, which was severe, ended the adventures of poor Nero.

I have often observed birds of this species in the Southern States, 14 and more especially in the Floridas, which were so much smaller than those met with in the Middle and Northern Districts, that I felt almost inclined to consider them different; but after studying their habits and voice, I became assured that they were the same. Another species allied to the present, and alluded to by Wilson, has never made its appearance in our Southern States.

Falco sparverius, Linn. Syst. Nat. vol. i. p. 128. Lath. *Ind. Ornith. vol. i. p. 42.*—Ch. Bonaparte, *Synops. of Birds of the United States, p. 27.*

American Sparrow-Hawk, Falco sparverius, Wils. *Amer. Ornith. vol. ii.*
p. 117. pl. 16. fig. 1, Female; and vol. iv. p. 57. pl. 32. fig. 2, Male.
Nuttall, *Manual, part i. p. 58.*
Falco sparverius, Little Rusty-crowned Falcon, Swains *and* Richards.
Fauna Bor. Amer. Part ii. p. 31.

Adult Male.   15
Bill short, cerate at the base, the dorsal line curved in its whole
length; upper mandible with the edges slightly inflected, and forming a
small projecting process, the tip trigonal, acute, descending; lower
mandible inflected at the edges, with a notch near the end, which is
abrupt. Nostrils roundish, with a central papilla, and placed close to
the edge of the cere. Head rather large, flattened, neck short, body of
moderate size. Legs of ordinary length; tarsi roundish with two rows of
large scales before, three only below being transverse, with small
scales on the sides; toes scutellate above, scabrous and tuberculate
beneath; middle toe much longer than the outer, which is connected
with it by a small web; claws longish, curved, rounded, very acute.

Plumage compact on the back, blended on the head and under 16
parts. Feathers of the head and neck narrow, of the breast oblong, of
the back broad and rounded. Space between the bill and eye covered
with bristly feathers. Wings long, much pointed, the primaries taper-
ing, the second and third with their outer webs, the first and second
their inner ones sinuated; second quill longest. Tail long, moderately
rounded, of twelve rather narrow, rounded feathers.

Bill light blue, the tip black, the cere yellow. Iris brown. Feet 17
yellow; claws black. A circular patch of deep orange-brown on the
crown of the head, which is surrounded by a band of dark greyish-blue,
which is in contact a black spot on the nape; a patch of black descends
from the fore part of the eye, another immediately behind it, the cheek
between them being white, and there is a third farther back, and
surrounded by pale brown. A narrow line between the forehead and the
bill, and another over the eye, white. The back and scapulars are
brownish-red, with a few transverse black bars, the rump unspotted
and deeper. Tail of the same colour as the rump, with a broad
sub-terminal band of black, the tips white, as is the outer web of the
lateral feather, which on its inner web has five black bars (including
the sub-terminal one), the spaces between them white. The next
feather has also frequently a few marks of black and white. The
wing-coverts are greyish-blue, spotted with black. Quills brownish-
black, their inner webs transversely spotted with white. The throat,
hind part of the belly, and under tail-coverts, white; the breast
brownish-white, its fore part and sides, with the lower part of the neck,
marked with the guttiform black spots. Under wing-coverts white,
spotted with black.

Length 12 inches, extent of wings; bill along the back; tarsus 1 18
5/12; middle toe and claw 1 3/12.

Adult Female.   19
The female is similarly coloured, but the crown of the head is

marked with longitudinal black lines, and the back, which is of a duller
tint, with regular transverse bars of the same. The tail is barred with
black, the subterminal bar not nearly so broad as in the male, and the
tips brownish-white. The under surface is like that of the male, but the
breast and flanks are marked with oblong pale yellowish-brown
streaks, the spots on the inner webs of the quills are pale brown.

Length 12 inches.   **20**

Study Questions

1. Audubon is one of our best naturalists. Does he reveal
   anything of his own personality while describing the
   sparrow-hawk? Is he completely objective?
2. Which of the paragraphs would be more effective if
   divided? If combined?
3. What does Audubon accomplish by including information
   from Bachman and Theodore Lincoln?
4. How does Audubon's style before the break on page 201
   differ from his style after that break?

The Bird and the Machine
LOREN C. EISELEY

Loren C. Eiseley (1907-1977) was born in Lincoln, Nebraska. He
received his B.A. (1933) from the University of Nebraska, and his
M.A. (1935) and Ph.D. (1937) from the University of Pennsylvania.
He taught at the University of Kansas and Oberlin College before
returning, in 1947, to Pennsylvania, where he became University
Professor in Anthropology and History of Science and head of the
Department of the History and Philosophy of Science. A
Guggenheim fellow, he published widely in both popular periodi-
cals and learned journals. *Darwins's Century* received the Phi Beta
Kappa science award in 1958, and *The Firmament of Time* (1960)
received the John Burroughs medal and the Lecomte de Nöuy
award. His other books include *The Immense Journey* (1957),
Francis Bacon and the Modern Dilemma (1962), *Galapagos: The
Flow of Wilderness* (1968), *The Invisible Pyramid* (1970) and *All
The Strange Hours* (1975).

I suppose their little bones have years ago been lost among   1
the stones and winds of those high glacial pastures. I suppose their
feathers blew eventually into the piles of tumbleweed beneath the
straggling cattle fences and rotted there in the mountain snows, along
with dead steers and all the other things that drift to an end in the
corners of the wire. I do not quite know why I should be thinking of
birds over *The New York Times* at breakfast, particularly the birds of
my youth half a continent away. It is a funny thing what the brain will
do with memories and how it will treasure them and finally bring them
into odd juxtapositions with other things, as though it wanted to make
a design, or get some meaning out of them, whether you want it or not,
or even see it.

It used to seem marvelous to me, but I read now that there are   2
machines that can do these things in a small way, machines that can
crawl about like animals, and that it may not be long now until they do
more things—maybe even make themselves—I saw that piece in the
Times just now. And then they will, maybe—well, who knows—but you
read about it more and more with no one one making any protest, and
already they can add better than we and reach up and hear things
through the dark and finger the guns over the night sky.

This is the new world that I read about at breakfast. This is the   3
world that confronts me in my biological books and journals, until
there are times when I sit quietly in my chair and try to hear the little
purr of the cogs in my head and the tubes flaring and dying as the
messages go through them and the circuits snap shut or open. This is
the great age, make no mistake about it; the robot has been born
somewhat appropriately along with the atom bomb, and the brain they
say now is just another type of more complicated feedback system. The
engineers have its basic principles worked out; it's mechanical, you
know; nothing to get superstitious about; and man can always improve
on nature once he gets the idea. Well, he's got it all right and that's
why, I guess, that I sit here in my chair, with the article crunched in
my hand, remembering those two birds and that blue mountain
sunlight. There is another magazine article on my desk that reads
"Machines Are Getting Smarter Every Day." I don't deny it, but I'll
still stick with the birds. It's life I believe in, not machines.

Maybe you don't believe there is any difference. A skeleton is all   4
joints and pulleys, I'll admit. And when man was in his simpler stages
of machine building in the eighteenth century, he quickly saw the
resemblances. "What," wrote Hobbes, "is the heart but a spring, and
the nerves but so many strings, and the joints but so many wheels,
giving motion to the whole body?" Tinkering about in their shops it
was inevitable in the end that men would see the world as a huge
machine "subdivided into an infinite number of lesser machines."

The idea took on with a vengeance. Little automatons toured the   5
country—dolls controlled by clockwork. Clocks described as little
worlds were taken on tours by their designers. They were made up of
moving figures, shifting scenes and other remarkable devices. The life
of the cell was unknown. Man, whether he was conceived as possessing

a soul or not, moved and jerked about like these tiny puppets. A human being thought of himself in terms of his own tools and implements. He had been fashioned like the puppets he produced and was only a more clever model made by a greater designer.

Then in the nineteenth century, the cell was discovered, and the 6 single machine in its turn was found to be the product of millions of infinitesimal machines—the cells. Now, finally, the cell itself dissolves away into an abstract chemical machine—and that into some intangible, inexpressible flow of energy. The secret seems to lurk all about, the wheels get smaller and smaller, and they turn more rapidly, but when you try to seize it the life is gone—and so, by popular definition, some would say that life was never there in the first place. The wheels and the cogs are the secret and we can make them better in time— machines that will run faster and more accurately than real mice to real cheese.

I have no doubt it can be done, though a mouse harvesting seeds on 7 an autumn thistle is to me a fine sight and more complicated, I think, in his multiform activity, than a machine "mouse" running a maze. Also, I like to think of the possible shape of the future brooding in mice, just as it brooded once in a rather ordinary mousy insectivore who became a man. It leaves a nice fine indeterminate sense of wonder that even an electronic brain hasn't got, because you know perfectly well that if the electronic brain changes, it will be because of something man has done to it. But what man will do to himself he doesn't really know. A certain scale of time and a ghostly intangible thing called change are ticking in him. Powers and potentialities like the oak in the seed, or a red and awful ruin. Either way, it's impressive; and the mouse has it, too. Or those birds, I'll never forget those birds—yet before I measured their significance, I learned the lesson of time first of all. I was young then and left alone in a great desert—part of an expedition that had scattered its men over several hundred miles in order to carry on research more effectively. I learned there that time is a series of planes existing superficially in the same universe. The tempo is a human illusion, a subjective clock ticking in our own kind of protoplasm.

As the long months passed, I began to live on the slower planes and 8 to observe more readily what passed for life there. I sauntered, I passed more and more slowly up and down the canyons in the dry baking heat of mid-summer. I slumbered for long hours in the shade of huge brown boulders that had gathered in tilted companies out on the flats. I had forgotten the world of men and the world had forgotten me. Now and then I found a skull in the canyons, and these justified my remaining there. I took a serene cold interest in these discoveries. I had come, like many a naturalist before me, to view life with a wary and subdued attention. I had grown to take pleasure in the divested bone.

I sat once on a high ridge that fell away before me into a waste of 9 sand dunes. I sat through hours of a long afternoon. Finally, as I glanced beside my boot an indistinct configuration caught my eye. It was a coiled rattlesnake, a big one. How long he had sat with me I do

not know. I had not frightened him. We were both locked in the
sleepwalking tempo of the earlier world, baking in the same high air
and sunshine. Perhaps he had been there when I came. He slept on as I
left, his coils, so ill discerned by me, dissolving once more among the
stones and gravel from which I had barely made him out.

Another time I got on a higher ridge, among tough little wind- 10
warped pines half covered over with sand in a basin-like depression
that caught everything carried by the air up to those heights. There
were a few thin bones of birds, some cracked shells of indeterminable
age, and the knotty fingers of pine roots bulged out of shape from their
long and agonizing grasp upon the crevices of the rock. I lay under the
pines in the sparse shade and went to sleep once more.

It grew cold finally, for autumn was in the air by then, and the few 11
things that lived thereabouts were sinking down into an even chillier
scale of time. In the moments between sleeping and waking I saw the
roots about me and slowly, slowly, a foot in what seemed many
centuries, I moved my sleep-stiffened hands over the scaling bark and
lifted my numbed face after the vanishing sun. I was a great awkward
thing of knots and aching limbs, trapped up there in some long, patient
endurance that involved the necessity of putting living fingers into
rock and by slow, aching expansion bursting those rocks asunder. I
suppose, so thin and slow was the time of my pulse by then, that I
might have stayed on to drift still deeper into the lower cadences of the
frost, or the crystalline life that glistens pebbles, or shines in a
snowflake, or dreams in the meteoric iron between the worlds.

It was a dim descent, but time was present in it. Somewhere far 12
down in that scale the notion struck me that one might come the other
way. Not many months thereafter I joined some colleagues heading
higher into a remote windy tableland where huge bones were reputed
to protrude like boulders from the turf. I had drowsed with reptiles and
moved with the century-long pulse of trees; now, lethargically, I was
climbing back up some invisible ladder of quickening hours. There had
been talk of birds in connection with my duties. Birds are intense,
fast-living creatures—reptiles, I suppose one might say, that have
escaped out of the heavy sleep of time, transformed fairy creatures
dancing over sunlit meadows. It is a youthful fancy, no doubt, but
because of something that happened up there among the escarpments
of that range, it remains with me a lifelong impression. I can never
bear to see a bird imprisoned.

We came into that valley through the trailing mists of a spring 13
night. It was a place that looked as though it might never have known
the foot of man, but our scouts had been ahead of us and we knew all
about the abandoned cabin of stone that lay far up on one hillside. It
had been built in the land rush of the last century and then lost to the
cattlemen again as the marginal soils failed to take to the plow.

There were spots like this all over the country. Lost graves marked 14
by unlettered stones and old corroding rim-fire cartridge cases lying
where somebody had made a stand among the boulders that rimmed
the valley. They are all that remain of the range wars; the men are

under the stones now. I could see our cavalcade winding in and out through the mist below us: torches, the reflection of the truck lights on our collecting tins, and the far-off bumping of a loose dinosaur thigh bone in the bottom of a trailer. I stood on a rock a moment looking down and thinking what it cost in money and equipment to capture the past.

We had, in addition, instructions to lay hands on the present. The 15 word had come through to get them alive—birds, reptiles, anything. A zoo somewhere abroad needed restocking. It was one of those reciprocal matters in which science involves itself. Maybe our museum needed a stray ostrich egg and this was the payoff. Anyhow, my job was to help capture some birds and that was why I was there before the trucks.

The cabin had not been occupied for years. We intended to clean it 16 out and live in it, but there were holes in the roof and the birds had come in and were roosting in the rafters. You could depend on it in a place like this where everything blew away, and even a bird needed some place out of the weather and away from coyotes. A cabin going back to nature in a wild place draws them till they come in, listening at the eaves, I imagine, pecking softly among the shingles till they find a hole and then suddenly the place is theirs and man is forgotten.

Sometimes of late years I find myself thinking the most beautiful 17 sight in the world might be the birds taking over New York after the last man has run away to the hills. I will never live to see it, of course, but I know just how it will sound because I've lived up high and I know the sort of watch birds keep on us. I've listened to sparrows tapping tentatively on the outside of air conditioners when they thought no one was listening, and I know how other birds test the vibrations that come up to them through the television aerials.

"Is he gone?" they ask, and the vibrations come up from below, 18 "Not yet, not yet."

Well, to come back, I got the door open softly and I had the 19 spotlight all ready to turn on and blind whatever birds there were so they couldn't see to get out through the roof, I had a short piece of ladder to put against the far wall where there was a shelf on which I expected to make the biggest haul. I had all the information I needed just like any skilled assassin. I pushed the door open, the hinges squeaking only a little. A bird or two stirred—I could hear them—but nothing flew and there was a faint starlight through the holes in the roof.

I padded across the floor, got the ladder up and the light ready, and 20 slithered up the ladder till my head and arms were over the shelf. Everything was dark as pitch except for the starlight at the little place back of the shelf near the eaves. With the light to blind them, they'd never make it. I had them. I reached my arm carefully over in order to be ready to seize whatever was there and I put the flash on the edge of the shelf where it would stand by itself when I turned it on. That way I'd be able to use both hands.

Everything worked perfectly except for one detail—I didn't know 21 what kind of birds were there. I never thought about it at all, and it wouldn't have mattered if I had. My orders were to get something interesting. I snapped on the flash and sure enough there was a great beating and feathers flying, but instead of my having them, they, or rather he, had me. He had my hand, that is, and for a small hawk not much bigger than my fist he was doing all right. I heard him give one short metallic cry when the light went on and my hand descended on the bird beside him; after that he was busy with his claws and his beak was sunk in my thumb. In the struggle I knocked the lamp over on the shelf, and his mate got her sight back and whisked neatly through the hole in the roof and off among the stars outside. It all happened in fifteen seconds and you might think I would have fallen down the ladder, but no, I had a professional assassin's reputation to keep up, and the bird, of course, made the mistake of thinking the hand was the enemy and not the eyes behind it. He chewed my thumb up pretty effectively and lacerated my hand with his claws, but in the end I got him, having two hands to work with.

He was a sparrow hawk and a fine young male in the prime of life. I 22 was sorry not to catch the pair of them, but as I dripped blood and folded his wings carefully, holding him by the back so that he couldn't strike again, I had to admit the two of them might have been more than I could have handled under the circumstances. The little fellow had saved his mate by diverting me, and that was that. He was born to it, and made no outcry now, resting in my hand hopelessly, but peering toward me in the shadows behind the lamp with a fierce, almost indifferent glance. He neither gave nor expected mercy and something out of the high air passed from him to me, stirring a faint embarrassment.

I quit looking into the eye and managed to get my huge carcass 23 with its fist full of prey back down the ladder. I put the bird in a box too small to allow him to injure himself by struggle and walked out to welcome the arriving trucks. It had been a long day, and camp still to make in the darkness. In the morning that bird would be just another episode. He would go back with the bones in the truck to a small cage in a city where he would spend the rest of his life. And a good thing, too. I sucked my aching thumb and spat out some blood. An assassin has to get used to these things. I had a professional reputation to keep up.

In the morning, with the change that comes on suddenly in that 24 high country, the mist that had hovered below us in the valley was gone. The sky was a deep blue, and one could see for miles over the high out-croppings of stone. I was up early and brought the box in which the little hawk was imprisoned out onto the grass where I was building a cage. A wind as cool as a mounting spring ran over the grass and stirred my hair. It was a fine day to be alive. I looked up and all around and at the hole in the cabin roof out of which the other little hawk had fled. There was no sign of her anywhere that I could see.

"Probably in the next county by now," I thought cynically, but 25 before beginning work I decided I'd have a look at my last night's capture.

Secretively, I looked again all around the camp and up and down **26**
and opened the box. I got him right out in my hand with his wings
folded properly and I was careful not to startle him. He lay limp in my
grasp and I could feel his heart pound under the feathers but he only
looked beyond me and up.

I saw him look that last look away beyond me into a sky so full of **27**
light that I could not follow his gaze. The little breeze flowed over me
again and nearby a mountain aspen shook all its tiny leaves. I suppose
I must have had an idea then of what I was going to do, but I never let
it come up into consciousness. I just reached over and laid the hawk on
the grass.

He lay there a long minute without hope, unmoving, his eyes still **28**
fixed on that blue vault above him. It must have been that he was
already so far away in heart that he never felt the release from my
hand. He never even stood. He just lay with his breast against the
grass.

In the next second after that long minute he was gone. Like a **29**
flicker of light, he had vanished with my eyes full on him, but without
actually seeing even a premonitory wing beat. He was gone straight
into that towering emptiness of light and crystal that my eyes could
scarcely bear to penetrate. For another long moment there was silence.
I could not see. The light was too intense. Then from far up somewhere
a cry came ringing down.

I was young then and had seen little of the world, but when I heard **30**
that cry my heart turned over. It was not the cry of the hawk I had
captured; for, by shifting my position against the sun, I was now seeing
further up. Straight out of the sun's eye, where she must have been
soaring restlessly above us for untold hours, hurtled his mate. And
from far up, ringing from peak to peak of the summits over us, came a
cry of such unutterable and ecstatic joy that it sounds down across the
years and tingles among the cups on my quiet breakfast table.

I saw them both now. He was rising fast to meet her. They met in a **31**
great soaring gyre that turned to a whirling circle and a dance of
wings. Once more, just once, their two voices, joined in a harsh wild
medley of question and response, struck and echoed against the
pinnacles of the valley. Then they were gone forever somewhere into
those upper regions beyond the eyes of men.

I am older now, and sleep less, and I have seen most of what there **32**
is to see and am not very much impressed any more, I suppose, by
anything. "What Next in the Attributes of Machines?" my morning
headline runs. "It Might Be the Power to Reproduce Themselves."

I lay the paper down and across my mind a phrase floats insinuat- **33**
ingly: "It does not seem that there is anything in the construction,
constituents, or behavior of the human being which it is essentially
impossible for science to duplicate and synthesize. On the other hand
. . ."

All over the city the cogs in the hard, bright mechanisms have **34**
begun to turn. Figures move through computers, names are spelled out,
a thoughtful machine selects the fingerprints of a wanted criminal

from an array of thousands. In the laboratory an electronic mouse runs swiftly through a maze toward the cheese it can neither taste nor enjoy. On the second run it does better than a living mouse.

"On the other hand . . ." Ah, my mind takes up, on the other hand 35 the machine does not bleed, ache, hang for hours in the empty sky in a torment of hope to learn the fate of another machine, nor does it cry out with joy or dance in the air with the fierce passion of a bird. Far off, over a distance greater than space, the remote cry from the heart of heaven makes a faint buzzing among my breakfast dishes and passes on and away.

Study Questions

1. If one sentence can be called the *thesis sentence* of this essay, which sentence is it? How effective is the *transition* between this sentence and the paragraph following it?
2. The *introduction* to this essay is set off from the *body* of the essay by extra spacing. Why isn't the *conclusion* similarly set off?
3. The essay is entitled "The Bird and the Machine." Does it compare birds and machines? Contrast them? Both *compare and contrast* them?
4. What is the relationship of the episode of the bird to the thesis sentence?
5. What is your reaction to the conversation between the sparrows and the vibrations? Is it too "cute"?
6. Why is Eiseley slightly embarrassed by the bird's glance? Why does he say, "I quit looking into that eye . . ." instead of "those eyes"?

Hook
WALTER VAN TILBURG CLARK

Walter Van Tilburg Clarke (1900–1971) was a highly regarded
writer and teacher of creative writing whose stories and novels
about the West helped rescue Western fiction from the popularizers
of the Western "myth." His *The Ox-Bow Incident* (1940) is considered a classic Western novel. Among his other well-known works
are *The City of Trembling Leaves* (1945), *The Track of the Cat*
(1949), and *The Watchful Gods and Other Stories* (1950). He was in
great demand as a teacher of writers. He was Writer in Residence
at the University of Nevada, Visiting Lecturer at the universities
of Iowa, Utah, Wyoming, California, Washington, Oregon, and
Stanford University and Reed College, and later Writer in Residence at San Francisco State College. In 1945 he won the O. Henry
Memorial Award for "The Wind and the Snow of Winter."

I

Hook, the hawks' child, was hatched in a dry spring among the oaks, 1
beside the seasonal river, and was struck from the nest early. In the
drouth his single-willed parents had to extend their hunting ground by
more than twice, for the ground creatures upon which they fed died and
dried by the hundreds. The range became too great for them to wish to
return and feed Hook, and when they had lost interest in each other
they drove Hook down into the sand and brush and went back to
solitary courses over the bleaching hills.

Unable to fly yet, Hook crept over the ground, challenging all large 2
movements with recoiled head, erected, rudimentary wings, and the
small rasp of his clattering beak. It was during this time of abysmal
ignorance and continual fear that his eyes took on the first quality of a
hawk, that of being wide, alert and challenging. He dwelt, because of
his helplessness, among the rattling brush which grew between the
oaks and the river. Even in his thickets and near the water, the white
sun was the dominant presence. Except in the dawn, when the land
wind stirred, or in the late afternoon, when the sea wind became strong
enough to penetrate the half-mile inland to this turn in the river, the
sun was the major force, and everything was dry and motionless under
it. The brush, small plants and trees alike husbanded the little
moisture at their hearts; the moving creatures waited for dark, when
sometimes the sea fog came over and made a fine, soundless rain which
relieved them.

The two spacious sounds of his life environed Hook at this time. **3**
One was the great rustle of the slopes of yellowed wild wheat, with over
it the chattering rustle of the leaves of the California oaks, already as
harsh and individually tremulous as in autumn. The other was the
distant whisper of the foaming edge of the Pacific, punctuated by the
hollow shoring of the waves. But these Hook did not yet hear, for he
was attuned by fear and hunger to the small, spasmodic rustlings of
live things. Dry, shrunken, and nearly starved, and with his plumage
delayed, he snatched at beetles, dragging in the sand to catch them.
When swifter and stronger birds and animals did not reach them first,
which was seldom, he ate the small, silver fish left in the mud by the
failing river. He watched, with nearly chattering beak, the quick, thin
lizards pause, very alert, and raise and lower themselves, but could not
catch them because he had to raise his wings to move rapidly, which
startled them.

Only one sight and sound not of his world of microscopic necessity **4**
was forced upon Hook. That was the flight of the big gulls from the
beaches, which sometimes, in quealing play, came spinning back over
the foothills and the river bed. For some inherited reason, the big,
shipbodied birds did not frighten Hook, but angered him. Small and
chewed-looking, with his wide, already yellowing eyes glaring up at
them, he would stand in an open place on the sand in the sun and
spread his shaping wings and clatter his bill like shaken dice. Hook
was furious about the swift, easy passage of gulls.

His first opportunity to leave off living like a ground owl came **5**
accidentally. He was standing in the late afternoon in the red light
under the thicket, his eyes half-filmed with drowse and the stupefac-
tion of starvation, when suddenly something beside him moved, and he
struck, and killed a field mouse driven out of the wheat by thirst. It
was a poor mouse, shriveled and lice ridden, but in striking, Hook had
tasted blood, which raised nest memories and restored his nature. With
started neck plumage and shining eyes, he tore and fed. When the
mouse was devoured, Hook had entered hoarse adolescence. He began
to seek with a conscious appetite, and to move more readily out of
shelter. Impelled by the blood appetite, so glorious after his long
preservation upon the flaky and bitter stuff of bugs, he ventured even
into the wheat in the open sun beyond the oaks, and discovered the
small trails and holes among the roots. With his belly often partially
filled with flesh, he grew rapidly in strength and will. His eyes were
taking on their final change, their yellow growing deeper and more
opaque, their stare more constant, their challenge less desperate. Once
during this transformation, he surprised a ground squirrel, and although he was ripped and wingbitten and could not hold his prey, he
was not dismayed by the conflict, but exalted. Even while the wing was
still drooping and the pinions not grown back, he was excited by other
ground squirrels and pursued them futilely, and was angered by their
dusty escapes. He realized that his world was a great arena for killing,
and felt the magnificence of it.

The two major events of Hook's young life occurred in the same **6** day. A little after dawn he made the customary essay and succeeded in flight. A little before sunset, he made his first sustained flight of over two hundred yards, and at its termination struck and slew a great buck squirrel whose thrashing and terrified gnawing and squealing gave him a wild delight. When he had gorged on the strong meat, Hook stood upright, and in his eyes was the stare of the hawk, never flagging in intensity but never swelling beyond containment. After that the stare had only to grow more deeply challenging and more sternly controlled as his range and deadliness increased. There was no change in kind. Hook had mastered the first of the three hungers which are fused into the single, flaming will of a hawk, and he had experienced the second.

The third and consummating hunger did not awaken in Hook until **7** the following spring, when the exultation of space had grown slow and steady in him, so that he swept freely with the wind over the miles of coastal foothills, circling, and ever in sight of the sea, and used without struggle the warm currents lifting from the slopes, and no longer desired to scream at the range of his vision, but intently sailed above his shadow swiftly climbing to meet him on the hillsides, sinking away and rippling across the brush-grown canyons.

That spring the rains were long, and Hook sat for hours, hunched **8** and angry under their pelting, glaring into the fogs of the river valley, and killed only small, drenched things flooded up from their tunnels. But when the rains had dissipated, and there were sun and sea wind again, the game ran plentiful, the hills were thick and shining green, and the new river flooded about the boulders where battered turtles climbed up to shrink and sleep. Hook then was scorched by the third hunger. Ranging farther, often forgetting to kill and eat, he sailed for days with growing rage, and woke at night clattering on his dead tree limb, and struck and struck and struck at the porous wood of the trunk, tearing it away. After days, in the draft of a coastal canyon miles below his own hills, he came upon the acrid taint he did not know but had expected, and sailing down it, felt his neck plumes rise and his wings quiver so that he swerved unsteadily. He saw the unmated female perched upon the tall and jagged stump of a tree that had been shorn by storm, and he stooped, as if upon game. But she was older than he, and wary of the gripe of his importunity, and banked off screaming, and he screamed also at the intolerable delay.

At the head of the canyon, the screaming pursuit was crossed by **9** another male with a great wing-spread, and the light golden in the fringe of his plumage. But his more skillful opening played him false against the ferocity of the twice-balked Hook. His rising maneuver for position was cut short by Hook's wild, upward swoop, and at the blow he raked desperately and tumbled off to the side. Dropping, Hook struck him again, struggled to clutch, but only raked and could not hold, and, diving, struck once more in a passage, and then beat up, yelling triumph, and saw the crippled antagonist side-slip away, half-tumble once, as the ripped wing failed to balance, then steady and glide obliquely into the cover of brush on the canyon side. Beating hard and stationary in the wind above the bush that covered his competitor, Hook waited an instant, but when the bush was still, screamed again, and let himself go off with the current, reseeking, infuriated by the burn of his own wounds, the thin choke-thread of the acrid taint.

On a hilltop projection of stone two miles inland, he struck her 10 down, gripping her rustling body with his talons, beating her wings down with his wings, belting her head when she whimpered or thrashed, and at last clutching her neck with his hook and, when her coy struggles had given way to stillness, succeeded.

In the early summer, Hook drove the three young ones from their 11 nest, and went back to lone circling above his own range. He was complete.

II

Throughout that summer and the cool, growthless weather of the 12 winter, when the gales blew in the river canyon and the ocean piled upon the shore, Hook was master of the sky and the hills of his range. His flight became a lovely and certain thing, so that he played with the treacherous currents of the air with a delicate ease surpassing that of the gulls. He could sail for hours, searching the blanched grasses below him with telescopic eyes, gaining height against the wind, descending in mile-long, gently declining swoops when he curved and rode back, and never beating either wing. At the swift passage of his shadow within their vision, gophers, ground squirrels and rabbits froze, or plunged gibbering into their tunnels beneath matted turf. Now, when he struck, he killed easily in one hard-knuckled blow. Occasionally, in sport, he soared up over the river and drove the heavy and weaponless gulls downstream again, until they would no longer venture inland.

There was nothing which Hook feared now, and his spirit was 13 wholly belligerent, swift and sharp, like his gaze. Only the mixed smells and incomprehensible activities of the people at the Japanese farmer's home, inland of the coastwise highway and south of the bridge across Hook's river, troubled him. The smells were strong, unsatisfactory and never clear, and the people, though they behaved foolishly, constantly running in and out of their built-up holes, were large, and appeared capable, with fearless eyes looking up at him, so that he instinctively swerved aside from them. He cruised over their yard, their gardens, and their bean fields, but he would not alight close to their buildings.

But this one area of doubt did not interfere with his life. He ignored 14 it, save to look upon it curiously as he crossed, his afternoon shadow sliding in an instant over the chicken-and-crate-cluttered yard, up the side of the unpainted barn, and then out again smoothly, just faintly, liquidly rippling over the furrows and then over the stubble of the grazing slopes. When the season was dry, and the dead earth blew on the fields, he extended his range to satisfy his great hunger, and again narrowed it when the fields were once more alive with the minute movements he could not only see but anticipate.

Four times that year he was challenged by other hawks blowing up 15 from behind the coastal hills to scud down his slopes, but two of these he slew in mid-air, and saw hurtle down to thump on the ground and lie still where he circled, and a third, whose wing he tore, he followed closely to earth and beat to death in the grass, making the crimson jet out from its breast and neck into the pale wheat. The fourth was a strong flier and experienced fighter, and theirs was a long, running battle, with brief, rising flurries of striking and screaming from which down and plumage soared off.

Here, for the first time, Hook felt doubts, and at moments wanted 16 to drop away from the scoring, burning talons and the twisted hammer strokes of the strong beak, drop away shrieking, and take cover and be still. In the end, when Hook, having outmaneuvered his enemy and come above him, wholly in control, and going with the wind, tilted and plunged for the death rap, the other, in desperation, threw over on his back and struck up. Talons locked, beaks raking, they dived earthward. The earth grew and spread under them amazingly, and they were not fifty feet above it when Hook, feeling himself turning toward the underside, tore free and beat up again on heavy, wrenched wings. The other, stroking swiftly, so close to down that he lost wing plumes to a bush, righted himself and planed up, but flew on lumberingly between the hills and did not return. Hook screamed the triumph, and made a brief pretense of pursuit, but was glad to return, slow and victorious, to his dead tree.

In all these encounters Hook was injured, but experienced only the 17 fighter's pride and exultation from the sting of wounds received in successful combat. And in each of them he learned new skill. Each time the wounds healed quickly, and left him a more dangerous bird.

In the next spring, when the rains and the night chants of the little 18 frogs were past, the third hunger returned upon Hook with a new violence. In this quest, he came into the taint of a young hen. Others too were drawn by the unnerving perfume, but only one of them, the same with which Hook had fought his great battle, was a worthy competitor. This hunter drove off two, while two others, game but neophytes, were glad enough that Hook's impatience would not permit him to follow and kill. Then the battle between the two champions fled inland, and was a tactical marvel, but Hook lodged the neck-breaking blow, and struck again as they dropped past the treetops. The blood had already begun to pool on the gray, fallen foliage as Hook flapped up between branches, too spent to cry his victory. Yet his hunger would not let him rest until, late in the second day, he drove the female to ground among the laurels of a strange river canyon.

When the two fledglings of this second brood had been driven from 19 the nest, and Hook had returned to his own range, he was not only complete, but supreme. He slept without concealment on his bare limb, and did not open his eyes when, in the night, the heavy-billed cranes coughed in the shallows below him.

III

The turning point of Hook's career came that autumn, when the brush 20
in the canyons rustled dryly and the hills, mowed close by the cattle,
smoked under the wind as if burning. One midafternoon, when the
black clouds were torn on the rim of the sea and the surf flowered white
and high on the rocks, raining in over the low cliffs, Hook rode the
wind diagonally across the river mouth. His great eyes, focused for
small things stirring in the dust and leaves, overlooked so large and
slow a movement as that of the Japanese farmer rising from the brush
and lifting the two black eyes of his shotgun. Too late Hook saw and,
startled, swerved, but wrongly. The surf muffled the reports, and
nearly without sound, Hook felt the minute whips of the first shot, and
the astounding, breath-taking blow of the second.

Beating his good wing, tasting the blood that quickly swelled into 21
his beak, he tumbled off with the wind and stuck into the thickets on
the far side of the river mouth. The branches tore him. Wild with rage,
he thrust up and clattered his beak, challenging, but when he had
fallen over twice, he knew that the trailing wing would not carry, and
then heard the boots of the hunter among the stones in the river bed
and, seeing him loom at the edge of the bushes, crept back among the
thickest brush and was still. When he saw the boots stand before him,
he reared back, lifting his good wing and cocking his head for the
serpent-like blow, his beak open but soundless, his great eyes hard and
very shining. The boots passed on. The Japanese farmer, who believed
that he had lost chickens, and who had cunningly observed Hook's
flight for many afternoons, until he could plot it, did not greatly want a
dead hawk.

When Hook could hear nothing but the surf and the wind in the 22
thicket, he let the sickness and shock overcome him. The fine film of
the inner lid dropped over his big eyes. His heart beat frantically, so
that it made the plumage of his shot-aching breast throb. His own
blood throttled his breathing. But these things were nothing compared
to the lightning of pain in his left shoulder, where the shot had
bunched, shattering the airy bones so the pinions trailed on the ground
and could not be lifted. Yet, when a sparrow lit in the bush over him,
Hook's eyes flew open again, hard and challenging, his good wing was
lifted and his beak strained open. The startled sparrow darted piping
out over the river.

Throughout that night, while the long clouds blew across the stars 23
and the wind shook the bushes about him, and throughout the next
day, while the clouds still blew and massed until there was no gleam of
sunlight on the sand bar, Hook remained stationary, enduring his
sickness. In the second evening, the rains began. First there was a
long, running patter of drops upon the beach and over the dry trees and
bushes. At dusk there came a heavier squall, which did not die
entirely, but slacked off to a continual, spaced splashing of big drops,
and then returned with the front of the storm. In long, misty curtains,
gust by gust, the rain swept over the sea, beating down its heavy, and

coursed up the beach. The little jets of dust ceased to rise about the drops in the fields, and the mud began to gleam. Among the boulders of the river bed, darkling pools grew slowly.

Still Hook stood behind his tree from the wind, only gentle drops **24** reaching him, falling from the upper branches and then again from the brush. His eyes remained closed, and he could still taste his own blood in his mouth, although it had ceased to come up freshly. Out beyond him, he heard the storm changing. As rain conquered the sea, the heave of the surf became a hushed sound, often lost in the crying of the wind. Then gradually, as the night turned toward morning, the wind also was broken by the rain. The crying became fainter, the rain settled toward steadiness, and the creep of the waves could be heard again, quiet and regular upon the beach.

At dawn there was no wind and no sun, but everywhere the roaring **25** of the vertical, relentless rain. Hook then crept among the rapid drippings of the bushes, dragging his torn sail, seeking better shelter. He stopped often and stood with the shutters of film drawn over his eyes. At midmorning he found a little cave under a ledge at the base of the sea cliff. Here, lost without branches and leaves about him, he settled to await improvement.

When, at midday of the third day, the rain stopped altogether, and **26** the sky opened before a small, fresh wind, letting light through to glitter upon a tremulous sea, Hook was so weak that his good wing trailed also to prop him upright, and his open eyes were lusterless. But his wounds were hardened, and he felt the return of hunger. Beyond his shelter, he heard the gulls flying in great numbers and crying their joy at the cleared air. He could even hear, from the fringe of the river, the ecstatic and unstinted bubblings and chirpings of the small birds. The grassland, he felt, would be full of the stirring anew of the close-bound life, the undrowned insects clicking as they dried out, the snakes slithering down, heads half erect, into the grasses where the mice, gophers and ground squirrels ran and stopped and chewed and licked themselves smoother and drier.

With the aid of his hunger, and on the crutches of his wings, Hook **27** came down to stand in the sun beside his cave, whence he could watch the beach. Before him, in ellipses on tilting planes, the gulls flew. The surf was rearing again, and beginning to shelve and hiss on the sand. Through the white foam-writing it left, the long-billed pipers twinkled in bevies, escaping each wave, then racing down after it to plunge their fine drills into the minute double holes where the sand crabs bubbled. In the third row of breakers two seals lifted sleek, streaming heads and barked, and over them, trailing his spider legs, a great crane flew south. Among the stones at the foot of the cliff, small red and green crabs made a little, continuous rattling and knocking. The cliff swallows glittered and twanged on aerial forays.

The afternoon began auspiciously for Hook also. One of the two **28** gulls which came squabbling above him dropped a freshly caught fish to the sand. Quickly Hook was upon it. Gripping it, he raised his good wing and cocked his head with open beak at the many gulls which had

circled and come down at once toward the fall of the fish. The gulls
sheered off, cursing raucously. Left alone on the sand, Hook devoured
the fish and, after resting in the sun, withdrew again to his shelter.

IV

In the succeeding days, between rains, he foraged on the beach. He **29**
learned to kill and crack the small green crabs. Along the edge of the
river mouth, he found the drowned bodies of mice and squirrels and
even sparrows. Twice he managed to drive feeding gulls from their
catch, charging upon them with buffeting wing and clattering beak. He
grew stronger slowly, but the shot sail continued to drag. Often, at the
choking thought of soaring and striking and the good, hot-blood kill, he
strove to take off, but only the one wing came up, winnowing with a
hiss, and drove him over onto his side in the sand. After these futile
trials, he would rage and clatter. But gradually he learned to believe
that he could not fly, that his life must now be that of the discharged
nestling again. Denied the joy of space, without which the joy of
loneliness was lost, the joy of battle and killing, the blood lust, became
his whole concentration. It was his hope, as he charged feeding gulls,
that they would turn and offer battle, but they never did. The
sandpipers, at his approach, fled peeping, or, like a quiver of arrows
shot together, streamed out over the surf in a long curve. Once, pent
beyond bearing, he disgraced himself by shrieking challenge at the
businesslike heron which flew south every evening at the same time.
The heron did not even turn his head, but flapped and glided on.

Hook's shame and anger became such that he stood awake at **30**
night. Hunger kept him awake also, for these little things of the gulls
could not sustain his great body in its renewed violence. He became
aware that the gulls slept at night in flocks on the sand, each with one
leg tucked under him. He discovered also that the curlews and the
pipers, often mingling, likewise slept, on the higher remnant of the
bar. A sensation of evil delight filled him in the consideration of
protracted striking among them.

There was only half of a sick moon in a sky of running but **31**
far-separated clouds on the night when he managed to stalk into the
center of the sleeping gulls. This was light enough, but so great was his
vengeful pleasure that there broke from him a shrill scream of
challenge as he first struck. Without the power of flight behind it, the
blow was not murderous, and this newly discovered impotence made
Hook crazy, so that he screamed again and again as he struck and tore
at the felled gull. He slew the one, but was twice knocked over by its
heavy flounderings, and all the others rose above him, weaving and
screaming, protesting in the thin moonlight. Wakened by their clamor,
the wading birds also took wing, startled and plaintive. When the
beach was quiet again, the flocks had settled elsewhere, beyond his
pitiful range, and he was left alone beside the single kill. It was
a disappointing victory. He fed with lowering spirit.

Thereafter, he stalked silently. At sunset he would watch where 32
the gulls settled along the miles of beach, and after dark he would come
like a sharp shadow among them, and drive with his hook on all sides
of him, till the beatings of a poorly struck victim sent the flock up.
Then he would turn vindictively upon the fallen and finish them. In his
best night, he killed five from one flock. But he ate only a little from
one, for the vigor resulting from occasional repletion strengthened only
his ire, which became so great at such a time that food revolted him. It
was not the joyous, swift, controlled hunting anger of a sane hawk, but
something quite different, which made him dizzy if it continued too
long, and left him unsatisfied with any kill.

Then one day, when he had very nearly struck a gull while driving 33
it from a gasping yellowfin, the gull's wing rapped against him as it
broke for its running start, and, the trailing wing failing to support
him, he was knocked over. He flurried awkwardly in the sand to regain
his feet, but his mastery of the beach was ended. Seeing him, in clear
sunlight, struggling after the chance blow, the gulls returned about
him in a flashing cloud, circling and pecking on the wing. Hook's
plumage showed quick little jets of irregularity here and there. He
reared back, clattering and erecting the good wing, spreading the
great, rusty tail for balance. His eyes shone with a little of the old
pleasure. But it died, for he could reach none of them. He was forced to
turn and dance awkwardly on the sand, trying to clash bills with each
tormentor. They banked up quealing and returned, weaving about him
in concentric and overlapping circles. His scream was lost in their
clamor, and he appeared merely to be hopping clumsily with his mouth
open. Again he fell sideways. Before he could right himself, he was
bowled over, and a second time, and lay on his side, twisting his neck to
reach them and clappering in blind fury, and was stuck three times by
three successive gulls, shrieking their flock triumph.

Finally he managed to roll to his breast, and to crouch with his 34
good wing spread wide and the other stretched nearly as far, so that he
extended like a gigantic moth, only his snake head, with its now silent
scimitar, erect. One great eye blazed under its level brow, but where
the other had been was a shallow hole from which thin blood trickled to
his russet gap.

In this crouch, by short stages, stopping repeatedly to turn and 35
drive the gulls up, Hook dragged into the river canyon and under the
stiff cover of the bitter-leafed laurel. There the gulls left him, soaring
up with great clatter of their valor. Till nearly sunset Hook, broken
spirited and enduring his hardening eye socket, heard them celebrat-
ing over the waves.

When his will was somewhat replenished, and his empty eye 36
socket had stopped the twitching and vague aching which had forced
him often to roll ignominiously to rub it in the dust, Hook ventured
from the protective lacings of his thicket. He knew fear again, and the
challenge of his remaining eye was once more strident, as in adolescence. He dared not return to the beaches, and with a new, weak
hunger, the home hunger, enticing him, made his way by short

hunting journeys back to the wild wheat slopes and the crisp oaks. There was in Hook an unwonted sensation now, that of the ever-neighboring possibility of death. This sensation was beginning, after his period as a mad bird on the beach, to solidify him into his last stage of life. When, during his slow homeward passage, the gulls wafted inland over him, watching the earth with curious, miserish eyes, he did not cower, but neither did he challenge, either by opened beak or by raised shoulder. He merely watched carefully, learning his first lessons in observing the world with one eye.

At first the familiar surroundings of the bend in the river and the 37 tree with the dead limb to which he could not ascend, aggravated his humiliation, but in time, forced to live cunningly and half-starved, he lost much of his savage pride. At the first flight of a strange hawk over his realm, he was wild at his helplessness, and kept twisting his head like an owl, or spinning in the grass like a small and feathered dervish, to keep the hateful beauty of the windrider in sight. But in the succeeding weeks, as one after another coasted his beat, his resentment declined, and when one of the raiders, a haughty yearling, sighted his upstaring eye, and plunged and struck him dreadfully, and failed to kill him only because he dragged under a thicket in time, the second of his great hungers was gone. He had no longer the true lust to kill, no joy of battle, but only the poor desire to fill his belly.

Then truly he lived in the wheat and the brush like a ground owl, 38 ridden with ground lice, dusty or muddy, even half-starved, forced to sit for hours by small holes for petty and unsatisfying kills. Only once during the final months before his end did he make a kill where the breath of danger recalled his valor, and then the danger was such as a hawk with wings and eyes would scorn. Waiting beside a gopher hole, surrounded by the high, yellow grass, he saw the head emerge, and struck, and was amazed that there writhed in his clutch the neck and dusty coffin-skull of a rattlesnake. Holding his grip, Hook saw the great, thick body slither up after, the tip an erect, strident blur, and writhe on the dirt of the gopher's mound. The weight of the snake pushed Hook about, and once threw him down, and the rising and falling whine of the rattles made the moment terrible, but the vaulted mouth, gaping from the closeness of Hook's grip, so that the pale, envenomed sabers stood out free, could not reach him. When Hook replaced the grip of his beak with the grip of the talons, and was free to strike again and again at the base of the head, the struggle was over. Hook tore and fed on the fine, watery flesh, and left the tattered armor and the long, jointed bone for the marching ants.

When the heavy rains returned, he ate well during the period of 39 the first escapes from flooded burrows, and then well enough, in a vulture's way, on the drowned creatures. But as the rains lingered, and the burrows hung full of water, and there were no insects in the grass and no small birds sleeping in the thickets, he was constantly hungry, and finally unbearably hungry. His sodden and ground-broken plumage stood out ragedly about him, so that he looked fat, even bloated, but underneath it his skin clung to his bones. Save for his great talons and clappers, and the rain in his down, he would have been like a handful of air. He often stood for a long time under some bush or ledge, heedless of the drip, his one eye filmed over, his mind neither asleep or awake, but between. The gurgle and swirl of the brimming river, and the sound of chunks of the bank cut away to splash and dissolve in the already muddy flood, became familiar to him, and yet a torment, as if that great, ceaselessly working power of water ridiculed his frailty, within which only the faintest spark of valor still glimmered. The last two nights before the rain ended, he huddled under the floor of the bridge on the coastal highway, and heard the palpitant thunder of motors swell and roar over him. The trucks shook the bridge so that Hook, even in his famished lassitude, would sometimes open his one great eye wide and startled.

V

After the rains, when things became full again, bursting with growth **40** and sound, the trees swelling, the thickets full of song and chatter, the fields, turning green in the sun, alive with rustling passages, and the moonlit nights strained with the song of the peepers all up and down the river and in the pools in the fields, Hook had to bear the return of the one hunger left him. At times this made him so wild that he forgot himself and screamed challenge from the open ground. The fretfulness of it spoiled his hunting, which was not entirely a matter of patience. Once he was in despair, and lashed himself through the grass and thickets, trying to rise when that virgin scent drifted for a few moments above the current of his own river. Then, breathless, his beak agape, he saw the strong suitor ride swiftly down on the wind over him, and heard afar the screaming fuss of the harsh wooing in the alders. For that moment even the battle heart beat in him again. The rim of his good eye was scarlet, and a little bead of new blood stood in the socket of the other. With beak and talon, he ripped at a fallen log, and made loam and leaves fly from about it.

But the season of love passed over to the nesting season, and **41** Hook's love hunger, unused, shriveled in him with the others, and there remained in him only one stern quality befitting a hawk, and that the negative one, the remnant, the will to endure. He resumed his patient, plotted hunting, now along a field of the Japanese farmer, but ever within reach of the river thickets.

Growing tough and dry again as the summer advanced, inured to **42** the family of the farmer, whom he saw daily, stooping and scraping with sticks in the ugly, open rows of their fields, where no lovely grass rustled and no life stirred save the shameless gulls, which walked at the heels of the workers, gobbling the worms and grubs they turned up, Hook became nearly content with his shard of life. The only longing or resentment to pierce him was that which he suffered occasionally when forced to hide at the edge of the mile-long bean field from the wafted cruising and the restive, down-bent gaze of one of his own kind. For the rest, he was without flame, a snappish, dust-colored creature, fading into the grasses he trailed through, and suited to his petty ways.

At the end of that summer, for the second time in his four years, **43** Hook underwent a drouth. The equinoctial period passed without a rain. The laurel and the rabbit-brush dropped dry leaves. The foliage of the oaks shriveled and curled. Even the night fogs in the river canyon failed. The farmer's red cattle on the hillside lowed constantly, and could not feed on the dusty stubble. Grass fires broke out along the highways, and ate fast in the wind, filling the hollows with the smell of smoke, and died in the dirt of the shorn hills. The river made no sound. Scum grew on its vestigial pools, and turtles died and stank among the rocks. The dust rode before the wind, and ascended and flowered to nothing between the hills, and every sunset was red with the dust in the air. The people in the farmer's house quarreled, and even struck one another. Birds were silent, and only the hawks flew much. The animals lay breathing hard for very long spells, and ran and crept jerkily. Their flanks were fallen in, and their eyes were red.

At first Hook gorged at the fringe of the grass fires on the **44** multitudes of tiny things that came running and squeaking. But thereafter there were the blackened strips on the hills, and little more in the thin, crackling grass. He found mice and rats, gophers and ground-squirrels, and even rabbits, dead in the stubble and under the thickets, but so dry and fleshless that only a faint smell rose from them, even on the sunny days. He starved on them. By early December he had wearily stalked the length of the eastern foothills, hunting at night to escape the voracity of his own kind, resting often upon his wings. The queer trail of his short steps and great horned toes zigzagged in the dust and was erased by the wind at dawn. He was nearly dead, and could make no sound through the horn funnels of his clappers.

Then one night the dry wind brought him, with the familiar, **45** lifeless dust, another familiar scent, troublesome, mingled and unclear. In his vision-dominated brain he remembered the swift circle of his flight a year past, crossing in one segment, his shadow beneath him, a yard cluttered with crates and chickens, a gray barn and then again the plowed land and the stubble. Traveling faster than he had for days, impatient of his shrunken sweep, Hook came down to the farm. In the dark wisps of cloud blown among the stars over him, but no moon, he stood outside the wire of the chicken run. The scent of fat and blooded birds reached him from the shelter, and also within the enclosure was water. At the breath of the water, Hook's gorge contracted, and his tongue quivered and clove in its groove of horn. But there was the wire. He stalked its perimeter and found no opening. He beat it with his good wing, and felt it cut but not give. He wrenched at it with his beak in many places, but could not tear it. Finally, in a fury which drove the thin blood through him, he leaped repeatedly against it, beating and clawing. He was thrown back from the last leap as from the first, but in it he had risen so high as to clutch with his beak at the top wire. While he lay on his breast on the ground, the significance of this came upon him.

Again he leapt, clawed up the wire, and, as he would have fallen, **46**
made even the dead wing bear a little. He grasped the top and tumbled
within. There again he rested flat, searching the dark with quick-
turning head. There was no sound or motion but the throb of his own
body. First he drank at the chill metal trough hung for the chickens.
The water was cold, and loosened his tongue and his tight throat, but it
also made him drunk and dizzy, so that he had to rest again, his claws
spread wide to brace him. Then he walked stiffly, to stalk down the
scent. He trailed it up the runway. Then there was the stuffy,
body-warm air, acrid with droppings, full of soft rustlings as his talons
clicked on the board floor. The thick, white shapes showed faintly in
the darkness. Hook struck quickly, driving a hen to the floor with one
blow, its neck broken and stretched out stringily. He leaped the still
pulsing body, and tore it. The rich, streaming blood was overpowering
to his dried senses, his starved leathery body. After a few swallows, the
flesh choked him. In his rage, he struck down another hen. The urge to
kill took him again, as in those nights on the beach. He could let
nothing go. Balked of feeding, he was compelled to slaughter. Clattering, he struck again and again. The henhouse was suddenly filled with
the squawking and helpless rushing and buffeting of the terrified,
brainless fowls.

Hook reveled in mastery. Here was game big enough to offer **47**
weight against a strike, and yet unable to soar away from his blows.
Turning in the midst of the turmoil, cannily, his fury caught at the
perfect pitch, he stuck unceasingly. When the hens finally discovered
the outlet, and streamed into the yard, to run around the fence, beating
and squawking, Hook followed them, scraping down the incline, clumsy
and joyous. In the yard, the cock, a bird as large as he, and much
heavier, found him out and gave valiant battle. In the dark, and both
earthbound, there was little skill, but blow upon blow, and only chance
parry. The still squawking hens pressed into one corner of the yard.
While the duel went on, a dog, excited by the sustained scuffling, began
to bark. He continued to bark, running back and forth along the fence
on one side. A light flashed on in an uncurtained window of the
farmhouse, and streamed whitely over the crates littering the ground.

Enthralled by his old battle joy, Hook knew only the burly cock **48**
before him. Now, in the farthest reach of the window light, they could
see each other dimly. The Japanese farmer, with his gun and lantern,
was already at the gate when the finish came. The great cock leapt to
jab with his spurs and, toppling forward with extended neck as he fell,
was struck and extinguished. Blood had loosened Hook's throat.
Shrilly he cried his triumph. It was a thin and exhausted cry, but
within him as good as when he shrilled in mid-air over the plummeting
descent of a fine foe in his best spring.

The light from the lantern partially blinded Hook. He first turned **49**
and ran directly from it, into the corner where the hens were huddled.
They fled apart before his charge. He essayed the fence, and on the
second try, in his desperation, was out. But in the open dust, the dog
was on him, circling, dashing in, snapping. The farmer, who at first
had not fired because of the chickens, now did not fire because of the

dog, and, when he saw that the hawk was unable to fly, relinquished the sport to the dog, holding the lantern up in order to see better. The light showed his own flat, broad, dark face as sunken also, the cheekbones very prominent, and showed the torn-off sleeves of his shirt and the holes in the knees of his overalls. His wife, in a stained wrapper, and barefooted, heavy black hair hanging around a young, passionless face, joined him hesitantly, but watched, fascinated and a little horrified. His son joined them too, encouraging the dog, but quickly grew silent. Courageous and cruel death, however it may afterward sicken the one who has watched it, is impossible to look away from.

In the circle of the light, Hook turned to keep the dog in front of 50 him. His one eye gleamed with malevolence. The dog was an Airedale, and large. Each time he pounced, Hook stood ground, raising his good wing, the pinions newly torn by the fence, opening his beak soundlessly, and, at the closest approach, hissed furiously, and at once struck. Hit and ripped twice by the whetted horn, the dog recoiled more quickly from several subsequent jumps and, infuriated by his own cowardice, began to bark wildly. Hook maneuvered to watch him, keeping his head turned to avoid losing the foe on the blind side. When the dog paused, safely away, Hook watched him quietly, wing partially lowered, beak closed, but at the first move lifted the wing and gaped. The dog whined, and the man spoke to him encouragingly. The awful sound of his voice made Hook for an instant twist his head to stare up at the immense figures behind the light. The dog again sallied, barking, and Hook's head spun back. His wing was bitten this time, and with a furious sideblow, he caught the dog's nose. The dog dropped him with a yelp, and then, smarting, came on more warily, as Hook propped himself up from the ground again between his wings. Hook's artificial strength was waning, but his heart still stood to the battle, sustained by a fear of such dimension as he had never known before, but only anticipated when the arrogant young hawk had driven him to cover. The dog, unable to find any point at which the merciless, unwinking eye was not watching him, the parted beak waiting, paused and whimpered again.

"Oh, kill the poor thing," the woman begged   51

The man, though, encouraged the dog again, saying, "Sick him; 52 sick him."

The dog rushed bodily. Unable to avoid him, Hook was bowled down, snapping and raking. He left long slashes, as from the blade of a knire, on the dog's flank, but before he could right himself and assume guard again, was caught by the good wing and dragged, clattering, and seeking to make a good stroke from his back. The man followed them to keep the light on them, and the boy went with him, wetting his lips with his tongue and keeping his fists closed tightly. The woman remained behind, but could not help watching the diminished conclusion.

In the little, palely shining arena, the dog repeated his successful 54 maneuver three times, growling but not barking, and when Hook thrashed up from the third blow, both wings were trailing, and dark, shining streams crept on his black-fretted breast from the shoulders. The great eye flashed more furiously than it ever had in victorious battle, and the beak still gaped, but there was no more clatter. He faltered when turning to keep front; the broken wings played him false even as props. He could not rise to use his talons.

The man had tired of holding the lantern up, and put it down to rub   55 his arm. In the low, horizontal light, the dog charged again, this time throwing the weight of his forepaws against Hook's shoulder, so that Hook was crushed as he struck. With his talons up, Hook raked at the dog's belly, but the dog conceived the finish, and furiously worried the feathered bulk. Hook's neck went limp, and between his gaping clappers came only a faint chittering, as from some small kill of his own in the grasses.

In this last conflict, however, there had been some minutes of the   56 supreme fire of the hawk whose three hungers are perfectly fused in the one will; enough to burn off a year of shame.

Between the great sails the light body lay caved and perfectly still.   57 The dog, smarting from his cuts, came to the master and was praised. The woman, joining them slowly, looked at the great wingspread, her husband raising the lantern that she might see it better.

"Oh, the brave bird," she said.   58

Study Questions

1. How does Clark's treatment of Hook differ from what would be presented in an essay?
2. "Hook" is divided into five sections. What major development of plot occurs in each of these sections?
3. How are sections I and IV related?
4. When is the first suggestion of Hook's approaching confrontation with the gulls? With the Japanese farmer?
5. Is there any consistent way in which Clark constructs his expository paragraphs?

Rhetoric Justifies Grammar: Extreme Sentence Length in "Hook"

RICHARD ALLEN

Richard Allen (1950–   ) was born in Buffalo, New York. He studied at Arizona State University, where he received his degree in chemical engineering in 1972. In 1969, while he was a freshman, Allen won both first and fourth prizes for best freshman essay in English classes. The first-prize essay is reprinted below.

1   Like the short, choppy sentence, the excessively long sentence is taboo in most grammar classes. The extremely long sentences Walter Van Tilburg Clark uses in "Hook" might seem to be open to a charge of ungrammaticality, but he has used the lengths of sentences rhetorically to achieve desired effect: emphasis on actions, climax of action, and the poetic effect of action.

2   Clark uses the sentence length to emphasize action. For example, when Hook battles with another hawk, Clark uses a long, zigzagging sentence which emphasizes the unorganized, flashing movements of the birds:

> In the end, when Hook, having outmaneuvered his enemy and come above him, wholly in control, and going with the wind, tilted and plunged for the death rap, the other, in desperation, threw over on his back and struck up.

3   The sentence basically states, ". . . when Hook . . . tilted and plunged for the death rap, the other, . . ., threw over on his back and struck up." Clark has added participial phrases, such as "having outmaneuvered his enemy and come above him," "wholly in control," and "and going with the wind," to obtain the zigzagging effect of the birds fighting and darting in air.

4   Immediately following this sentence, Clark, to emphasize the action again, uses a short sentence. "Talons locked, beaks raking, they dived earthward." This sentence begins specifically—"Talons locked, beaks raking,"—then ends in suspense. A similar example would be:

"Engines ignited, gears shifting, they raced down the dragway." Both sentences leave the reader curiously asking "Who will win?"

The suspenseful sentence builds the reader up to a climax which 5 leaves him at a high degree of tension and hungering interest. Clark also uses long climactic sentences which build the reader up, then bring him down again. There are two good examples of this.

> On a hilltop projection of stone two miles inland, he struck her down, gripping her rustling body with his talons, beating her wings down with his wings, belting her head when she whimpered or thrashed, and at last clutching her neck with his hook and, when her coy struggles had given way to stillness, succeeded.

In this one-sentence paragraph, Clark opens with a moderate state of 6 action—"On a hilltop projection of stone . . ."—then builds to a climax—"gripping her rustling body with his talons, beating her wings down with his wings . . ."—then back down to relief—"succeeded." He expresses this action in the same procedure as the sexual act itself; it reaches a peak, then recedes.

Another example of climactic action conveyed by the sentence 7 structure is found after Hook is shot by the farmer.

> Wild with rage, he thrust up and clattered his beak, challenging, but when he had fallen over twice, he knew that the trailing wing would not carry, and then heard the boots of the hunter among the stones in the river bed and, seeing him loom at the edge of the bushes, crept back among the thickest brush and was still.

This sentence follows the same pattern of the previous example except that it begins near the climax and eases down slowly to the end—"and was still"; the sentence is actually anti-climatic.

Clark uses the long sentence again, but this time to achieve a 8 poetic effect. He relates this effect to the movement of the bird in flight.

> The third and consummating hunger did not awaken in Hook until the following spring, when the exultation of space had grown slow and steady in him, so that he swept freely with the wind over miles of coastal foothills, circling, and ever in sight of the sea, and used without struggle the warm currents lifting from the slopes, and no longer desired to scream at the range of his vision, but intently sailed above his shadow swiftly climbing to meet him on the hillsides, sinking away and rippling across the brush-grown canyons.

This long, one-sentence paragraph glides along like the flight of the 9 bird, Hook. Clark uses the long sentence here to describe the action of the gliding bird through a poetic stringing together of clauses which gives the reader a sense of floating in air. Here again, Clark has used the structure of his sentence to parallel, and therefore to convey, the action of the bird.

Devices typical of poetry, such as the mixing of the senses, 10 alliteration, and rhythm, are found in this paragraph. Clark mixes the senses—"scream at the range of his vision"—and on page 312 he mentions Hook's "choking thought." Alliteration, another device of poetry is found in this passage. The phrases "slow and steady," "shadow swiftly," and "sight of the sea" are found in the following sentence. These phrases also have a rhythm. The rhythm of these phrases is choppy as is the rhythm of this sentence: "Talons locked, beaks raking," which was discussed earlier. While many of the individual phrases have a staccato rhythm, the sentences, especially in this last paragraph, flow with lulling sentence structure.

Although Clark uses long sentences, he never becomes redundant. 11 He has mastered the long—as well as the short—sentence and has broken the taboo. In strict grammatical terms, extremely long sentences may be undesirable, but Clark has clearly demonstrated that rhetoric justifies grammatical liberties.

Study Questions

1. Which sentence is the *thesis statement?*
2. What three points does Allen choose to discuss? In what order does he discuss them?
3. How many paragraphs are devoted to each of the three points?
4. How does the conclusion draw us back to the introduction?

Education
UNWILLINGLY TO SCHOOL

5

Education continues to be a major concern in America, and perhaps more so today than in the past. Problems and questions we faced decades ago remain unresolved. In addition we must deal with new ones—rising costs, demographic shifts that affect school populations, preparing students and faculty for the age of high technology, and many others. The eight essays and one short story selected for this section deal with both practical and philosophic issues in education, and illustrate a variety of approaches, modes, and styles in the presentation of ideas on these issues.

Eric Hoffer's "Beware the Intellectual" will trouble members of the academic community, students and faculty alike. His indictment of the intellectual as partly responsible for the evils that plague this century raises a number of questions. Hoffer's faith in formal education is at best fragile, for he argues that survival of the species depends on a capacity for compassion, a quality that cannot be acquired by education. Derek Bok's "Can Ethics Be Taught?" is a statement of faith in education, for he sees that schools and colleges can play an important role in restoring eroded moral values. Specifically, he describes by illustration and analysis how ethics can be taught, in ways far more effective than in the past. As a bit of comic relief to the tone and substance of the Hoffer and Bok essays, Russell Baker's "School vs. Education" is a playful satire of education in America today, both in the home and at school.

Sloan Wilson's "Why Jessie Hates English" and Sheridan Baker's "Writing As Discovery" treat a practical issue in education—the teaching of English. Wilson decries the way it is taught and the texts used to teach it. Baker describes the process whereby the act of writing can help us expand our ideas. His ideas on writing and his methods of teaching it are what Wilson finds lacking in his daughter's experience in English. These two essays offer two different approaches and presentations of a specific issue and could serve as models for students in their theme assignments on similar subjects.

Opposing views on an unresolved educational issue are found in John Silber's "The Flight from Excellence" and Shirley Chisholm's "Needed: Equal Educational Opportunity for All." Silber argues for a restoration of excellence in higher education. He concedes that many people consider this antidemocratic, but he answers this charge by citing the ready acceptance and admiration of high excellence in other endeavors, such as sports and entertainment. Here elitism is desirable. Chisholm stands for opening up educational opportunities, so that people may obtain the upward mobility a college degree will give them. These pro-and-con essays offer a wide range of argument to be analyzed and evaluated.

The short story that concludes this section deals with another educational issue, underlying the portrait of the author's father. Jesse Stuart's "My Father Is an Educated Man" is a very sympathetic study of a man who would be judged by many people as uneducated, even illiterate. But in the author's view he and the countless others who helped develop this country were educated in a very special way and are therefore very special people. Stuart indirectly raises questions about what constitutes an education and by what standards a person's real worth is measured.

Beware the Intellectual

ERIC HOFFER

Eric Hoffer (1902–   ) was born in New York City. A philosophical writer who has had a lifelong passion for books, he has been compared to such diverse personalities as Machiavelli and the Duc de LaRochefoucauld. Hoffer early felt the stifling complexities of the big city and moved to California at the first opportunity. There he worked in a box factory, as a migrant field hand, in the gold mines and in construction, finally coming to rest in San Francisco, where he was a longshoreman for some twenty years. At present he holds weekly seminars at the University of California at Berkeley, where he has refused a full-time professorship. A logical, somewhat cold, and pessimistic writer, Hoffer nonetheless sees great potential for human growth. His first book, *The True Believer* (1951), won for him the Commonwealth Club of California Gold Medal in 1952. Other publications include *The Passionate State of Mind* (1955), *First Things, Last Things* (1971), *Reflections on the Human Condition* (1972), and *Before the Sabbath* (1976). *Working and Thinking on the Waterfront,* a journal of his experiences with longshoremen, was published in 1969.

From the early days of the Industrial Revolution, intellec- 1
tuals of every sort predicted that the machine would make man superfluous. Right now, it would be difficult to find a social scientist who does not believe that automated machines and computers are eliminating man as a factor in the social equation.

The belief that the machine turns men into robots is an a priori 2
assumption that prevents social scientists from seeing that technology is doing precisely the opposite of what they predicted it would do. There is evidence on every hand that the human factor has never been so central as it is now in technologically advanced countries. And it is the centrality of the human factor that makes industrial societies at present so unpredictable.

In the 19th century, which saw a Promethean effort to master and 3
harness nature, little thought was given to the management of man. The ruling middle class could proceed on the principle that government is best when it governs least. Everyday life had a fabulous regularity. Obedience of authority was as automatic as a reflex movement. Social processes were almost as rational and predictable as the processes of

Reprinted by permission of Eric Hoffer. Originally appeared in *Harper's Magazine,* October 1979.

nature. It was reasonable to believe in the possibility of a social science as exact as a natural science.

There was also boundless hope, a belief in automatic progress that 4 imbued people with patience.

Then came the 20th century! Have there ever been two successive 5 centuries so different from each other as the 19th and the 20th?

The 19th century was stable, predictable, rational, hopeful, free, 6 fairly peaceful and lumpy with certitudes.

The 20th century has been hectic, soaked with the blood of 7 innocents, fearful of the future, stripped of certitudes, unpredictable and absurd. The history of the 20th century is a succession of disastrous absurdities: the First World War, the Russian Revolution, the Versailles Peace Treaty, Prohibition, the wild '20s, the Great Depression, the Roosevelt Administration, the Hitler Revolution, the Second World War, the Holocaust, the absurd 1960s and now the Carter Presidency.

What was it that made the 20th century so different from the 19th? 8 The First World War was the sharp dividing line between the two centuries. But it was not the First World War itself, but its aftermath, that shaped our century. Without the breakdown of Czarist Russia and the humiliation of Germany by the Versailles Treaty, there would have been neither a Lenin nor a Hitler Revolution.

We have the testimony of highly reliable observers on the fabulous 9 stability and hopefulness of the pre-war decade. To Alfred North Whitehead, who was immersed in the new physics, "the period 1880 to 1914 was one of the happiest times in the history of mankind."

It is impressive how logic and hope kept 19th-century thinkers 10 from contemplating an unpleasant, let alone apocalyptic, denouement as the fulfillment of the Industrial Revolution. Few in the 19th century were aware of the explosive irrationality of the human condition. No one suspected that once nature had been mastered, industrial societies would enter a psychological age in which man would become a threat to mankind's survival.

No one foresaw the disintegration of values and the weakening of 11 social discipline caused by the elimination of scarcity. A logician like Marx could not foresee the downfall of capitalism by ever-increasing efficiency rather than by ever-increasing misery. Hardly anyone in the 19th century foresaw the chronic unemployment and the loss of a sense of usefulness caused by increased ambition. No one feared that drastic change would upset traditions, customs and other arrangements that make life predictable. Finally, no one foresaw that the education explosion made possible by advanced technology would swamp societies with hordes of educated nobodies who want to be somebodies and end up being mischief-making busybodies.

Strangely, those whom thinkers of the 19th century viewed with 12 alarm were the masses. Some thought that the masses loathed continuity and that their clamor for change would topple all that was noble and precious. Others believed that, once the masses were given political power, only education and prosperity could preserve social stability. How naive to believe in a stabilizing power of prosperity and education after we have seen what affluence and education have done!

To Freud, it seemed that individuals composing the masses support 13 one another in giving free reign to their indiscipline. No one had an inkling that anarchy, when it came, would originate not in the masses but in violent minorities, including the minority of the educated. Everything that was said about the anarchic propensities of the masses fits perfectly with the behavior of students, professors, writers, artists and the hangers-on during the righteous '60s.

The masses are the protagonists of stability, continuity and law 14 and order. It is curious that Disraeli—remarkable man—should have had a truer worldview of the nature of the masses than his liberal contemporaries. He sensed the conservatism and patriotism of common people. Could it be that, as a genuine conservative, Disraeli was more attuned to the eternal verities of man's existence? Considering also how timely and relevant were Disraeli's ideas about what makes nations strong and great, it is legitimate to wonder whether you have to be a conservative if you want to be up to date.

The 20th century saw not only the fulfillment of the Industrial 15 Revolution but also the fulfillment of wars planted in the preceding century. There is hardly an atrocity perpetrated in the 20th century that had not been advocated by some intellectual in the 19th.

The 19th century was dominated by men of action; the intellectu- 16 als just talked. And no one expected savage words to have consequence. The intellectuals entered the 19th century convinced that it was going to be their century. Had they not made the French Revolution? They saw themselves as the coming ruling class. But the Industrial Revolution gave power to the middle class, and the intellectuals were left out in the cold.

It is the predicament of the middle class that, although it excels in 17 mastering things, it is awkward and almost helpless when it comes to managing men. Thus, when the human factor became more and more central, the middle class, drained of confidence by the First World War and a great Depression, found itself in deep trouble.

The stage was set for the entrance of the intellectuals. To an 18 intellectual, power means power over man. He cannot conceive of power moving mountains and telling rivers where to flow. He is in his element commanding, brainwashing and in general making people love what they hate. He glories in the role of medicine man and charismatic leader. And feels godlike when he makes words become flesh. Thus, he has made the 20th century a century of words par excellence. In no other century have words become so dangerous. A failure to recognize this fact can have disastrous consequences.

Now, viewed from any vantage point, the 19th century was a sharp 19 historical deviation. About 150 years ago, the Occident was catapulted into a trajectory away from the ancient highway of history. We can now see that the trajectory is the loop that turns upon itself and is curving back to where it started. We can see all around us the lineaments of a pre-industrial pattern emerging in post-industrial society. We are not plunging ahead into the future, but falling back into the past. The explosion of the young, the dominance of the intellectuals, the savagery of our cities, the revulsion from work are all characteristics of the decades that preceded the Industrial Revolution. We are returning to the rocky highway of history and are rejoining the ancient caravan.

The significant point is that the people who are rejoining the 20 ancient caravan are not what they were in pre-industrial days. They are more dangerous. The unspeakable atrocities of the 20th century have demonstrated that man is the originator of a great evil that threatens the survival of mankind. The central problem of the post-industrial age is how to cope with this human evil.

It is conceivable that if the exhaustion of raw materials and 21 sources of energy make it imperative for a society to tap the creative energies of its people, it may in doing so also tap a new source of social discipline, for the creative individual, no matter how highly endowed, must be hard-working and disciplined if he's to accomplish much.

There is no invention that will take the hard work out of creating. 22 Moreover, since the creative flow is never abundant, the greatest society is likely to be disciplined by a new chronic scarcity. The trouble is that the coming of the creative society will be slow and faltering, and we must find other defenses against evil.

What I'm going to advocate may seem far-fetched. But in this case, 23 all suggestions are legitimate. As things are now, it may well be that the survival of the species will depend upon the capacity to foster a boundless capacity for compassion. In the alchemy of man's soul, almost all noble attributes—courage, love, hope, faith, beauty, loyalty—can be transmuted into ruthlessness. Compassion alone stands apart from the continuous traffic between good and evil proceeding within us. Compassion is the antitoxin of the soul. Where there is compassion, even the poisonous impulses remain relatively harmless.

Compassion seems to have its roots in the family. It is conceivable 24 that the present weakening of the family may allow compassion to leak out into wider circles. So, too, the cultivation of esprit de corps, which is the creation of family ties between strangers, may spread compassion.

The question is: can we make people compassionate by education? 25 It is natural to assume that the well-educated are more humane and compassionate than the uneducated. But, believe it or not, the reverse seems to be true. When Gandhi was asked what it was that worried him most, he replied, "The hardness of heart of the educated."

We have seen the highly educated German nation give its al- 26 legiance to the most murderously vengeful government in history. The bloody-minded professors in the Kremlin, as Churchill called them, liquidated 60 million Russian men, women and children. We have also seen a band of graduates of the Sorbonne, no less, slaughter and starve millions of innocents in Cambodia and Vietnam. The murder weapons that may destroy our society are being forged in the work factories of our foremost universities. In many countries, universities have become the chief recruiting ground of mindless terrorists.

I've never been a teacher or a parent, and my heart is savage by 27
nature and therefore unfit to tell people how to implant compassion.
Still, I have the feeling that perhaps the adoption of a certain view of
life might bear the fruit of compassion. We feel close to each other
when we see our planet as a tiny island of life in an immensity of
nothingness. We also draw together when we become aware that night
must close in on all living things, that we are condemned to death at
birth and that life is a bus ride to the place of execution. All of our
struggling and vying is about seats in the bus, and the ride is over
before we know it.

Study Questions

1. This is a variation on the problem-solution essay. In
   presenting the problem, how does Hoffer use cause-and-
   effect and comparison-and-contrast?
2. How does the metaphor Hoffer uses in the last two
   sentences of the concluding paragraph serve his argument about compassion and education?
3. What is the rhetorical effect of making paragraphs 4, 5,
   and 6 so short? What would be the effect if these had been
   combined into one paragraph?
4. Note the sentence structures in paragraphs 10 and 11.
   What effect is produced by the repetition of "No one" as
   subject?
5. What type of development is used in paragraphs 3, 8, and
   11?
6. Identify the historical allusions Hoffer makes. What do
   they tell us about the type of audience he addresses?

School vs. Education
RUSSELL BAKER

Russell Baker (1925–   ) was born in Virginia and graduated
from Johns Hopkins in 1947. As a newspaperman, he has served on
The Baltimore Sun and *The New York Times* for which he writes
the *Observer* column. His many awards include the Pulitzer Prize
in 1976. He has published *An American in Washington* (1961), *No
Cause for Panic* (1964), *All Things Considered* (1965), *Our Next
President* (1968), *Poor Russell's Almanac* (1972), and *The Upside
Down Man* (1977).

By the age of six the average child will have completed the   1
basic American education and be ready to enter school. If the child has
been attentive in these pre-school years, he or she will already have
mastered many skills.

From television, the child will have learned how to pick a lock,   2
commit a fairly elaborate bank holdup, prevent wetness all day long,
get the laundry twice as white and kill people with a variety of
sophisticated armaments.

From watching his parents, the child, in many cases, will already   3
know how to smoke, how much soda to mix with whiskey, what kind of
language to use when angry and how to violate the speed laws without
being caught.

At this point, the child is ready for the second stage of education,   4
which occurs in school. There, a variety of lessons may be learned in
the very first days.

The teacher may illustrate the economic importance of belonging   5
to a strong union by closing down the school before the child arrives.
Fathers and mothers may demonstrate to the child the social cohesion
that can be built on shared hatred by demonstrating their dislike for
children whose pigmentation displeases them. In the latter event, the
child may receive visual instruction in techniques of stoning buses,
cracking skulls with a nightstick and subduing mobs with tear gas.
Formal education has begun.

During formal education, the child learns that life is for testing.   6
This stage lasts twelve years, a period during which the child learns
that success comes from telling testers what they want to hear.

Early in this stage, the child learns that he is either dumb or   7
smart. If the teacher puts intelligent demands upon the child, the child
learns he is smart. If the teacher expects little of the child, the child
learns he is dumb and soon quits bothering to tell the testers what they
want to hear.

At this point, education becomes more subtle. The child taught by   8
school that he is dumb observes that neither he, she, nor any of the
many children who are even dumber, ever fails to be promoted to the
next grade. From this, the child learns that while everybody talks a lot
about the virtue of being smart, there is very little incentive to stop
being dumb.

What is the point of school, besides attendance? the child wonders.   9
As the end of the first formal stage of education approaches, school
answers this question. The point is to equip the child to enter college.

Children who have been taught they are smart have no difficulty.   10
They have been happily telling testers what they want to hear for
twelve years. Being artists at telling testers what they want to hear,
they are admitted to college joyously, where they promptly learn that
they are the hope of America.

Children whose education has been limited to adjusting them-   11
selves to their schools' low estimates of them are admitted to less
joyous colleges which, in some cases, may teach them to read.

At this stage of education, a fresh question arises for everyone. If   12
the point of lower education was to get into college, what is the point of

college? The answer is soon learned. The point of college is to prepare the student—no longer a child now—to get into graduate school. In college, the student learns that it is no longer enough simply to tell the testers what they want to hear. Many are tested for graduate school; few are admitted.

Those excluded may be denied valuable certificates to prosper in 13 medicine, at the bar, in the corporate boardroom. The student learns that the race is to the cunning and often, alas, to the unprincipled.

Thus, the student learns the importance of destroying competitors 14 and emerges richly prepared to play his role in the great simmering melodrama of American life.

Afterward, the former student's destiny fulfilled, his life rich with 15 Oriental carpets, rare porcelain and full bank accounts, he may one day find himself with the leisure and the inclination to open a book with a curious mind, and start to become educated.

Study Questions

1. In what ways does Baker establish the tone of this essay?
2. The first four paragraphs contain only six sentences. What effect is achieved by this type of structure?
3. Identify the topic sentence of paragraph 5.
4. Identify the words and phrases that link paragraphs 1–8.
5. What type of development does Baker use in paragraph 12?
6. Other than bringing the essay to conclusion, what is the function of the last paragraph?

Can Ethics Be Taught?
DEREK C. BOK

Derek C. Bok (1930–   ) was born in Ardmore, Pennsylvania. His degrees include a B.A. from Stanford (1951), an L.L.B. from Harvard (1954), and an M.A. from George Washington (1958). He joined the faculty of Harvard Law School in 1958, became dean in 1968, and president of the university in 1971. His numerous publications include the coauthored book *Labor Law* (with Archibald Cox, 1962) and *Labor and the American Community* (with John T. Dunlop, 1970).

Reprinted from *Change,* October 1976, by permission.

Americans have few rivals in their willingness to talk 1
openly about ethical standards. They are preached in our churches,
proclaimed by public officials, debated in the press, and discussed by
professional societies to a degree that arouses wonder abroad. Yet there
has rarely been a time when we have been so dissatisfied with our
moral behavior or so beset by ethical dilemmas of every kind. Some of
these problems have arisen in the backwash of the scandals that have
recently occurred in government, business, and other areas of national
life. Others are the product of an age when many new groups are
pressing claims of a distinctly moral nature—racial minorities,
women, patients, consumers, environmentalists, and many more.

It will be difficult to make headway against these problems 2
without a determined effort by the leaders of our national institutions.
But the public is scarcely optimistic over the prospects, for society's
faith in its leaders has declined precipitously in recent years. From
1966 to 1975, the proportion of the public professing confidence in
Congress dropped from 42 to 13 percent; in major corporate presidents
from 55 to 19 percent; in doctors from 72 to 43 percent; and in leaders of
the bar from 46 to 16 percent. Worse yet, 69 percent of the public
agreed in 1975 that "over the past 10 years, this country's leaders have
consistently lied to the people."

It is also widely believed that most of the sources that transmit 3
moral standards have declined in importance. Churches, families, and
local communities no longer seem to have the influence they once
enjoyed in a simpler, more rural society. While no one can be certain
that ethical standards have declined as a result, most people seem to
think that they have, and this belief in itself can erode trust and spread
suspicion in ways that sap the willingness to behave morally toward
others.

In struggling to overcome these problems, we will surely need help 4
from many quarters. Business organizations and professional associations will have to take more initiative in establishing stricter codes of
ethics and providing for their enforcement. Public officials will need to
use imagination in seeking ways of altering incentives in our legal and
regulatory structure to encourage moral behavior.

But it is also important to look to our colleges and universities and 5
consider what role they can play. Professors are often reluctant even to
talk about this subject because it is so easy to seem censorious or banal.
Nevertheless, the issue should not be ignored if only because higher
education occupies such strategic ground from which to make a
contribution. Every businessman and lawyer, every public servant and
doctor will pass through our colleges, and most will attend our
professional schools as well. If other sources of ethical values have
declined in influence, educators have a responsibility to contribute in
any way they can to the moral development of their students.

Unfortunately, most colleges and universities are doing very little 6
to meet this challenge. In several respects, they have done even less in
recent decades than they did a hundred years ago. In the nineteenth
century, it was commonplace for college presidents to present a series

of lectures to the senior class expounding the accepted moral principles of the time. This practice may seem quaint today, but in its time it served reasonably well as a method of moral education. In 1850, it was easier to discern a common moral code that could be passed along from one generation to the next. Partly because of their positions of authority, and partly because of the force of their personalities, many presidents seemed increasingly arbitrary and doctrinaire when they characters of their students.

In the intervening years, society changed in ways that eventually 7 discredited these lectures. Students became less inclined to fear authority or to be greatly impressed by those who held it. More serious still, the sense of a prevailing moral code broke down. As early as the 1850s, the president of Oberlin College could declare with certitude that slavery was immoral, even as his counterpart at Mercer College was vigorously upholding the practice on biblical and pragmatic grounds. As social change led to new sources of conflict, college presidents seemed increasingly arbitrary and doctrinaire when they attempted to convey a set of proper ethical precepts. And since their lectures were didactic in style, they failed to prepare students to think for themselves in applying their moral principles to the new controversies and new ethical issues that an industrializing society seemed constantly to create. By World War I, the tradition had all but ended.

In its place, many colleges introduced survey courses on moral 8 philosophy. These offerings have acquainted students with a great intellectual tradition in a manner that could scarcely be called doctrinaire. But they have rarely attempted to make more than a limited contribution to moral education. Since the classes usually consist of lectures, they do not develop the power of moral reasoning. To the extent that these courses are simply suveys of ethical theory, they likewise do little to help the student cope with the practical moral dilemmas he may encounter in his own life.

Professional schools have never shown much interest in providing 9 lectures on moral conduct or surveys of ethical theory. Many of them have simply ignored moral education altogether. But others have tried to approach the subject in another way by attempting to weave moral issues throughout a variety of courses and problems in the regular curriculum. This method has the advantage of suggesting to students that ethical questions are not isolated problems but an integral part of the daily life and experience of the profession. As such, the efforts are valuable and should be encouraged. But it is doubtful whether this approach by itself can have more than limited success in bringing students to reason more carefully about moral issues. Most professors have so much ground to cover that they will rarely take the time to acquaint their students with the writings of moral philosophers on the ethical issues under discussion.

Still more important, if a professional school divides the responsi- 10 bility for moral education among a large number of faculty members, most instructors will not have a knowledge of ethics that is equal to the task. Many of them will give short shrift to the moral problems and concentrate on other aspects of the course materials that they feel more equipped to teach. The difficulties are clearly illustrated by the findings of a recent report from a prominent business school. After listing a wide variety of moral issues distributed throughout the curriculum, the report described the reactions of a sample of students and faculty: "Almost without exception, the faculty members indicated that they touch on one or more of these issues frequently . . . but while they were certain they covered the issues, they often had second thoughts about how explicit they had been. Almost equally without exception, students felt the issues are seldom touched on, and when they are, are treated as afterthoughts or digressions."

In view of the disadvantages of the traditional approaches, more 11 attention is being given today to developing problem-oriented courses in ethics. These classes are built around a series of contemporary moral dilemmas. In colleges, the courses tend to emphasize issues of deception, breach of promise, and other moral dilemmas that commonly arise in everyday life. In schools of law, public affairs, business, and medicine, the emphasis is on professional ethics. Medical students will grapple with abortion, euthanasia, and human experimentation, while students of public administration will discuss whether government officials are ever justified in lying to the public, or leaking confidential information, or refusing to carry out the orders of their superiors. In schools of business, such courses may take up any number of problems—corporate bribes abroad, deceptive advertising, use of potentially hazardous products and methods of production, or employment practices in South Africa.

Whatever the problem may be, the classes generally proceed by 12 discussion rather than lecturing. Instructors may present their own views, if only to demonstrate that it is possible to make carefully reasoned choices about ethical dilemmas. But they will be less concerned with presenting solutions than with carrying on an active discussion in an effort to encourage students to perceive ethical issues, wrestle with the competing arguments, discover the weaknesses in their own position, and ultimately reach thoughtfully reasoned conclusions.

What can these courses accomplish? One objective is to help 13 students become more alert in discovering the moral issues that arise in their own lives. Formal education will rarely improve the character of a scoundrel. But many individuals who are disposed to act morally will often fail to do so because they are simply unaware of the ethical problems that lie hidden in the situations they confront. Others will not discover a moral problem until they have gotten too deeply enmeshed to extricate themselves. By repeatedly asking students to identify moral problems and define the issues at stake, courses in applied ethics can sharpen and refine the moral perception of students so that they can avoid these pitfalls.

Another major objective is to teach students to reason carefully 14 about ethical issues. Many people feel that moral problems are matters of personal opinion and that it is pointless even to argue about them since each person's views will turn on values that cannot be established or refuted on logical grounds. A well-taught course can demonstrate that this is simply not true, and that moral issues can be discussed as rigorously as many other problems considered in the classroom. With the help of carefully selected readings, students can then develop their capacity for moral reasoning by learning to sort out all of the arguments that bear upon moral problems and apply them to concrete situations.

A final objective of these courses is to help students clarify their 15 moral aspirations. Whether in college or professional school, many students will be trying to define their identity and to establish the level of integrity at which they will lead their professional lives. By considering a series of ethical problems, they can be encouraged to consider these questions more fully. In making this effort, students will benefit from the opportunity to grapple with moral issues in a setting where no serious personal consequences are at stake. Prospective lawyers, doctors, or businessmen may set higher ethical standards for themselves if they first encounter the moral problems of their calling in the classroom instead of waiting to confront them at a point in their careers when they are short of time and feel great pressure to act in morally questionable ways.

Despite these apparent virtues, the problem-oriented courses in 16 ethics have hardly taken the curriculum by storm. A few experimental offerings have been introduced, but they are still regarded with indifference or outright skepticism by many members of the faculty. What accounts for these attitudes? To begin with, many skeptics question the value of trying to teach students to reason about moral issues. According to these critics, such courses may bring students to perceive more of the arguments and complexities that arise in moral issues, but this newfound sophistication will simply leave them more confused than ever and quite unable to reach any satisfactory moral conclusions.

This attitude is puzzling. It may be impossible to arrive at answers 17 to certain ethical questions through analysis alone. Even so, it is surely better for students to be aware of the nuance and complexity of important human problems than to act on simplistic generalizations or unexamined premises. Moreover, many ethical problems are not all that complicated if students can only be taught to recognize them and reason about them carefully. However complex the issue, analysis does have important uses, as the following illustrations make clear:

> In one Harvard class, a majority of the students thought it proper for a 18 government official to lie to a congressman in order to forestall a regressive piece of legislation. According to the instructor, "The students seem to see things essentially in cost-benefit terms. Will the lie serve a good policy? What are the chances of getting caught? If you get caught, how much will it hurt you?" This is a very narrow view of deception. Surely these students might revise their position if they were

asked to consider seriously what would happen in a society that invited everyone to lie whenever they believed that it would help to avoid a result which they believed to be wrong.

The New York Times reports that many young people consider it permissi- 19 ble to steal merchandise because they feel that they are merely reducing the profits of large corporations. At the very least, analysis will be useful in pointing out that theft is not so likely to diminish profits as to increase the price to other consumers.

Courses in moral reasoning can also help students to avoid moral difficul- 20 ties by devising alternate methods of achieving their ends. This is a simple point, but it is often overlooked. For example, many researchers commonly mislead their human subjects in order to conduct an important experiment. Careful study can often bring these investigators to understand the dangers of deception more fully and exert more imagination in devising ways of conducting their experiments which do not require such questionable methods.

Even in the most difficult cases—such as deciding who will have access to 21 some scarce, life-sustaining medical technique—progress can be made by learning to pay attention not only to the ultimate problem of who shall live, but to devising procedures for making such decisions in a manner that seems reasonable and fair to all concerned.

There are other skeptics who concede that courses can help 22 students reason more carefully about ethical problems. But these critics argue that moral development has less to do with reasoning than with acquiring proper moral values and achieving the strength of character to put these values into practice. Since such matters are not easily taught in a classroom, they question whether a course on ethics can accomplish anything of real importance. It is this point of view that accounts for the statement of one business school spokesman in explaining why there were no courses on ethics in the curriculum: "On the subject of ethics, we feel that either you have them or you don't."

There is clearly some force to this argument. Professors who teach 23 the problem-oriented courses do not seek to persuade students to accept some preferred set of moral values. In fact, we would be uneasy if they did, since such an effort would have overtones of indoctrination that conflict with our notions of intellectual freedom. As for building character, universities can only make a limited contribution, and what they accomplish will probably depend more on what goes on outside the classroom than on the curriculum itself. For example, the moral aspirations of Harvard students undoubtedly profited more from the example of Archibald Cox than from any regular course in ethics. Moreover, if a university expects to overcome the sense of moral cynicism among its students, it must not merely offer courses; it will have to demonstrate its own commitment to principled behavior by making a serious effort to deal with the ethical aspects of its investment policies, its employment practices, and the other moral dilemmas that inevitably confront every educational institution.

But it is one thing to acknowledge the limitations of formal 24 learning and quite another to deny that reading and discussion can have any effect in developing ethical principles and moral character. As I have already pointed out, problem-oriented courses encourage students to define their moral values more carefully and to understand more fully the reasons that underlie and justify these precepts. Unless one is prepared to argue that ethical values have no intellectual basis whatsoever, it seems likely that this process of thought will play a useful role in helping students develop a clearer, more consistent set of ethical principles that takes more careful account of the needs and interests of others. And it is also probable that students who fully understand the reasons that support their ethical principles will be more inclined to put their principles into practice and more uncomfortable at the thought of sacrificing principle to serve their own private ends.

To be sure, no one would deny that ethical values and moral **25** character are profoundly dependent on many forces beyond the university—on family influences, religious experience, and the personal example of friends and public figures. But this is true of all of education. Everyone knows that outstanding lawyers, businessmen, and public servants succeed not only because of the instruction they received as students but because of qualities of leadership, integrity, judgment, and imagination that formal education cannot hope to supply. Nevertheless, we still have faith in the value of professional schools because we believe that most students possess these personal qualities in sufficient measure to benefit from professional training and thereby become more effective practitioners. In the same way, we should be willing to assume that most students have sufficient desire to live a moral life that they will profit from instruction that helps them to become more alert to ethical issues, and to apply their moral values more carefully and rigorously to the ethical dilemmas they encounter in their professional lives.

Even if we are prepared to agree that these problem-oriented **26** courses on ethics have a valuable contribution to make, there is a final, practical objection to consider. To put it bluntly, much of the skepticism about these courses probably arises not from doubts about their potential value but from deeper reservations as to whether those who teach the courses are really qualified to do so. Unfortunately, it is simply a fact that many courses in applied ethics have been taught by persons with little qualification beyond a strongly developed social conscience. Of all the problems that have been considered, this is the most substantial. Poor instruction can harm any class. But it is devastating to a course on ethics, for it confirms the prejudices of those students and faculty who suspect that moral reasoning is inherently inconclusive and that courses on moral issues will soon become vehicles for transmitting the private prejudices of the instructor.

What does a competent professor need to know to offer a course of **27** this type? To begin with, instructors must have an adequate knowledge of moral philosophy so that they can select the most useful readings for their students and bring forth the most illuminating theories and arguments that have been devised to deal with recurrent ethical dilemmas. In addition, teachers must have an adequate knowledge of the field of human affairs to which their course is addressed. Otherwise, they will neither be credible to students nor succeed in bringing students to understand all of the practical implications and consequences of choosing one course of action over another. Finally, instructors must know how to conduct a rigorous class discussion that will elicit a full consideration of the issues without degenerating into a windy exchange of student opinion.

These requirements are not insuperable, but they present real 28 difficulties because in most universities there is no single department or program that is equipped to train a fully qualified instructor. Professors of law or business may understand judicial procedures and corporate finance—they may even be masters of the Socratic method—but they will rarely have much background in moral philosophy. Philosophers in turn will usually know virtually nothing about any of the professions and may even lack experience in teaching problem-oriented classes. If moral education is ever to prosper, we will have to find ways of overcoming these deficiencies by creating serious interdisciplinary programs for students seeking careers of teaching and scholarship in this field. Fortunately, the time is ripe for developing such programs, since professional schools are beginning to recognize the moral demands being made on their professions while philosophy departments are finding it more and more difficult to place their PhDs in traditional teaching posts.

But is the effort worth making? I firmly believe that it is. Even if 29 courses in applied ethics turned out to have no effect whatsoever on the moral development of our students, they would still make a contribution. There is value to be gained from any course that forces students to think carefully and rigorously about complex human problems. The growth of such courses will also encourage professors to give more systematic study and thought to a wide range of contemporary moral issues. Now that society is expressing greater concern about ethics in the professions and in public life, work of this kind is badly needed, for it is surprising how little serious, informed writing has been devoted even to such pervasive moral issues as lying and deception. But beyond these advantages, one must certainly hope that courses on ethical problems will affect the lives and thought of students. We cannot be certain of the impact these courses will have. But certainty has never been the criterion for educational decisions. Every professor knows that much of the information conveyed in the classroom will soon be forgotten. The willingness to continue teaching rests on an act of faith that students will retain a useful conceptual framework, a helpful approach to the subject, a valuable method of analysis, or some other intangible residue of intellectual value. Much the same is true of courses on ethical problems. Although the point is still unproved, it does seem plausible to suppose that the students in these courses will become more alert in perceiving ethical issues, more aware of the reasons underlying moral principles, and more equipped to reason carefully in applying these principles to concrete cases. Will they behave more ethically? We may never know. But surely the experiment is worth trying, for the goal has never been more important to the quality of the society in which we live.

Study Questions

1. This is another variation on the problem-solution essay. What type of development does Bok use in presenting the problem?
2. What rhetorical purpose is served by paragraphs 5–10?
3. Underline the words and phrases that link paragraphs 1–10.
4. What type of development does Bok use in paragraphs 13, 27, and 29?
5. What paragraphs are primarily transitional?
6. In what ways does Bok's presentation indicate the type of audience he is addressing?

Is a Crime Against the Mind No Crime at All?

JUDITH PLOTZ

Judith Plotz (1938–   ) was born in Brooklyn. She received an A.B. from Radcliffe College in 1960 and a Ph.D. from Harvard in 1965. In 1968–1969 an American Association of University Women Fellowship sent her to England, after which she returned to teaching English at George Washington University. Her *Ideas of the Decline of Poetry* was published in 1965.

Twenty research papers are submitted in one freshman   1
composition section; nine are plagiarized. A sharp-eyed history profes-

Reprinted from *The Chronicle of Higher Education*, February 2, 1976, by permission of the author.

sor, disheartened by yearly bumper crops of plagiarists, gives up on the term paper: "I even have graduate students do annotated bibliographies now." Another professor in the social sciences retains papers, but with cynical fatalism: "Plagiarism? Sure, there's lots of it, but I'm busy and try not to look too closely." An allegedly original English paper is submitted bearing a fresh top-sheet over the unaltered text of a roommate's year-old paper, unaltered even to the roommate's name and the original instructor's comments and grade.

These are representative examples of university life in the '70s, **2** where plagiarism is epidemic. The academic community has proffered a number of explanations for the plague, each more dismal than the last. The general decline in moral standards is a recurrent theme: something is rotten—the students, the country, even the university. The students, one argument goes, are intellectually corrupt; growing up in unearned ease, they have never learned to respect the hard-earned achievements of intellect. Or, more vastly, the nation, as the Watergate affair illustrates, is corrupt and has taught its children to seek success at any price. Alternatively, or additionally, the university is corrupt in employing a judgmental grading system that encourages students to jockey for grades rather than to seek truth. Less moralistically, others trace the problem to a presumed drop in standards of admissions. Traditional university programs demand too much of poorly prepared students, who plagiarize out of panic.

These explanations may account for some cases, but not all. **3** Actually, the very concept of plagiarism, a relatively new phenomenon, has grown up with modern ideas of individuality.

In the medieval and Renaissance periods, the concept of **4** plagiarism—the *illegitimate* borrowing from another author—was virtually unknown. With the exception of direct comma-for-comma copying of another writer's work, most sorts of borrowing were legitimate, even laudable. An authoritarian social system nurtured literary authoritarianism. To model one's style, one's plots, one's ideas on a literary master was the time-honored way of learning to write well. One rather boasted of than tried to hide one's appropriations from the masters. Medieval poets, recognizing Virgil as a supreme craftsman, believing that one could not have too much of a good thing, translated and versified great swatches of the *Aeneid;* rather than condemning such poets for theft, their audiences praised them for pleasing versions of an honored favorite.

The classical masters were regarded, as nature itself was regarded, **5** as a writer's resource. The writer foolish enough to aim at total individuality was not admirable, but an eccentric deliberately impoverishing himself.

Plagiarism first came into existence as a significant literary **6** problem only toward the end of the 17th century. Like Renaissance writers, critics of this period were predominantly authoritarian and held that all the major subjects for literature had already been pre-empted, seized upon by writers of genius when the world was young, when "nature," as Samuel Johnson said of Shakespeare, "was still open" to them. But a favorite Latin tag of the age, *"Pereant qui ante nos nostra dixerunt"* (Damn those who had all our best ideas before we did), captures the increasing discontent with this situation. Eighteenth-century writers, despite their traditionalism, also felt an envious esteem for originality, the power to look at something in a new way, and for invention, the power to discover a new subject. Originality, now held to be a prime literary virtue, was despairingly deemed typical only of young civilizations and virtually unattainable in a modern age. Despite their desire for originality, modern writers could never be much more than copyists of the past, or so the prevailing theory went.

It was during this period of reluctant traditionalism and longing   7 for originality that critics began fervidly to hunt down plagiarists. Whether out of a thirst for originality or out of an aggrieved desire to show originality impossible to anyone, critics began to make accusations of plagiarism against writers who did no more than echo a word or phrase from an earlier writer. The presence of plagiarism was held to be an inevitability in a period which was a reluctant heir to the treasures of the ages. Nevertheless, it was fiercely derided as an enemy of originality. The failure to be original became culpable only when originality became desirable.

By the Romantic age plagiarism should have become unnecessary.   8 The early 19th-century Romantics took a high view of the potential creativity of every human soul. Originality, they argued, is the birthright of every individual. So liberating, so antiauthoritarian a theory of creativity should have set a writer free from the necessity of literary theft. Yet the greatest plagiarist in literary history—great in the number of his depredations, great in his genius—Samuel Taylor Coleridge, is a product of the age of originality. As Normal Fruman's recent book, *Coleridge, the Damaged Archangel*, makes plain, Coleridge compulsively appropriated the materials of other writers, notably German critics and philosophers, and equally compulsively protested his absolute originality.

Like Coleridge, contemporary undergraduates labor under a dou-   9 ble burden: the burden of originality imposed by the age and the burden of intellectual coherence imposed by the university. That the burdens often prove intolerable, the present state of academic morality attests.

American undergraduates of the '70s are heirs to the by-now sleazy   10 and dilapidated Romantic ideal of creativity. I call the ideal sleazy because it was degenerated from its original heroic summons to immense productive and synthetic efforts into a slack and sentimental invitation to self-complacent ease. It is one thing to hold that every child is innately imaginative and another to argue that all self-expression, no matter how feeble, is artistic creation. To believe that the inner spirit, the childlike soul in and of itself, untouched by any particular knowledge, is alone creative, has led in much contemporary secondary education to a loss of confidence in forms and in substantive knowledge. Since creativity comes from the naked self, it is no longer necessary to furnish that self with facilitating knowledges (grammar, German, Latin, calculus, physics) and forms (syntax, the sonnet, the book report). With "writing" in secondary schools largely confined to English class (though extracts copied from encyclopedias and other unimpeachable sources frequently surface as "research" papers in various other subject areas) and with English dedicated to evoking individual creativity, students are losing the habit of unself-conscious writing as a means of communication, as a mechanical knack in which the deepest self is not necessarily involved.

Habitually to write free verse, impressionistic responses to litera- 11 ture, and ruminative short stories without any compensatory training in the mere prose of communication is to hole up the self in a very narrow cell. Originality has been confounded with the spontaneous, unmediated productions of the sole self and the real experience of the sole self has been identified with pre-verbal incommunicable states which are impossible to express discursively. To be true to one's self, therefore, to be appropriately original, is to draw back from the world of facts and forms, the world of science and high culture. Authenticity lies in expressing the self rather than in expressing the world.

Parallel with the development of this solipsistic idea of originality 12 has been the knowledge explosion. The first-hand knowledge of any individual, even if he has the curiosity of a Leonardo and the stamina of a Casanova, is puny beside the vast stores of genuine scholarship that are piling up with unprecedented speed and to an unprecedented density in our libraries. The act of synthesizing preceding knowledge requires humility, ardor, and dedication to the life of the mind. Even a seasoned scholar feels intimidated by the mass of materials he must master and comprehend.

When a student is asked to write an essay synthesizing or 13 assessing literary or historical or political data, he finds himself facing materials on which considerable authoritative commentary may already exist. To write a good essay, the student must digest the data and commentary, synthesize them, and then go beyond them. The process, once second nature to well-trained college students, has by now become remarkably difficult for them. My guess is that the act of writing is increasingly tied up with the idea of self-expression and has little connection with the comprehension of any external aspect of the world. Because the presumably true, the creative self, exists most fully in isolation from the multiple intellectual constructions and historical accumulations with which liberal education is concerned, many students find all questions involving comment on a body of knowledge artificial, mechanical, and alien. When a student regards a paper assignment as merely mechanical, he quite consistently feels something of a hypocrite in devoting his full strength to so empty a pursuit. To many students it seems no greater a self-violation to commit fraud and plagiarize their papers than to push themselves through an exercise personally meaningless.

If my hypothesis is correct, if plagiarism does derive from a 14 perverted ideal of creativity, is there anything at all the university can do? Clearly, the plagiarist's contempt for earned intellectual distinction, his assumption that a crime against the mind is no crime, his theft from his sources and his fraud against his professors destroy any possible value from his education.

The quick way to abolish the problem, of course, is to abolish term 15 papers; but this is decapitation for a headache. The problem goes so deep that individual actions may be only palliative, but some new approaches to writing might help. Three kinds of papers might be useful. In order to combat the association between the act of writing and self-expression, I suggest that numerous small exercises be demanded—quizzes, summaries, paraphrases—all cast in consecutive prose. I also suggest the revival of the deliberate Imitation, an educational device so old, so aboriginal, as to be new. Students might be asked to write about English history in the manner of Macaulay, about the Vietnam war as Karl Marx. This would give the aid an established form always provides while still demanding the expression of individual judgment.

With exercises and imitations encouraging impersonal prose, 16 major paper assignments might be made more personal. The rote assignment, the question unreal both to instructor and student, might be replaced by assignments that deliberately cross the subjective self with the objective world, assignments that demand a reaching out into the world from a frankly acknowledged personal center. One might even try tapping the tremendous energy of animus, of anger, and ask students to write on those aspects of subjects they find most objectionable.

One might, one might . . . In any case, one must. The epidemic of 17 plagiarism is sad testimony to student estrangement from the goals of education. The increasing inability of students to leap the gap between their sole selves and the realm of knowledge means that it is vital to build more bridges, more crossings, to ease the passage.

Study Questions

1. In which paragraph does the thesis of this essay appear?
2. Does the first paragraph set the tone? If so, how?
3. What is the function of paragraphs 4–8?
4. Identify the topic sentence in paragraph 2. What type of development is used in this paragraph?
5. Note the first sentence of paragraph 17. What effect is achieved by the structure of this sentence?

Writing as Discovery
SHERIDAN BAKER

Sheridan Baker (1918–   ) was born in Santa Rosa, California. He received an A.B. (1939), M.A. (1946), and Ph.D. (1950) from the University of California at Berkeley. He has taught at Berkeley and the University of Michigan, and was a Fulbright lecturer in Japan in 1961–1962. He has contributed poems and critical articles, many of them on eighteenth-century English literature, to numerous periodicals. His influential books include *The Practical Stylist* (1962) and *Ernest Hemingway: An Introduction and Interpretation* (1967).

My idea here is simple, even self-evident: that the process 1 of writing is a process of discovery. Everyone who writes has experienced this process, has discovered, through writing it out, what he has in mind. Yet this simple fact is one not frequently propounded in our textbooks, and it seems utterly alien to the students who come to us from high-school courses in English, some of which may have included almost no writing at all. Even the growing emphasis on creative writing seems to cut against such a concept, which is one I urge upon my students, and would like to urge upon you as an almost desperate necessity if we are to make our courses in composition truly valuable and lead our students—and their teachers—to see the full value of writing in intellectual education and the intellectual life.

I believe, quite simply, that writing is our chief means, as indi- 2 viduals, of discovering knowledge, and eventually of discovering values and what is valid. Reading, of course, takes us well into that territory, as do lectures and TV and films and talk and all the rest of our experience, raw and otherwise. But only by *realizing*—making real—our new ideas by writing them out do we really discover them fully and as our own. We discover what we know by writing it out, bringing up from our tumbling mists of thought and intuition, our perpetual daydreams, those concepts we hardly knew we had. On blank paper we shape thoughts from what we thought were our blank minds. We discover that we know something after all. Only on paper can we hold those thoughts still, straighten them out, test them out. Like our inner dialogues, speech helps, of course, so we warm up our ideas with discussion. But only writing makes the full discovery of thought.

"How can I know what I think till I see what I say?" writes W.H. Auden in explaining how poetry is a "game of knowledge, a bringing to

Reprinted by permission of the Modern Language Association of America from "Writing as Discovery," *ADE Bulletin* (November 1974), pp. 34–37.

consciousness, by naming them, of emotions and their hidden relationships."[1] *Seeing* thought, *seeing* meaning: "Oh, I see," we say when we understand, and writing makes this literally true, makes our thoughts visible to the eye. All writing bears out Auden's observations, bringing to consciousness, by naming them, not only our emotions and their hidden relationships but all our wordless visual pictures and all our pictureless ideas as well. Writing is seeing, or seeing anew and in a more enduring way. In a sense, we do not see the woods and the trees, nor the valid and the invalid, until we conceptualize them in words and sentences and paragraphs on paper, telling one from the other, discovering them.

Dis-cover means to uncover. We uncover to ourselves what we had **4** somewhere in mind, and we then uncover it further, *discovering* it to the reader, as the eighteenth-century writers would say. I have, in the past, suggested that language *is* thought.[2] I think this is only partially true, however, and only of what we might call rational thought, or rationalized thought (to borrow a seminal idea from James Harvey Robinson's book of some years ago, *The Mind in the Making*). We need words to get hold of, to grasp, in a rational, conceptual way, ideas provided by our minds below the level of language. Language comes from the left lobe of the brain that controls our right thinking, from the hemisphere able to achieve analytic thought, but it also comprehends, as best it can, the clouds and lightning in the darks of the right-lobed intuitions formed in the part of the brain controlling holistic and nonverbal activity. Language thus gets things together—reason and instinct, left and right—and writing our language out is like spinning a straight thread from the woolly heaps of whatever we have in our minds. Ideas and language are not identical, as any effort to express our ideas in writing soon illustrates. As the transformational grammarians have reminded us, we can express the same idea in a number of different ways. We have something to say, even though we don't quite know what it is or how to say it. Then we find the words that lift the thought up into the light, that fit it, like the shell of a snail, embodying it, giving it form and being. Again, only on paper, by writing and rewriting, can we get the fit, make the thought visible, bring it into some kind of nonsubjective being where it will bear inspection from both ourselves and others. In short, we discover it fully for the first time.

I am really talking about two things, both of which are discoveries. **5** The first is having a conviction: for instance, that writing is somehow vitally important to our conceptual and rational thinking, our most distinctive characteristic as humans in this animated kingdom. All

---

[1]"Squares and Oblongs," *Poets at Work,* Rudolf Arnheim et al. (New York: Harcourt, Brace and Co., 1948), pp. 174, 173. This quotation, and the rest of this paragraph, I have borrowed and adapted slightly from preface to *The Crowell College Reader,* with David B. Hamilton (New York: Thomas Y. Crowell Co., 1974), p. vii.
[2]*The Written Word,* with Jacques Barzun and I. A. Richards (Rowley, Mass.: Newbury House Publishers, Inc., 1971), p. 5.

right, we have an idea, a conviction. Then we must find the language to express it, to make it clear both to others and ourselves. This process is a discovery, because in writing it out, in expressing it, we discover not only its conceptual being but its depths and ramifications. We have discovered, through writing, our idea's meaning and force. We have made it tangible. We have established it as something either to embrace or challenge, or to qualify and deepen for new discoveries. This is the first discovery of ideas in language, possible only through the process of writing which gives fibre to the process of thought.

The second process of discovery is akin to the first, part of the 6 inevitable process set in motion by the first, in fact—the actual creating of thought in our minds as we work thought into some graspable statement on paper. The blank paper and the blank mind seem to conspire, like white clouds, to generate the flash of an idea and all its zigzags of implication—light out of chaos, just as the Biblical writers pictured being and light as forming simultaneously in the initial act of creation, the discovery of order and clarity and harmony. The words draw forth the idea, separate the mud from the water, populate teeming emptiness with categories of being, and with a measure of beauty and order in the process.

Now this idea that language brings thought into being, and that 7 writing brings this being into something like palpable permanence, clarifying it further as it holds it still for consideration—this idea is quite contrary to what I find my students assuming about freshman conposition. Their first assumption is that everyone knows how to write, at least after twelve years of schooling, just as everyone knows how to talk. Their second is that writing is something specialized, something for the specialist or the classroom, not really related to life as they live it. Composition is thus something dry and schoolmarmish, a kind of superficial fussing with inessential details like commas, something utterly elementary, something to be excused from.

A couple of years ago, I came back to the freshman program at 8 Michigan after about a decade away from it. The freshmen seemed as bright as ever, and much the same as ever (and mercifully more docile than students in some of those intervening years). But they could not write even as well as their peers of a decade earlier, which was indeed not well. Many simply could not see, and never learned with any certainty that a phrase is not a sentence, that they had not completed the idea they had in mind. They could not distinguish the meaning of a comma from the meaning of a period. Some had never written an essay.

One was a young man named Rand. He stood out that first 9 hour—alert, interested, keen of question—and I remember his name, as frequently I do not, because of the Rand Corporation's famous think-tank. "Wow," I thought, "maybe I have the Son of Rand in hand." Then I read his first paper, a simple fifteen-minute impromptu deriving from that opening discussion. He had written two or three painful and garbled sentences, and, judging from his smile as he handed them in, had thought he had written well.

"What did you do in high-school English?" I asked him later. 10

"Well, we had some great discussions about how we see things, 11 about perception. You know, when you see green and I see green do we see the same green, and how do we know we do if we do."

"It's a fascinating question," I said. "It really is. But didn't you 12 write about it? Didn't you look up some articles and maybe write something about what you thought as to whether green was green?"

"No, not really. We really didn't write anything. The teacher 13 brought in some stuff, some pictures and slides and stuff, and we had some great discussions."

Well, my class was reading other things than the physiology and 14 psychology of perception, and I didn't follow it up. But I know now I should have prompted the student to write an essay on the subject. It interested him, even though he could say, at the time, very little about it. I should have encouraged him to write his ideas and knowledge into being, to discover the idea he must have had somewhere in mind from all that interest, to assert that green was or was not green and to find the evidence and the reasons to prove it, discovering the idea that he seemed to have but not to know, to test its validity, to argue it into being, discovering and creating thought from all that interesting vagueness he was content to let drift off into thin air. Writing in an atmosphere already mildly charged would have discovered thought, would have created it.

Writing is essentially creative. And here I want to make a further 15 distinction that many of our students and many of our teachers do not see or do not believe in. Creative writing is all the rage these days. Students and teachers—all of us, I suppose—give it a higher value than poor old plodding freshman composition. When I rose to the call to take on our freshman program, I discovered to my dismay that we had been exempting a number of freshmen, in addition to those exempted by examination in participating high schools, on individual pleas to the director, that is, to me. Some came armed with sheafs of essays, others with a short story or poem or two, others with nothing but perfect confidence in their case and their charm. What surprised me most was the number of high schools that seemed to have converted composition into creative writing, and the almost universal assumption that anyone who has written a poem or story has already passed to a sphere far beyond the dusty pedestrian world of composition.

Now, I am an old creative writer myself, and a teacher of creative 16 writing too. I got deeply hooked on the writing of poetry in my early years of teaching, when I inherited a creative writing class at the same time I was really getting excited about poetry for the first time by teaching it in another course. I know the intensities of trying to create a poem, and I know I learned in that cauldron something about verbal economies and the meanings of words and the potencies of metaphor that I would not have learned otherwise. But I also know that settling for self-expression as the whole of writing will leave in darkness another whole continent that writing can and should discover for each and every one of our students—the realm of rational thinking, the realm of reason.

I believe that education should be primarily intellectual, since the **17** intuitional, passional, sensational side of our existence is where we start—in sin, as St. Augustine would put it, the sin of the self-centered ego. We need to stretch upward and away from our sole selves toward the enlightened intellect, which is also part of ourselves, the fullest potential of every person. Creative writing at the elementary level— beyond which it rarely goes in elementary courses—usually leaves us trapped in self-expression. Even worse, it leaves us with the illusion that we know all we need to know about writing. We are doubly trapped in ourselves because pleased with ourselves, and thus incapable of getting beyond ourselves into rational thought, into ideas, into the truths and truth about this mysterious and wonderful and perhaps frightening life and universe of which we are a part.

I am quite content to start with self-expression, with automatic **18** stream-of-consciousness writing, with anything to get the pencils and thoughts in motion, but only as a pump-primer, as something other than, or auxiliary to, the real business of the course—certainly not as something to exclude the rational discovery and validification of ideas through writing, which is the primary contribution of writing to one's education and intellectual life. I also frequently try an excursion into self-expression later in the term to help the students infuse the power of personality into their reasoning.

One of the results of emphasizing creative writing at the expense of **19** expository writing is to separate the two and to encourage the assumption that expository prose should be bloodless and dry as dust, with no personality whatsoever. Perhaps the most valuable discovery through writing one's ideas into being is that good ideas are both personal (meaningful in here) and impersonal (meaningful out there, generally valid out there), and that the satisfaction of writing them out well, of bringing others to see the validity one has discovered, comes also in finding a language, an expression, alive with one's own personality and conviction. Good writing contains that personal joy in having hit the right words, the right rhythms, and the right figures of speech to catch the ideas that are being discovered fully in the process of attempting to make them as persuasive and attractive to others as to oneself. From the first, I urge each student to find his own written voice, to give his writing personality (his own), to write as he speaks, but with everything tightened up a notch, all the hems and haws chipped out, all uncertainties and repetitions cleaned up, everything smoother, clearer, more sure, more attractive, more fully stated, more completely expressed in words everyone will understand and respect. Perhaps the final discovery in writing is precisely this pleasure in discovering that private convictions can be affirmed as public validities in a language that carries the fullest possible force—the force of human personality, one's own personality.

Ideas are valuable only insofar as they are humanly valuable, of **20** course. And self-expression is valuable—aside from the psychic therapy of letting off steam, or soothing or bolstering the needy ego—only when it discovers validities beyond the self. To expand one's grasp of these validities is education. And in this educational process the very process of writing is of the highest value as it helps us discover those validities and to realize them, to make them realities for us and for others.

The process of writing, in fact, expands our capacity to think as 21 nothing else can. Aside from trying to solve mathematical problems and puzzles and playing tough intellectual games like chess, our intellectual beings—our physical brains, in fact—are never so intensely engaged as in the process of writing an essay. Writing is hard, and we shy away from it precisely because it demands such intense engagement. It is solving continuous sets of complex problems, finding the idea, from among myriad choices, by fitting the word to it. Writing is so highly valuable because it exercises our highest capacity so fully. And it increases the capacity. The old-fashioned notion that thinking makes our brains grow seems indeed to be true. Professor Mark Rosenzweig and his associates at the University of California have for some time been demonstrating by scalpel, calipers, and scales that the brains of thinking rats grow as compared to those of rats who don't have to think to eat.[3] The problem-solvers developed bumps on their cerebral cortexes, enlarging that cortex far beyond those of the nonthinkers, to whom everything was given but the necessity to think. The brain is muscular after all. Problems develop its brawny powers. And writing is a kind of moment-by-moment problem-solving that exercises us along the very frontiers of thought itself, developing our most valuable capacities.

Thus writing does physically develop our ability to think, as it also 22 helps us in each instance to discover and clarify our thoughts. I suppose we all know this from our own experience of writing and rewriting, but most of us somehow fail to get this simple truth across to our students, perhaps because we ourselves do not write persistently enough. Like many others, Charles Darwin discovered this obvious but neglected truth:

> I have as much difficulty as ever in expressing myself clearly and 23 concisely; . . . but it has had the compensating advantage of forcing me to think long and intently about every sentence, and thus I have been led to see errors in reasoning and in my own observations or those of others.[4]

In an era that prizes the irrational and praises blowing the mind, 24 we have an immense task to convince our students, all over again, of what Charles Darwin discovered: writing can bring one to think rationally, to uncover errors not only in reasoning but in what seems to be factual, empirical observation, until the struggle with words and thought reveals those observations to have been misinterpretations of what we thought we saw.

So, to conclude, writing will discover ideas for us, will bring them 25 to realization, and with them will increase our capacity to realize. To

---

[3] From here on, I borrow from my portion of *The Written Word*, rephrasing slightly and clearing up typographical errors, some serious, in a book that got into print without at least this author's seeing galley proof, through an unfortunate editorial oversight.

[4] *Autobiography*, The Life of Science Library, ed. George Gaylord Simpson (New York: Schuman Publishers, 1950), p. 65.

bring every student to fulfill his capacities is the teacher's aim, and the process of writing is our most immediate and important way to that fulfillment. We need to remember that, to convince our students of it, and to keep the process of writing prominently in the forefront of what we require to be educated. Otherwise we may discover we have frittered away and abandoned our very best means of intellectual discovery.

Study Questions

1. Considering Baker's audience, purpose, and subject, why is the first-person point of view more appropriate than the third person?
2. What is Baker's thesis? Is it stated? If so, where? Is it implied? If so, how?
3. In paragraphs 2 and 4 what is the relationship of the first and last sentence in each paragraph?
4. What is the purpose of the type of development used in paragraphs 10–13?
5. In paragraphs 1–4 what type of sentence occurs most frequently?
6. Identify the topic of paragraph 21 and the type of development.

Why Jessie Hates English
SLOAN WILSON

Sloan Wilson (1920–   ) was born in Norwalk, Connecticut, and received an A.B. from Harvard University (1946). During World War II he was an officer in the Coast Guard. Then he wrote for the *Providence Journal* and later Time, Inc. In 1953 he taught English at Buffalo University. He was assistant director for the White House Conference on Education (1955) and a member of the National Citizens Committee for Public Schools (1949–1953). His books include *Voyage to Somewhere* (1946), *The Man in the Gray Flannel Suit* (1955), *A Summer Place* (1958), *Away From It All* (1969), *All the Best People* (1970), *What Shall We Wear to This Party?* (1976), and *Ice Brothers* (1979). Moviegoers will remember the film versions of *The Man in the Gray Flannel Suit* and *A Summer Place*.

Reprinted from *Saturday Review,* September 18, 1976, by permission.

Not long ago, my youngest daughter, Jessica, who is twelve 1
years old, came home from school, dropped her book bag in the middle
of our living room, and yelled, "I hate English!"

In some families this might not cause much of a stir, but I am an 2
old English teacher, as well as a writer. My father was an English
teacher and so was *his* father. As a matter of fact, my father, who
enjoyed exaggeration, used to claim that all his progenitors had been
English teachers, going clear back to a lone Wilson aboard the *Santa
Maria,* who died horribly while attempting to give a lesson in English
grammar to the Indians. They skinned him alive, Dad said, and boiled
him.

When Jessie came home with her shocking announcement, my 3
first impulse was to find the teacher who had made her hate English
and give her the same treatment that the aborigines had given my
ancestor. I should add here my objective, impartial view that my
youngest daughter is extremely bright, especially gifted in English,
and a surprisingly dedicated scholar. All right, the opinion of a father
concerning his youngest daughter has to be discounted at least 50
percent. Even so, Jessie is a child who reads far more than most adults
do at home, and she writes well enough to get the highest marks
whenever she pens a report for a course other than English. In her
English course she never has had to write much of anything. In many
modern sixth-grade English courses, I had already discovered, writing
does not occupy a large part of the curriculum, if any.

But what had the teacher been doing to make Jessie hate English? 4
She was not, Jessie hastened to tell me, the kind of classroom ogre who
can make a student hate anything.

"It's not the teacher, Daddy," she said with some exasperation, as 5
though I were a very slow pupil, "it's just *English.*"

"Don't you enjoy all the stories and poems you get in English?" 6

"We hardly ever get stories and poems. All we get, Daddy, in 7
grammar. That's all we're supposed to study, right through high
school. I'll show you my books.

That night I spent several hours poring over my daughter's 8
textbooks after she had finished her homework.

"What do you think?" my wife asked, poking her head into my 9
study when it was time for bed.

"I hate English!" I replied. "These books have converted me from a 10
lifelong lover of the language to a truant."

"What's the matter with them?" 11

I showed her two books. They were the official kind of modern 12
textbook that apparently is contrived to look as little like a textbook as
possible. The layout looks as though it is the brainstorm of the art
director of a struggling new advertising agency after a three-martini
lunch. Much of the copy was apparently supplied by a deposed editor of
the New York *Daily News.* Headlines scream. There are eye-catching
photographs of football players and full-page reproductions of old
advertisements for expensive coats, cosmetics, and automobiles. In one
book, my favorite horror, there is an entire section on the grammar of
Madison Avenue, which the authors obviously admire.

For a long time I have been aware that we all live in a nightmare 13
world, but I had not realized that the schools have substituted
advertising copy for the prose and poetry of the masters, which
students in my antique day used to study and occasionally enjoy. Why
are they doing this sort of thing?

To find out, I telephoned my *oldest* daughter, Lisa, who followed 14
the family trade and is or, rather, was an English teacher. Unlike me,
she has recent knowledge of what goes on in the public schools.

"A lot of advertising copy is used to teach English nowadays," she 15
said. "The words are short and the sentences simple—"

"I'm not talking about a class for retarded children," I objected.   16

"Neither am I. That's the depressing part of it. Even in classes for 17
the brightest children, the advertising copy is sometimes useful, just to
keep the kids awake."

"I hate the whole system!" I exploded. "Jessie spends hours at home 18
looking at television, and when she finally goes to school, they teach
her advertisements as though they were gems of English prose! Pretty
soon she's going to think and talk like a deodorant commercial!"

"Do I?" Lisa asked with a laugh. "What do you think I had to 19
study? The lucky thing is that most kids ignore school."

Perhaps in an effort to preserve some facade of respectability, 20
Jessie's English textbooks also included some brief snippets of good
books by recognizable authors. A few paragraphs by the masters, from
Mark Twain to Ray Bradbury, were sandwiched between the gaudy
photographs and the advertising copy, free samples of a product that
many of the students may never see in its entirety.

The jazzy layout, which made a textbook look like a sales brochure, 21
and the snippets of real writing were all sugarcoating for the main
subject of Jessie's English books, which was, of course, grammar. Page
after page was devoted to this dismal exercise, chapter after chapter.
Many little tests in grammar were offered. Most of them I could not
pass despite a lifetime of making a living by writing English.

What are "derivational suffixes"? How about a "subjective comple- 22
tion"? While I puzzled over "subjective completion," I thought it might
be some sort of euphemism for "premature ejaculation," but the
textbook tells me that it is "a word which completes the verb and refers
back to the subject." Understand now?

I have here a whole bagful of nuggets of information mined from 23
Jessie's textbook. Here is one sentence: "Just as there are determiners
to signal the presence of nouns in a sentence, so too are there signal
words which point to the presence of verbs—structure words called
auxiliaries."

That is the kind of sentence that I cannot understand and do not 24
want to understand. People who understand sentences like that are
thrown out of the Authors League and the Roma Bar, my favorite
hangout.

Do you have "terminal clusters"? They are not a form of cancer, but 25
something that adds to the descriptive power of prose, the book assures
me. Are you a master of the "multi-level sentence"? Apparently it has

nothing to do with the critics' favorite, the multi-level novel. Are you good at "parallel repetition" and "chain linking"? We are still talking about English prose, mind you, not wire fences. Are you a master of that new addition of marlinespike scholarship, the "comma splice"?

My twelve-year-old daughter has to be able to interpret all this 26 nonsense. If she can't, she will fail her examinations in English, no matter how much she reads at home, no matter how well she writes for other classes.

Who invented all this hideous jargon used by grammarians? I don't 27 know, but my quotations are from that favorite horror book of Jessie's, *Grammar Lives*. The title becomes more nonsensical the more one thinks about it. This mercifully slender volume, which presumably has been sold to many school systems, was published in 1975 by McDougal, Littell & Company. The names of the people responsible for this reverse masterpiece go on like the "crawl" preceding a pornographic movie, constituting a list of individuals eagerly seeking credit for the discreditable. The "consultant" is Karen J. Kuehner. The "authors" are Ronald T. Shephard and John MacDonald. The "editorial direction," which must have been remarkable, was supplied by Claudia Norlin. These people presumably all got together, invented or borrowed phrases like "terminal clusters," reprinted some old advertisements and snippets of legitimate prose, and then really demonstrated their talents by finding a way to make this stuff compulsory reading for hundreds of thousands, if not millions, of innocent children. They should not, however, feel alone in their guilt. Plenty of other "educators" are helping them to make children hate English and to be illiterate.

I could quote many more examples of the grammarian's art, but I 28 have to take it easy on my blood pressure.

"Why does grammar make you so angry?" my wife asked. "Doesn't 29 everybody have to study it?"

The answer, of course, is that for the last few thousand years 30 nobody was asked to study grammar anywhere near as much as the pupils in most American public schools, where it often occupies most of the English curriculum. In my own youth I studied formal grammar briefly in the fifth grade. I remember it because it seemed so silly. Who but a schoolteacher would diagram sentences and make simple prose so complex? Fortunately my teacher hated grammar as much as I did. Soon she returned to assigning us themes and correcting them in detail, a much better way to teach the mechanics of the language. She also asked us to read good books—*whole books,* not snippets. When we wrote book reports, the teacher got another shot at correcting our English. I often wonder what she would have said if someone had asked her to give us advertisements for study.

I have heard it said that the students of my generation and of prior 31 ones did not need to learn grammar because we studied so much Latin. I believe that this contradicts everything that has been learned about learning, part of which can be summed up with the astonishing news that when a boy studies Latin, he just learns Latin. My own case provides only one correction to that. For eight years I studied Latin, but I didn't acquire any lasting knowledge of Latin. I just learned to hate school, except for English, which made sense. I do not owe my knowledge of English to Latin, except for the fact that Latin made everything else appear easy.

Those who are in charge of planning English courses in the public 32 schools do not seem to be aware of the fact that those who study grammar do not learn English—they just learn the crazy jargon of the grammarians and all their rules and regulations for English when studied as a dead language. Grammar is an attempt to codify the English language, reduce it to abstractions devoid of meaning or beauty, break it into "rules," "laws," and pseudomathematical "rights" and "wrongs." The fact that it is necessary to learn to speak and write grammatically does not mean that one must devote much time to the abstract study of grammar. One should, instead, study, of all things, speaking and writing.

Some youngsters can find real joy in writing a good theme and 33 welcome a teacher's attempts to show them how to improve it, even if the corrections involve the use of a few basic rules of grammar. In a properly run English composition class, grammar has specific applications and is not taught as an abstract "science." As it should be, it is always subordinate to the basic urge to communicate, not an end in itself.

I think I know how the public schools came to rely more and more 34 heavily on the teaching of grammar as an abstract science. As the children of parents who themselves spoke broken English flooded the public schools, something had to be done to help countless students learn whole new speech patterns. The study of grammar is not good remedial English, as the performance of so many high school graduates sadly proves, but it must have seemed a good solution at first and a much cheaper one than the complex programs necessary for helping a person change speech patterns acquired in infancy.

Although classes in grammar didn't teach children anything but 35 how to pass examinations devised by the grammarians, they offered certain practical advantages. Tests in grammar can be graded by machines. A teacher who asks his class to write themes every day may be deluged with papers that have to be corrected line after line by the human hand. It is also true that almost any adult, after a few months of specialized instruction, can teach grammar. To be a good teacher of English composition, one has to be able to write good English oneself. As has been often remarked, English has rarely been a strong point of the teachers' colleges and departments of education, which have produced most of our public school teachers. The jargon of the educator is not conducive to teaching good, clear English.

The current discovery that high school graduates on the whole 36 read and write with more difficulty than even their recent predecessors hits educators hard. The public schools have been supported and defended as an act of faith by most Americans all during their periods of rapid growth, especially since World War II. Criticisms have been shrugged off as the work of crackpots or intellectual snobs. When the book *Why Johnny Can't Read* came out, more than twenty years ago, it sold a lot of copies, but it was never quite respectable among people who were seriously concerned with the schools. If the schools were not teaching reading well at the moment, the feeling was, the difficulties would soon be overcome.

Now decades have passed, and there is evidence that the schools **37** are teaching reading worse than they have in the past and that writing among recent high school graduates is almost a lost art. There have been loud cries for "a return to the fundamentals." And what are the fundamentals? Reading? Writing? Of course not! In the minds of the educators, *grammar* is the real fundamental. If the proliferation of courses in grammar has resulted in the graduation of countless youngsters who can hardly read or write, the obvious answer is to give the youngsters even more grammar. If one aspirin doesn't stop your headache, take two.

Apparently no one puts himself in the position of the student who **38** sits squirming while the teacher drills him in grammar day after day, year after year. It's easy to see why such a student doesn't want to read anything—he is taught to regard the text as a boneyard of grammar problems on which he will probably be quizzed. Writing, too, becomes a test of fitting together words and phrases in a way that is *grammatical*, not interesting, funny, or meaningful. My youngest daughter is not the only pupil in her school who hates English, and as a result, she gives it as little time as possible.

Like many other parents, I have tried to do something about this **39** situation for my child. I wrote a long letter to my old friend David S. Siegel, the superintendent of schools in Ticonderoga, N.Y., the upstate village where we live. Dave really wanted to help. He referred the matter to the "language arts coordinator," a title that apparently means "head English teacher" in the language of contemporary public schools. He turned out to be a pleasant, intelligent young chap who is alarmingly well versed in the theories of modern public schools, but ambitious and idealistic concerning the English courses nonetheless. He organized a class for students from three grades who are especially gifted in English and invited my youngest daughter to join it. The class is known as a speed group, and now, poor Jessie reports, she is being fed about three times as much grammar as before. Her new ambition is to be a veterinarian. With animals, after all, she will be asked neither to write, to read, nor even to talk.

Study Questions

1. What rhetorical advantage does Wilson gain by writing this essay in the first person? By the use of dialogue in paragraphs 5–19?
2. What type of development is used in paragraphs 20–25?

3. In dealing with a situation he feels should be corrected, what is the author's strategy in his presentation?
4. Identify the topics of paragraphs 27 and 35. What type of development is used in these paragraphs?
5. What is Wilson's strategy in presenting his solution implicitly rather than explicitly?
6. What is the effect of the humor Wilson uses? Does it detract from a serious intent? Would the effect be different without the humor?

The Flight from Excellence
JOHN R. SILBER

John Robert Silber (1926–   ) was born in San Antonio, Texas, and earned degrees from Trinity and Yale universities. His publications in ethics and education have earned him many honorary degrees, as well as awards from the Fulbright committee and the Guggenheim Foundation. He taught at the University of Texas and Boston University before becoming president of BU in 1971. Silber's works include *The Ethical Significance of Kant's Religion* (1968) and numerous articles in periodicals including *Ethics* and the *University of Chicago Law Review*.

The only standard of performance that can sustain a free 1 society is excellence. It is increasingly claimed, however, that excellence is at odds with democracy; increasingly we are urged to offer a dangerous embrace to mere adequacy.

By this I do not mean that our performance is necessarily becoming 2 worse. In the sports in which precise comparison is possible we excel our predecessors with a consistency and regularity that threaten to become monotonous. Athletes have never run so fast, jumped so high, or sunk so many baskets. Even as we recognize what appears to be our prevailing inability to teach most children to read and write, we reassure ourselves that educational opportunity has never been greater and that science and mathematics have never been taught more effectively. Consumer goods have been developed to such a degree of sophistication, low cost, and reliability that one can now buy for a few dollars a tiny device whose capabilities were unavailable forty years ago in any size and at any price: the pocket calculator.

Our flight from excellence is different and apart from this prog- 3

Reprinted by permission.

ress. It is profoundly philosophical. Out of a well-intentioned but inept concern with equality of opportunity, we have begun to reject anything that exceeds anyone's grasp. Some might argue that it is our right to engage in this curious flight, and so it is, the right of free men to be fools. But do we have the right as citizens in a free society to reject excellence on behalf of others who may not be so foolish?

Much of the present-day rejection of standards is precisely by **4** people and institutions that act in trust for others. This is flagrantly true of higher education, and especially regrettable because higher education purports to be and has been a repository for the highest standards.

One of the most obvious examples here is the war against grading. **5** While there are many motives and rationales behind the movement to substitute pass/fail or pass/no-entry "grading" for the traditional scales, all begin with the same crucial assumption: that there is no compelling reason to distinguish between excellence and adequacy, and that it is wrong—either educationally or morally—to record evidence of inadequacy or failure. A related phenomenon is grade inflation, whereby teachers behave as if all students are equally gifted and hardworking. Declining standards are also reflected in the relaxed indifference shown by many professors and institutions to the wholesale and retail distribution of plagiarized materials by corporations selling term papers and other academic assignments. In all cases the threat to excellence is obvious, for our refusal to reject inauthentic work or to identify excellence will eventually render us unable to recognize it or care about it.

Last year the City University of New York abandoned open **6** enrollment. It did not, however, return to its earlier admissions standards, but instead established as the minimum qualification for admission the competence expected of an eighth-grade education. This is less an indictment of the standards of CUNY, which was, after all, seeking rather tentatively to step back from the abyss, than it is of the high schools. For while prospective students at CUNY must now have reached an eighth-grade level, they must also be high-school graduates—so, in theory, they must also have attained a twelfth-grade education. Implicit in the admissions standards of CUNY is a one-third devaluation of the New York high-school diploma.

It is to the credit of the City University that it has introduced very **7** extensive remedial programs to upgrade the competence of incoming freshmen. But should this extensive remedial work, requiring at least one full year to complete, be carried on in the context of a great university? It is hardly higher education, since it is no higher than the work expected of high-school students. Surely this work could be done more economically and appropriately by the high schools or community colleges.

Every day it becomes more obvious that a technologically sophisti- **8** cated society will need more, not fewer, educated citizens. Postindustrial society will be grim for a functional illiterate, and it will itself be badly disrupted by the presence of large numbers of semiliterates whose skills, if any, are suited to a world that no longer exists. A restoration of excellence is therefore in the interest of society at large and of each of its members.

Some people believe that the pursuit of excellence is essentially 9 antidemócratic. This fallacy is most obvious in the commonly voiced charge that educational institutions with high standards of excellence in admissions and faculty recruitment are "elitist," a term that for most people is redolent of special and unearned privilege and suggests that these institutions are havens for the incompetent offspring of the rich.

Our society is ambivalent about elitism. We refer easily and 10 unself-consciously to Ruth, Gehrig, and Mays as the elite of baseball, to Simpson and Baugh as the elite of football, to Jones, Palmer, and Trevino as the elite of golf, and to Zaharias, Thorpe, and Owens as the elite of athletics itself; but outside of sports we use the word as a reproach. This confusion did not afflict Jefferson or Adams. "That all men are born to equal rights is true," said Adams.

> *Every being has a right to his own, as clear, as moral, as sacred, as any other being has. . . . But to teach that all men are born with equal powers and faculties . . . is as gross a fraud, as glaring an imposition on the credulity of people as ever was practiced.*

Jefferson recognized a natural aristocracy based on virtue and 11 talents. He contrasted to this aristocracy an artificial one, founded on wealth and birth without regard to virtue or talent. The natural aristocracy, Jefferson believed, was "the most precious gift of nature." He not only acknowledged, but embraced, the idea that people are born with varying degrees of intelligence and talent.

Speaking on the occasion of receiving an Alumnae Award recently 12 at Boston University, Rep. Barbara Jordan pointed out that our confusion has had deleterious effects on the federal government's effort to aid higher education. She said:

> *We have been so brainwashed by an erroneous definition of democracy that we have difficulty prescribing any program or formula, or giving any grant which is better or more than some other grant, because we don't want to be accused of being antidemocratic because we recognize that some people are excellent. . . . As members of Congress, we should not be engaged in a leveling process. . . . We ought to enunciate and promote those policies which would lead absolutely, categorically, and without hesitation, to the best this country has to offer.*

Calls for the maintenance of standards are often denounced as 13 racist and sexist, but only a sexist or racist could believe that women or members of minorities are in fact inferior to everyone else, and would be unable to compete on an equal basis if judged by performance alone. If our society really did hold and maintain high standards, we would expect up to 51 percent of all partners in Wall Street law firms to be women and 11 percent of all surgeons to be blacks. The extent to which we fall short of these figures shows how far we are from honoring excellence as a criterion. Rejecting excellence in the interest of women and minorities is in effect a condescending adoption of a lower standard for them.

The movement to establish the United States as a bilingual nation 14 provides a striking example of this condescension. Until recently, the United States was unique in the world as a very large nation covering a great land mass that maintained a single national language with dialects that were easily mutually intelligible. It is remarkable that a nation of such ethnic diversity has not been torn apart by intercommunal violence. Our comparative peace and the single language are almost certainly related: unlike Canada, Belgium, and other nations with explosive linguistic problems, the United States has been able to sustain its diverse culture within the context of one official language. Recent attempts to require bilingual ballots erode the position of the national language by assuming that it is possible to be a citizen even if one is literate only in the language of one's ethnic group.

The proposal is designed to exempt one large group of citizens from 15 a requirement that has hitherto been expected of all citizens, the acquisition of some modest competence in the national language. This reduces the standard of performance expected of citizens to a derisory level. It patronizes the Hispanic culture by implying that it cannot survive coexistence with the English language. And it has racist overtones, suggesting that Spanish-speaking American citizens cannot be expected to acquire the same level of competence that was acquired by immigrants from Germany, Italy, Russia, Poland, Greece, and many other countries, and that was until recently expected of Spanish-speaking citizens. (Such an ill-advised notion should not be confused with the thoughtfully established programs of bilingual education which have been designed to induct children into the use of the national language. This process is a burden that obviously ought to be assumed by our society as a logical consequence of having a national language in the first place, and as essential to the provision of equal educational opportunity.)

A similar question arises with regard to the various dialects of 16 English. In 1974 the National Council of Teachers of English issued a position paper maintaining that students who grow up speaking dialectal variants of English should not be required to learn standard English. On a recent television program an obviously intelligent and educated young black student said it was plain that students who grew up speaking dialects arrived in school ill prepared to function in the standard dialect. He did not think that attempts to require these students to use the standard dialect grew out of "overt racism or elitism. ... That's the way it's mapped out by society." Recognizing that the good intentions of such attempts precluded their being *overtly* racist, he nevertheless left the impression that he considered them part of unconscious societal racism.

Nothing could be farther from racism or elitism than requiring 17 students from the ghetto to learn standard English. For this is to treat them as the equals of the great majority of students.

It is particularly reprehensible for white professors and white 18
middle-class students to encourage black students in the mistaken
belief that it does not matter whether they learn to speak and write
with educated middle-class proficiency. The black student who speaks
only ghetto English is not able to communicate fully. He can communicate effectively only with those who speak his own dialect, but an
educated black can converse with anyone in the English-speaking
world. White professors and students, already proficient in standard
English, retain their monopoly in it and protect themselves from black
competition by encouraging blacks to renounce their educational
opportunities. Thus blacks may remain tragically isolated from the
mainstream of their national culture, and pay the price for the
ideological whims of whites.

Lowered expectations are a threat to all our students, since their 19
ability to develop is very largely dependent upon the goals we establish
for them. But it is not students alone who need a vision of excellence.
Writing in 1830, Alexis de Tocqueville noted that in times of faith,
people concern themselves with a distant supreme goal beyond this
life. In so doing,

> they learn by imperceptible degrees to repress a crowd of petty passing
> desires in order ultimately to best satisfy the one great permanent longing
> which obsesses them. When these same men engage in worldly affairs, such
> habits influence their conduct. . . . That is why religious nations have often
> accomplished such lasting achievements. For in thinking of the other world,
> they have found out the great secret of success in this.

But in skeptical ages, Tocqueville continued, the vision of the life 20
to come is lost, a problem that is exacerbated in democracies, where
people are set free to compete with each other to improve their
situations. In such a combination of circumstances, "the present looms
large and hides the future, so that men do not want to think beyond
tomorrow." Tocqueville thought it especially important that the
philosophers and rulers in skeptical democracies should always "strive
to set a distant aim as the object of human efforts; that is their most
important business." He did not specify the nature of the goals which
need to be set in such ages, but we can hardly doubt that such goals
require the best efforts not merely of individuals but of the society as a
whole. In a secular age in which few believe in a life to come and in
which God is, if not dead, at most indifferent, a vision of excellence—a
secular kingdom of God—in which individuals fulfill themselves
through education and useful public service may be essential.

Study Questions

1. Paragraphs 1, 4, 9 , and 21 introduce the various sections
   of the essay. Analyze the ways they serve this purpose.
2. What type of development is used in sections introduced
   by paragraphs 4 and 9?

3. What is implied by the word "elite" in the title, and why is it necessary for Silber to devote a section of his essay to explain what he means by the term?
4. What in the presentation indicates the audience Silber is addressing? Explain.
5. What is Silber's strategy in the second paragraph, in which he notes that our performances in some areas are directed toward excellence?
6. What basic type of argument does Silber use to advance his position?

Needed: Equal Educational Opportunity for All
SHIRLEY CHISHOLM

Shirley Chisholm (1924–   ) was born in Brooklyn. She graduated *cum laude* from Brooklyn College, later received an M.A. from Columbia, and has been the recent recipient of numerous honorary degrees. She has served in both the New York State Assembly and in the 91st–94th Congresses, representing New York. Her books include *Unbought and Unbossed* (1970) and *The Good Fight* (1970).

A democratic society depends upon the intelligence and 1 wisdom of the mass of people to keep the country moving. A government of the people, by the people, and for the people necessarily depends upon the people's judgment to make decisions that affect the growth of the country. In America, we have delegated to institutions of higher education the responsibility to train the minds of those who will make scientific and medical discoveries; who will give us an intellectual basis for law, order, and justice; and who will propagate an appreciation for the arts—thus, supplying us with cultural training.

While the fulfillment of these responsibilities remains the central 2 purpose of institutions of higher education, American society casts another, less theoretical responsibility upon institutions of higher

Reprinted from *School and Society*, April 1972, by permission.

learning—that of granting "union cards" for upward social mobility. The slogan, "education is the key to success," is interpreted, in the United States, to mean that graduation from college opens up job possibilities at a salary range which is above that of the average American. Indeed, this very practical consideration of what one can do with a college degree—usually referred to as a college education—too often interferes with the more esoteric concern of how one's mind is strengthened by studying a particular curriculum at school.

It is the mundane and practical consideration of acquiring a college 3 degree for the purpose of upward mobility which is inescapably on the minds of minority groups in their demand for equal participation in the mainstream of American society. Higher education is the key to this goal; and institutions of higher learning must address themselves to a relatively new constituency.

Toward this end, there must be universal acceptance of the 4 premise that higher education is the right of every American who has demonstrated the ability of potential for doing academic work at the college level. Many Americans have come to accept this in theory, but few have become directly involved in seeking ways of implementation. The municipal government of New York City, in conjunction with the Board of Education, has taken a bold step in practically applying the theory. New York City now has a policy of open admissions, where high school graduates who are residents of the city are guaranteed admission to one of the colleges in the city's college system upon application. The program was devised after the demands of the blacks from Bedford-Stuyvesant and Harlem and of Puerto Ricans from the Bronx, but it has proved to be as valuable to the white residents of Queens and Staten Island as it has to minorities from ghettoes.

Neither the quality of education offered nor respect for the integ- 5 rity of a college diploma has been impaired by the institution of open enrollment. It is certainly a program worthy of implementation throughout the country, and one which is absolutely necessary for allowing the economically disadvantaged to assume their right of education. But, at this point, our nation lacks the commitment to invest the proper resources in higher education.

Resources from the government and private sources are manda- 6 tory, for open enrollment as well as any other program designed to open college doors to minorities places an extra financial burden upon the institutions. Thus, institutions of higher education must be given plenty of financial assistance if they are to fulfill the new obligations of allowing minorities and the poor access to higher education—toward the ultimate end of entrance into the mainstream of American society.

Will we have the courage and commitment to stop utilizing our 7 resources on warfare and to work on the intellectual and economic development of the American people? Will we desist from practices that deprive minorities and women of the opportunity to participate fully in our society? These are questions which the great majority of Americans will have to answer; and higher education must do the same.

There must be a willingness on the part of college administrators 8
to propose policies on admission that will take into consideration the
obligation of higher education to address itself to the needs of
minorities, women, and the poor. There also must be steps taken to
make sure that the course of study effectively treats the contributions
of minorities to the growth and development of American society and
that courses are offered which will educate college students to the
abuses and inequalities in our system and which will urge their
involvement in activities designed to promote equality of rights for all
Americans.

Such education should be part of the curriculum in any democratic 9
society; and it does not involve, in my view, the institutions, themselves, in social activity. Rather, it presents the students with the
opportunity to apply certain theories to practical situations, which is in
keeping with the notion that the only valuable education is one which
promotes an understanding of what is necessary in order for human
beings to make a contribution to the growth, prosperity, and durability
of an orderly society.

Study Questions

1. What is the basic difference in the types of arguments
   Chisholm and Silber use?
2. Which paragraph contains the conclusion of Chisholm's
   argument?
3. Identify the topic of paragraph 4. What type of development does the author use?
4. Paragraph 8 is composed of two long sentences. Would
   the effect be different if there were three or four shorter
   sentences? Explain.
5. What is the function of paragraph 7? Why are questions
   used in this paragraph?

My Father Is an Educated Man

JESSE STUART

Jesse Stuart (1907 —   ) was born in West Hollow, Kentucky, and still lives there. He received an A.B. from Lincoln Memorial University and later attended Vanderbilt University and Peabody College. He worked in a circus, in a steel mill, and as a farmer before taking education as his profession. He has taught English at numerous American universities, and lectured all over the world, particularly in the Far East. His books have won him grants, honors, and honorary degrees galore, and also endeared him to millions of readers. Among these books are *Trees of Heaven* (1940), *Taps for Private Tussie* (1943), *The Beatinest Boy* (1953), *Hold April* (1962), *Tomorrow's People* (1968), and *The Kingdom Within* (1979). He has written texts and children's books, and contributes articles, verse, and stories to numerous magazines.

Yesterday I was in town with my father. This town has been 1 the center of his universe. He has never traveled a fifty-mile radius from this town. He goes on Saturdays, dressed in his overalls, clean blue work shirt, overall jacket, his soiled weathered cap with a shrinking bill and his turned-at-the-toes stump-scarred brogan shoes. Often, he goes through the weekdays to town if he wants something from the stores or a bottle of beer. He walks a path four miles over the bony hills to the town as he has done since I can remember. And I can remember him for thirty-three years. He has dressed the same way, has walked the same path to the same town.

My father talked to a group of men on the courthouse square where 2 the men from all over the county meet on Saturdays with the men from the town, where they talk, tell their stories, chew their tobacco, try to whittle the longest shaving with their pocketknives while they listen to the courthouse bell calling men inside the courthouse for justice. While they talked and chewed tobacco from long home-grown twists of burley and spit mouthfuls of ambeer spittle on the courthouse square, I heard a man say, who was standing in another group of men not far from my father's group, "There's old overalled Mitch Stuart. . . . See 'im in town every Saturday." This fairly well-dressed man, teacher of a rural school, pointed to my father and the men in his group looked and listened while he talked. "Never amounted to anything in his life.

Reprinted by permission.

Never will amount to anything. But he's got smart children. His boy is a book-writer, you may've heard about."

Pert Maldin didn't see me as he went on telling the men in his **3** group how my father loved to come to town on Saturdays and loaf, just loaf and try to whittle the longest shavings, how he loved the sound of the courthouse bell and how he'd listened to it for a half century. And he told them he'd known my father that long and how my father had gone to the same little tavern, run by the same people for a half century and got his beer on Saturdays and after he had a few beers how he talked to his old friends and told them big windy tales. He told about his seeing my father have a few fights in his younger days and how time had now slowed him down. Since Pert Maldin talked confidentially to the men that surrounded him, I couldn't hear all he said. I did hear him say my father wouldn't know his name if he would meet it in the road, that he couldn't read a beer sign and he couldn't write his name.

I thought once that I would walk over to Pert Maldin and tell him a **4** few things. One thing that I would tell him was my father would know his name if he'd meet it in the big road or saw it printed on a sign beside the road but if it were in a paper he would not see it for I'd never seen him look inside a newspaper in my life. Yet, he knew his name, for my mother had taught him the letters in his name and that he knew these letters same as he knew from memory a rock cliff, an oak tree, beech, sassafras or persimmon. . . . And that if he saw his name, he would know it immediately since my mother had taught him letters in our alphabet, that he would slowly go over the letters in a word and piece them together and pronounce some of the hardest words correctly.

I thought about walking over and popping Pert Maldin on the nose **5** when he talked about my father. But I stood silently and listened as long as I could and many thoughts flashed through my brain as the ambeer spittle flashed brown in the November sunlight from the mouths of the men in the group where my father was talking, where they were laughing at some story one of his group had told. I thought a pop on the nose would serve Pert Maldin right and then I thought, "What's the use? What does he know about my father? And what does he know about education though he is a school-teacher?"

While I stood on the courthouse square watching these figures of **6** the hill earth that came to town on Saturdays to swap their windy tales and try each other's twists of homegrown burley, I thought about the members of the human family I had known. I thought about my own people and the path they had come over the earth. I thought about my father and my father's people, beardy-faced, tall, figures of the earth, tillers of earth, men who had cut the timber, cleared the fields of brush and sprouts and who had plowed the root and rock-infested mountain slopes with oxen hitched to yellow-locust-beamed cutter plows. And the longer thoughts flashed across my brain, the more I knew Pert Maldin didn't know what he was talking about . . . for my people, my father's people, had helped to build the railroads up the Big Sandy and into the

mountains of West Virginia. They had helped to build the coal drags of
the nation. . . . They had helped to build the cities, though not any that
I knew lived there now or had ever lived there. My father's people had
helped to build the highways. And the schools where children only of
the late generations have attended. They had helped to build church-
houses where but few attended since such limitations had been put on
the kind of a life they had loved, tobacco chewing, smoking, drinking of
wine, whiskey, and even beer.

Such would never suit his people. They raised their own tobacco   7
and they used it; they made their own whiskey and they drank it. They
carried firearms and used them in time of danger while they helped to
build America. What did they know about letters of the alphabet?
These little things didn't mean a lot to them! And what did they care
about books? Why should they spend their time in a closed-up schoolroom, controlled by school authorities, and strive to learn to read
secondhand life in books when they had firsthand life before them to
live?

The older men in my father's family, now sleeping in the Virginia,   8
West Virginia, and Kentucky mountains, if they were alive today
would pity their offspring, entangled in the spider web of civilization.
They would despise and fight with all their might, if they could raise
from their graves, any barriers that would confine their freedom.

What would they care about my books? They would not even read   9
them. To them, I would be an oddling.

Though I belong to them, they would not claim me since I have had   10
my chance and unlike them I have not killed one of my enemies. I am
one of the book-educated ones and I have thought this thing through.
And it took me many days and nights walking among the hills to make
my decision that I would not kill an enemy only in the time of war. . . .
And even when I was going through these days and nights of walking
the hills and thinking about what to do, my father was telling me that
since he didn't have as many years to live as I had that he would take
care of my enemies. I told him that I would do my own fighting. And
when I thought these things through, maybe, it was the book education
and the spider-web civilization his people didn't take to that helped me
to make my decision.

Let Pert Maldin talk on the courthouse square. Let him talk about   11
my father's not having an education, that he wouldn't know his name if
he'd meet it in the big road. I could tell Pert that he didn't know about
education. He was speaking about these secondhanded things called
books when my father's people had lived an education while they were
helping to build a nation and a civilization. Yes, they had taken the
law in their own hands for they had to do it since the law didn't protect
them while they fought their enemies; helped to build the railroads
through the mountains, bridges to span the rivers and blast the
turnpikes around the rocky slopes. They cleared the fields and broke
the first furrows through the roots. They built the log cabins from the
giant trees they didn't split into fence rails; they hauled giant sawlogs
with yokes of oxen to the edge of the Big Sandy and waited for the
spring rains when with spiked boots and with long poles with spikes in

the end they took their log rafts down the Big Sandy and the Ohio River to the little town of Cincinnati, the Queen City of the West.

I could tell Pert Maldin that my father, son of these figures of the 12 earth, with the blood of these men flowing through his veins, was an educated man. He was educated same as they were educated . . . but maybe his education didn't fit the time he was living. He couldn't sit behind a desk wearing a white shirt, a necktie, a neatly pressed tailored suit and shined shoes, with a pencil behind his ear. He couldn't live in a world of figures and words. They would be playthings on the wind to him. All he'd say, even if his mind were trained to do these things is "To hell with this." I know him well enough to know that he would say these words. For what does he say about my books? "A lot of damned foolishness."

I could tell anybody that my father is an educated man. Though he 13 is a small man with a wind-parched face color of the autumn earth, my father has the toughness in his muscles of the hickory sprout. He has a backbone like a saw-log. In his make-up fear was left out. That word is not in his limited vocabulary. I never heard him say, in my lifetime, that he was afraid of anything.

My father can take a handful of new-ground dirt in his hand, smell 14 of it, then sift it between his fingers and tell whether to plant the land in corn, tobacco, cane or potatoes. He has an intuition that I cannot explain. Maybe Pert Maldin, with all his education, could explain it. And my father knows when to plant, how to plant and cultivate and the right time to reap. He knows the right trees to cut from his timber for wood to burn and the trees to leave for timber. He knows the names of all the trees, flowers and plants that grow on his rugged acres. My father is able to live from sterile rugged mountain soil. He has raised enough food for his family to eat and his family has eaten about all he has raised. Money does not mean food to him as it does to many in America today. Money is some sort of a luxury to him. It is something he pays his taxes with. Money is something to him to buy land with. And the land and everything thereon is more than a bank account would be to him; land is something durable, something his eyes can see and his hands can feel. It is not the secondhand substance he would find in a book if he could read.

I could tell anybody in America if my father isn't an educated 15 man, we don't have educated men in America. And if his education isn't one of the best educations a man can have then I am not writing these words and the rain is not falling today in Kentucky. If his education isn't as important as mine—this son of his he used to tell every day to go to school since he had found the kind of education he had didn't work as well this day and time in America as the kind of education where a man had a pencil behind his ear and worked in a world of figures, words, dollars and cents, when to buy, what to buy, when, where, and how to sell—then I am not writing these words.

And as I think of my father's autumn-colored face, of this small 16 hickory-tough figure on the earth, I think of the many men in America still like him. And I say they are educated men.

Study Questions

1. What strategy does Stuart use in characterizing his father? What function does Pert Maldin serve in this?
2. Identify the ways the author reveals his attitude toward his father. How does he avoid becoming sentimental? Or does he? Explain.
3. What is the purpose of paragraph 9 in the development of this story?
4. Summarize the topic of paragraph 14 and describe the type of development the author uses.
5. What is Stuart's strategy in using his father to present his ideas on education? What advantage does this gain over a less personal, more detached method?

Language
THE SOUL OF WIT

6

To most college freshmen, the prospect of having to read about language holds little appeal, and understandably so. Their reading on language has usually been limited to textbooks and other related materials that, with rare exceptions, do little to make the subject palpable, much less interesting. With this in mind, we selected essays that illustrate a variety of tones, styles, and approaches, and it is no accident that half of them were written with a humorous intent.

Six of the essays deal, in part or wholly, with questions of usage, each with a different approach to the subject and with different views on what is and what is not acceptable and appropriate. Barbara Lawrence, in "Four-Letter Words Can Hurt You," and Wallace Stegner, in "Good-Bye to All T--T," differ in their positions on the use of obscenities. Written for women, the Lawrence essay traces the etymology of the most commonly used four-letter words and finds them blatantly sexist. Addressing a more general audience, Stegner employs a lighter and more humorous tone to argue that the words are not obscene. According to him, the sin is not in using what people consider obscenity, but in using it at the wrong time and place.

Jim Quinn and William Zinsser show that questions of what is acceptable in grammar and usage are not easily answered. Quinn in "Hopefully, They Will Shut Up," draws on historical authority to argue that certain idioms outlawed by what he calls "pop grammarians" should be considered acceptable. Zinsser's "Is It an O.K. Word, Usewise?" whimsically describes the work of *The American Heritage Dictionary of the English Language* usage panel. It is evident that by Quinn's standards the panel represented the thinking of the "pop grammarians."

The Mark Twain and H. Allen Smith selections illustrate the professional humorist's interest in language matters. Twain's "Buck Fanshaw's Funeral" comically illustrates communication difficulties caused by different dialects and Smith's "The Ugliest Word" humorously deals with the connotation of certain words.

The essays by Pei, Langer, and Orwell are more formally structured and are intended more to inform than to entertain. In "How Language and Languages Can Help You," Pei explains why we should be more concerned with what is widely acceptable than with what is correct. Langer's essay is a touching and sensitive analysis of how honest feelings expressed in simple language run the risk of being misunderstood by those who use and require in others a jargon-ridden, nonhuman official prose. Time has proven the Orwell essay, "Politics and the English Language" to be a minor classic. It is written with authority and grace and is so rich in substance that it could serve as the text for an entire semester's work on language study.

How Language— and Languages— Can Help You

MARIO PEI

Mario Pei was born in Rome in 1901 and became a United States citizen in 1925. He graduated *magna cum laude* from City College of New York (1925) and received his Ph.D. (1932) from Columbia University. His teaching career at Columbia ended in 1970, after nearly thirty-five years. In those years he established himself as a scholar and perceptive critic of the Romance languages and literatures. His writings won him the recognition of numerous national leaders. Pei's books include *Language Today* (1967), *Words in Sheep's Clothing* (1969), *Double Speak in America* (1973), and *The Story of Latin and the Romance Languages* (1976).

A well-known linguist advises you to "leave your language 1 alone"; that is, speak naturally, even if incorrectly, letting the chips fall where they may. Go ahead and use "ain't," "it's me," "who did you see?," "I laid on the bed," he advocates. Another distinguished authority in the field suggests that it would be a splendid thing if no more spelling were taught for half a century, and people were allowed to spell as they please; at the end of that period, he adds, the chances are we would have worked out a new system of spelling that would reflect the pronunciation.

Statements like these are spectacular, and they sound good on the 2 surface. They encourage the tendency inborn in each of us, to follow the line of least resistance and avoid work and effort.

Also, they have in them a grain of sense. Consider, for example, the 3 different sorts of car driving you see on the road; some are glaringly bad and lead to crashes; but certainly, within the range of safety, there is room for various ways of holding the steering wheel, applying the brakes, making a turn. Not all good golf players hold their clubs in precisely the same fashion; one man who could never break ninety as long as he held his club in the way taught him by the pro found himself down in the low eighties as soon as he threw instruction overboard and handled the club in the way that was most natural for him. Some people pound the typewriter with two fingers of each hand and their eyes on the keyboard, and are almost as speedy and accurate as devotees of the touch system.

However, there are limits to the effectiveness of doing as you 4 please. This is particularly true in language. Even the man who wants you to "leave your language alone" admits that if you use "ain't" and "I done it" in the "best" circles, you won't get invited to tea again. As for the matter of spelling, we may get away with "thru" and "nite," but phonetic spellings like "natcherly," "watchagonnado," and "I should of done it" will mark you as an illiterate.

Rightly or wrongly, most people consider language as an index of 5 culture, breeding, upbringing, personality, sometimes even of intelligence, decency, and integrity. Under the circumstances, it is unwise, not to say harmful, to pay no heed to your language. The present status of the language being what it is, the use of wrong words and forms, or the inability to produce the right ones, may do as much damage to your chances of getting ahead (and along) as using a knife on your peas or slurping your soup.

Language is something more than a system of communications; it 6 is also a social convention which one must observe, under penalty of being misjudged. Ignorance or improper use of language can easily interfere with your success and advancement. It can take money out of your pocket.

Conversely, the proper use of the proper language in the environ- 7 ment for which it is designed can lead to success in both business and social relations. For this, there is a well-grounded psychological reason.

Language is a set of rules tacitly agreed to and accepted by 8 common consent of all the speakers. There is no intrinsic connection between the *object* "hat" and the *word* "hat" save that the word has been set apart by the English-speaking community to serve as the *symbol* of the object. A French-speaking community will use not "hat" but *chapeau* to represent the object we call a hat. The validity of the language symbol for the object is subjective and unstable, in precisely the same way that a dollar bill, or a pound note, is a subjective and unstable token of purchasing power, and not at all identical with the things it can buy.

If you find yourself alone in a desert you will quickly realize that 9 the value of such dollar bills as you may have in your pocket shrinks to nil, and that a slab of bacon or a canteen of water is infinitely more valuable than a handful of hundred-dollar notes. You will also find that your language equipment is of no particular value, since there is no one to use it on.

But human beings normally do not live alone in deserts. They live 10 in communities of their fellowmen, and in such communities symbol values come into play. The dollar bill has no value in itself; it is only a piece of paper. But it is everywhere accepted as a *symbol* of purchasing power. In the same way, language becomes of value because it is accepted as the symbol of thought, the medium by which thought is transferred from one person to another.

It is at this point that the symbol comes in for close scrutiny. Why 11

is a forged dollar bill not accepted, while one produced by the
government presses is? Intrinsically, the privately produced dollar
note is just as valuable (or valueless) as the good note. But the
community has decided that only such dollar bills as bear the authentic imprint of the U.S. government shall be valid as media of exchange
and symbols of metal currency. This is because we know that government has the silver with which to redeem the paper note.

In language, the community has decided that certain words and 12
forms are valid as symbols of thought and shall be accepted by all
members of the community, while others, for one reason or another
(not necessarily a logical one), are not valid. Those not valid may serve
the purpose of temporary exchange of meaning in a limited way, just as
some forms of scrip served the purposes of money in small communities
during the depression days, or in certain army units during the
occupation of foreign lands. Their use, however, is limited, while the
fully standard forms have universal currency throughout the entire
speech community.

The type of language you ought to strive to write and speak should 13
therefore be the one that has the widest, not the narrowest, currency,
that is universally accepted and understood wherever there are English speakers. You should not be content with a kind of language that
is restricted to one locality, or one social class.

To discover what is universally current throughout the speech 14
community calls for some effort. Through ignorance, you may sometimes delude yourself into believing that the local or class speech form
you happen to be using is standard when as a matter of fact it is not. If
you are wrong and don't know it, there is no way of correcting your
error. But if you are wrong and are aware of the fact, you can do
something about it.

The question is not so much one of striving to achieve "correctness" 15
in accordance with some arbitrary or antiquated model, but of striving
to come as close as possible to the general usage of the community. To
speak without gross and glaring localisms, and with a minimum of
class features, slang, and jargon, is desirable. This can only be
achieved by watching your language, not by "leaving it alone."

The person who speaks, easily and correctly, the standard speech of 16
the broad language community to which he belongs will normally find
himself better off all around. He will be able to express his ideas and
personality and get what he wants. He will be able to make friends and
influence people. He will find that his opinions carry greater weight
with the men and women he associates with. He will also find that he
has greater understanding of others, their ideas, and their problems.

In addition to the comparison between authentic U.S. currency and 17
scrip or forged notes, another comparison is possible, between an
authentic dollar bill and an authentic British pound note. Both are
fully valid and fully accepted in their own areas. But the areas don't
coincide. Dollar, pound, franc, mark, lira, ruble, yen are all legitimate
forms of currency, but you cannot translate one into purchasing power
in the area of another without going through the process of exchange.

Something quite similar happens in the case of foreign languages 18 as compared with your own native tongue. The other languages are valid media of thought transfer in their respective countries, just as yours is valid in your land. The process by which you get your linguistic money exchanged in the foreign area is to have translators and interpreters at your disposal to convey your thoughts to the local people and get theirs in return. But just as you may also provide yourself, before you set forth on your travels, with amounts of foreign money, you may, in like manner, provide yourself with greater or smaller amounts of foreign languages, which will save you the trouble of stopping at the local exchange office or securing the services of a translator or interpreter.

Materially speaking, a knowledge of foreign languages makes your   19
traveling easier and more comfortable and allows you to carry on your activities in the foreign country as naturally as you would in your own.

On another plane, a knowledge of foreign languages gives you a   20
keener insight into the world-wide human mind, permits you to compare ways of expression and modes of thought, gives you a greater understanding of other peoples, and makes for far more pleasant and friendly relations, and this is true whether you travel or not. A good deal of the antipathy and intolerance existing in the world today hinges upon lack of linguistic understanding.

It is therefore desirable to know, as well as possible, both your own   21
language and the languages of other groups. Language, once it is gained, can be put to work for you. It can help you in your business or occupation, in your social life, in your travels, in your enjoyment of the world in general. It expands your horizons, and makes accessible to you the treasuries of world thought, both in your own chosen line of endeavor and in that broad field of leisure which modern technology has put within reach of practically all men.

Study Questions

1. To explain the functions and importance of acceptable language Pei uses an extended analogy. Identify the analogy and explain his strategy in using it.
2. Analyze the method Pei uses to introduce and lead into his subject. What are the advantages of this method?
3. What is the function of paragraph 13?
4. Identify the words or phrases that link paragraphs 1–2, 2–3, 3–4, 6–7, 9–10.
5. Identify paragraphs that contain series of parallel sentences. What effect is achieved by these types of sentences?
6. What is the topic of paragraph 8? What type of development does Pei use in this paragraph?

Four-Letter Words Can Hurt You

BARBARA LAWRENCE

Barbara Lawrence was born in Hanover, New Hampshire. She received a B.A. in French literature from Connecticut College, and later an M.A. in philosophy from New York University. Her professional writing experience includes stints as editor for *McCall's, Redbook, Harper's Bazaar,* and the *New Yorker.* Lawrence is currently an Associate Professor of Humanities at the State University of New York's Old Westbury College. She has published fiction, nonfiction, and poetry in, among others, *Choice,* the *New Yorker, The New York Times, Commonweal,* and *Columbia Poetry.*

Why should any words be called obscene? Don't they all 1 describe natural human functions? Am I trying to tell them, my students demand, that the "strong earthy, gut-honest"—or, if they are fans of Norman Mailer, the "rich, liberating, existential"—language they use to describe sexual activity isn't preferable to "phony-sounding, middle-class words like 'intercourse' and 'copulate'?" "Cop You Late!" they say with fancy inflections and gagging grimaces. "Now, what is *that* supposed to mean?"

Well, what is it supposed to mean? And why indeed should one 2 group of words describing human functions and human organs be acceptable in ordinary conversation and another, describing presumably the same organs and functions, be tabooed—so much so, in fact, that some of these words still cannot appear in print in many parts of the English-speaking world?

The argument that these taboos exist only because of "sexual 3 hang-ups" (middle-class, middle-age, feminist), or even that they are a result of class oppression (the contempt of the Norman conquerors for the language of their Anglo-Saxon serfs), ignores a much more likely explanation, it seems to me, and that is the sources and functions of the words themselves.

The best known of the tabooed sexual verbs, for example, comes 4 from the German *ficken,* meaning "to strike"; combined, according to Partridge's etymological dictionary *Origins,* with the Latin sexual verb *futuere;* associated in turn with the Latin *fustis,* "a staff or cudgel"; the Celtic *buc,* "a point, hence to pierce"; the Irish *bot,* "the male member"; the Latin *battuere,* "to beat"; the Gaelic *batair,* "a cudgeller"; the Early Irish *bualaim,* "I strike"; and so forth. It is one of what etymologists sometimes call "the sadistic group of words for the man's part in copulation."

The brutality of this word, then, and its equivalents ("screw," 5 "bang," etc.), is not an illusion of the middle class or a crotchet of Women's Liberation. In their origins and imagery these words carry undeniably painful, if not sadistic, implications, the object of which is almost always female. Consider, for example, what a "screw" actually does to the wood it penetrates; what a painful, even mutilating, activity this kind of analogy suggests. "Screw" is particularly interesting in this context, since the noun, according to Partridge, comes from words meaning "groove," "nut," "ditch," "breeding sow," "scrofula" and "swelling," while the verb, besides its explicit imagery, has antecedent associations to "write on," "scratch," "scarify," and so forth—a revealing fusion of a mechanical or painful action with an obviously denigrated object.

Not all obscene words, of course, are as implicitly sadistic or 6 denigrating to women as these, but all that I know seem to serve a similar purpose: to reduce the human organism (especially the female organism) and human functions (especially sexual and procreative) to their least organic, most mechanical dimension; to substitute a trivializing or deforming resemblance for the complex human reality of what is being described.

Tabooed male descriptives, when they are not openly denigrating 7 to women, often serve to divorce a male organ or function from any significant interaction with the female. Take the word "testes," for example, suggesting "witnesses" (from the Latin *testis)* to the sexual and procreative strengths of the male organ; and the obscene counterpart of this word, which suggests little more than a mechanical shape. Or compare almost any of the "rich," "liberating" sexual verbs, so fashionable today among male writers, with that much-derided Latin word "copulate" ("to bind or join together") or even that Anglo-Saxon phrase (which seems to have had no trouble surviving the Norman Conquest) "make love."

How arrogantly self-involved the tabooed words seem in compari- 8 son to either of the other terms, and how contemptuous of the female partner. Understandably so, of course, if she is only a "skirt," a "broad," a "chick," a "pussycat" or a "piece." If she is, in other words, no more than her skirt, or what her skirt conceals; no more than a breeder, or the broadest part of her; no more than a piece of a human being or a "piece of tail."

The most severely tabooed of all the female descriptives, inciden- 9 tally, are those like a "piece of tail," which suggests (either explicitly or through antecedents) that there is no significant difference between the female channel through which we are all conceived and born and the anal outlet common to both sexes—a distinction that pornographers have always enjoyed obscuring.

This effort to deny women their biological identity, their individu- 10 ality, their humanness, is such an important aspect of obscene language that one can only marvel at how seldom, in an era preoccupied with definitions of obscenity, this fact is brought to our attention. One problem, of course, is that many of the people in the best position to do this (critics, teachers, writers) are so reluctant today to admit that they are angered or shocked by obscenity. Bored, maybe, unimpressed, aesthetically displeased, but—no matter how brutal or denigrating the material—never angered, never shocked.

And yet how eloquently angered, how piously shocked many of 11 these same people become if denigrating language is used about any minority group other than women; if the obscenities are racial or ethnic, that is, rather than sexual. Words like "coon," "kike," "spic," "wop," after all, deform identity, deny individuality and humanness in almost exactly the same way that sexual vulgarisms and obscenities do.

No one that I know, least of all my students, would fail to question 12 the values of a society whose literature and entertainment rested heavily on racial or ethnic pejoratives. Are the values of a society whose literature and entertainment rest as heavily as ours on sexual pejoratives any less questionable?

Study Questions

1. Note the number of questions in the first two paragraphs. What is the rhetorical purpose in this type of paragraph development?
2. Identify the type of development used in paragraphs 5, 7, and 8.
3. What effect is achieved by the first-person point of view?
4. In what specific ways does Lawrence reveal her attitude toward her subject? Her audience?
5. Identify the type of argument used to establish that words and phrases are taboo.
6. Which paragraph contains the thesis sentence?

Good-Bye to All T- -T!

WALLACE STEGNER

Wallace Stegner (1909–   ) was born in Lake Mills, Iowa. He
received a B.A. from the University of Iowa (1930) and both an
M.A. and a Ph.D. from the University of Iowa (1932, 1935). He has
served as an editor for Houghton Mifflin, as Assistant Secretary of
the Interior, and as consultant to the Library of Congress. Stegner
received fellowships from the Rockefeller and Guggenheim Foun-
dations, from the Center for Advanced Studies in Behavioral
Sciences, and from the National Endowment for the Humanities.
He was instrumental in founding the Creative Writing Program at
Stanford University, where he taught for many years. Stegner's
books have earned him numerous awards including the Pulitzer
Prize, the O. Henry Memorial Award, and the National Book
Award. Among those books are *Remembering Laughter* (1937), *The
Big Rock Candy Mountain* (1943), *The City of the Living* (1956),
Shooting Star (1961), and *The Uneasy Chair* (1974).

1 Not everyone who laments what contemporary novelists
have done to the sex act objects to the act itself, or to its mention. Some
want it valued higher than fiction seems to value it; they want the
word "climax" to retain some of its literary meaning. Likewise, not
everyone who has come to doubt the comtemporary freedom of language objects to strong language in itself. Some of us object precisely
because we value it.

2 I acknowledge that I have used four-letter words familiarly all my
life, and have put them into books with some sense that I was insisting
on the proper freedom of the artist. I have applauded the extinction of
those d- - - -d emasculations of the Genteel Tradition and the intrusion
into serious fiction of honest words with honest meanings and emphasis. I have wished, with D. H. Lawrence, for the courage to say shit
before a lady, and have sometimes had my wish.

3 Words are not obscene: naming things is a legitimate verbal act.
And "frank" does not mean "vulgar," any more than "improper" means
"dirty." What vulgar does mean is "common"; what improper means is
"unsuitable." Under the right circumstances, any word is proper. But
when any sort of word, especially a word hitherto taboo and therefore

noticeable, is scattered across a page like chocolate chips through a tollhouse cookie, a real impropriety occurs. The sin is not the use of an "obscene" word; it is the use of a loaded word in the wrong place or in the wrong quantity. It is the sin of false emphasis, which is not a moral but a literary lapse, related to sentimentality. It is the sin of advertisers who so plaster a highway with neon signs that you can't find the bar or liquor store you're looking for. Like any excess, it quickly becomes comic.

If I habitually say shit before a lady, what do I say before a flat tire   4
at the rush hour in Times Square or on the San Francisco Bay Bridge? What do I say before a revelation of the inequity of the universe? And what if the lady takes the bit in her teeth and says shit before *me?*

I have been a teacher of writing for many years and have watched   5
this problem since it was no bigger than a man's hand. It used to be that with some Howellsian notion of the young-girl audience one tried to protect tender female members of a mixed class from the coarse language of males trying to show off. Some years ago Frank O'Connor and I agreed on a system. Since we had no intention whatever of restricting students' choice of subject or language, and no desire to expurgate or bowdlerize while reading their stuff aloud for discussion, but at the same time had to deal with these young girls of an age our daughters might have been, we announced that any stuff so strong that it would embarrass us to read it aloud could be read by its own author.

It was no deterrent at all, but an invitation, and not only to coarse   6
males. For clinical sexual observation, for full acceptance of the natural functions, for discrimination in the selection of graffiti, for boldness in the use of words that it should take courage to say before a lady, give me a sophomore girl every time. Her strength is as the strength of ten, for she assumes that if one shocker out of her pretty mouth is piquant, fifty will be literature. And so do a lot of her literary idols.

Some acts, like some words, were never meant to be casual. That is   7
why houses contain bedrooms and bathrooms. Profanity and so-called obscenities are literary resources, verbal ways of rendering strong emotion. They are not meant to occur every ten seconds, any more than—Norman Mailer to the contrary notwithstanding—orgasms are.

So I am not going to say shit before any more ladies. I am going to   8
hunt words that have not lost their sting, and it may be I shall have to go back to gentility to find them. Pleasant though it is to know that finally a writer can make use of any word that fits his occasion, I am going to investigate the possibilities latent in restraint.

I remember my uncle, a farmer who had used four-letter words ten   9
to the sentence ever since he learned to talk. One day he came too near the circular saw and cut half his fingers off. While we stared in horror, he stood watching the bright arterial blood pump from his ruined hand. Then he spoke, and he did not speak loud. "Aw, the dickens," he said.

I think he understood, better than some sophomore girls and better   10
than some novelists, the nature of emphasis.

Study Questions

1. How does the tone of this essay differ from the tone of the Lawrence essay?
2. What type of development is used in paragraphs 3 and 5?
3. What does Stegner gain by writing in the first person instead of the third person?
4. What effect does Stegner achieve by the account of his uncle in paragraph 9?
5. Where does Stegner express the central idea of his essay?
6. Note the concluding sentences in paragraphs 1, 3, and 6. What rhetorical effect does Stegner achieve with these?

The Ugliest Word
H. ALLEN SMITH

H. Allen Smith (1906–   ) was born in McLeansboro, Illinois, and educated in parochial schools. His writing career began at age 15 on a newspaper in Huntington, Indiana; in a few years he became a feature writer for United Press and soon established himself as a humorist of note. Smith's speciality has been writing about odd characters—Fred Allen called him the screwball's Boswell—and his humor is in the midwestern tradition of Twain, George Ade, et al. Among Smith's works are *Son of Rhubarb* (1967), *The Great Chili Confrontation* (1969), *Low Man Rides Again* (1973), *Return of the Virginian* (1974), and *The Life and Legend of Gene Fowler* (1976).

Lullaby. *Golden. Damask. Moonlight.* Do these words seem   1
aesthetically attractive to you? They have appeared with some regularity on lists of "the ten most beautiful words in our language." Along with *luminous, hush, anemone, mother,* and various others. These lists appear from time to time in the public prints, and there is almost always disagreement among the scholarly people who mine the dictionaries looking for lovely words. Sometimes these disagreements reach a point where ugly words are used. I can't recall ever having seen a list of the ten ugliest words in the language but I do remember that the late Ring Lardner, coming upon one of the beautiful word lists in a newspaper, remarked with chagrin and bitterness: "Why did they leave out *gangrene?*"

The people who assemble these lists actually can't make up their 2
minds what they are after. Is a beautiful word beautiful because of its
musical sound or because of the thing it describes? If *moonlight* was the
name of the diamond-back rattlesnake, would *moonlight* be considered
a romantic-sounding and pretty word? If there were no such word as
mother, and your mother was your *sludge,* would *sludge* be poetically
beautiful? You ask my opinion and I'll tell you that *gangrene* is a
downright lovely word, provided you keep your mind off gangrene. You
want to hear a *real* ugly word? *Ugly.*

My own choice for the most beautiful word of them all would not 3
appeal to the generality of people; it is a word of glowing, glimmering
loveliness and arouses intense feelings of well-being and even sensual-
ity within me. The word is *End.* With a capital "E." As a professional
writer of books and magazine aritcles, I almost swoon with gladness
when, on the last page of the third draft of a long manuscript, I write:
The End. I sit and stare at it, and the longer I do so, the more
excruciatingly beautiful it becomes. *Lullaby* my ass! I have left
instructions that *The End* be chiseled on my gravestone.

As for ugly words, almost every literate person has in his head an 4
agglomeration of them—words that can cause him to wince, and even
shudder, such as *agglomeration.* I lay claim to several hundred of the
uglies. *Mulcted* almost nauseates me. I cringe in the face of *albeit,
and/or, yelept, obsequies, whilom,* and *tinsmith.*

My own nomination for the meanest and low-downest and ugliest 5
word of them all is *Oh.* Said twice, with maybe a hyphen, this way.
Oh-oh. In its maximal ugliness, it is customarily spoken softly with
inflections that would curl the toes of a South Georgia mule.

Something is wrong, let us say, with the engine of your car. You 6
take it to the garage. The mechanic lifts the hood and pokes around a
bit and then you hear him murmur: "Oh-oh." The wretched creature
says it in such a restrained dramatic manner that you know instantly
that your whole motor has to be derricked out and thrown away and a
new one put in.

Oh-oh almost suggests tragedy, or impending tragedy. I remember 7
standing with another man at a cocktail party when he, glancing
across the crowded room, said, "Oh-oh." I followed his gaze. A prominent actor and an equally prominent newspaperman were squaring off,
and blows began raining, and a nose was bloodied, and it took some
doing to pry the two gentlemen apart.

Consider again our friends the dentists. Most of them have enough 8
gumption to conceal their opinions and judgments, but sometimes
you'll run across one who forgets his chairside manner. He'll be
inspecting a big molar in the back and suddenly he'll say, "Oh-oh." Or
he'll come out of his darkroom carrying an X-ray taken a few minutes
earlier, and he'll put it up against the light, and he'll look at it briefly,
and then his head will give a jerk and he'll say, "Oh-oh." You know at
once, without ESP, precisely what is meant. Out. All of them. From
now on, plates. And you know what Aunt Gert says about plates. No
apples. No corn on the cob. No a lot of things. You are a captive in the

dentist's chair but you feel like busting out of the place and hiding in the woods.

Physicians as a general thing have schooled themselves carefully 9 to conceal any sinister condition they may find during an examination. Yet I have run across one offender in my checkered medical career. He was giving me the annual checkup. He took my blood pressure and tapped me for knee jerks and scratched me on the bottoms of my feet for God knows what and stethoscoped me front and back and had me blow into a machine to test my "vital capacity" and then he turned the electrocardiograph loose on me. As he studied the saw-toothed dossier on my heart, his brow crinkled and I heard him say quite softly but with an undercurrent of alarm, "Oh-oh." Everything inside me suddenly bunched together in one large knot.

"What is it?" I gulped. "Whad you find there?"   10

"Nothing really," he said. "Nothing important."   11

Nothing! Cancer of the heart is *nothing?* It had to be that at the 12 very least.

"I heard you say 'Oh-oh,' " I told him. "Come on. Give it to me. I'm a 13 man. I can take it. Let me have it straight."

"Okay," he said, and I steeled myself manfully for seven seconds 14 and then began to turn chicken. He resumed: "I said 'Oh-oh' because I just happened to think that I haven't made out my tax return yet, and the deadline is tomorrow."

I quit him the next day. Took my aches and agues elsewhere. I 15 can't use a doctor who is mooning over his income tax problems while he is looking at the record of my frightful heart disorders. I don't want a doctor *ever* to say "Oh-oh" in my presence, unless perhaps he has dropped his sphygmomanometer on the floor and busted it all to hell. Even in that contingency I think he should employ a more masculine and earthy expression. I surely would.

The saying of "Oh-oh" should be forbidden by federal statute. It is 16 the most frightening, nerve-shattering locution to come into general usage since Noah Webster quit slopping pigs on his father's farm in Connecticut. It is, in fact, so low-down mean in its usual implications that even the dictionaries won't let it in. I scorn it, and deride it, and let my mind dwell on its opposite—that most beautiful of words . . .

Study Questions

1. What characterizes the tone of this essay?
2. Why is the first-person point of view more appropriate in this type of essay than the third-person point of view?
3. What is gained by dramatizing the illustration in paragraphs 9–15?
4. Compare the structure of this essay with the structure of the Lawrence essay.
5. Identify the type of development used in the first two paragraphs.

The Human Use of Language

Insensitive Ears Can't Hear Honest Prose

LAWRENCE L. LANGER

Lawrence L. Langer (1929–   ) was born in New York City and
educated at City College of New York and Harvard University. He
has taught at the University of Connecticut, was for a year a
Fulbright Lecturer in Austria, and is currently a Professor of
English at Simmons College in Boston. His earlier scholarly
interests in the "moral and material imagination" of post-Civil
War America and in Russian literature has continued, but his
more recent critical work has included studies in such contemporary authors as James Baldwin and in the literature of the
holocaust. In 1975 he published *The Holocaust and the Literary
Imagination* and *Beyond Atrocity: Perspectives on Death in Modern
Literature* in 1978.

A friend of mine recently turned in a paper to a course on 1
behavior modification. She had tried to express in simple English some
of her reservations about this increasingly popular approach to education. She received it back with the comment: "Please rewrite this in
behavioral terms."

It is little wonder that human beings have so much trouble saying 2
what they feel, when they are told that there is a specialized vocabulary for saying what they think. The language of simplicity and
spontaneity is forced to retreat behind the barricades of an official
prose developed by a few experts who believe that jargon is the most
precise means of communication. The results would be comic, if they
were not so poisonous; unfortunately, there is an attitude toward the
use of language that is impervious to human need and drives some
people back into silence when they realize the folly of risking human
words on insensitive ears.

The comedy is easy to come by. Glancing through my friend's 3
textbook on behavior modification, I happened on a chapter beginning
with the following challenging statement: "Many of the problems
encountered by teachers in the daily management of their classes could

be resolved if. . . ." Although I was a little wary of the phrase "daily management," I was encouraged to plunge ahead, because as an educator I have always been interested in ideas for improving learning. So I plunged. The entire sentence reads: "Many of the problems encountered by teachers in the daily management of their classes could be resolved if the emission of desirable student behaviors was increased."

Emission? At first I thought it was a misprint for "omission," but   **4** the omission of desirable student behaviors (note the plural) hardly seemed an appropriate goal for educators. Then I considered the possibility of metaphor, both erotic and automotive, but these didn't seem to fit, either. A footnote clarified the matter: " 'Emission' is a technical term used in behavioral analysis. The verb, 'to emit,' is used specifically with a certain category of behavior called 'operant behavior.' Operant behaviors are modified by their consequences. Operant behaviors correspond closely to the behavior colloquially referred to as voluntary." Voluntary? Is jargon then an attack on freedom of the will?

Of course, this kind of abuse of language goes on all the time—   **5** within the academic world, one regrets to say, as well as outside it. Why couldn't the author of this text simply say that we need to motivate students to learn willingly? The more I read such non-human prose, and try to avoid writing it myself, the more I am convinced that we must be in touch with ourselves before we can use words to touch others.

Using language meaningfully requires risk; the sentence I have   **6** just quoted takes no risks at all. Much of the discourse that poses as communication in our society is really a decoy to divert our audience (and often ourselves) from that shadowy plateau where our real life hovers on the precipice of expression. How many people, for example, have the courage to walk up to someone they like and actually *say* to them: "I'm very fond of you, you know"?

Such honesty reflects the use of language as revelation, and that   **7** sort of revelation, brimming with human possibilities, is risky precisely because it invites judgment and rebuff. Perhaps this is one reason why, especially in academe, we are confronted daily with so much neutral prose: Our students are not yet in touch with themselves; not especially encouraged by us, their instructors, to move in that direction; they are encouraged indeed to expect judgment and hence perhaps rebuff, too, in our evaluation of them. Thus they instinctively retreat behind the anonymity of abstract diction and technical jargon to protect themselves against us—but also, as I have suggested, against themselves.

This problem was crystallized for me recently by an encounter only   **8** peripherally related to the issue. As part of my current research, I have been interviewing children of concentration-camp survivors. One girl I have been meeting with says that her mother does not like to talk about the experience, *except with other survivors*. Risk is diminished when we know in advance that our audience shares with us a sympathy for our theme. The nakedness of pain *and* the nakedness of love require gentle responses. So this survivor is reticent, except with fellow victims.

But one day a situation arose which tempted her to the human use   9 of language although she could not be sure, in advance, of the recception her words would receive. We all recognize it. This particular woman, at the age of 40, decided to return to school to get a college degree. Her first assignment in freshman composition was to write a paper on something that was of great importance to her personally. The challenge was immense; the risk was even greater. For the first time in 20 years, she resolved to confront a silence in her life that she obviously needed to rouse to speech.

She was 14 when the Germans invaded Poland. When the roundup 10 of the Jews began a year later, some Christian friends sent their young daughter to "call for her" one day, so that they might hide her. A half hour later, the friends went themselves to pick up her parents, but during that interval, a truck had arrived, loaded aboard the Jewish mother and father—and the daughter never saw them or heard from them again. Their fate we can imagine. The girl herself was eventually arrested, survived several camps, and after the war, came to America. She married, had children of her own, and except for occasional reminiscences with fellow survivors, managed to live adequately without diving into her buried personal past. Until one day her instructor in English composition touched a well-insulated nerve, and it began to throb with a painful impulse to express. I present verbatim the result of that impulse, a paper called "People I Have Forgotten":

"Can you forget your own Father and Mother? If so—how or why? 11

"I thought I did. To mention their names, for me is a great 12 emotional struggle. The brutal force of this reality shakes my whole body and mind, wrecking me into ugly splinters; each crying to be mended anew. So the silence I maintain about their memory is only physical and valid as such but not true. I could never forget my parents, nor do I want to do it. True, I seldom talk about them with my husband or my children. How they looked, who they were, why they perished during the war. The love and sacrifices they have made for me during their lifetime, never get told.

"The cultural heritage to which each generation is entitled to have 13 access to seems to be nonexistant [*sic*], since I dare not talk about anything relating to my past, my parents.

"This awful, awesome power of not-remembering, this heart- 14 breaking sensation of the conspiracy of silence is my dilemma.

"Often, I have tried to break through my imprisoning wall of 15 irrational silence, but failed: now I hope to be able to do it.

"Until now, I was not able to face up to the loss of my parents, 16 much less talk about them. The smallest reminder of them would set off a chain reaction of results that I could anticipate but never direct. The destructive force of sadness, horror, fright would then become my master. And it was this subconscious knowledge that kept me paralyzed with silence, not a conscious desire to forget my parents.

"My silent wall, my locked shell existed only of real necessity; I 17 needed time.

"I needed time to forget the tragic loss of my loved ones, time to 18 heal my emotional wound so that there shall come a time when I can again remember the people I have forgotten."

The essay is not a confrontation, only a prelude, yet it reveals 19 qualities which are necessary for the human use of language: In trying to reach her audience, the author must touch the deepest part of herself. She risks self-exposure—when we see the instructor's comment, we will realize how great was her risk—and she is prepared for judgment and perhaps even rebuff, although I doubt whether she was prepared for the form they took. This kind of prose, for all its hesitant phraseology, throws down a gauntlet to the reader, a challenge asking him to understand that life is pain as well as plenty, chaos as well as form. Its imagery of locked shells and imprisoning walls hints at a silent world of horror and sadness far less enchanting than the more familiar landscape of love where most of us dwell. Language is a two-edged tool, to pierce the wall which hides that world, or build high abstract barriers to protect us from its threats.

The instructor who graded the paper I have just read preferred 20 walls to honest words. At the bottom of the last page she scrawled a large "D-minus," emphatically surrounded by a circle. Her only comment was: "Your theme is not clear—you should have developed your 1st paragraph. You talk around your subject." At this moment, two realms collide: a universe of unarticulated feeling seeking expression (and the courage and encouragement to express) and a nature made so immune to feeling by heaven-knows-what that she hides behind the tired, tired language of the professional theme-corrector.

Suddenly we realize that reading as well as writing requires risks, 21 and that the metaphor of insulation, so central to the efforts of the Polish woman survivor to re-establish contact with her past, is a metaphor governing the response of readers, too. Some writing, like "the emission of desirable student behaviors," thickens the insulation that already separates the reader from the words that throw darts at his armor of indifference. But even when language unashamedly reveals the feeling that is hidden behind the words, it must contend with a different kind of barrier, the one behind which our instructor lies concealed, unwilling or unable to hear a human voice and return a human echo of her own.

Ironically, the victor in this melancholy failure at communication 22 is the villain of the piece, behavior modification. For the Polish survivor wrote her next theme on an innocuous topic, received a satisfactory grade, and never returned to the subject of her parents. The instructor, who had encountered a problem in the daily management of her class in the form of an essay which she could not respond to in a human way, altered the attitude of her student by responding in a non-human way, thus resolving her problem by increasing the emission of desirable student behavior. The student now knows how vital it is to develop her first paragraph, and how futile it is to reveal her first grief.

Even more, she has learned the danger of talking around her 23 subject: She not only refuses to talk *around* it now, she refuses to talk *about* it. Thus the human use of language leads back to silence—where perhaps it should have remained in the first place.

Study Questions

1. How does the author attempt to capture the reader's attention in the four introductory paragraphs?
2. What effect is achieved by the use of the theme written by the refugee mother?
3. Analyze the structure of sentences in paragraphs 2, 7, 20, and 21. Note especially the subordinate structures and the way Langer links the sentences.
4. What does Langer gain by writing in the first person? What would be the effect if this essay were written in the third person?
5. Note the last sentence in paragraph 19. To test the effectiveness of the metaphor in this sentence, rewrite it without the use of figurative language.
6. Does Langer address the same type of audience that Orwell does? Stegner? Explain.

Politics and the English Language
GEORGE ORWELL

George Orwell (1903–1950) was the pen name of Eric Blair, who was born in Bengal, India. He graduated from Eton, served with the Indian Imperial Police in Burma from 1922 to 1927, and then returned to England to begin his career as a writer. His works include *Burmese Days* (1934), *Homage to Catalonia* (1938), *Dickens, Dali, and Others* (1946), and *Shooting an Elephant* (1950). His fame, however, is primarily the result of *Animal Farm* (1945) and *1984* (1949), the former one of the most famous modern satires and the latter a classic novel of social protest. His *Collected Essays* was published in 1969.

Most people who bother with the matter at all would admit   1
that the English language is in a bad way, but it is generally assumed
that we cannot by conscious action do anything about it. Our civilization is decadent and our language—so the argument runs—must
inevitably share in the general collapse. It follows that any struggle
against the abuse of language is a sentimental archaism, like preferring candles to electric light or hansom cabs to aeroplanes. Underneath
this lies the half-conscious belief that language is a natural growth and
not an instrument which we shape for our own purposes.

Now, it is clear that the decline of a language must ultimately   2
have political and economic causes: it is not due simply to the bad
influence of this or that individual writer. But an effect can become a
cause, reinforcing the original cause and producing the same effect in
an intensified form, and so on indefinitely. A man may take a drink
because he feels himself to be a failure, and then fail all the more
completely because he drinks. It is rather the same thing that is
happening to the English language. It becomes ugly and inaccurate
because our thoughts are foolish, but the slovenliness of our language
makes it easier for us to have foolish thoughts. The point is that the
process is reversible. Modern English, especially written English, is
full of bad habits which spread by imitation and which can be avoided
if one is willing to take the necessary trouble. If one gets rid of these
habits, one can think more clearly, and to think clearly is a necessary
first step towards political regeneration: so that the fight against bad
English is not frivolous and is not the exclusive concern of professional
writers. I will come back to this presently, and I hope that by that time
the meaning of what I have said here will have become clearer.
Meanwhile, here are five specimens of the English language as it is
now habitually written.

These five passages have not been picked out because they are   3
especially bad—I could have quoted far worse if I had chosen—but
because they illustrate various of the mental vices from which we now
suffer. They are a little below the average, but are fairly representative samples. I number them so that I can refer back to them when
necessary:

> *(1) I am not, indeed sure whether it is not true to say that the Milton*   4
> *who once seemed not unlike a seventeenth-century Shelley had not become,*
> *out of an experience ever more bitter in each year, more alien* [sic] *to the*
> *founder of Jesuit Jesect which nothing could induce him to tolerate.*
> —*Harold Laski, Essay in* Freedom of Expression

> *(2) Above all, we cannot play ducks and drakes with a native battery of*   5
> *idioms which prescribes such egregious collocations of vocables as the Basic*
> put up with *for* tolerate *or* put at a loss *for* bewilder.
> —*Lancelot Hogben,* Interglossa

> *(3) On the one side we have the free personality: by definition it is not*   6
> *neurotic, for it has neither conflict nor dream. Its desires, such as they are,*
> *are transparent, for they are just what institutional approval keeps in the*
> *forefront of consciousness; another institutional pattern would alter their*

number and intensity; there is little in them that is natural, irreducible, or culturally dangerous. But on the other side, the social bond itself is nothing but the mutual reflection of these self-secure integrities. Recall the definition of love. Is not this the very picture of a small academic? Where is there a place in this hall of mirrors for either personality or fraternity?

—Essay on psychology in Politics *(New York)*

(4) *All the "best people" from the gentlemen's clubs, and all the frantic* **7** *fascist captains, united in common hatred of Socialism and bestial horror of the rising tide of the mass revolutionary movement, have turned to acts of provocation, to foul incendiarism, to medieval legends of poisoned wells, to legalize their own destruction of proletarian organizations, and rouse the agitated petty-bourgeoisie to chauvinistic fervour on behalf of the fight against the revolutionary way out of the crisis.*

—Communist pamphlet.

(5) *If a new spirit is to be infused into this old country, there is one* **8** *thorny and contentious reform which must be tackled, and that is the humanization and galvanization of the B.B.C. Timidity here will bespeak cancer and atrophy of the soul. The heart of Britain may be sound and of strong beat, for instance, but the British lion's roar at present is like that of Bottom in Shakespeare's* Midsummer Night's Dream—*as gentle as any sucking dove. A virile new Britain cannot continue indefinitely to be traduced in the eyes or rather ears, of the world by the effete languors of Langham Place, brazenly masquerading as "standard English." When the Voice of Britain is heard at nine o'clock, better far and infinitely less ludicrous to hear aitches honestly dropped than the present priggish, inflated, inhibited, school-ma'amish arch braying of blameless bashful mewing maidens!*

—Letter in Tribune.

Each of these passages has faults of its own, but, quite apart from **9** avoidable ugliness, two qualities are common to all of them. The first is staleness of imagery: the other is lack of precision. The writer either has a meaning and cannot express it, or he inadvertently says something else, or he is almost indifferent as to whether his words mean anything or not. This mixture of vagueness and sheer incompetence is the most marked characteristic of modern English prose, and especially of any kind of political writing. As soon as certain topics are raised, the concrete melts into the abstract and no one seems able to think of turns of speech that are not hackneyed: prose consists less and less of *words* chosen for the sake of their meaning, and more and more of *phrases* tacked together like the sections of a prefabricated henhouse. I list below, with notes and examples, various of the tricks by means of which the work of prose-construction is habitually dodged:

Dying Metaphors

A newly invented metaphor assists thought by evoking a visual image, **10** while on the other hand a metaphor which is technically "dead" (e.g., *iron resolution)* has in effect reverted to being an ordinary word and can generally be used without loss of vividness. But in between these two classes there is a huge dump of worn-out metaphors which have lost all evocative power and are merely used because they save people the trouble of inventing phrases for themselves. Examples are: *Ring the changes on, take up the cudgels for, toe the line, ride roughshod over, stand shoulder to shoulder with, play into the hands of, no axe to grind, grist to the mill, fishing in troubled waters, on the order of the day, Achilles' heel, swan song, hotbed.* Many of these are used without knowledge of their meaning (what is a "rift," for instance?), and incompatible metaphors are frequently mixed, a sure sign that the writer is not interested in what he is saying. Some metaphors now current have been twisted out of their original meaning without those who use them even being aware of the fact. For example, *toe the line* is sometimes written *tow the line.* Another example is *the hammer and the anvil,* now always used with the implication that the anvil gets the worst of it. In real life it is always the anvil that breaks the hammer, never the other way about: a writer who stopped to think what he was saying would be aware of this, and would avoid perverting the original phrase.

Operators or Verbal False Limbs

These save the trouble of picking out appropriate verbs and nouns, and 11 at the same time pad each sentence with extra syllables which give it an appearance of symmetry. Characteristic phrases are: *render inoperative, militate against, make contact with, be subjected to, give rise to, give grounds for, have the effect of, play a leading part (role) in, make itself felt, take effect, exhibit a tendency to, serve the purpose of, etc., etc.* The keynote is the elimination of simple verbs. Instead of being a single word, such as *break, stop, spoil, mend, kill,* a verb becomes a *phrase,* made up of a noun or adjective tacked on to some general-purposes verb such as *prove, serve, form, play, render.* In addition, the passive voice is wherever possible used in preference to the active, and noun constructions are used instead of gerunds *(by examination of* instead of *by examining).* The range of verbs is further cut down by means of the *-ize* and *de-* formation, and the banal statements are given an appearance of profundity by means of the *not un-*formation. Simple conjunctions and prepositions are replaced by such phrases as *with respect to, having regard to, the fact that, by dint of, in view of, in the interests of, on the hypothesis that;* and the ends of sentences are saved from anticlimax by such resounding commonplaces as *greatly to be desired, cannot be left out of account, a development to be expected in the near future, deserving of serious consideration, brought to a satisfactory conclusion,* and so on and so forth.

Pretentious Diction

Words like *phenomenon, element, individual* (as noun), *objective,* 12 *categorical, effective, virtual, basic, primary, promote, constitute, exhibit, exploit, utilize, eliminate, liquidate,* are used to dress up simple statements and give an air of scientific impartiality to biased judgments. Adjectives like *epoch-making, epic, historic, unforgettable, triumphant, age-old, inevitable, inexorable, veritable,* are used to dignify the sordid processes of international politics, while writing that aims at glorifying war usually takes on an archaic colour, its characteristic words being: *realm, throne, chariot, mailed fist, trident, sword, shield, buckler, banner, jack-boot, clarion.* Foreign words and expressions such as *cul de sac, ancien regime, deus ex machina, mutatis mutandis, status quo, gleichshaltung, weltanschauung,* are used to give an air of culture and elegance. Except for the useful abbreviations *i.e., e.g.,* and *etc.,* there is no real need for any of the hundreds of foreign phrases now current in English. Bad writers, and especially scientific, political and sociological writers, are nearly always haunted by the notion that Latin or Greek words are grander than Saxon ones, and unnecessary words like *expedite, ameliorate, predict, extraneous, deracinated, clandestine, subaqueous* and hundreds of others constantly gain ground from their Anglo-Saxon opposite numbers.[1] The jargon peculiar to Marxist writing *(hyena, hangman, cannibal, petty bourgeois, these gentry, lacquey, flunkey, mad dog, White Guard,* etc.) consists largely of words and phrases translated from Russian, German or French; but the normal way of coining a new word is to use a Latin or Greek root with the appropriate affix and, where necessary, the -ize formation. It is often easier to make up words of this kind *(deregionalize, impermissible, extramarital, nonfragmentary* and so forth) than to think up the English words that will cover one's meaning. The result, in general, is an increase in slovenliness and vagueness.

Meaningless Words

In certain kinds of writing, particularly in art criticism and literary 13 criticism, it is normal to come across long passages which are almost completely lacking in meaning.[2] Words like *romantic, plastic, values, human, dead, sentimental, natural, vitality,* as used in art criticism, are strictly meaningless in the sense that they not only do not point to any discoverable object, but are hardly ever expected to do so by the reader. When one critic writes, "The outstanding feature of Mr. X's work is its living quality," while another writes, "The immediately striking thing about Mr. X's work is its peculiar deadness," the reader accepts this as a simple difference of opinion. If words like *black* and *white* were

---

[1]An interesting illustration of this is the way in which the English flower names which were in use till very recently are being ousted by Greek ones, *snapdragon* becoming *antirrkinum, forget-me-not* becoming *myostis,* etc. It is hard to see any practical reason for this change of fashion: it is probably due to an instinctive turning-away from the more homely word and a vague feeling that the Greek word is scientific.

[2]Example: "Comfort's catholicity of perception and image, strangely Whitmanesque in range, almost the exact opposite in aesthetic compulsion, continues to evoke that trembling atmospheric accumulative hinting at a cruel, an inexorably serene timelessness ... Wrey Gardiner scores by aiming at simple bull's-eyes with precision. Only they are not so simple, and through this contented sadness runs more than the surface bitter-sweet of resignation." *(Poetry Quarterly.)*

involved, instead of the jargon words *dead* and *living,* he would see at once that language was being used in an improper way. Many political words are similarly abused. The word *Fascism* has now no meaning except in so far as it signifies "something not desirable." The words *democracy, socialism, freedom, patriotic, realistic, justice,* have each of them several different meanings which cannot be reconciled with one another. In the case of a word like *democracy,* not only is there no agreed definition, but the attempt to make one is resisted from all sides. It is almost universally felt that when we call a country democratic we are praising it: consequently the defenders of every kind of regime claim that it is a democracy, and fear that they might have to stop using the word if it were tied down to any one meaning. Words of this kind are often used in a consciously dishonest way. That is, the person who uses them has his own private definition, but allows his hearer to think he means something quite different. Statements like *Marshall Petain was a true patriot, The Soviet Press is the freest in the world, The Catholic Church is opposed to persecution,* are almost always made with intent to deceive. Other words used in variable meanings, in most cases more or less dishonestly, are: *class, totalitarian, science, progressive, reactionary, bourgeois, equality.*

Now that I have made this catalogue of swindles and perversions, **14** let me give another example of the kind of writing that they lead to. This time it must of its nature be an imaginary one. I am going to translate a passage of good English into modern English of the worst sort. Here is a well-known verse from *Ecclesiastes:*

> I returned and saw under the sun, that the race is not to the swift, nor the battle to the strong, neither yet bread to the wise, nor yet riches to men of understanding, nor yet favour to men of skill; but time and chance happeneth to them all.

Here it is in modern English:

> Objective considerations of contemporary phenomena compels the conclu- **15** sion that success or failure in competitive activities exhibits no tendency to be commensurate with innate capacity, but that a considerable element of the unpredictable must invariably be taken into account.

This is a parody, but not a very gross one. Exhibit (3), above, for **16** instance, contains several patches of the same kind of English. It will be seen that I have not made a full translation. The beginning and ending of the sentence follow the original meaning fairly closely, but in the middle the concrete illustrations—race, battle, bread—dissolve into the vague phrase "success or failure in competitive activities." This had to be so, because no modern writer of the kind I am discussing—no one capable of using phrases like "objective consideration of contemporary phenomena"—would ever tabulate his thoughts in that precise and detailed way. The whole tendency of modern prose is away from concreteness. Now analyse these two sentences a little more closely. The first contains forty-nine words but only sixty syllables, and all its words are those of everyday life. The second contains thirty-eight words of ninety syllables: eighteen of its words are from Latin roots, and one from Greek. The first sentence contains six vivid images, and only one phrase ("time and chance") that could be called vague. The second contains not a single fresh, arresting phrase, and in spite of its ninety syllables it gives only a shortened version of the meaning contained in the first. Yet without a doubt it is the second kind of sentence that is gaining ground in modern English. I do not want to exaggerate. This kind of writing is not yet universal, and outcrops of simplicity will occur here and there in the worst-written page. Still, if you or I were told to write a few lines on the uncertainty of human fortunes, we should probably come much nearer to my imaginary sentence than to the one from *Ecclesiastes*.

As I have tried to show, modern writing at its worst does not 17 consist in picking out words for the sake of their meaning and inventing images in order to make the meaning clearer. It consists in gumming together long strips of words which have already been set in order by someone else, and making the results presentable by sheer humbug. The attraction of this way of writing is that it is easy. It is easier—even quicker, once you have the habit—to say *In my opinion it is a not unjustifiable assumption that* than to say *I think*. If you use ready-made phrases, you not only don't have to hunt about for words; you also don't have to bother with the rhythms of your stenences, since these phrases are generally so arranged as to be more or less euphonious. When you are composing in a hurry—when you are dictating to a stenographer, for instance, or making a public speech—it is natural to fall into a pretentious, Latinized style. Tags like *a consideration which we should do well to bear in mind* or *a conclusion to which all of us would readily assent* will save many a sentence from coming down with a bump. By using stale metaphors, similes and idioms, you save much mental effort, at the cost of leaving your meaning vague, not only for your reader but for yourself. This is the significance of mixed metaphors. The sole aim of a metaphor is to call up a visual image. When these images clash—as in *The Fascist octopus has sung its swan song, the jackboot is thrown into the melting pot*—it can be taken as certain that the writer is not seeing a mental image of the objects he is naming; in other words he is not really thinking. Look again at the examples I gave at the beginning of this essay. Professor Laski (1) uses five negatives in fifty-three words. One of these is superfluous, making nonsense of the whole passage, and in addition there is the slip *alien* for *akin*, making further nonsense, and several avoidable pieces of clumsiness which increase the general vagueness. Professor Hogben (2) plays ducks and drakes with a battery which is able to write prescriptions, and, while disapproving of the everyday phrase *put up with*, is unwilling to look *egregious* up in the dictionary and see what it means. (3), if one takes an uncharitable attitude towards it, it is simply meaningless: probably one could work out its intended meaning by reading the whole of the article in which it occurs. In (4), the writer knows more or less what he wants to say, but an accumulation of stale phrases chokes him like tea leaves blocking a sink. In (5), words and meaning have almost parted company. People who write in this manner usually have a general emotional meaning—they dislike one thing and want to express solidarity with another—but they are not interested in the detail of what they are saying. A scrupulous writer, in every sentence that he writes, will ask himself at least four questions, thus: What am I trying to say? What words will express it? What image or idiom will make it clearer? Is this image fresh enough to have an effect? And he will probably ask himself two more: Could I put it more shortly? Have I said anything that is avoidably ugly? But you are not obliged to go to all this trouble. You can shirk it by simply throwing your mind open and letting the ready-made phrases come crowding in. They will construct your sentences for you—even think your thoughts for you, to a certain extent—and at need they will perform the important service of partially concealing your meaning even from yourself. It is at this point that the special connection between politics and the debasement of language becomes clear.

In our time it is broadly true that political writing is bad writing. 18 Where it is not true, it will generally be found that the writer is some kind of rebel, expressing his private opinions and not a "party line." Orthodoxy, of whatever colour, seems to demand a lifeless, imitative style. The political dialects to be found in pamphlets, leading articles, manifestos, White Papers and the speeches of under-secretaries do, of course, vary from party to party, but they are all alike in that one almost never finds in them a fresh, vivid, homemade turn of speech. When one watches some tried hack on the platform mechanically repeating the familiar phrases—*bestial atrocities, iron heel, bloodstained tyranny, free peoples of the world, stand shoulder to shoulder*—one often has a curious feeling that one is not watching a live human being but some kind of dummy: a feeling which suddenly becomes stronger at moments when the light catches the speaker's spectacles and turns them into blank discs which seem to have no eyes behind them. And this is not altogether fanciful. A speaker who uses that kind of phraseology has gone some distance towards turning himself into a machine. The appropriate noises are coming out of his larynx, but his brain is not involved as it would be if he were choosing his words for himself. If the speech he is making is one that he is accustomed to make over and over again, he may be almost unconscious of what he is saying, as one is when one utters the responses in church. And this reduced state of consciousness, if not indispensible, is at any rate favourable to political conformity.

In our time, political speech and writing are largely the defence of 19 the indefensible. Things like the continuance of British rule in India, the Russian purges and deportations, the dropping of the atom bombs on Japan, can indeed be defended, but only by arguments which are too brutal for most people to face, and which do not square with the professed aims of political parties. Thus political language has to consist largely of euphemism, question-begging and sheer cloudy vagueness. Defenceless villages are bombarded from the air, the inhabitants driven out into the countryside, the cattle machine-gunned, the huts set on fire with incendiary bullets: this is called *pacification*. Millions of peasants are robbed of their farms and sent trudging along the roads with no more than they can carry: this is called *transfer of population* or *rectification of frontiers*. People are imprisoned for years without trial, or shot in the back of the neck or sent to die of scurvy in Arctic lumber camps: this is called *elimination of unreliable elements*. Such phraseology is needed if one wants to name things without calling up mental pictures of them. Consider for instance some comfortable English professor defending Russian to-talitarianism. He cannot say outright, "I believe in killing off your opponents when you can get good results by doing so." Probably, therefore, he will say something like this:

> While freely conceding that the Soviet regime exhibits certain fea-tures which the humanitarian may be inclined to deplore, we must, I think, agree that a certain curtailment of the right to political opposition is an unavoidable concomitant of transitional periods, and that the rigours which the Russian people have been called upon to undergo have been amply justified in the sphere of concrete achievement.

The inflated style is itself a kind of euphemism. A mass of Latin words fall upon the facts like soft snow, blurring the outlines and covering up all the details. The great enemy of clear language is insincerity. When there is a gap between one's real and one's declared aims, one turns as it were instinctively to long words and exhausted idioms, like a cuttlefish fish squirting out ink. In our age there is no such thing as "keeping out of politics." All issues are political issues, and politics itself is a mass of lies, evasions, folly, hatred and schizo-phrenia. When the general atmosphere is bad, language must suffer. I should expect to find—this is a guess which I have not sufficient knowledge to verify—that the German, Russian and Italian languages have all deteriorated in the last ten or fifteen years, as a result of dictatorship.

But if thought corrupts language, language can also corrupt 21 thought. A bad usage can spread by tradition and imitation, even among people who should and do know better. The debased language that I have been discussing is in some ways very convenient. Phrases like *a not unjustifiable assumption, leaves much to be desired, would serve no good purpose, a consideration which we should do well to bear in mind,* are a continuous temptation, a packet of aspirins always at one's elbow. Look back through this essay, and for certain you will find that I have again and again committed the very faults I am protesting against. By this morning's post I have received a pamphlet dealing with conditions in Germany. The author tells me that he "felt im-pelled" to write it. I open it at random, and here is almost the first sentence that I see: "(The Allies) have an opportunity not only of achieving a radical transformation of Germany's social and political structure in such a way as to avoid a nationalistic reaction in Germany itself, but at the same time of laying the foundations of a cooperative and unified Europe." You see, he "feels impelled" to write—feels, presumably, that he has something new to say—and yet his words, like cavalry horses answering the bugle, group themselves automatically into the familiar dreary pattern. This invasion of one's mind by ready-made phrases (*lay the foundations, achieve a radical transformation*) can only be prevented if one is constantly on guard against them, and every such phrase anaesthetizes a portion of one's brain.

I said earlier that the decadence of our language is probably 22 curable. Those who deny this would argue, if they produced an argument at all, that language merely reflects existing social conditions, and that we cannot influence its development by any direct tinkering with words and constructions. So far as the general tone or spirit of a language goes, this may be true, but it is not true in detail. Silly words and expressions have often disappeared, not through any evolutionary process but owing to the conscious action of a minority. Two recent examples were *explore every avenue* and *leave no stone unturned,* which were killed by the jeers of a few journalists. There is a long list of flyblown metaphors which could similarly be got rid of if enough people would interest themselves in the job; and it should also be possible to laugh the *not un-* formation out of existence,[3] to reduce the amount of Latin and Greek in the average sentence, to drive out foreign phrases and strayed scientific words, and, in general, to make pretentiousness unfashionable. But all these are minor points. The defence of the English language implies more than this, and perhaps it is best to start by saying what it does *not* imply.

To begin with it has nothing to do with archaism, with the 23 salvaging of obsolete words and turns of speech, or with the setting up of a "standard English" which must never be departed from. On the contrary, it is especially concerned with the scrapping of every word or idiom which has outworn its usefulness. It has nothing to do with correct grammar and syntax, which are of no importance so long as one makes one's meaning clear, or with the avoidance of Americanisms, or with having what is called a "good prose style." On the other hand it is not concerned with fake simplicity and the attempt to make written English colloquial. Nor does it even imply in every case preferring the Saxon word to the Latin one, though it does imply using the fewest and shortest words that will cover one's meaning. What is above all needed is to let the meaning choose the word, and not the other way about. In prose, the worst thing one can do with words is to surrender to them. When you think of a concrete object, you think wordlessly, and then, if you want to describe the thing you have been visualizing you probably hunt about till you find the exact words that seem to fit. When you think of something abstract you are more inclined to use words from the start, and unless you make a conscious effort to prevent it, the existing dialect will come rushing in and do the job for you, at the expense of blurring or even changing your meaning. Probably it is better to put off using words as long as possible and get one's meaning as clear as one can through pictures or sensations. Afterwards one can choose—not simply *accept*—the phrases that will best cover the mean-

[3]One can cure onself of the *not un-* formation by memorizing this sentence: *A not unblack dog was chasing a not unsmall rabbit across a not ungreen field.*

ing, and then switch round and decide what impression one's words are likely to make on another person. This last effort of the mind cuts out all stale or mixed images, all prefabricated phrases, needless repetitions, and humbug and vagueness generally. But one can often be in doubt about the effect of a word or a phrase, and one needs rules that one can rely on when instinct fails. I think the following rules will cover most cases:

1. Never use a metaphor, simile or other figure of speech which you are used to seeing in print.
2. Never use a long word where a short one will do.
3. If it is possible to cut a word out, always cut it out.
4. Never use the passive where you can use the active.
5. Never use a foreign phrase, a scientific word or a jargon word if you can think of an everyday English equivalent.
6. Break any of these rules sooner than say anything outright barbarous.

These rules sound elementary, and so they are, but they demand a 24 deep change of attitude in anyone who has grown used to writing in the style now fashionable. One could keep all of them and still write bad English, but one could not write the kind of stuff that I quoted in those five specimens at the beginning of this article.

I have not here been considering the literary use of language, but 25 merely language as an instrument for expressing and not for concealing or preventing thought. Stuart Chase and others have come near to claiming that all abstract words are meaningless, and have used this as a pretext for advocating a kind of political quietism. Since you don't know what Fascism is, how can you struggle against Fascism? One need not swallow such absurdities as this, but one ought to recognize that the present political chaos is connected with the decay of language, and that one can probably bring about some improvement by starting at the verbal end. If you simplify your English, you are freed from the worst follies of orthodoxy. You cannot speak any of the necessary dialects, and when you make a stupid remark its stupidity will be obvious, even to yourself. Political language—and with variations this is true of all political parties, from Conservatives to Anarchists—is designed to make lies sound truthful and murder respectable, and to give an appearance of solidity to pure wind. One cannot change this all in a moment, but one can at least change one's own habits, and from time to time one can even, if one jeers loudly enough, send some worn-out and useless phrase—some *jackboot, Achilles' heel, hotbed, melted pot, acid test, veritable inferno* or other lump of verbal refuse—into the dustbin where it belongs.

Study Questions

1. Identify the various types of paragraph development Orwell uses in this essay.

2. Judging from the allusions (especially in the examples), the level of diction, structure of sentences, and other rhetorical elements in this essay, what audience would you say Orwell addresses?
3. Analyze the development of paragraphs 16–18.
4. What is the most obvious difference in the diction of paragraphs 14 and 15?
5. What words and phrases link paragraphs 13–23?
6. What is the tone of this essay, and how is it established and maintained?

Is It an O.K. Word, Usewise?

WILLIAM ZINSSER

William Zinsser (1922–   ) was born in New York City, attended Deerfield Academy, and received an A.B. from Princeton University in 1944. He has been a critic for both the *New York Herald Tribune* and NBC's "Sunday." For nearly a decade he taught English at Yale, but he now makes his living as a free-lance writer. Zinsser's books include *Any Old Place With You* (1957), *Search and Research* (1961), *Pop Goes America* (1966), *The Lunacy Boom* (1970), and *On Writing Well* (1976).

Will I accept the verb "to host"? Or "escalate" or "finalize"   1
or "enthuse"? Do I approve of nouns posing as adjectives: "health reasons" or "disaster proportions"? How do I feel about "it's me"? Will I allow "like" to be used as a conjunction—like so many people do? Will I give my O.K. to "mighty," as in "mighty fine"? Will I give my O.K. to "O.K."?

I received these questions in the mail for four years, and so did 103   2
other men and women, a group of people—mostly writers, poets, editors and teachers—who care about the language and try to use it well. We are the "panel on usage" formed by a new dictionary—*The American Heritage Dictionary of the English Language*—to appraise the new words and dubious constructions that have come knocking at the door. Which should be ushered in, which thrown out on their ear?

Now that the Dictionary has been born we can see what we   3
decided. Even before publication it was clear that our passions ran

high, for some of the comments that we wrote on our questionnaires were released to the press. "Good God, no! Never!" cried Barbara W. Tuchman, asked about the verb "to author." Scholarship hath no fury like that of a language purist confronted with sludge, and I share Miss Tuchman's vow that "author" shall never be authorized, just as I agree with Lewis Mumford that the adverb "good" should be "left as the exclusive property of Hemingway" and with Gerald Carson that "normalcy" should be "permitted only to admirers of the late Warren G. Harding."

But a usage panel is only doing half its job if it merely keeps the 4 language from becoming sloppy. Any boob can rule that the suffix "wise," as in "mediawise," is boobwise, or that being "rather unique" is no more possible than being rather pregnant. The other half of the job is to help the language grow by welcoming any newcomer that will bring strength or color.

Therefore I was glad to see in the Dictionary that 97 percent of us 5 voted to admit "dropout," which is clean and vivid, but only 47 percent would accept "senior citizen," which is pretentious and patronizing, typical of all the pudgy new intruders from the land of sociology, where a clod is an underachiever and a slum is a depressed socioeconomic area. I'm glad we accepted "escalate," the kind of verbal contraption which I ordinarily dislike, but which the Vietnam war has given a precise meaning, complete with overtones of blunder.

I'm glad we took into full membership all sorts of robust words that 6 were formerly degraded as "colloquial": adjectives like "rambunctious," verbs like "stall" and "trigger" and "rile," nouns like "shambles" and "tycoon" and "trek," the latter approved by 78 percent to mean any difficult trip, as in "the commuter's daily trek to Manhattan." Originally, of course, it was a Cape Dutch word applied to the Boers' harsh journey by ox wagon. But who is to say that the Manhattan commuter's daily trek is any less arduous, or made on trains that are much better than an ox wagon? Not us.

This is the virtue of having a usage panel and tabulating its 7 opinions in the dictionary: it puts our differences on display as well as our agreements. Thus our 95 percent vote against "myself," as in "he invited Mary and myself to dinner," condemned as "prissy," "horrible" and "a genteelism," ought to warn off anyone who doesn't want to be prissy, horrible and genteel. As Red Smith put it, " 'Myself' is the refuge of idiots taught early that 'me' is a dirty word."

On the other hand, only 66 percent of us rejected the verb "to 8 contact," and only half opposed the split infinitive and the verbs "to fault" and "to bus." So nobody can really fault you if you decide to willingly contact your school board and bus your children to another town. Our apparent rule of thumb was stated by Theodore M. Bernstein: "We should apply the test of convenience and necessity. Does the word fill a real need? If it does, let's give it a franchise."

All of this merely confirms what any lexicographer knows: that the 9 laws of usage are relative, bending with the taste of the lawmaker. Katherine Anne Porter calls "O.K." a "detestable vulgarity" and claims that she has never spoken the word in her life, whereas I will freely admit that I have spoken the word "O.K." "Most," as in "most everyone," was derided as "cute farmer talk" by Isaac Asimov and embraced as a "good English idiom" by Virgil Thomson. "Regime," meaning any administration, as in "the Kennedy regime," drew the approval of most everyone on the panel—as did "dynasty"—and the wrath of Jacques Barzun, who said, "These are technical terms, you blasted non-historians!" I railed against the bloated noun "personality," as in a "TV personality," but now I wonder if it isn't the only word for that vast new breed of people who are famous for being famous— and, quite possibly, for nothing else. What does Art Linkletter, for instance, really *do?* Or Zsa Zsa Gabor?

In the end it comes down to one question: what is "correct" usage? 10 We have no king to establish the King's English; we only have the President's English—which we don't want. Webster, long a defender of the faith, roiled the waters in 1961 with its permissive Third Edition, which argued that almost anything goes as long as somebody uses it, noting that "ain't" is "used orally in most parts of the U.S. by many cultivated speakers."

Just where Webster cultivated those speakers I ain't sure. 11 Nevertheless it's true that the spoken language is always looser than the written language, and *The American Heritage Dictionary* properly put its questions to us in both forms. Often we gladly allowed an oral idiom which we forbade in print as too informal, fully realizing, however, that "the pen must at length comply with the tongue," as Samuel Johnson said, and that today's garbage may be gold tomorrow. Usewise, some of it just can't be finalized.

We also recognized that usage can vary within a given word. We 12 voted heavily against "cohort" as a synonym for "colleague"—except where the tone was jocular. Thus a professor would not be among his cohorts at a faculty meeting, but they would abound at his college reunion, probably wearing funny hats. We rejected "too" as a common synonym for "very," as in "his health is not too good." Whose health is? But we approved it in wry or humorous use: "He was not too happy when she ignored him."

On the whole our panel turned out to be liberal in accepting new 13 words and phrases, but conservative in grammar. We strictly upheld most of the classic distinctions ("can" and "may," "fewer" and "less," etc.) and decried the classic errors, insisting that "flaunt" still doesn't mean "flout," or "infer" mean "imply," that "fortuitous" still means "accidental" and "disinterested" means "impartial," no matter how many people use them wrong. Or wrongly. Here we were motivated by our love of the language's beautiful precision. Like any craftsmen, we enjoy using exact tools and hate to see them maltreated. "Simple illiteracy," Dwight Macdonald said, "is no basis for linguistic evolution."

"I choose always the grammatical form unless it sounds affected," 14 explained Marianne Moore, and that, finally, is where we took our stand. We are not pedants, so hung up on correctness that we don't want the language to keep refreshing itself with phrases like "hung up." That doesn't mean, however, that we have to accept every atrocity that comes along, like "hopefully." Prayerfully these usages can be kept out, but fearfully many of them won't be.

Study Questions

1. Describe the method Zinsser uses to develop the central idea in this essay.
2. Identify sentences in which the author illustrates usage the panel accepted or rejected. What effect does he achieve in these sentences?
3. What is the author's strategy in the way he introduces his subject?
4. Is the humorous treatment of the subject simply to entertain? If not, what is the purpose of the humor?
5. Why is the first-person point of view more appropriate than the third person?

Hopefully, They Will Shut Up
JIM QUINN

Jim Quinn (1935–   ) graduated from Temple University with a degree in English Literature in 1968. From 1968 to 1971 he was coeditor of the *Collegiate Guide to Philadelphia*. Other books soon followed: *Word of Mouth* (1971) and *American Tongue and Cheek* (1981); *Never Eat Out on a Saturday Night* will be published in 1983. His continuing columns appear in the *Nation*, the *Soho Weekly News, Welcomat*, and the *Philadelphia Magazine*. In 1980 Quinn was a finalist in the Columbia School of Journalism Awards for magazine criticism.

Almost everybody in America has an illiteracy they love to 1
hate because it makes them feel superior to other Americans: "Anyone can do what they like," "between you and I," "input," "different than," "hopefully." Sometimes the list seems endless. We are in the middle of

a great national crusade to protect the language from the people who speak it.

The crusaders certainly seem to be having fun. Though they claim 2 to see the Death of English approaching at any moment, there's a kind of rosy romantic glow to their despair. You get a picture of this gallant little band of the last literates going down to defeat with *Warriner's Grade Four Grammar* in one hand and *Best Loved Poems of College English Departments* in the other. There are only two things wrong with this great conservative crusade of correctors: it is not conservative, and it is not correct. Though our popularizers of good grammar (let's call them pop grammarians for short) think they are defending standards and traditions, they keep attacking idioms that are centuries old. Here are a few examples:

Anyone Can Do What They Like. We must never combine *anyone* 3 with *they,* says John Simon in his book, *Paradigms Lost:* "that way madness lies." Simon seems to think this madness is brand-new, produced in part at least by feminists who want to overturn the old male grammar of "anyone can do what *he* wants" (and *she* better shut up about it). In fact, a wholesale confusion of number and case in pronouns has been a feature of standard English since Elizabethan times. This never hurt the writing of Shakespeare, Marlowe, Ben Jonson, Defoe, Swift, Jane Austen, Dickens, George Bernard Shaw and Oscar Wilde ("Experience is the name that everyone gives to their mistakes"). The use of *they* instead of *he,* in cases where both men and women are meant, is defended by such conservative, pre-liberation authorities as the *Oxford English Dictionary (OED),* our greatest historical dictionary, and Otto Jespersen, the distinguished scholarly grammarian of our language. If that be madness, as Simon says, it is a venerable and literary lunacy.

Between You and I. "Horrible!" wrote poet W. H. Auden, giving his 4 expert opinion in *The Harper Dictionary of Contemporary Usage.* "All debts are cleared between you and I," wrote poet William Shakespeare (*Merchant of Venice,* Act III, Scene 2). Whom are we to trust? D. H. Lawrence points the way for us here. Never trust the artist, said Lawrence; always trust the art. A poet's idea of how language works is as likely to be correct as his idea of how a typewriter works. "You and I" in the accusative is an ancient (and indestructible) idiom. See the opening line of T. S. Eliot's *The Love Song of J. Alfred Prufrock:* "Let us go then, you and I."

Input. "Computer cant," said Theodore Bernstein in *Dos, Don't & 5 Maybes of English Usage;* "laymen sometimes take it over to sound impressive." In fact, "input" has been around since the eighteenth century. Sir Walter Scott used it to mean "contribution" in *The Heart of Midlothian* (1818). The Supplement to the *OED* shows noncant uses in such fields as economics long before the first computer use (1948). Input is not a computer word—it's an old word borrowed by computer scientists. No harm in borrowing it back.

Different Than. *Different than* rather than *different from* is wrong," 6
wrote Edwin Newman in *Strictly Speaking*. Short, simple, to the point
and utterly without foundation. H. W. Fowler, in *Modern English
Usage* (the bible of most pop grammarians), classes insistence on
"different from" as a superstition. The *OED* notes that "different than"
is considered by many to be incorrect, but that "different than" can be
found in writers of all ages. Among them: Addison, Steele, Defoe,
DeQuincey, Coleridge, Carlyle, and Thackeray. Use "different from" if
you want—but criticize "different than" and you're messing with the
big guys.

Rhetoric. "Not so long ago," says William Safire, in his book, *On* 7
Language, "the predominant meaning of rhetoric was *the science of
persuasion.*" Now we tend to use rhetoric to mean empty talk. Safire
would like to rescue this good old word from our abuse and has a cure:
use "bloviation," an old slang word dating back before 1851, for empty
talk. The abuse of "rhetoric" dates back before 1851, too—to the
sixteenth century. Among users cited in the *OED:* Spenser, Milton,
Swift, and Swinburne, who warns against "the limp loquacity of
long-winded rhetoric, so natural to men and soldiers in an hour of
emergency." And so natural, also, to pop grammarians when they
invent cures for which there is no disease.

Hopefully, Better-Coordinated Programs Will Result. To John 8
Simon, that use of "hopefully" is an infallible sign of illiteracy.
" 'Hopefully' so used is an abomination, its adherents should be
lynched," says poet Phyllis McGinley. Adherents include Theodore
Bernstein, William Safire, and the editors of the *Concise Oxford,
Random House, Merriam-Webster, Webster's New World* and *Standard
College* dictionaries. Did Phyllis McGinley really want all of them
lynched? The author of the sentence that begins this paragraph was
Dr. Nathan Pusey, the former president of Harvard. Does John Simon
really believe that Dr. Pusey cannot read or write? Of course not. Both
Simon and McGinley were merely using the limp and fuzzy rhetoric of
pop grammar, where "illiterate" means only "hasn't read my
stylebook."

A New Non-Worry: The Danger From the Right. Should we all 9
worry that the pop grammarians will succeed and that someday soon
we'll have to talk what they call Good English? Not at all. Wrong-
headed objections to idioms are as much a part of the history of
English as the idioms themselves—and probably always will be. There
will always be gallant little bands to fling themselves, and their
violent rhetoric, in front of some age-old word they have made a fad of
trying to stop. And there will always be the rest of us to run right over
them. That's why English is still alive.

Study Questions

1. What is Quinn's method of development in this essay?
2. How does he establish and maintain his authority on the subject?
3. Identify the basic type of argument he uses in this essay.
4. Compare and contrast the tone of this essay with the tone of "Is It an O.K. Word, Usewise?"
5. Note the diction of the second paragraph. What effect is achieved by such words and phrases as "crusaders," "gallant little band of the last literates," and "pop grammarians"?

Buck Fanshaw's Funeral
MARK TWAIN

Mark Twain, pen name for Samuel Langhorne Clemens (1835–1910), internationally known humorist and satirist, was born in Florida, Missouri, and spent his boyhood in Hannibal, Missouri. In his youth and early manhood he worked at a variety of occupations—journeyman printer, steamboat pilot, newspaper reporter, prospector, free-lance writer, and lecturer. His experiences gave him a lifetime of material for his writings. In his own time he enjoyed an international reputation as a wit and social commentator. In his later years he became bitterly cynical, but he is remembered by most Americans as the author of *Tom Sawyer* (1876) and *The Adventures of Huckleberry Finn* (1884).

Somebody has said that in order to know a community, one   1
must observe the style of its funerals and know what manner of men they bury with most ceremony. I cannot say which class we buried with most eclat in our "flush times," the distinguished public benefactor or the distinguished rough—possibly the two chief grades or grand divisions of society honored their illustrious dead about equally; and hence, no doubt, the philosopher I have quoted from would have needed to see two representative funerals in Virginia before forming his estimate of the people.

"Buck Fanshaw's Funeral," Chapter VI from *Roughing It*, Volume II, by Mark Twain. Reprinted by permission of Harper & Row, Publishers, Inc.

There was a grand time over Buck Fanshaw when he died. He was   **2**
a representative citizen. He had "killed his man"—not in his own
quarrel, it is true, but in defense of a stranger unfairly beset by
numbers. He had kept a sumptuous saloon. He had been the proprietor
of a dashing helpmeet whom he could have discarded without the
formality of a divorce. He had held a high position in the fire
department and been a very Warwick in politics. When he died there
was great lamentation throughout the town, but especially in the vast
bottom-stratum of society.

On the inquest it was shown that Buck Fanshaw, in the delirium of   **3**
a wasting typhoid fever, had taken arsenic, shot himself through the
body, cut his throat, and jumped out of a four-story window and broken
his neck—and after due deliberation, the jury, sad and tearful, but
with intelligence unblinded by its sorrow, brought in a verdict of death
"by the visitation of God." What could the world do without juries?

Prodigious preparations were made for the funeral. All the vehi-   **4**
cles in town were hired, all the saloons put in mourning, all the
municipal and fire-company flags hung at half-mast, and all the
firemen ordered to muster in uniform and bring their machines duly
draped in black. Now—let us remark in parentheses—as all the
peoples of the earth had representative adventurers in the Silverland,
and as each adventurer had brought the slang of his nation or his
locality with him, the combination made the slang of Nevada the
richest and the most infinitely varied and copious that had ever existed
anywhere in the world, perhaps, except in the mines of California in
the "early days." Slang was the language of Nevada. It was hard to
preach a sermon without it, and be understood. Such phrases as "You
bet!" "Oh, no, I reckon not!" "No Irish need apply," and a hundred
others, became so common as to fall from the lips of a speaker
unconsciously—and very often when they did not touch the subject
under discussion and consequently failed to mean anything.

After Buck Fanshaw's inquest, a meeting of the short-haired   **5**
brotherhood was held, for nothing can be done on the Pacific coast
without a public meeting and an expression of sentiment. Regretful
resolutions were passed and various committees appointed; among
others, a committee of one was deputed to call on the minister, a
fragile, gentle, spiritual new fledgling from an Eastern theological
seminary, and as yet unacquainted with the ways of the mines. The
committeeman, "Scotty" Briggs, made his visit; and in after days it was
worth something to hear the minister tell about it. Scotty was a
stalwart rough, whose customary suit, when on weighty official business, like committee work, was a firehelmet, flaming red flannel shirt,
patent-leather belt with spanner and revolver attached, coat hung over
arm, and pants stuffed into boot-tops. He formed something of a
contrast to the pale theological student. It is fair to say of Scotty,
however, in passing, that he had a warm heart, and a strong love for
his friends, and never entered into a quarrel when he could reasonably
keep out of it. Indeed, it was commonly said that whenever one of
Scotty's fights was investigated, it always turned out that it had

originally been no affair of his, but that out of native good-heartedness he had dropped in of his own accord to help the man who was getting the worst of it. He and Buck Fanshaw were bosom friends, for years, and had often taken adventurous "pot-luck" together. On one occasion, they had thrown off their coats and taken the weaker side in a fight among strangers, and after gaining a hard-earned victory, turned and found that the men they were helping had deserted early, and not only that, but had stolen their coats and made off with them. But to return to Scotty's visit to the minister. He was on a sorrowful mission, now, and his face was the picture of woe. Being admitted to the presence he sat down before the clergyman, placed his fire-hat on an unfinished manuscript sermon under the minister's nose, took from it a red silk handkerchief, wiped his brow and heaved a sigh of dismal impressiveness, explanatory of his business. He choked, and even shed tears; but with an effort he mastered his voice and said in lugubrious tones:

"Are you the duck that runs the gospel-mill next door?"   6

"Am I the—pardon me, I believe I do not understand?"   7

With another sigh and a half sob, Scotty rejoined: 8

"Why you see we are in a bit of trouble, and the boys thought   9 maybe you would give us a lift, we'd tackle you—that is, if I've got the rights of it and you are the head clerk of the doxology-works next door."

"I am the shepherd in charge of the flock whose fold is next door."   10

"The which?"   11

"The spiritual adviser of the little company of believers whose   12 sanctuary adjoins these premises."

Scotty scratched his head, reflected a moment, and then said: 13

"You ruther hold over me, pard. I reckon I can't call that hand.   14 Ante and pass the buck."

"How? I beg pardon. What did I understand you to say?"   15

"Well, you've ruther got the bulge on me. Or maybe we've both got   16 the bulge, somehow. You don't smoke me and I don't smoke you. You see, one of the boys has passed in his checks, and we want to give him a good send-off, and so the thing I'm on now is to roust out somebody to jerk a little chin-music for us and waltz him through handsome."

"My friend, I seem to grow more and more bewildered. Your   17 observations are wholly incomprehensible to me. Cannot you simplify them in some way? At first I thought perhaps I understood you, but I grope now. Would it not expedite matters if you restricted yourself to categorical statements of fact unencumbered with obstructing accumulations of metaphor and allegory?"

Another pause, and more reflection. Then, said Scotty: 18

"I'll have to pass, I judge."   19

"How?"   20

"You've raised me out, pard."   21

"I still fail to catch your meaning."   22

"Why, that last lead of yourn is too many for me—that's the idea. I   23 can't neither trump nor follow suit."

The clergyman sank back in his chair perplexed. Scotty leaned his   24 head on his hand and gave himself up to thought. Presently his face came up, sorrowful but confident.

"I've got it now, so's you can savvy," he said. "What we want is a 25
gospel-sharp. See?"

"A what?"   26

"Gospel-sharp. Parson."   27

"Oh! Why did you not say so before? I am a clergyman—a parson." 28

"Now you talk! You see my blind and straddle it like a man. Put it 29
there!"—extending a brawny paw, which closed over the minister's
small hand and gave it a shake indicative of fraternal sympathy and
fervent gratification.

"Now we're all right, pard. Let's start fresh. Don't you mind my 30
snuffling a little—becuz we're in a power of trouble. You see, one of the
boys has gone up the flume—"

"Gone where?"   31

"Up the flume—throwed up the sponge, you understand."   32

"Thrown up the sponge?"   33

"Yes—kicked the bucket—"   34

"Ah—has departed to that mysterious country from whose bourne 35
no traveler returns."

"Return! I reckon not. Why, pard, he's *dead!*"   36

"Yes, I understand."   37

"Oh, you do? Well I thought maybe you might be getting tangled 38
some more. Yes, you see he's dead again—"

"Again! Why, has he ever been dead before?"   39

"Dead before? No! Do you reckon a man has got as many lives as a 40
cat? But you bet you he's awful dead now, poor old boy, and I wish I'd
never seen this day. I don't want no better friend than Buck Fanshaw. I
knowed him by the back; and when I know a man and like him, I freeze
to him—you hear *me.* Take him all round, pard, there never was a
bullier man in the mines. No man ever knowed Buck Fanshaw to go
back on a friend. But it's all up, you know, it's all up. It ain't no use.
They've scooped him."

"Scooped him?"   41

"Yes—death has. Well, well, well, we've got to give him up. Yes, 42
indeed. It's a kind of a hard world, after all, *ain't* it? But pard, he was a
rustler! You ought to seen him get started once. He was a bully boy
with a glass eye! Just spit in his face and give him room according to
his strength, and it was just beautiful to see him peel and go in. He was
the worst son of a thief that ever drawed breath. Pard, he was *on* it! He
was on it bigger than an Injun!"

"On it? On what?"   43

"On the shoot. On the shoulder. On the fight, you understand. *He* 44
didn't give a continental for *any*body. *Beg* your pardon, friend, for
coming so near saying a cuss-word—but you see I'm on an awful strain,
in this palaver, on account of having to cramp down and draw
everything so mild. But we've got to give him up. There ain't any
getting around that. I don't reckon. Now if we can get you to help plant
him—"

"Preach the funeral discourse? Assist at the obsequies?"   45

"Obs'quies is good. Yes. That's it—that's our little game. We are 46
going to get the thing up regardless, you know. He was always nifty

himself, and so you bet you his funeral ain't going to be no slouch—solid-silver doorplate on his coffin, six plumes on the hearse, and a nigger on the box in a biled shirt and a plug hat—how's that for high? And we'll take care of *you*, pard. We'll fix you all right. There'll be a kerridge for you; and whatever you want, you just 'scape out and we'll 'tend to it. We've got a shebang fixed up for you to stand behind, in No. 1's house, and don't you be afraid. Just go in and toot your horn, if you don't sell a clam. Put Buck through as bully as you can, pard, for anybody that knowed him will tell you that he was one of the whitest men that was ever in the mines. You can't draw it too strong. He never could stand it to see things going wrong. He's done more to make this town quiet and peaceable than any man in it. I've seen him lick four Greasers in eleven minutes, myself. If a thing wanted regulating, *he* warn't a man to go browsing around after somebody to do it, but he would prance in and regulate it himself. He warn't a Catholic. Scasley. He was down on 'em. His word was, 'No Irish need apply!' But it didn't make no difference about that when it came down to what a man's rights was—and so, when some roughs jumped the Catholic boneyard and started in to stake out town lots in it he *went* for 'em! And he *cleaned* 'em, too! I was there, pard, and I seen it myself."

"That was very well indeed—at least the impulse was—whether 47 the act was strictly defensible or not. Had the deceased any religious convictions? That is to say, did he feel a dependence upon, or acknowledge allegiance to a higher power?"

More reflection.   48

"I reckon you've stumped me again, pard. Could you say it over 49 once more, and say it slow?"

"Well, to simplify it somewhat, was he, or rather had he ever been 50 connected with any organization sequestered from secular concerns and devoted to self-sacrifice in the interests of morality?"

"All down but nine—set 'em up on the other alley, pard."   51

"What did I understand you to say?"   52

"Why, you're most too many for me, you know. When you get in 53 with your left I hunt grass every time. Every time you draw, you fill; but I don't seem to have any luck. Let's have a new deal."

"How? Begin again?"   54

"That's it."   55

"Very well. Was he a good man, and—"   56

"There—I see that; don't put up another chip till I look at my hand. 57 A good man, says you? Pard, it ain't no name for it. He was the best man that ever—pard, you would have doted on that man. He could lam any galoot of his inches in America. It was him that put down the riot last election before it got a start; and everybody said he was the only man that could have done it. He waltzed in with a spanner in one hand and a trumpet in the other, and sent fourteen men home on a shutter in less than three minutes. He had that riot all broke up and prevented nice before anybody ever got a chance to strike a blow. He was always for peace, and he would *have* peace—he could not stand disturbances. Pard, he was a great loss to this town. It would please the boys if you

could chip in something like that and do him justice. Here once when
the Micks got to throwing stones through the Methodis' Sunday-school
windows, Buck Fanshaw, all of his own notion, shut up his saloon and
took a couple of six-shooters and mounted guard over the Sunday-
school. Says he, 'No Irish need apply!' And they didn't. He was the
bulliest man in the mountains, pard! He could run faster, jump higher,
hit harder, and hold more tanglefoot whisky without spilling it than
any man in seventeen counties. Put that in, pard—it'll please the boys
more than anything you could say. And you can say, pard, that he
never shook his mother."

    "Never shook his mother?"   58

    "That's it—any of the boys will tell you so."   59

    "Well, but why *should* he shake her?"   60

    "That's what *I* say—but some people does."   61

    "Not people of any repute?"   62

    "Well, some that averages pretty so-so."   63

    "In my opinion the man that would offer personal violence to his 64
own mother, ought to—"

    "Cheese it, pard; you've banked your ball clean outside the string. 65
What I was drivin' at, was, that he never *throwed off* on his mother—
don't you see? No indeedy. He give her a house to live in, and town lots,
and plenty of money; and he looked after her and took care of her all
the time; and when she was down with the smallpox I'm d——d if he
didn't set up nights and nuss her himself! *Beg* your pardon for saying
it, but it hopped out too quick for yours truly. You've treated me like a
gentleman, pard, and I ain't the man to hurt your feelings intentional.
I think you're white. I think you're a square man, pard. I like you, and
I'll lick any man that don't. I'll lick him tell he can't tell himself from a
last year's corpse! put it *there*!" [Another fraternal handshake—and
exit.]

    The obsequies were all that "the boys" could desire. Such a marvel 66
of funeral pomp had never been seen in Virginia. The plumed hearse,
the dirge-breathing brass-bands, the close marts of business, the flags
dropping at half-mast, the long, plodding procession of uniformed
secret societies, military battalions and fire companies, draped engines, carriages of officials, and citizens in vehicles and on foot,
attracted multitudes of spectators to the sidewalks, roofs, and windows; and for years afterward, the degree of grandeur attained by any
civic display in Virginia was determined by comparison with Buck
Fanshaw's funeral.

    Scotty Briggs, as a pall-bearer and a mourner, occupied a promi- 67
nent place at the funeral, and when the sermon was finished and the
last sentence of prayer for the dead man's soul ascended, he responded,
in a low voice, but with feeling:

    "AMEN. No Irish need apply."   68

    As the bulk of the response was without apparent relevancy, it was 69
probably nothing more than a humble tribute to the memory of the
friend that was gone; for, as Scotty had once said, it was "his word."

    Scotty Briggs, in after days, achieved the distinction of becoming 70 the only convert to religion that was ever gathered from the Virginia roughs; and it transpired that the man who had it in him to espouse the quarrel of the weak out of inborn nobility of spirit was no mean timber whereof to construct a Christian. The making him one did not warp his generosity or diminish his courage; on the contrary it gave intelligent direction to the one and a broader field to the other. If his Sunday-school class progressed faster than the other classes, was it matter for wonder? I think not. He talked to his pioneer small-fry in a language they understood! It was my large privilege, a month before he died, to hear him tell the beautiful story of Joseph and his brethren to his class "without looking at the book." I leave it to the reader to fancy what it was like, as it fell, riddled with slang, from the lips of that grave, earnest teacher, and was listened to by his little learners with a consuming interest that showed that they were as unconscious as he was that any violence was being done to the sacred proprieties!

Study Questions

1. Contrast the language of the narrator in paragraphs 1–5 and 61–64 with the language used by Scotty and by the minister. What are the major differences?
2. How are Scotty and the minister characterized by their language?
3. What is the narrator's attitude toward Scotty? How does he reveal this attitude?
4. What type of development is used in paragraph 5?
5. In addition to the situation between Scotty and the minister, what are the other sources of humor?

7 Popular Culture and the Arts
THE WINTER OF OUR DISCONTENT

Cultural historians will no doubt remember the 1980s as the decade when Americans spent an increasing number of hours and dollars on entertainment and leisure-time activities; when the value of culture and the arts stood in doubt; when the ideas and opinions of Americans were increasingly formed by images selected for them by the media; and when, as a result, the integrity of the media was called into question. Although a cursory reading of *The New York Times* might indicate that the dance is the most popular of contemporary arts, statistics demonstrate that Americans take the greatest interest in sports, television, and the film. Television showings of mini-series such as "Shogun" attract some of the largest viewing audiences in history. On the big screen, box office records tumble and tumble again, as films like *The Empire Strikes Back* and *Raiders of the Lost Ark* push some former box-office champions as *Gone with the Wind* and *The Sound of Music* way down the list. This is an era of culture for the masses, with cable television promising to change our lives profoundly.

Our first selection, "The Computer and the Poet," raises the age-old question of whether the machine can replace the human mind; in it, Norman Cousins investigates the nature of creativity. Then Ann Nietzke and Ralph Schoenstein examine contemporary song lyrics from a fem lib point of view; they remind us that contemporary issues will often force us to reconsider hitherto viable art forms. In "Powerhouse" and "The Monster" Eudora Welty and Deems Taylor respectively study two musical figures and the forces that motivate them. The results are provocative, not only for what they tell us about the artists but also for their stylistic approaches to the material: "Powerhouse" is a short story, while "The Monster" is an essay.

The other essays in "Popular Culture and the Arts" explore such pastimes as sports and television, kinds of pop culture that attract great numbers of people. Big-time athletics are scrutinized by Arnold J. Mandell and David Friedman. Because Mandell looks at those who play and Friedman at those who watch violent sports, the two essays make an interesting pair for comparison and contrast.

Jean Kerr then finds her addiction to television soap opera amusing and harmless, while Marya Mannes finds television and television commercials in particular harmful and divisive. Michael Arlen is disquieted by the passivity which television engenders in the viewer, while Leslie Bennetts questions the connection between violence in the arts and violent America. Finally, Charles Kuralt tours the United States and looks at a national custom—the barbeque; he writes a paean to lost simplicity, as by implication do many of the writers in this section.

Together, the essays in this final section should provoke the thoughtful reader into an examination of the role and importance of the arts in the decade ahead.

The Computer and the Poet

NORMAN COUSINS

Norman Cousins (1915–   ) was born in New Jersey. He received a Litt.D. from the American University in 1948, and has been awarded honorary degrees by many other colleges and universities, including Notre Dame, Brandeis, and Washington and Jefferson. Although probably best known as the editor of *Saturday Review,* Cousins has performed in a similar capacity for *Current History* and served as chairman of programming for PBS. He has received awards too numerous to list for journalism, and for his efforts in education and humanitarian endeavors. His works include *Talks with Nehru* (1951), *Who Speaks for Man?* (1952), *Doctor Schweitzer of Lambarene* (1960), and *The Celebration of Life* (1975).

The essential problem of man in a computerized age remains the same as it has always been. That problem is not solely how to be more productive, more comfortable, more content, but how to be more sensitive, more sensible, more proportionate, more alive. The computer makes possible a phenomenal leap in human proficiency; it demolishes the fences around the practical and even the theoretical intelligence. But the question persists and indeed grows whether the computer will make it easier or harder for human beings to know who they really are, to identify their real problems, to respond more fully to beauty, to place adequate value on life, and to make their world safer than it now is.   1

Electronic brains can reduce the profusion of dead ends involved in vital research. But they can't eliminate the foolishness and decay that come from the unexamined life. Nor do they connect a man to the things he has to be connected to—the reality of pain in others; the possibilities of creative growth in himself; the memory of the race; and the rights of the next generation.   2

The reason these matters are important in a computerized age is that there may be a tendency to mistake data for wisdom, just as there has always been a tendency to confuse logic with values, and intelligence with insight. Unobstructed access to facts can produce unlimited good only if it is matched by the desire and ability to find out what they mean and where they would lead.   3

Facts are terrible things if left sprawling and unattended. They are   4

319

too easily regarded as evaluated certainties rather than as the rawest of raw materials crying to be processed into the texture of logic. It requires a very unusual mind, Whitehead said, to undertake the analysis of a fact. The computer can provide a correct number, but it may be an irrelevant number until judgment is pronounced.

To the extent, then, that man fails to make the distinction between 5 the intermediate operations of electronic intelligence and the ultimate responsibilities of human decision and conscience, the computer could prove a digression. It could obscure man's awareness of the need to come to terms with himself. It may foster the illusion that he is asking fundamental questions when actually he is asking only functional ones. It may be regarded as a substitute for intelligence instead of an extension of it. It may promote undue confidence in concrete answers. "If we begin with certainties," Bacon said, "we shall end in doubts but if we begin with doubts, and we are patient with the., we shall end in certainties."

The computer knows how to vanquish error, but before we lose 6 ourselves in celebration of the victory, we might reflect on the great advances in the human situation that have come about because men were challenged by error and would not stop thinking and probing until they found better approaches for dealing with it. "Give me a good fruitful error, full of seeds, bursting with its own corrections," Ferris Greenslet wrote. "You can keep your sterile truth for yourself."

The biggest single need in computer technology is not for improved 7 circuitry, or enlarged capacity, or prolonged memory, or miniaturized containers, but for better questions and better use of the answers. Without taking anything away from the technicians, we think it might be fruitful to effect some sort of junction between the computer technologist and the poet. A genuine purpose may be served by turning loose the wonders of the creative imagination on the kinds of problems being put to electronic tubes and transistors. The company of poets may enable the men who tend the machines to see a larger panorama of possibilities than technology alone may inspire.

A poet, said Aristotle, has the advantage of expressing the univer- 8 sal; the specialist expresses only the particular. The poet, moreover, can remind us that man's greatest energy comes not from his dynamos but from his dreams. The notion of where a man ought to be instead of where he is; the liberation from cramped prospects; the intimations of immorality through art—all these proceed naturally out of dreams. But the quality of a man's dreams can only be a reflection of his subconscious. What he puts into his subconscious, therefore, is quite literally the most important nourishment in the world.

Nothing really happens to a man except as it is registered in the 9 subconscious. This is where event and feeling become memory and where the proof of life is stored. The poet—and we use the term to include all those who have respect for and speak to the human spirit—can help to supply the subconscious with material to enhance its sensitivity, thus safeguarding it. The poet, too, can help to keep man from making himself over in the image of his electronic marvels.

For the danger is not so much that man will be controlled by the computer as that he may imitate it.

The poet reminds men of their uniqueness. It is not necessary to 10 possess the ultimate definition of this uniqueness. Even to speculate on it is a gain.

Study Questions

1. What is the thesis of Cousins's essay?
2. Comment on how Cousins uses quotations to further his argument.
3. Suggest alternate paragraphing for what are now paragraphs 1–4.
4. Cousins tells us what he means by "poet" in paragraph 9. Should he have done this earlier? Where?
5. Find examples of parallel construction in this essay.
6. The last paragraph contains either a fragment or a nontraditional sentence, depending on your point of view. Which sentence is it, and what modification might you suggest?

. . . Doin' Somebody Wrong
ANN NIETZKE

Ann Nietzke (1945–   ) was born in Alton, Illinois. She has been a free-lance writer since 1972, when her first article—a psychological analysis of Coke and Pepsi commercials—was published in the *Saturday Review*. For five years she was a contributing editor to *Human Behavior;* many of her articles from that magazine have been reprinted. An interview with Loretta Lynn appeared in the *Village Voice,* and *Windowlight: A Woman's Journal from the Edge of America* was honored with the Southern California P.E.N. award. Nietzke holds a Master of Arts in English and currently earns her living as a typist.

There was a time when country-and-western music was 1 known outside the rural South and Southwest only as hillbilly or redneck music, foot-stomping or, if you will, shit-kicking music. Now that its popularity has mushroomed nationwide (even New York has about 20 exclusively country stations), and the country-music business has become a giant industry, people are a little kinder in their references to the genre. In fact, there is a lot of talk now about country being *the* true American sound, and the Country Music Association (CMA) would have us believe it is "America's only native art form."

If that is true, it's ironic that country music has become more   2
popular in the past decade or so precisely because it has become less "country," having been influenced—to the dismay of many older fans—by rock, pop, folk and whatever else has been in (or on) the air. Current pop-country stars such as Kris Kristofferson, Mac Davis, Glenn Campbell, John Denver, Anne Murray and Olivia Newton-John, for example, have quite a different sound from such current solid country stars as Merle Haggard, Johnny Cash, Freddy Hart and Loretta Lynn, just as these differ from the more traditional sounds of the late Hank Williams or Ernest Tubb, Mother Maybelle Carter or Kitty Wells.

Nowadays, many country singers dream of recording a "crossover"   3
single that will be a hit on both the country and pop charts, although at the same time they worry about becoming too "pop" and thus tarnishing their image with the hard-core country audience. This is a very legitimate concern because country audiences, more than any others (with the possible exception of political supporters and thus the parallel in Robert Altman's film *Nashville),* are vitally interested in the personal lives of the stars and seem to feel that the singers should be truly grateful to fans. They insist that singers who "make it big" appear to stay "country" and humble and poor at heart, in spite of the fact that many earn fantastic amounts of money, run big business enterprises and live in mansions.

The motto of the Illinois Country Opry, for example, is "Stay   4
Country," but the difficulty in trying to stay country lies at least partly in figuring out what *country* means. Even a committee appointed by the CMA to work up a definition of a country song finally gave up. Kris "Me and Bobby McGee" Kristofferson says, "If it sounds country, man, it's country," but his own country credentials are highly suspect, his image being a little too hip and intellectual for many country fans (having been a former Rhodes scholar and English instructor at West Point). Tom T. Hall, composer of "Harper Valley PTA," insists that content is more important than sound in determining what's country—it's what *happens* in a country song that counts. In broader terms, the framework of country music has been described by Christopher Wren of *The New York Times* as rural southern in origin, conservative in politics, fundamentalist in religion, and blue-collar in economics. I myself think the CMA is right on target when it states that "country music is no longer strictly rural, as the name implies, but has become the folk music of the working classes."

If you really want to know what country music is, though, you have   5
to find out for yourself by listening to it. Set your radio dial at your

country station for a few days and, if you feel any affinity for what you hear there, stop by your local discount drugstore, where you will probably find at least a few not-so-current albums by top country stars for as little as two or three dollars. Then, with the money you've "saved" on the records, buy yourself a 12-pack of beer so you'll have something to cry in while you listen to them, for you will probably discover, just as I did, that the world of country music is essentially a world of "heartaches by the number, troubles by the score."

My own interest in country was first aroused early this year when I **6** read of the controversy stirred up by Loretta Lynn's single called "The Pill" in which a wife is telling her husband, all in chicken-farm metaphors, that she's tired of his screwing around with other hens while she stays at home constantly pregnant and that, in fact, now that she has the Pill, she's going out to have some fun of her own unless he wants to "make a deal" and start behaving himself ("There's gonna be some changes made right here on nursery hill/You've set this chicken your last time 'cause now I've got the Pill").

I found Lynn's manifestor of liberation so funny and touching that **7** I became an instant fan. How could any feminist, whatever medical reservations she might have about the Pill, resist loving such lines as "I'm tearin' down your brooder house" or "This chicken's done tore up her nest" or, finally, "This incubator's overused because you kept it filled/But feelin' good comes easy now since I got the Pill"? The very sentiments that made the song irresistible to me, however, made it very resistible to many country deejays across the nation, and the record was banned by so many stations that sales were actually boosted by the controversy—all of which shook up the Nashville establishment, since Loretta Lynn is probably the current queen of the country music and has won just about every award in the business.

You might think that the song would be banned because of its **8** "earthness" and, indeed, some deejays did use that as an excuse. But the truth is that a lot of country music is earthy—more sexually explicit than rock, I think, if only because in country the words are so simple and direct and clearly sung that you understand immediately just what's being said. Stations that refused to air "The Pill" had no qualms about playing Conway Twitty's "You've Never Been This Far Before," during the course of which somebody's virginity is lost ("I don't know what I'm saying as my fingers touch forbidden places"). And 17-year-old Little Tanya Tucker gets away with "Would You Lay with Me in a Field of Stone?" in which she asks, "Should my lips grow dry would you wet them, dear/In the midnight hour, if my lips were dry?" So it could hardly have been sex per se that folks found to be offensive in "The Pill."

Out of curiosity, I called my local country station request line and **9** asked for the song. I was told that the entire staff had decided not to air it because it was too "commercial." This seemed a bit farfetched to me, since the station repeatedly plays such songs as Ray Steven's faddish and corny "The Streak" and an incredibly, *literally* commercial number called "Red Necks, White Socks and Blue Ribbon Beer." It began to seem that Lynn's own outspoken estimate of the situation at the radio stations was indisputably true: "If all the disc jockeys were women there wouldn't be no confusion. The song's not dirty—it's threatening because it says what's good for the gander is good for the goose."

After listening to more and more country music, I began to realize 10 that a great portion of the heartache and trouble in the songs stems from disastrous relationships of one kind or another between men and women, from the disastrous ways in which men and women see themselves and each other. I think one reason the world of country music is often such a sad one—despite all its humor, corn and high spirit—is that it is so often a world of diminished personhood and, although the world at large is sad for the same reason, I think the working-class lifestyle and mentality, as depicted in most country music, accentuates it.

To begin with, the only really acceptable role for decent women 11 seems to be that of housewife and mother. The indecent women who work are all waitresses, barmaids, or prostitutes who travel from "Barrooms to Bedrooms," as David Wills sings it, and are in many songs referred to collectively as "honky-tonk angels." The men, decent and indecent, work hard and play hard, travel or wander, drink a lot, and sometimes end up in prison, while the women stay home and take care of the kids. To the tune of Roger Miller's big hit "King of the Road," Jody Miller sings "Queen of the House," in which she describes the life of the hardworking housewife and mother who rules a domain of children, dirty floors, and bathtub rings—the regalia that yet ennoble her.

This image is reinforced by the lives of the women country stars as 12 described in various country music publications and in their album notes. No matter that these women had to be extremely strong and determined in order to make successful careers for themselves, or that they may spend as many as 250 nights a year in a bus, traveling to reach their fans all over the United States. What matters, so far as their public images go, is how devoted they are as wives and mothers. This description of Dottie West is typical in tone and content of much of the publicity I've seen on Lynn Anderson, Tammy Wynette, Jeanne Pruett, Brenda Lee, Loretta Lynn and others: "To her mother, she's the oldest of 10 children; to her husband, the greatest wife in the world; to her four lovely children, she's a devoted mother; and to her friends, an excellent cook." Even Canadian pop-country star Anne Murray has said she'll quit the business at 30 to get married and have children because she believes that "career and marriage don't mix."

One star who managed literally to mix her career with marriage is 13 Tammy Wynette, formerly a cosmetologist named Wynette Pugh who, after she started singing, married her childhood idol and one of the kings of country music—George Jones. Both made something of a career out of the marriage itself as they performed together, even including a reenactment of their wedding ceremony as a climax to their act. Their recent divorce or "D-I-V-O-R-C-E," as Tammy would sing it, is her third and proves that she is unable to live out the

philosophy that underlies so many of her songs, a philosophy
epitomized in "Stand By Your Man," the largest-selling single ever
recorded by a woman in the history of country music, that bad times
are often the lot of a woman, particularly when her man is out enjoying
himself or doing things she finds incomprehensible. But if you love
him, ladies, you're supposed to "be proud of him" and give him "all the
love you can" for, above everything else it's important to "stand by
your man."

Nowhere in country, I think, does the relationship between di- 14
minished personhood and sadness become more apparent than in the
work of Tammy Wynette, for her voice conveys a little teardrop in
every syllable, and most of the syllables add up to portrayals of women
who feel "I am nothing, my man is everything." So Tammy is full of
advice on how to hold your man. "There's no secret, just some little
things to do," she says and recommends that you start his day out right
with a loving smile, support him, understand him and let him know
that you think he's "better than the rest." A woman is supposed to
maintain this attitude no matter how badly the man treats her.
"Sometimes," Tammy sings, "I lay in bed and cry, cry, cry," but she
insists, "for better or worse, I took him 'til the day I die."

Women who treat men similarly, however, women who do any 15
"slippin' around," may very well get shot as punishment (Johnny
Cash's "Kate" and Claude King's "Laura"), because men view women
as their sexual property. Surely this is partly because the men work so
hard to pay for everything else that they must feel they are paying as
well for their women, who wait passively at home. Tex Ritter sings, for
example, "I've had enough of your two-timing/You've had enough of
my bankroll," and Bobby Bare complains of "Alimony, same old blues
in it/I'm payin' for it while someone else is usin' it." For whatever
reasons, a woman who cheats, even if she isn't killed for it, is very
rarely forgiven in country. Over and over and over again men are
driven to the bottle by their unfaithful women ("My heart is breaking
like the tiny bubbles/She's actin' single, I'm drinkin' doubles").

The Good Woman—Bad Woman split is, in fact, a major theme in 16
the music, because the married men are constantly tempted by
"honky-tonk angels" of various types who, I gather, are generally
better lays than their wives ("She's the one I love," Mel Street tells one,
"but you make me feel more like a man"). While many do give in to
temptation, they often suffer from the conflict within themselves:
"Lord, I'm only human, and I can feel the glow," Jim Mundy sings. "My
body's saying yes but my heart is saying no."

The happiest songs narrated by married men, therefore, are those 17
in which the conflict is resolved for them by a wife who can be sexy at
the appropriate times. The best-known example of these is probably
Charlie Rich's "Behind Closed Doors," in which his woman is always a
"lady" until he gets her behind closed doors where no one sees what
goes on, where she lets her hair hang down and makes him glad he's a
man. Jerry Wallace brags of a similar ideal setup in "I've Got So Many
Wives At Home," for his wife, too, is both lady and satisfying lover, and

"If I need a devil, as all men sometimes do/You got just enough to make me love the devil out of you."

It is taken for granted by both men and women in country music 18 that men have to be "the way they are," while women have to be what their men want them to be. In "I Can't Be Myself," Merle Haggard implies he'll be leaving a woman who wants him to change. George Jones demands, "Take Me As I Am," and Billy Edd Wheeler says straight out, "If you're expectin' me to change my old ways for the new/Baby, don't hold your breath until I do." Dottie West, however, is pictured on one of her album covers as a paper doll about to be cut out by a huge pair of scissors held by a big male hand ("Take your scissors and take your time/And cut along the dotted line"). She begs her man to keep his scissors handy and trim her edges now and then, and "Fit me in with all your plans/For I want to be what I'm cut out to be."

It would appear from such examples that the men have a good deal 19 of ego strength and personal pride, but a close look at many lyrics by both male and female singers reveals to what a great extent men rely on their women for emotional support and for a sense of "manhood" ("Whenever I'm down you come around/And you make me feel like a man"). The male counterpart of Tammy Wynette's "Stand By Your Man" is not "Stand By Your Woman" but rather "Only A Woman Like You (Can Make A Man of Me)," a woman capable of turning even small dreams into "the greatest thing."

Whatever power women do have in the world of country music 20 stems, I think, from this twisted emotional setup, and I find a subtle but definite thread of contempt for men running through a number of female songs. Tammy Wynette advises, "If you love him, be proud of him/'Cause after all he's *just a man,*" and elsewhere admits that she's "quit lookin' for a perfect man/'Cause there ain't any more of them." Obviously, if men need women to make men of them, then without women they are nothing but little boys ("I'd love to just deceive 'em, playin' with 'em like a toy/Then leave 'em like a little boy"). So, although "It's A Man's World," as Diana Trask sings, "He's got an awful lot of little boy in him/He wants to have his way." And little boys, of course, have to be mothered ("Baby me, baby, as only you can do").

One reason men need so much emotional support is that they are 21 not supposed to do anything so "unmanly" as to feel or express deep emotion themselves. Although men in country do a whole lot of crying, mostly boozy crying, they are nearly always ashamed of it and a little surprised at their own capacity for hurt. Johnny Cash sings of a man "six-foot-six" who weighed 235 lb. but who cried "like a whipped pup" and was "brought down to his knees" by "A Thing Called Love." It is implied that this is a very strange occurrence. The idea is stated as bluntly as possible by Waylon Jennings, when he warns his woman, "Don't mistake my tenderness for any sign of weakness in your man." All of this places the burden of emotion squarely on the woman. "I will feel your loneliness and I will feel your pain," Jennie C. Riley promises, and Jerry Wallace loves his woman, he tells her, because "If I hurt, it makes you cry."

The price men pay, however, for the questionable benefit of 22 keeping women at home to be mothers and emotional buffers for themselves is a great one, for in order to maintain some kind of balance, this arrangement also requires men to be daddies to their little girl—women, who can't take care of themselves financially or any other way. Dottie West sings an incredible song called "Everything's a Wreck (Since You're Gone)," in which a home turns into a disaster area when the man of the house leaves. The wife can't start the mower or unstop the sink or change a fuse or paint a room or even call a TV repairman so she can watch "Edge of Night." (My gut reaction was, "Christ, no wonder he left her—she's an idiot.")

In song after song by such singers as Charlie Rich and Charley 23 Pride, men express anxieties about whether they are materially successful enough to keep their women happy ("I don't know how to tell her I didn't get that raise in pay today/I know how much she wanted that dress in Baker's window"). The men age fast and wear themselves down trying to pay for the fancy clothes and new cars and houses they are convinced their wives want. George Jones thinks of giving up since he can't get ahead: "I work hard and I work overtime/And I'm still deep in debt."

Even if a man gets rich, however, there is no guarantee he can 24 keep his woman, for he also has the pressure of responsibility to satisfy her sexuality. Tammy Wynette sings of having "satin sheets to lie on" and a "big long Cadillac" and "tailor-mades upon her back," yet she is going to leave her rich man for another because he doesn't "keep her satisfied." For their part, the women have to learn all the tricks of catching and holding a man, because the Other Woman, portrayed in country music as Enemy Number One, is always out there waiting to steal him away ("She's a whole lot better lookin' than me and you/And she can do things to a man you never dreamed a woman can do").

In short, both men and women in country music have a hard life, 25 made worse by the limited ways in which they see themselves and each other. For comfort they retreat into their respective fantasy worlds. The women "watch their stories on TV every day/And eat at McDonald's once a week to get away," and read movie magazines ("They say to have her hair done Liz flies all the way to France/And Jackie's seen in a discotheque doin' a brand new dance"). The men romanticize themselves as "lovable losers, no-account boozers and honky-tonk heroes," studs who value their "Low Down Freedom," who can love women and leave 'em and be happy on the road as wandering gypsies. The prison records and down-and-out images of such singers as Merle Haggard and Johnny Paycheck and Johnny Cash (before he got on the religion bandwagon) appeal to these fantasies.

The central male image in country, alas, is probably still the 26 cowboy. "It ain't easy bein' a cowboy in this day and time," say the album notes of Waylon Jennings's *Honky-Tonk Heroes*. But Jennings ("tough and mean and wild") manages to be one, and "the cowboy will live on just as long as there is the sound of music." The authentic cowboys of the country-music world, though, are the truck drivers, who represent a perfect fusion of the cowboy myth and working-class reality.

There are scores and scores of trucking songs and, in many of them, 27 it becomes obvious that the truckers are cowboys, trucks are their horses, highways are the plains, truck stops are saloons and waitresses are saloon girls. In song after song, the monotony and sheer hard work of being a trucker are romanticized into something noble and exciting through stories of how trucks serve the nation, of how drivers help and rescue fellow travelers, of how they speed and manage to outsmart Smokey the Bear (state police) with their CB radios and especially of how every waitress in every truck stop finds every driver absolutely irresistible. Although often the men remain loyal to their wives at home and don't take advantage of this, they do seem to think about it quite a bit ("I could have a lot of women, but I'm not that kind of a guy"). Narrating as a trucker's wife, Tammy Wynette sings, "Last night he called from Dallas/He was havin' a beer at the Crystal Palace/And he said, honey, you won't be alone for long." He's calling to tell her he's going to bring his "big ol' engine" home to her, even though there are "a million chicks" out there who want to make love with him. And Tammy, as always, is patiently waiting, waiting, waiting at home for her man in order to give him "everything he needs."

And so my journey through the world of men and women in 28 country music, inspired by Loretta Lynn's "The Pill," was entertaining and funny and touching, but for a feminist it was pleasurable only in a masochistic sort of way. Only the work of Lynn herself provided me with any comfort or any hope that things might someday be different. In an interview I found Lynn, who was the model for Barbara Jean in Altman's *Nashville,* to be a charming combination of fragility and spunk (in the movie, Ronee Blakely conveyed the fragility and left out the spunk). She has unquestionably "paid her dues" as a woman, having married at 13, totally ignorant of sex, and having had four babies by age 17, plus twins several years later ("If I'd known about the Pill back then, I'd've popped 'em like popcorn"). By age 28 she was a grandmother. Nearly illiterate, she worked for years as a domestic to help pay the rent, as she puts it, and admits, "I had very few things bought from a store that wasn't from the Salvation Army 'til way after I started singin'."

Now Lynn is a millionaire, albeit a very hard-working one, and she 29 finally is beginning to feel strong enough to defy her manager-husband ("one of these kind that when he hollers he thinks you should jump"). One of her most remarkable songs, called "Two Mules Pull This Wagon," is about equality, of sorts, in marriage. A working-class wife-and-mother tells her husband in no uncertain terms that she is sick of his not appreciating the fact that she works as hard at home as he does on his job: "I wash and iron and cook and sew and find time for your naggin'/But you seem to forget, big boy, that two mules pull this wagon."

Lynn sings many different kinds of songs, from gospel to autobio- 30 graphical stories of being a coal miner's daughter in Butcher Hollow, Kentucky, but my favorites, naturally, are her high-spirited declarations of "what's good for the gander is good for the goose." A major theme in her work is that women should be as free as men are sexually—she told me that women should be able to do whatever men do outside of marriage, "because, as far as the Bible is concerned, it's just as wrong for one as it is for the other." In a great many of her songs, such as "The Pill," she threatens to seek pleasure for herself if her man doesn't quit "steppin' out" on her ("Better listen to what I say now/'Cause there's gonna come a day now/You'll have a hanky-panky woman on your hands").

If her man does come home for his sex, though, Lynn wants him 31 sober. Her "Don't Come Home Adrinkin [With Lovin' on Your Mind]" is a courageous if humorous statement of sexual self-respect bound to touch the heart of any woman who's ever been to bed with a drunken man. You may recall the besotted porter in *Macbeth* describing how drink "provokes and unprovokes" lechery—"it provokes the desire, but it takes away the performance." In "Your Squaw Is on the Warpath," Loretta Lynn expresses in this way: "That firewater that you've been drinkin'/Makes you feel bigger, but chief, you're shrinkin'." Interestingly, "Don't Come Home Adrinkin'" is one of Lynn's songs that Tammy Wynette has also recorded, although in "Stand By Your Man" she seems to imply that a woman should be passive and always ready to give her man "something warm to come to."

But whatever else Loretta Lynn might be in her music, she is 32 seldom passive. While other women, as in all country music, are depicted only as devils and manstealers in her songs, she at least has the spunk to fight for her man instead of suffering quietly, "You ain't woman enough to take my man," she tells one rival and threatens another. "You better close your face and stay out of my way/If you don't want to go to Fist City." In "Rated X," though, she sings sympathetically of the plight of the divorced woman ("The women all look at you like you're bad/And the men all hope you are") and advises her to go ahead and live her life and "let 'em talk."

However bright a ray of hope Loretta Lynn may symbolize for 33 women (and therefore men) through country music, though, the final stanza of her song called "One's on the Way" unfortunately tells it like it is for now, that while cosmopolitan women fight for equal rights, while glossy magazines promote the latest decor and while birth control may revolutionize the world of tomorrow, still, today, in Topeka, where "the flies are abuzzin'," a woman's life revolves around her chores and her children, and the child that's on the way.

Obviously the state of relationships between men and women in 34 the world of country music, as in the world at large, is pretty depressing. "Hey, won't you play another somebody done somebody wrong song," sings B. J. Thomas, and indeed there are so many such songs because men and women, through the diminishing, rigid ways in which they see themselves and each other, are constantly "doing each other wrong" in quiet, terrible fashion. And that, my friends, is the *real* tearjerker.

Study Questions

1. In which paragraph does Nietzke get to the heart of her essay? Are the paragraphs that precede it necessary?
2. Comment on the use of quotation marks in this essay.
3. To what extent does Nietzke utilize various *rhetorical modes* in developing her thesis?
4. For whom is this essay written? What do the content and style tell you about its potential audience?

Look What You've Done to My Songs, Girls

RALPH SCHOENSTEIN

Ralph Schoenstein (1933–   ) was born in New York City and attended Hamilton College and then Columbia University, from which he received a B. A. in 1953. After two years in the US Army, he began his career as a professional writer. Schoenstein has been a syndicated newspaper columnist; a television satirist, for ABC News and NET, among others; and a contributer of humor to many major American magazines, including the *New Yorker, Playboy, Cosmopolitan,* and *TV Guide.* Among his books are *Time Lurches On, My Year in the White House Doghouse, I Hear America Mating, The I-Hate-Preppies Handbook,* and *Kamikaze Management.* He is the recipient of the Grantland Rice Award for Best Sports Stories (1962) and the Playboy Award for Humor (1970).

I have always considered myself a liberated man, washing   1
windows, hauling garbage and hauling children with asexual glee. But

the women's movement has finally lost me by cruelly removing the song from my heart.

It all began one night last winter when I was immersed in the 2 enchantment of CBS's salute to Richard Rodgers. During one of the commercials, I found myself singing in tender counterpoint to a pitch for a hair spray:

A fellow needs a girl
To sit by his side
At the end of a weary day.

"If a fellow needs a girl to sit by his side, let him *rent* one from 3 Forty-second Street," my wife, Judy, replied to my song. "The American woman is *finished* being a two-legged beagle for a man!"

"No," I said, "Rodgers and Hammerstein just meant that . . ." 4

"We're supposed to be mascots, servants and psychiatrists for you. I 5 notice that *Mrs.* Rodgers wasn't sitting by *his* side. She was out inventing a mop!"

That night, after Judy had gone to sleep, I lay awake in a 6 melancholy mood. Were Richard Rodgers, Oscar Hammerstein and I really such bad guys? And even if we were, should we still not have been loved? As Rodgers and Hammerstein had put it so movingly in *Carousel:*

And somethin' gave him the things that are his.
One of those things is you.
So when he wants your kisses,
You will give them to the lad,
And anywhere he leads you, you will walk.
And anytime he needs you,
You'll go runnin' there like mad.
You're his girl and he's your feller—
And all the rest is talk.

Oh, nuts! I thought. All those words are now forbidden too. And I 7 could hear Judy saying to me:

"Running to a man and loving him no matter how rotten he is? You 8 think that we're all in the Salvation Army?"

The following day, after sadly deciding to become a closet Richard 9 Rodgers fan, I turned on a telecast of Irving Berlin's masterpiece, *Annie Get Your Gun.* I was so transported by the songs that I found myself joining Howard Keel in a duet that I must admit he carried:

The girl that I marry
Will have to be
As soft and as pink as a nursery.

"Yeech!" cried my daughter Lori, who had just come into the room. 10 "As *soft* and as *pink* as a *nursery?* The guy's collecting *stuffed animals.* Who *wrote* that nonsense anyway?"

"The greatest songwriter America has ever known," I said, proudly 11 taking my stand with the "God Bless America" man.

"Well, the thing that's soft and pink is his *brain,*" she replied. 12

And then Howard Keel made the mistake of singing:　13

A doll I can carry
The girl that I marry
Will be.

"He wants Matrimonial Barbie!" Lori cried.　14

"Look, you can't analyze these words like a William Buckley 15
speech," I said. "This is *poetry,* this is *romance.*"

"This is *junk.* If you guys want to play with dolls, then join a 16
nursery school. But don't expect to carry *us* around because soft and
pink we're not. Black and blue might be closer to the shade."

My musical nostalgia was no longer melancholy, it was grim, for I 17
saw that the problem was bigger than just the songs of Rodgers and
Berlin. Anything written before the time that Betty Friedan returned
enlightened from the wilderness had become a subversive memory.
NOW was destroying my precious then.

Two nights later, with the cunning of an addict, I waited until all 18
the women in my house had gone to sleep and then sneaked to the set
for the glorious *Kiss Me, Kate.* With the volume low, I began to bootleg
two hours of macho melody. And soon I was savoring Cole Porter's:

Won't you turn that new leaf over
So your baby can be your slave?
Oh, why can't you behave?

Then I imagined Gloria Steinem crying through the glow in my 19
mind: "What the hell is that? A sentimental salute to child labor?"

"But, Gloria, can't I hold on to *any* of it?" I mournfully pleaded. 20
"Listen, *you're* my age. Didn't a guy ever bring you a corsage and then
take you dancing on 'The Arthur Murray Show' while the horns and
saxophones wailed 'Bye Bye, Baby'?"

The following day, Robert Goulet stepped before the camera and 21
sang:

The way to handle a woman,
Is to love her . . . simply love her . . .
Merely love her . . . love her . . . love her.

I know. I *know,* I cried. He means "The way to handle a person is 22
love it, simply love it." I've *learned,* I thought! God helped me, I've
learned.

And, alas, I had: the sisterhood had revised all the lyrics in my 23
formerly mooning male chauvinist mind. And I bit my tongue every
time that I started to sing the medieval words of "The Man That Got
Away," "The Blues in the Night" and "A Man Chases a Girl (Until She
Catches Him)." Instead I continued to work on a song for Alan Alda to
sing on a CBS salute to Joan of Arc:

The girl that I marry will have to be
Someone constructed a lot like me.
The girl I call my own

Will maintain an apartment outside of Cologne.
Her nails will be nondescript like her hair,
She'll have a bewitchingly neuter air.
I'll be praisin'
Her amazin'
Flair for incessant consciousness raisin.'
Still rooming with Harry
The girl that I marry
Will be.

Study Questions

1. On the whole, what is Schoenstein's attitude toward fem lib?
2. Is this essay a satire? Why or why not?
3. Does Schoenstein have a stated thesis? If so, where is it?
4. In its original printing, this essay utilized spacing to divide paragraphs 16 and 17, and paragraphs 22 and 23. What purpose does such spacing serve?
5. How does Schoenstein use Gloria Steinem, Joan of Arc, Alan Alda, his wife, and his daughter to help his argument?

Powerhouse
EUDORA WELTY

Eudora Welty (1909–   ) was born in Jackson, Mississippi, where she now lives. She attended Mississippi State College for Women, the University of Wisconsin, and Columbia. Her first short stories were published in the 1930s in the *Southern Review;* her considerable skill resulted in Katherine Anne Porter's writing the introduction to *A Curtain of Green* (1941). Welty's other books include *The Robber Bridegroom* (1942), *Delta Wedding* (1946), *The Ponder Heart* (1954), *Losing Battles* (1970), *The Optimist's Daughter* (1972), *A Pageant of Birds* (1974), *The Eye of the Story* (1978), and *Ida M'tory* (1979). She is a member of the National Institute of Arts and Letters and an honorary consultant to the Library of Congress.

I

Powerhouse is playing! He's here on tour, from the city—   1
Powerhouse and His Keyboard—Powerhouse and His Tasmanians—

all the things he calls himself! There's no one in the world like him.
You can't tell what he is. He looks Asiatic, monkey, Babylonian,
Peruvian, fanatic, devil. He has pale gray eyes, heavy lids, maybe
horny like a lizard's, but big glowing eyes when they're open. He has
feet size twelve, stomping both together on either side of the pedals.
He's not coal black—beverage-colored; looks like a preacher when his
mouth is shut, but then it opens—vast and obscene. And his mouth is
going every minute, like a monkey's when it looks for fleas. Improvising, coming upon a very light and childish melody, *smooch*—he loves it
with his mouth. Is it posssible that he could be this! When you have
him there performing for you, that's what you feel. You know people on
a stage—and people of a darker race—so likely to be marvelous,
frightening.

This is a white dance. Powerhouse is not a show-off like the   2
Harlem boys—not drunk, not crazy, I think. He's in a trance; he's a
person of joy, a fanatic. He listens as much as he performs—a look of
hideous, powerful rapture on his face. Big arched eyebrows that never
stop traveling. When he plays, he beats down piano and seat and wears
them away. He is in motion every moment—what could be more
obscene? There he is with his great head, big fat stomach, little round
piston legs, and long yellow-sectioned strong fingers, at rest about the
size of bananas. Of course you know how he sounds—you've heard him
on records; but still you need to see him. He's going all the time, like
skating around the skating rink or rowing a boat. It makes everybody
crowd around, here in this shadowless steel-trussed hall with the
rose-like posters of Nelson Eddy and the testimonial for the mind-
reading horse in handwriting magnified five hundred times.

Powerhouse is so monstrous he sends everybody into oblivion.   3
When any group, any performers, come to town, don't people always
come out and hover near, leaning inward about them, to learn what it
is? What is it? Listen. Remember how it was with the acrobats. Watch
them carefully; hear the least word, especially what they say to one
another, in another language; don't let them escape you—it's the only
time for hallucination, the last time. They can't stay. They'll be
somewhere else this time tomorrow.

Powerhouse has as much as possible done by signals. Everybody,   4
laughing as if to hide a weakness, will sooner or later hand him up a
written request. Powerhouse reads each one, studying with a secret
face: that is the face which looks like a mask, anybody's; there is a
moment when he makes a decision. Then a light slides under his
eyelids and he says, "Ninety-two!" or some combination of figures—
never a name. Before a number the band is all frantic, misbehaving,
pushing, like children in a schoolroom, and he is the teacher getting
silence. His hands over the keys, he says sternly, "You-all ready?
You-all ready to do some serious walking?"—waits—then, STAMP.
Quiet. STAMP, for the second time. This is absolute. Then a set of
rhythmic kicks against the floor to communicate the tempo. Then, "Oh
Lord," say the distended eyes from beyond the boundary of the
trumpets; "Hello and good-bye"—and they are all down the first note
like a waterfall.

This note marks the end of any known discipline. Powerhouse 5
seems to abandon them all; he himself seems lost—down in the
song—yelling up like somebody in a whirlpool—not guiding them,
hailing them only. But he knows, really. He cries out, but he must
know exactly. "Mercy! . . . What I say! . . . Yeah!" and then drifting,
listening,—"Where that skinbeater?" (wanting drums),—and starting
up and pouring it out in the greatest delight and brutality. On the
sweet pieces, such a leer for everybody! He looks down so benevolently
upon all the faces and whispers the lyrics, and if you could hear him at
this moment on "Marie, the Dawn Is Breaking"! He's going up the
keyboard with a few fingers in some very derogatory triplet routine; he
gets higher and higher, and then he looks over the end of the piano, as
if over a cliff. But not in a show-off way: the song makes him do it.

He loves the way they all play, too—all those next to him. The far 6
section of the band is all studious—wearing glasses, every one; they
don't count. Only those playing around Powerhouse are the real ones.
He has a bass fiddler from Vicksburg, black as pitch, named Valentine,
who plays with his eyes shut and talking to himself, very young.
Powerhouse has to keep encouraging him: "Go on, go on, give it up,
bring it on out there!" When you heard him like that on records, did
you know he was really pleading?

He calls Valentine out to take a solo. 7

"What you going to play?" Powerhouse looks out kindly from 8
behind the piano; he opens his mouth and shows his tongue, listening.

Valentine looks down, drawing against his instrument, and says 9
without a lip movement, "Honeysuckle Rose."

He has a clarinet player named Little Brother, and loves to listen 10
to anything he does. He'll smile and say, "Beautiful!" Little Brother
takes a step forward when he plays and stands at the very front, with
the whites of his eyes like fishes swimming. Once when he played a low
note Powerhouse muttered in dirty praise, "He went clear downstairs
to get that one!"

After a long time, he holds up the number of fingers to tell the band 11
how many choruses still to go—usually five. He keeps his directions
down to signals.

It's a bad night outside. It's a white dance, and nobody dances, 12
except a few straggling jitterbugs and two elderly couples; everybody
just stands around the band and watches Powerhouse. Sometimes they
steal glances at one another. Of course, you know how it is with
them—they would play the same way, giving all they've got, for an
audience of one. . . . When somebody, no matter who, gives everything,
it makes people feel ashamed for him.

II

Late at night, they play the one waltz they will ever consent to play. By 13
request, "Pagan Love Song." Powerhouse's head rolls and sinks like a
weight between his waving shoulders. He groans and his fingers drag

into the keys heavily, holding on to the notes, retrieving. It is a sad song.

"You know what happened to me?" says Powerhouse.   14

Valentine hums a response, dreaming at the bass.   15

"I got a telegram my wife is dead," says Powerhouse, with   16
wandering fingers.

"Uh-huh?"   17

His mouth gathers and forms a barbarous O, while his fingers walk   18
up straight, unwillingly, three octaves.

"Gipsy? Why, how come her to die? Didn't you just phone her up in   19
the night last night long distance?"

"Telegram say—here the words: 'Your wife is dead.' " He puts   20
four-four over the three-four.

"Not but four words?" This is the drummer, an unpopular boy   21
named Scoot, a disbelieving maniac.

Powerhouse is shaking his vast cheeks. "What the hell was she   22
trying to do? What was she up to?

"What name has it got signed, if you got a telegram?" Scott is   23
spitting away with those wire brushes.

Little Brother, the clarinet player, who cannot now speak, glares   24
and tilts back.

"Uranus Knockwood is the name signed." Powerhouse lifts his eyes   25
open. "Ever heard of him?" A bubble shoots out on his lip, like a plate
on a counter.

Valentine is beating slowly on with his palm and scratching the   26
strings with his long blue nails. He is fond of a waltz; Powerhouse
interrupts him.

"I don't know him. Don't know who he is." Valentine shakes his   27
head with the closed eyes, like an old mop.

"Say it again."   28

"Uranus Knockwood."   29

"That ain't Lenox Avenue."   30

"It ain't Broadway."   31

"Ain't ever seen it wrote out in any print, even for horse-racing."   32

"Hell, that's on a star, boy, ain't it?" Crash of the cymbals.   33

"What the hell was she up to?" Powerhouse shudders. "Tell me, tell   34
me, tell me." He makes triplets, and begins a new chorus. He holds
three fingers up.

"You say you got a telegram." This is Valentine, patient and   35
sleepy, beginning again.

Powerhouse is elaborate. "Yas, the time I go out—go way   36
downstairs along a long *corridor* to where they put us. Coming back,
steps out and hands me a telegram: 'Your wife is dead.' "

"Gipsy?" The drummer is like a spider over his drums.   37

"Aaaaaa!" shouts Powerhouse, flinging out both powerful arms for   38
three whole beats to flex his muscles, then kneading a dough of bass
notes. His eyes glitter. He plays the piano like a drum sometimes—
why not?

"Gipsy? Such a dancer?"   39

"Why you don't hear it straight from your agent? Why it ain't come 40
from headquarters? What you been doing, getting telegrams in the
corridor, signed nobody?"

They all laugh. End of that chorus. 41

"What time is it?" Powerhouse calls. "What the hell place is that? 42
Where is my watch and chain?"

"I hang it on you," whimpers Valentine. "It still there." 43

There it rides on Powerhouse's great stomach, down where he can 44
never see it.

"Sure did hear some clock striking twelve while ago. Must be 45
midnight."

"It going to be intermission," Powerhouse declares, lifting up his 46
finger with the signet ring.

He draws the chorus to an end. He pulls a big Northern hotel towel 47
out of the deep pocket in his vast, special-cut tux pants and pushes his
forehead into it.

"If she went and killed herself!" he says with a hidden face. "If she 48
up and jumped out that window!" He gets to his feet, turning vaguely,
wearing the towel on his head.

"Ha, ha!" 49

"Sheik, sheik!" 50

"She wouldn't do that." Little Brother sets down his clarinet like a 51
precious vase, and speaks. He still looks like an East Indian queen,
implacable, divine, and full of snakes. "You ain't going to expect people
doing what they say over long distance."

"Come on!" roars Powerhouse. He is already at the back door; he 52
has pulled it wide open, and with a wild, gathered-up face is smelling
the terrible night.

III

Powerhouse, Valentine, Scoot, and Little Brother step outside into the 53
drenching rain.

"Well, they emptying buckets," says Powerhouse in a mollified 54
voice. On the street he holds his hands out and turns up the blanched
palms like sieves.

A hundred dark, ragged, silent, delighted Negroes have come 55
around from under the eaves of the hall, and follow wherever they go.

"Watch out, Little Brother, don't shrink," says Powerhouse. "You 56
just the right size now—clarinet don't suck you in. You got a dry
throat, Little Brother, you in the desert?" He reaches into the pocket
and pulls out a paper of mints. "Now hold 'em in your mouth—don't
chew 'em. I don't carry around nothing without limit."

"Go in that joint and have beer," says Scoot, and walks ahead. 57

"Beer? Beer? You know what beer is? What do they say is beer? 58
What's beer? Where I been?"

"Down yonder where it say World Cafe, that do?" They are across 59
the tracks now.

Valentine patters over and holds open a screen door warped like a   60
seashell, bitter in the wet, and they walk in, stained darker with the
rain and leaving footprints. Inside, sheltered dry smells stand like
screens around a table covered with a red-checkered cloth, in the
centre of which flies hang onto an obelisk-shaped ketchup bottle. The
midnight walls are checkered again with admonishing. "Not Responsible" signs and black-figured smoky calendars. It is a waiting, silent,
limp room. There is a burnt-out-looking nickelodeon, and right beside
it a long-necked wall instrument labeled "Business Phone, Don't Keep
Talking." Circled phone numbers are written up everywhere. There is
a worn-out peacock feather hanging by a thread to an old, thin, pink,
exposed light bulb, where it slowly turns around and around, whoever
breathes.

A waitress watches.   61

"Come here, living statue, and get all this big order of beer we   62
fixing to give."

"Never seen you before anywhere." The waitress moves and comes   63
forward and slowly shows little gold leaves and tendrils over her teeth.
She shoves up her shoulders and breasts. "How I going to know who
you might be—robbers? Coming in out of the black night right at
midnight, setting down so big at my table!"

"Boogers" says Powerhouse, his eyes opening lazily as in a cave.   64

The girl screams delicately with pleasure. Oh Lord, she likes talk 65
and scares.

"Where you going to find enough beer to put out on this-here   66
table?"

She runs to the kitchen with bent elbows and sliding steps.   67

"Here's a million nickels," says Powerhouse, pulling his hand out   68
of his pocket and sprinkling coins out, all but the last one, which he
makes vanish like a magician.

Valentine and Scoot take the money over to the nickelodeon,   69
which is beginning to look as battered as a slot machine, and read all
the names of the records out loud.

"Whose 'Tuxedo Junction'?" asks Powerhouse.   70

"You know whose."   71

"Nickelodeon, I request you please to play 'Empty Bed Blues' and   72
let Bessie Smith sing."

Silence: they hold it, like a measure.   73

"Bring me all those nickels on back here," says Powerhouse. "*Look* 74
at that! What you tell me the name of this place?"

"White dance, week night, raining—Alligator, Mississippi—long   75
ways from home."

"Uh-huh."   76

"Sent for You Yesterday and Here You Come Today" plays.   77

The waitress, setting the tray of beer down on a back table, comes   78
up taut and apprehensive as a hen. "Says in the kitchen, back there
putting their eyes to little hole peeping out, that you is Mr. Powerhouse. . . . They knows from a picture they seen."

"They seeing right tonight—that is him," says Little Brother.   79

"You him?"   80

"That is him in the flesh," says Scoot.   81
"Does you wish to touch him?" asks Valentine. "Because he don't   82
bite."
"You passing through?"   83
"Now you got everything right."   84
She waits like a drop, hands languishing together in front.   85
"Babe, ain't you going to bring the beer?"   86
She brings it, and goes behind the cash register and smiles,   87
turning different ways. The little fillet of gold in her mouth is
gleaming.
"The Mississippi River's here," she says once.   88
Now all the watching Negroes press in gently and bright-eyed   89
through the door, as many as can get in. One is a little boy in a straw
sombrero which has been coated with aluminum paint all over.
Powerhouse, Valentine, Scoot, and Little Brother drink beer, and their
eyelids come together like curtains. The wall and the rain and the
humble beautiful waitress waiting on them and the other Negroes
watching enclose them.
"Listen!" whispers Powerhouse, looking into the ketchup bottle   90
and very slowly spreading his performer's hands over the damp
wrinkling cloth with the red squares. "How it is. My wife gets missing
me. Gipsy. She goes to the window. She looks out and sees you know
what. Street. Sign saying 'Hotel.' People walking. Somebody looks up.
Old man. She looks down, out the window. Well? . . . *Ssst! Plooey!*
What she do? Jump out and bust her brains all over the world."
He opens his eyes.   91
"That's it," agrees Valentine. "You gets a telegram."   92
"Sure she misses you," Little Brother adds.   93
"Now, it's nighttime." How softly he tells them! "Sure. It's the   94
nighttime. She say, 'What do I hear? Footsteps walking up the hall?
That him?' Footsteps go on off. It's not me, I'm in Alligator, Mississippi;
she's crazy. Shaking all over. Listens till her ears and all grow out like
old music-box horns, but still she can't hear a thing. She says, 'All
right! I'll jump out the window then.' Got on her nightgown. I know
that nightgown, and she thinking there. Says, 'Ho hum, all right,' and
jumps out the window. Is she mad at me! Is she crazy! She don't leave
nothing behind her!"
"Ya! Ha!"   95
"Brains and insides everywhere—Lord, Lord."   96
All the watching Negroes stir in their delight, and to their higher   97
delight he says affectionately, "Listen! Rats in here."
"That must be the way, Boss."   98
"Only, naw, Powerhouse, that ain't true. That sound too *bad*."   99
"Does? I even know who finds her," cries Powerhouse. "That 100
no-good pussy-footed crooning creeper, that creeper that follow around
after me, coming up like weeks behind me, following around after me
everything I do and messing around on the trail I leave. Bets my
numbers, sings my songs, gets close to my agent like a betsy-bug—
when I going out he just coming in. I got him now! I got him spotted!"
"Know who he is?"   101

"Why, it that old Uranus Knockwood!"   102
"Ya! Ha!"   103
"Yeah, and he coming now, he going to find Gipsy. There he is, 104
coming around that corner, and Gipsy kadoodling down—oh-oh! Watch
out! *Sssst-flooey!* See, there she is in her little old nightgown, and her
insides and brains all scattered round."
A sigh fills the room.   105
"Hush about her brains. Hush about her insides."   106
"Ya! Ha! You talking about her brains and insides—old Uranus 107
Knockwood," says Powerhouse, "look down and say, 'Lord!' He say,
'Look here what I'm walking in!' "
They all burst into halloos of laughter. Powerhouse's face looks 108
like a big hot iron stove.
"Why, he picks her up and carries her off!" he says.   109
"Ya! Ha!"   110
"Carries her *back* around the corner . . ."   111
"Oh, Powerhouse!"   112
"You know him."   113
"Uranus Knockwood!"   114
"Yeahhh!"   115
"He take our wives when we gone!"   116
"He come in when we goes out!"   117
"Uh-huh!"   118
"He go out when we comes in!"   119
"Yeahhh!"   120
"He standing behind the door!"   121
"Old Uranus Knockwood!"   122
"You know him."   123
"Middle-size man."   124
"Wears a hat."   125
"That's him."   126
Everybody in the room moans with reassurance. The little boy in 127
the fine silver hat opens a paper and divides out a jelly roll among his
followers.
And out of the breathless ring somebody moves forward like a 128
slave, leading a great logy Negro with bursting eyes, and says,
"This-here is Sugar-Stick Thompson, that dove down to the bottom of
July Creek and pulled up all those drownded white people fall out of a
boat. Last summer—pulled up fourteen."
"Hello," says Powerhouse, turning and looking around at them all 129
with his great daring face until they nearly suffocate.
Sugar-Stick, their instrument, cannot speak; he can only look back 130
at the others.
"Can't even swim. Done it by holding his breath," says the fellow 131
with the hero.
Powerhouse looks at him seekingly.   132
"I his half-brother," the fellow puts in.   133
They step back.   134
"Gipsy say," Powerhouse rumbles gently again, looking at *them,* 136

" 'What is the use? I'm gonna jump out so far—so far—*Ssst*—' "

"Don't, Boss, don't do it again," says Little Brother.   136

"It's awful," says the waitress. "I hates that Mr. Knockwoods. All   137
that the truth?"

"Want to see the telegram I got from him?" Powerhouse's hand   138
goes to the vast pocket.

"Now wait, now wait, Boss." They all watch him.   139

"It must be the real truth," says the waitress, sucking in her lower   140
lip, her luminous eyes turning sadly, seeking the windows.

"No, Babe, it ain't the truth." His eyebrows fly up and he begins to   141
whisper to her out of his vast oven mouth. His hand stays in his pocket.
"Truth is something worse—I ain't said what, yet. It's something
hasn't come to me, but I ain't saying it won't. And when it does, then
want me to tell you?" He sniffs all at once, his eyes come open and turn
up, almost too far. He is dreamily smiling.

"Don't Boss. Don't, Powerhouse!"   142

"Yeahhh!"   143

"Oh!" The waitress screams.   144

"Go on, git out of here!" bellows Powerhouse, taking his hand out of   145
his pocket and clapping after her red dress.

The ring of watchers breaks and falls away.   146

"Look at that! Intermission is up," says Powerhouse.   147

He folds money under a glass, and after they go out Valentine   148
leans back in and drops a nickel in the nickelodeon behind them, and it
lights up and begins to play, and the feather dangles still. That was
going to be a Hawaiian piece.

"Take a telegram!" Powerhouse shouts suddenly up into the rain.   149
"Take a answer.—Now what was that name?"

They get a little tired.   150

"Uranus Knockwood."   151

"You ought to know."   152

"Yas? Spell it to me."   153

They spell it all the ways it could be spelled. It puts them in a   154
wonderful humor.

"Here's the answer. Here it is right here. 'What in the hell you   155
talking about? Don't make any difference: I gotcha.' Name signed:
Powerhouse."

"That going reach him, Powerhouse?" Valentine speaks in a   156
maternal voice.

"Yas, yas."   157

All hushing, following him up the dark street at a distance, like old   158
rained-on black ghosts, the Negroes are afraid they will die laughing.

Powerhouse throws back his vast head into the steaming rain, and   159
a look of hopeful desire seems to blow somehow like a vapor from his
own dilated nostrils over his face and bring a mist to his eyes.

"Reach him and come out the other side."   160

"That's it, Powerhouse, that's it. You got him now."   161

Powerhouse lets out a long sigh.   162

"But ain't you going back there to call up Gipsy long distance, the   163

way you did last night in that other place? I seen a telephone. . . . Just
to see if she there at home?"

There is a measure of silence. That is one crazy drummer that's 164
going to get his neck broken some day.

"No," growls Powerhouse. "No! How many thousand times tonight 165
I got to say *No?*"

He holds up his arm in the rain, like someone swearing.   166

"You sure-enough unroll your voice some night, it about reach up 167
yonder to her," says Little Brother, dismayed.

They go on up the street, shaking the rain off and on them like 168
birds.

Back in the dance hall they play "San" (99). The jitterbugs stiffen 169
and start up like windmills stationed over the floor, and in their orbits
(one circle, another, a long stretch and zigzag) dance the elderly
couples with old smoothness, undisturbed and stately.

When Powerhouse first came back from intermission (probably full 170
of beer, everyone said) he got the band tuned up again and not by
striking the piano keys for the pitch: he just opened his mouth and
gave falsetto howls—in A,D, and so on. They tuned by him. Then he
took hold of the piano, like seeing it for the first time, and tested it for
strength, hit it down in the bass, played an octave with his elbow, and
opened it and examined its interior, and leaned on it with all his might.
He played it for a few minutes with terrific force and got it under his
power—then struck into something fragile and smiled. You couldn't
remember any of the things he said—just inspired remarks that came
out of his mouth like smoke.

They've requested "Somebody Loves Me," and he's already done 171
twelve or fourteen choruses, piling them up nobody knows how, and it
will be a wonder if he ever gets through. Now and then he calls the
shouts, "Somebody loves me! Somebody loves me—I wonder who!" His
mouth gets to be nothing but a volcano when he gets to the end.

"Somebody loves me—I wonder who!"   172

"Maybe—" He uses all his right hand on a trill.   173

"Maybe—" He pulls back his spread fingers and looks out upon the 174
place where he is. A vast, impersonal, and yet furious grimace
transfigures his wet face.

"—Maybe it's you!"   175

Study Questions

1. Why does Welty use the *present tense?* How would *past
tense* change the effect of her story?

2. The author is careful to tell the reader what songs
Powerhouse and his combo play. Is there any significance
in these particular songs insofar as they contribute to the
development of the plot?

3. Is Uranus Knockwood real? Did Gipsy really die? Are the
members of the combo merely improvising on a theme
provided by Powerhouse?

4. What is humorous about, "Brains and insides everywhere—Lord, Lord" (paragraph 96)?
5. What is the reason for Powerhouse's "furious grimace"? What is the effect of the words *vast, impersonal,* and *transfigures* (paragraph 174)?
6. How accurate is Welty's use of black dialogue?

The Monster
DEEMS TAYLOR

Deems Taylor (1885–1966) was born in New York City and received an A.B. from New York University in 1906. His professional career began as a member of the editorial staff for various encyclopedias, house organs, and newspapers. For two years he was the associate editor for *Collier's Weekly.* His expertise in music resulted in his becoming intermission commentator for the New York Philharmonic Symphony broadcasts from 1936 to 1943. His own compositions include "Portrait of a Lady," "The King's Henchman," and "Christmas Overture." Among his books are *Of Men and Music* (1937), *The Well-Tempered Listener* (1940), *A Pictorial History of the Movies* (1943), *Music to My Ears* (1949), *Some Enchanted Evenings* (1953) and *The One-Track Mind* (1953).

He was an undersized little man, with a head too big for his 1 body— a sickly little man. His nerves were bad. He had skin trouble. It was agony for him to wear anything next to his skin coarser than silk. And he had delusions of grandeur.

He was a monster of conceit. Never for one minute did he look at 2 the world or at people, except in relation to himself. He was not only the most important person in the world, to himself; in his own eyes he was the only person who existed. He believed himself to be one of the greatest dramatists in the world, one of the greatest thinkers, and one of the greatest composers. To hear him talk he was Shakespeare, and Beethoven, and Plato, rolled into one. And you would have had no difficulty in hearing him talk. He was one of the most exhausting conversationalists that ever lived. An evening with him was an evening spent in listening to a monologue. Sometimes he was brilliant; sometimes he was maddeningly tiresome. But whether he was being brilliant or dull, he had one sole topic of conversation: himself. What *he* thought and what *he* did.

He had a mania for being in the right. The slightest hint of 3 disagreement, from anyone, on the most trivial point, was enough to set him off on a harangue that might last for hours, in which he proved himself right in so many ways, and with such exhausting volubility, that in the end his hearer, stunned and deafened, would agree with him, for the sake of peace.

It never occurred to him that he and his doing were not of the most 4 intense and fascinating interest to anyone with whom he came in contact. He had theories about almost any subject under the sun, including vegetarianism, the drama, politics, and music; and in support of these theories he wrote pamphlets, letters, books . . . thousands upon thousands of words, hundreds and hundreds of pages. He not only wrote these things, and published them—usually at somebody else's expense—but he would sit and read them aloud, for hours, to his friends and his family.

He wrote operas; and no sooner did he have the synopsis of a story, 5 but he would invite—or rather summon—a crowd of his friends to his house and read it aloud to them. Not for criticism. For applause. When the complete poem was written, the friends had to come again, and hear *that* read aloud. Then he would publish the poem, sometimes years before the music that went with it was written. He played the piano like a composer, in the worst sense of what that implies, and he would sit down at the piano before parties that included some of the finest pianists of his time, and play for them, by the hour, his own music, needless to say. He had a composer's voice. And he would invite eminent vocalists to his house, and sing them his operas, taking all the parts.

He had the emotional stability of a six-year-old child. When he felt 6 out of sorts, he would rave and stamp, or sink into suicidal gloom and talk darkly of going to the East to end his days as a Buddhist monk. Ten minutes later, when something pleased him, he would rush out of doors and run around the garden, or jump up and down on the sofa, or stand on his head. He could be grief-stricken over the death of a pet dog, and he could be callous and heartless to a degree that would have made a Roman emperor shudder.

He was almost innocent of any sense of responsibility. Not only did 7 he seem incapable of supporting himself, but it never occurred to him that he was under any obligation to do so. He was convinced that the world owed him a living. In support of this belief, he borrowed money from everybody who was good for a loan—men, women, friends, or strangers. He wrote begging letters by the score, sometimes groveling without shame, at others loftily offering his intended benefactor the privilege of contributing to his support, and being mortally offended if the recipient declined the honor. I have found no record of his ever paying or repaying money to anyone who did not have a legal claim upon it.

What money he could lay his hands on he spent like an Indian 8 rajah. The mere prospect of a performance of one of his operas was enough to set him running up bills amounting to ten times the amount of his prospective royalties. On an income that would reduce a more scrupulous man to doing his own laundry, he would keep two servants. Without enough money in his pocket to pay his rent, he would have the walls and ceiling of his study lined with pink silk. No one will ever know—certainly he never knew—how much money he owed. We do know that his greatest benefactor gave him 6,000 dollars to pay the most pressing of his debts in one city, and a year later had to give him 16,000 dollars to enable him to live in another city without being thrown into jail for debt.

He was equally unscrupulous in other ways. An endless procession **9** of women marched through his life. His first wife spent twenty years enduring and forgiving his infidelities. His second wife had been the wife of his most devoted friend and admirer, from whom he stole her. And even while he was trying to persuade her to leave her first husband he was writing to a friend to inquire whether he could suggest some wealthy woman—*any* wealthy woman—whom he could marry for her money.

He was completely selfish in his other personal relationships. His **10** liking for his friends was measured solely by the completeness of their devotion to him, or by their usefulness to him, whether financial or artistic. The minute they failed him—even by so much as refusing a dinner invitation—or began to lessen in usefulness, he cast them off without a second thought. At the end of his life he had exactly one friend left whom he had known even in middle age.

He had a genius for making enemies. He would insult a man who **11** disagreed with him about the weather. He would pull endless wires in order to meet some man who admired his work, and was able and anxious to be of use to him—and would proceed to make a mortal enemy of him with some idiotic and wholly uncalled-for exhibition of arrogance and bad manners. A character in one of his operas was a caricature of one of the most powerful music critics of his day. Not content with burlesquing him, he invited the critic to his house and read him the libretto aloud in front of his friends.

The name of this monster was Richard Wagner. Everything that I **12** have said about him you can find on record—in newspapers, in police reports, in the testimony of people who knew him, in his own letters, between the lines of his autobiography. And the curious thing about this record is that it doesn't matter in the least.

Because this undersized, sickly, disagreeable, fascinating little **13** man was right all the time. The joke was on us. He *was* one of the world's great dramatists; he *was* a great thinker; he *was* one of the most stupendous musical geniuses that, up to now, the world has ever seen. The world did owe him a living. People couldn't know those things at the time, I suppose; and yet to us, who know his music, it does seem as though they should have known. What if he did talk about himself all the time? If he talked about himself for twenty-four hours every day for the span of his life he would not have uttered half the number of words that other men have spoken and written about him since his death.

When you consider what he wrote—thirteen operas and music **14** dramas, eleven of them still holding the stage, eight of them unquestionably worth ranking among the world's great musico-dramatic masterpieces—when you listen to what he wrote, the debts and heartaches that people had to endure from him don't seem much of a price. Eduard Hanslick, the critic whom he caricatured in *Die Meistersinger* and who hated him ever after, now lives only because he was caricatured in *Die Meistersinger*. The women whose hearts he broke are long since dead: and the man who could never love anyone but himself has made them deathless atonement, I think, with *Tristan und Isolde*. Think of the luxury with which for a time, at least, fate rewarded Napoleon, the man who ruined France and looted Europe; and then perhaps you will agree that a few thousand dollars' worth of debts were not too heavy a price to pay for the *Ring* trilogy.

What if he was faithless to his friends and to his wives? He had one 15 mistress to whom he was faithful to the day of his death: music. Not for a single moment did he ever compromise with what he believed, with what he dreamed. There is not a line of his music that could have been conceived by a little mind. Even when he is dull, or downright bad, he is dull in the grand manner. There is a greatness about his worst mistakes. Listening to his music, one does not forgive him for what he may or may not have been. It is not a matter of forgiveness. It is a matter of being dumb with wonder that his poor brain and body didn't burst under the torment of the demon of creative energy that lived inside him, struggling, clawing, scratching to be released; tearing, shrieking at him to write the music that was in him. The miracle is that what he did in the little space of seventy years could have been done at all, even by a great genius. Is it any wonder that he had no time to be a man?

Study Questions

1. Why is the identification of the subject withheld until paragraph 12?
2. What is the point of this essay?
3. Does Taylor provide us with any clues to the sources for the information presented here?
4. Are the topic sentences explicit or implicit within paragraphs?
5. What is the effect of so many sentences begun with *he, his, it*?

A Psychiatric Study of Professional Football

ARNOLD J. MANDELL

Arnold J. Mandell (1934–   ) was born in Chicago, received a B.A. from Stanford University, and his M.D. from Tulane. His professional training as a psychiatrist has been utilized by the Peace Corps, the NASA Space Biology Laboratory, and the San Diego Chargers. National and International organizations have honored him for his research. Mandell's books include *The Coming of Middle Age* (1969), *The Nightmare Season* (1976), and *The Bio-Chemistry of Mental Disorders* (1977). His studies on psychiatry, psychopaths, and dreams may be found in numerous popular and medical journals.

Two years ago Harland Svare, then head coach of the San 1 Diego Chargers, asked me to lunch to talk about football. I was then, as I am now, chairman of the Department of Psychiatry at the University of California, San Diego. I had never paid much attention to football. During my five years of basic medical training, when we lived in the shadow of New Orleans's Sugar Bowl, I didn't attend a single game. I had been in San Diego as many years, and I still wasn't paying attention to football. The Chargers were a losing team, and Coach Svare, an imaginative man, wondered if my training might equip me to notice things about the attitudes and the behavior of his players that could help give the team what is often called "the winning edge."

Our lunch lasted three hours, and the result was that the Chargers 2 retained me as a sort of psychiatrist-in-residence—the first, I believe, for a National Football League team. At Svare's invitation I began to hang around the team. I joined the members of the Charger squad in the locker room, at team lectures, at practice, on the plane to and from away games, and on the sidelines during the games. In all, I conducted over 200 hours of individual interviews with them. My function was to provide the coaches with a clearer understanding of the players and their positions and, more practically, to make actual personnel comments and recommendations.

When I first sat on the bench, I realized I was hearing the sounds of 3 a Stone Age battleground. You can't pick them up on television or from a seat in the stadium. But on the bench you hear grunts, groans, hits—mankind's most fundamental sounds. I quickly learned what many Sunday widows already realized—that football is not a game but a religion, a metaphysical island of fundamental truth in a highly verbal, disguised society, a throwback of 30,000 generations of anthropological time.

When I was first around the team, the players thought I was 4 spooky because I just stood there and watched. It was to take me more than a year to break down barriers and build trust between the players and me. But after only a few weeks, I rushed to Coach Svare with my first systematic insight. "Harland," I said, "I think I can tell whether a player is on offense or defense just by looking at his locker. The offensive players keep their lockers clean and orderly, but the lockers of the defensive men are a mess. In fact, the better the defensive player, the bigger the mess."

As I pored over scouting reports and interviewed players and 5 coaches from numerous NFL teams, it became clear that offensive football players like structure and discipline. They want to maintain the status quo. They tend to be conservative as people, and as football players they take comfort in repetitious practice of well-planned and well-executed plays. The defensive players, just as clearly, can't stand structure; their attitudes, their behavior, and their lifestyles bear this out. They operate as though they've been put out of the tribe and are trying to show people that tribal structure is worthless anyway. Ostracism does not bother them; it serves as a source of fuel for their destructive energies. Rules or regulations put forward by anybody, anyplace, are to be challenged. Coaches find defensive players notably more difficult to control than their offensive teammates.

Offensive and defensive football players, I noticed, often had little 6 or nothing to do with one another. There was one exception on the Chargers. Walt Sweeney, an all-pro offensive guard, had the personality of a defensive player, and his friends were all on the defensive team. (In fact, Sweeney wasn't that much of an exception. The Chargers drafted him to be a linebacker, and that was the position he himself preferred.)

When I mentioned my new "rule," Svare, a former linebacker, 7 responded, "Sure, I never put it in words, but I'm basically a defensive player, and I find myself liking defensive players more than offensive players as people. I have very little patience with the rituals and repetition involved in the offense. We just don't look at the world the same way."

So I found that, despite the nomenclature, the offensive squad is 8 made up of defenders of structure and the defensive squad is garrisoned with attack troops. I began to differentiate the personality profiles of these men independently of any prior knowledge about the specific requirements of their individual positions. Before long a personality classification in relation to position began to emerge. The consistency of the patterns seems explainable on the basis of the selection that occurs before any professional football player gains a regular starting position in the NFL.

Every year several thousand college football players are eligible; 9 not more than 600 are seriously considered, and of those, 50 to 100 make it to the NFL. The selection goes on year after year. A player maintains his position by winning individual battles week after week on the field, where his performance is witnessed, filmed, and "graded." The crop of players is weeded systematically. The athletic difference between those who remain and those who are dropped is amazingly small. When it comes to making it in the NFL, practically every owner or coach with whom I've talked says, reverently and resignedly, "The game is in the mind." In addition to athletic ability, motivation, and commitment, the player needs a personality that meets the requirements of his position. This Darwinian process leaves each participant as an island of psychobiological organization in a circumstance that tests physical, psychological, intellectual, and spiritual strength— man-on-man—and in which psychological pressure from peers is even more potent a motivation than the challenge from the enemy. A suitable personality becomes the most significant and necessary component of survival. Making a proper match between player and position, then, is necessary for personal happiness, because players working in the wrong position are uneasy and attempt to correct their uneasiness. Or, as aggressive and territorial individuals are very prone to do, they become depressed, turning their aggression inward. Like the rest of us, they become demoralized and lose effectiveness when they aren't in the right place to function at their best.

It is important to realize that professional football players are, to **10** mint a term, "homoclites." That is, they are extremely normal people—stable and anxiety-free, accustomed to handling pressures and performing extraordinarily and quickly. Many of them are also paranoid, but my use of that term—and of others from psychology— does not imply pathology; it implies a personality trait within normal limits.

The men who fill particular positions on the offensive team can be **11** described by clusters of personality traits. The offensive linemen in general (centers, guards, tackles, and, to an extent, tight ends) are ambitious, tenacious, precise, attentive to detail. They manifest a kind of toughness that I would call stubborn rather than explosive. They work hard. Their traits clearly suit them for their work. As blocking assignments become ever more intricate, the linemen must practice like a ballet corps to coordinate perfectly the necessary spatial and temporal movements of blocking patterns. They also have to stand firm and cool when an opposing defensive line rushes their passer, no matter what verbal or physical abuse is thrown at them; they must care only about protecting their quarterback, not about proving their masculinity in an explosive way. A sacrificial attitude toward the welfare of the team is integral to the offensive linemen.

Within the offensive line itself, the typical personalities of centers, **12** guards, tackles, and tight ends are readily distinguishable. The center, who often has to call signals, is usually the brightest. His loquaciousness in relation to other members of the line reflects his leadership. The guard may be bright, and he is quicker than the center. He may also be more aggressive—in the violent, rather than the stubborn, sense—because on sweeps he may be called upon to block downfield. His assertiveness is more persistent; the center's is more volatile. The tackle is slower, more patient, and even more persistent than the guard. He is not called on to be as mobile as the guard, and he doesn't have to get the middle linebacker with an explosive block, as the center does. He maintains and sustains. Stubborn tenacity is prototypical of the offensive tackle; his loyalty and commitment to the welfare of the team know no match.

The wide receiver is a very special human being. He shares many 13 features with actors and movie stars. He is narcissistic and vain, and basically a loner.

Whereas the offensive linemen may hang around together (the 14 center is particularly gregarious), the wide receiver often lives alone, dates alone, and remains a bit of a mystery. He is tactful in interpersonal encounters but elusive and hard to locate as a person. Like the track star, the good wide receiver is disciplined because the precision required to run intricate pass patterns and hold onto passes while he is getting clobbered requires discipline. Yet the courage of the wide receiver is more brittle than that of the other offensive linemen. His elusiveness may move beyond unpredictability to treachery. Typically, the wide receiver doesn't mind getting hurt on the body, but he doesn't like his face to be touched—he's afraid of disfigurement. Essential, brilliant, vain, and not too friendly, he's rarely a popular member of the team. Disaffinity may be particularly acute between wide receivers and linebackers.

I have found two kinds of running backs. One is like the wide 15 receiver: tough, treacherous, quick, lonely, and perhaps even paranoid, like the much-traveled Duane Thomas, perhaps the most gifted runner of all time. That paranoia is adaptive for a man whom everybody on defense is out to get. His particular unpredictability makes him even more difficult than a wide receiver to locate as a person. He's never where you expect him to be. In his days with the Chargers, Thomas was as difficult to locate off the field as on; if you made a date with him, he was likely not to be there. He is a good example of how a really great football player's personality is welded to his job.

The other kind of offensive back—the Larry Csonka kind—runs 16 straight ahead. He's honest, tough, strong, disciplined, and if his toughness is a touch brutal, he may be great. He's not as quick, and he might not be as treacherous or paranoid, as the flanking back. He will work long and hard; he has some offensive tackle in him.

Back to the line, to the tight end. It's difficult to find an ideal tight 17 end because the chores he is required to do are virtually incompatible and therefore demand incompatible personality traits. The tight end must block like an offensive lineman or a fullback yet catch passes like a wide receiver. Blocking well requires bodily sacrifice for the welfare of others and does not gratify vanity; so the tight end can't have *too* much wide receiver in him. He does well to replace that with a bit of the distrust found in the Duane Thomas-type running back.

The most difficult of the offensive players to categorize are the 18 quarterbacks. I have studied the scouting reports of a number of quarterbacks and talked about them with scouts, teammates, reporters, owners, and coaches. Given the physical ability, passing talent, and intelligence, the major determinant of success as a quarterback appears to be self-confidence—a self-confidence that is more akin to super-arrogance. The physical threat to a quarterback passing from the "pocket" is intolerable. To stand there to the last millisecond, waiting for your receiver to reach the place the ball is supposed to go while you are being rushed by mammoth defensive linemen—that takes sheer courage. A single mistake might negate all the efforts and sacrifices of your teammates—as well as lay you open to a fearful pounding.

To stand that kind of responsibility requires poise beyond that 19 possessed by most men. How is the poise of the successful type of quarterback achieved? From my observations, there appear to be at least two routes. One is that of the naturally arrogant man who does not feel bound by the rules governing other men. He makes his own. He exploits the environment in a tough, tricky way and with very little compunction. Such men have run their talents and capacities to incredible self-advantage with no apparent anxiety or guilt. And they win football games—yea, even championships. The Joe Namaths and the Sonny Jurgensens fit well into this category.

The other way to turn in that kind of performance under those 20 battle conditions is with assurance from On High. The Cowboys' Roger Staubach and the peerless John Unitas, who has finished his outstanding career, are in this group. So is Fran Tarkenton, the Vikings' renowned scrambler. We might call them and their comrades the religious quarterbacks. They attend church regularly, are active in such organizations as the Fellowship of Christian Athletes, and have a truly evangelical mission that they carry forward with the calm certitude of the believer, the chosen one. (In my two seasons with the Chargers, I got a chance to see Unitas up close and was struck by his religious commitment, as well as by his humility. These qualities helped insulate him from what was obviously a particularly stressful situation: the struggle of a player of his stature and past achievements to remain a first-stringer.)

The believer-quarterbacks win championships, too. But any quar- 21 terback who leads with kindness and concern for others, who feels anxious about his responsibility to the 47 other men on the team and guilty over the outcome of his own actions, may collapse at critical moments—at the climax of a game or as his team moves closer to the playoffs. Students of the game point to John Hadl, the Rams' all-pro quarterback, whose pass-completion percentages dropped off drastically in the critical final games of last season.

The increasing use of computers to analyze the plays called by 22 individual quarterbacks in various situations may change the personality requirements of successful quarterbacking. Except for audible signals (which can be employed in a significant percentage of the plays), computer-versus-computer may eventually lead to all plays being called from the bench. The defensive team may be able to guess what the opposing quarterback is going to do before he himself knows it—by a computer calculation of what he has done 77 percent of the time on "third and long" early in the fourth quarter when his team is behind by seven points.

Will this usurpation change the need for super-arrogance in 23 quarterbacks? Maybe the super-arrogant will not obey readily. Many disciplined college quarterbacks who obeyed readily have not been able to make it in pro football; their opportunities may increase when plays are called from the bench.

The defensive team members are the renegades. They attack 24 structure, and they feel that little is to be gained by identification with the establishment. They are basically angry and rebellious, primed to explode. The degree of inhibition controlling the trigger varies with the distance from the line of scrimmage. The defensive linemen, in contrast to offensive linemen, are restless, peevish, irritable, impatient, intolerant of detail, and barely under control. Usually, it is the defensive players (especially the linemen) who have committed the impulsive, flamboyant acts that make newspaper headlines. The defensive linemen have the least-well-organized inhibitory systems. They are wild and free of conflict on the attack. The tackles may be reserved in some ways, but they, too, relish the hostilities. I remember one defensive tackle, a wonderful human being with his wife and family and friends, telling me gleefully in the heat of a game, "Look at that [a rookie quarterback entering the game for the opposing team]. It's like letting me into a candy store!"

Defensive ends have even more spleen, and they are quicker. They 25 display swagger and showmanship. Defensive end Deacon Jones, the former Ram superstar now with the Chargers, demonstrated at least the spleen at last year's training camp. He parked his car in the same no-parking zone for 40 consecutive days, even though he got a ticket—and paid the fine—each day. The defensive lineman takes great joy in his unbridled assault on organization. Guilt or depression are not normally in his repertoire, although sometimes, as during the Monday blues, one can see vague hints. His temper, brutality, bluntness, and sarcastic sense of humor predict his success.

Linebackers experience more conflict about the aggression they 26 manifest and by the same token achieve more precision of time and place in their attack. The linebacker in particular struggles with this balance of aggression and inhibition. Often he achieves a public image as a solid citizen; yet simultaneously he's a killer. When I asked a number of NFL scouts whom they would send behind the lines in wartime to assassinate an important enemy, they said a linebacker: his cleverness and air of legitimacy would get him into the country and let him pass as a good citizen, and his brutality would let him kill when the time came. The linebacker pays heavily for his control. Keeping so much hostility on short rein occasionally forces the aggression inward, and the linebacker typically has periods of depression. He needs a seventh sense and special visual capacities to diagnose plays and to go where he is needed. The defensive linemen either stay or charge, but the linebackers may need to stay, charge, or go back.

In linebackers I found two kinds of intelligence. Some have the 27 capacity to memorize a sequence of rules of behavior for themselves. Following certain keys—movements by opposing centers, guards, or fullbacks—they behave according to that set of rules. Other linebackers achieve the same effectiveness without knowing the rules very well. They actually visualize the action of the entire field and have the capacity to follow the developing patterns of movement. These men often make brilliant plays; but, as in the case of all positions, if the opposing team knows their habits well, they can be badly fooled. The linebacker is a fascinating combination of control, brutality, and internal conflict. He does not lack vanity, but unlike the wide receiver, whose witnesses are his parents or the fans, the linebacker evaluates his own performance. He wants to look good to himself. When he fails, he can almost destroy himself in depression.

In the defensive backfield the aggression gets buried under more 28 and more inhibition and discipline. These men are like long-distance runners: they are loners, but they are nowhere near as hungry for glory as are the wide receivers. In place of the vanity and fantasies of the wide receivers, the defensive backs experience depression and rage. They have traits that can be found in offensive linemen, wide receivers, and linebackers. They are tenacious. They must learn zone and man-to-man pass-defense patterns that require incredible self-discipline in the furor of battle. They must not be led by their natural inclination, which is to follow receivers out of their zone before the quarterback releases the ball on a pass play. They must execute patterns precisely. To counter running plays, however, they must move up fast and, though lighter and weaker than the running backs they are trying to stop, hit very hard. So they need controlled and timed brutality and anger.

In my research team's recent study of more than 600 potential NFL 29 draft choices, six men were found to be almost suicidally depressed; all of them were defensive backs. The depression of a corner back who has been "beaten" on a pass play may last for days, though the great ones shake it somehow. The depression resulting from the inhibition of so much aggression can put such men in constant danger of self-destruction.

Professional football, because there are objective criteria for per- 30 formance, provides a model situation in which to observe an ultimate test of function. Given the same amount of athletic ability, why do some men fail and others succeed? Inevitably it is because the personality orientations of the latter better fit the tasks. No amount of coaching seems to alter these basic traits. Pragmatically, the NFL system quickly separates the misfits—even the athletically competent ones—from the team. My experiences with the men who play NFL football renewed my conviction that the psychobiological organization of personality, when it coincides with the appropriate role, is perhaps the most significant single determinant of personal success and happiness in life. De Gaulle was obviously a quarterback. Woody Allen is a defensive back. According to a recent profile in *The New Yorker,* Allen lives to "endlessly fend off guilt" with his continuous commitment to effort and performance. There is little or none of the vanity of the wide receiver in Woody Allen. Former President Nixon's stubbornly persistent and tenacious (not brilliant or explosive) management of his crisis reminds me of the instincts of an offensive lineman. His attempts to be blunt, quick, and clever would have suited him to be an offensive guard.

My mother is an offensive lineman, a center-guard; my father, a 31 classical wide receiver. My wife is a gifted center-guard. My medical school dean, John Moxely III, is a linebacker; my university chancellor, William McElroy, is a defensive personality, too, perhaps a linebacker. President Ford is a natural offensive lineman, which is in fact what he was at the University of Michigan. Truman Capote is a wide receiver. Kate Smith is a fullback, in more than size. Leonard Bernstein is a cross between a quarterback and a wide receiver.

I am often asked what I accomplished for the Chargers. The answer 32 has to be: very little. The team's dismal record over the past two years—6 victories in 28 games—indicates that. So does my own professional observation. When attack troops hit the beach of the enemy's territory, some may benefit from benedictory reassurance, others from biochemical madness, few if any from a reminder that their current fear is reminiscent of the "castration anxiety" of their early childhood. Psychiatry and pro football, I conclude, probably don't mix. Or if they do, the blend is best left to the brewmaster, the head coach. The shrinks should stay with the rest of the armchair experts— in front of their television sets.

Study Questions

1. Where and how does Mandell establish his credentials?
2. Which paragraph serves to organize the rest of the essay?
3. Comment on the extent of and the significance of Mandell's comparison of the football field to a Stone Age battleground.
4. What paragraphs might be better combined into one paragraph?
5. On what evidence does Mandell reach his conclusions, or rather his divisions, among types of players?
6. Comment on the comparisons to De Gaulle, Woody Allen, and President Nixon in paragraph 30.

Ball Games or Brawl Games?

DAVID FRIEDMAN

David Friedman (1949–   ) was born in New York City. He received a B.A. from Hobart College in 1969 and an M.A. from the University of Colorado in 1972. From 1973 to 1981 he was sports editor for *TV Guide*.

In a ruling late last season, National League president 1 Charles (Chub) Feeney fined outfielder Cesar Cedeno, then of the Houston Astros, $5000 for entering the stands to argue with a patron in Atlanta—but terminated Cedeno's "indefinite suspension" after only two days. "The fan's remarks," Feeney explained, "went beyond the realm of decency."

The "realm of decency"? Is that somewhere near Camelot, pray 2 tell? Does it have a king? A round table? A zip code?

No matter what the answers to such queries might be, there's no 3 questioning one fact about Feeney's "realm": it's a small community, getting smaller all the time.

The Phillies' Pete Rose and Reggie Smith of the Dodgers were also 4 involved in altercations with fans last season. Dave Parker of the Pirates dodged batteries hurled from the stands. The Orioles' Dennis Martinez, poor soul, was kabonged by a bottle. Yes, baseball fans are growing wild in the seats—and sometimes even out of them, as a disturbing occurrence at Yankee Stadium last year showed all too well.

Angered by what he felt was a bad call during a Brewers–Yankees 5 playoff game, a Yankee fan vaulted onto the field and assaulted umpire Mike Reilly. The Reilly incident, like the others, illuminated the fine line separating fan from fanatic. But it raised other issues as well—for the crime was witnessed not only by the more than 56,000 in the park that night, but by the millions at home watching ABC's telecast of the game.

Should ABC have covered the incident? Or ignored it? How valid is 6 the position, articulated on the air by Howard Cosell, that "we had to show this scene. We wouldn't be journalists if we didn't"?

Does TV coverage imply approval? Does it encourage viewers to 7 mimic what they've seen?

These and similar questions have elicited various—and 8 complex—responses.

Reprinted by permission of David Friedman. Originally appeared in *TV Guide*, March 27, 1982.

One critic of ABC's decision to show all is Tom Villante, director of   9
broadcasting for major league baseball. "By putting the spotlight on
these cuckoo birds, you're glorifying them," says Villante. Villante's
view is seconded by Rep. Ronald M. Mottl (D-Ohio), sponsor of the
Sports Violence Act pending in Congress. If passed, the act would
attempt to curb violence among athletes by setting up a special
arbitration procedure to assess financial penalties against the teams of
the belligerents. (The act does not cover fan violence, however.) "The
networks certainly have freedom of speech," says Mottl. "But TV is so
pervasive that it has a duty to try to prevent violence in society. Such a
duty would be well served by a decision not to cover such incidents."

Ironically, the loudest voice coming to ABC's defense is that of   10
Mike Weisman, who coordinates baseball coverage for rival NBC. "You
have to make a distinction between exhibitionsts and those people who
are violence-prone," he insists. "Exhibitionists *are* encouraged by
exposure, so we try to avoid them whenever possible. On the other
hand, I'm convinced that violent fans couldn't care less whether they're
on TV or not."

Weisman's view is supported by psychiatrist Stanley Cheren of the   11
Boston University School of Medicine, an expert in the field. "There is
no conclusive evidence," says Dr. Cheren, "that fan violence is related
to the desire to get on TV." Rather, the doctor attributes the rise of fan
violence to a number of factors. Among them: the ambivalence of hero
worship. "Athletes are admired," says Dr. Cheren, "but they're envied
as well."

Nor does Richard Phillips, attorney for the Major League Umpires   12
Association, blame television for the current spate of fan violence.
"Violent fans," he says, "are encouraged when they see managers like
Earl Weaver and Billy Martin bump, push or taunt umpires."

Many social scientists agree with Phillips' assertion that violence   13
or abusive behavior on the playing field triggers violence in the stands.
And as proof, they cite the numerous instances of rowdyism that have
occurred in the stands at National Football League games, where the
mayhem on the field can be considerable. Indeed, during the first five
Monday-night games of the past NFL season, more than 100 people
were arrested, most of them on assault-and-battery charges.

Many of these incidents, to be sure, were related to alcohol   14
abuse—a problem that certainly is no stranger to baseball. Only a few
seasons back, a besotted "Dime Beer Night" crowd in Cleveland ran
amok through the stands and onto the field, causing the Indians to
forfeit.

It's quite clear that unless something changes, sports fans may   15
soon find themselves left out of the fun altogether—as has already
happened on at least one occasion in England.

It seems that when the first of two games in a scheduled home-   16
and-home series between England's West Ham United soccer club and
Spain's Castilla of Madrid was marred by excessive fan violence, a
ruling was handed down that the second game in the series could go on
at West Ham's home field *only if no paying spectators were present.* And

so it did, at Upton Grounds (capacity 35,000) before an assortment of team officials and journalists estimated at about 100.

No incidents of fan violence were reported.   17

Study Questions

1. Where is the thesis of this essay?
2. What is Friedman's purpose in paragraph 2?
3. How relevant is paragraph 9 to his argument?
4. What do Friedman's quotations and examples contribute to his argument?
5. How many different causes for fan violence are suggested?
6. Provide an outline for this essay.

Confessions of a Soap-Opera Addict
JEAN KERR

Jean Kerr (1923–   ) was born in Scranton, Pennsylvania, and earned degrees at Maywood College and the Catholic University of America. She has said that her two ambitions were to make a lot of money and to make people laugh; she has been eminently successful at both. Numerous universities have awarded Kerr honorary degrees for her humorous studies of the American family, studies often based on her own family. To get away from her family, she drives somewhere and writes in the car. Her books include *Please Don't Eat the Daisies* (1957) and *The Snake Has All the Lines* (1960). Kerr has been equally successful on the Broadway stage, with such plays (many of them coauthored), as *Mary, Mary; Poor Richard; Jenny Kissed Me;* and *Finishing Touches.*

"The world was passing me by. I was giving the most bizarre explanations for why I never could go out in the afternoons on weekdays."

I'll tell you the exact moment I knew I had to give up my   1
soap opera. One of my best friends called me on the telephone recently,

From *How I Got to Be Perfect* (New York: Doubleday, 1978). Reprinted by permission.

and I said, "Hey, Peggy, can I call you back? My other phone is ringing." There was a silence, and then she said, rather plaintively, "Jean, you don't *have* another phone." And of course I don't. It was all a tissue of lies, part of a cover-up that wasn't really fooling anybody. But there it was. Even to Peggy, who has been a solace for twenty-eight years, I couldn't blurt out the truth, which was that I was watching "One Life to Live."

Furthermore, the day she called wasn't just an ordinary day in   2
Landview, the locale of "One Life. . . ." You see, the Craigs were having this wedding reception for Larry and Karen and, right smack in the middle of things, Mrs. Magruder arrived with Viki and Joe's baby, who had been kidnaped—oh, months ago—by Cathy Craig, who was disturbed by the loss of her baby, which was also Joe's baby. And everything would have been marvelous except that while Viki was hugging her now-recovered baby, Kevin, Joe was drunk in a bar punching out a stranger. Well, you can see why I had to be there.

The funny thing is that until about two years ago I had never seen   3
even one episode of a soap opera. I had a definite idea, though, of the kind of woman who would watch them: a gin-soaked slattern in her husband's old bathrobe, dirty dishes mounting in the sink, waxy buildup piling up on the linoleum. Actually, the gin-soaked part is patently absurd. You have to be alert to follow these plots.

But, in spite of all my highfalutin attitudes, I have lived, I have   4
learned. It's not just pride. *Everything* goeth before the fall.

Like most affairs, the whole thing began so innocently. I looked at   5
"One Life to Live" just once (ha!) to catch a glimpse of Erika Slezak, who plays Viki Lord. I should tell you that Erika lived right across the street from us when she was a little girl (no, this part is true; in fact, one of our boys was in love with her when he was ten). Anyway, I wanted to see if Erika was still so pretty. As it turned out, she was even prettier. But I couldn't tell right away because the first time I looked she was in a coma from a car accident, which occurred while she was rushing Megan, Joe's illegitimate daughter who had a congenital heart condition, to the hospital, where she (Megan) perished. And, for that matter, it was touch and go with Viki for about six weeks. I felt that I should keep looking until she (Erika/Viki) was well enough to open her eyes and get her hair done. And by the time Viki, radiant once more, was taking her first halting steps in a walker, I was hopelessly hooked.

Not just with Viki's and Joe's problems (she's a saint, and God   6
knows he *means* well) but also with the hazards facing Timmy Siegel, who wanted to marry Jenny—who was a nun—as soon as he got out of jail. And I really became fond of Victor Lord, who was slipping into the clutches of rotten Dorian. By the way, I can't bring myself to tell you how many of these characters have since expired. That hospital in Landview is a death trap.

No matter. In those days the show ran only one-half hour, which   7
means twenty-two minutes if you take off eight minutes for commercials. Now, when they take off eight minutes for commercials, I take off eight minutes for commercials, leaving the area entirely. There is no

need for me to stay, since I am already convinced beyond the need for further persuasion that if you wash with "ordinary detergent alone" you are a slob and your children's spotted, messy clothing will be the scandal of the entire neighborhood.

But I did feel I was entitled to my full twenty-two minutes of actual **8** diversion. It was Thomas Aquinas, or somebody sensible, who said that "no man can exist without pleasure." And there were no calories involved, no hangovers. Look at it another way. Every single day of his life, my husband wastes twenty minutes on the *Times* crossword puzzle (he says it's more like seven minutes, but then he's not the one waiting for the paper), and he isn't looked down upon as a pariah or a second-class ctizen. Of course, he is willing to take phone calls during the puzzle, but what, in fact, is he learning? I asked him that once, and he said he was learning that a nef is a ship-shaped clock and an oda is a room in a harem.

But we're not talking about his conscience and his wasted life. **9** We're talking about me and how the whole thing escalated and finally got out of hand. First, "One Life to Live" extended to forty-five minutes. Then last winter I was confined to my bed with some kind of grippe and, feeling rather too languid to turn off the set when my show was over, I discovered what millions may already have known. "General Hospital" follows immediately after "One Life to Live" and is, in turn, followed by "The Edge of Night." Now, about "General Hospital." *There* is a perfect maelstrom of seething personalities. I myself think that Terri and Dr. Mark Dante will get together in spite of Mark's meddling wife, Mary Ellen, who has tried to kill two people (since she was released from a mental institution), including Terri, who then lapsed into the customary coma before brain surgery.

Before you say it, I'll say it. *I* was in a coma. The world was passing **10** me by. I was giving the most bizarre explanations for why I *never* could go out in the afternoons on weekdays. I was even testy with my charming dentist, because he claimed that he only saw patients on Saturday afternoons if there were a real emergency. The whole thing was actually beginning to cost me money. With the car just sitting in the garage while I was glued to the set, I sent a taxi to the vet to pick up Frosty, our dog (he wasn't sick, he was just in for a shampoo and a set). I know that sounds awful, but I figured Frosty would understand (certainly the cab driver didn't understand) that I had to be present for Lesley's Caesarean section.

Now that it's all behind me, now that I have quit forever, I am not **11** taking a holier-than-thou attitude. Luckier-than-thou, perhaps, but not holier. Nor would I dream of suggesting that there is anything "wrong" about following a soap opera. Listen. Miss Lillian, President Carter's remarkable mother, watches one. My idol, the late, great P.G. Wodehouse, who was still working at full tilt at ninety, *never* missed an episode of "The Edge of Night." I simply address myself to those among us who find, for whatever reasons, that they simply cannot handle it any more.

Now, I don't recommend just quitting cold turkey. In my experi- **12** ence, the only thing you can quit cold turkey is cold turkey. No, the best thing to do is to wean yourself gradually away from the soap opus, soap opera, of your choice. A good way to start is to tell your husband the plot every night at dinner. He'll have the weekends to recover. And if the children are listening, so much the better for your eventual rehabilitation.

If your husband is supportive and wants to help you lick this thing, 13 he will encourage you to babble on by asking provocative questions, like, "Herniating, *what* is herniating?" You probably should have looked that up, but it's always safe to say that in "General Hospital" if a person is unconscious and a doctor pops a tiny flashlight in her eye and says, "She's herniating," that's *real* trouble. And you can go on to explain that they're going to have to suction out a hematoma, which, as anyone could guess, is a pretty iffy proposition. If the left temporal lobe is breached, the patient could suffer a speech deficit, which would certainly affect the whole plot. By the time I had finished weaving my tale one evening, I thought I could detect a certain bemused—no, wary—look in my husband's eyes. On the other hand, my son, who has just completed medical school, was so impressed he had to leave the room.

Another thing that will help in your rehabilitation is to discuss the 14 matter at dinner parties. Should you be introduced to a celebrated surgeon, you might say, "Oh, Doctor Cahan, I've always wanted to meet you because I have a question. Lee Baldwin's stepson in 'General Hospital' is suffering from Malenkov's Disease. Is that a real disease and, if so, what is the prognosis?" This will bring all conversation to a halt, and in the silence you can reflect upon the gravity of your situation. Furthermore, you won't need to write a thank-you note because you *won't* be asked back.

Finally, I find it helpful to invite somebody, preferably a house- 15 guest (who can't exactly get out of it), to watch along with me. Make girlish, fluttery excuses: "You may not enjoy this all that much because, you know, you'll be starting in the middle." (There's no point in explaining that down through all eternity there will be no beginning and no end—just always, always the middle.) And then make note of what your friend says even if it enrages you.

My friend Charles, whom I love like a brother, and my brother, 16 whom I love like a brother, both watched with me one afternoon. My brother, rather intemperate by nature, suddenly looked at me in some confusion and exclaimed, "I don't believe this—you've gone mad." Charles, who writes for a living (I think that makes him kind of jumpy sometimes), kept shaking his head from side to side and finally muttered, "Did I hear that line, did I really and truly hear that line?" "What line?" I asked, honestly perplexed. He was quick to clarify: "That man on the sofa just pointed his finger and said, 'Okay, Dorian, but if Viki loses this baby she's carrying, it'll be on your head.' "

He didn't really like the second program, either. In fact, he seemed 17 to find something humorous in this perfectly straightforward state- ment: "I know you don't like Monica, but before you evaluate her personality, please remember her skill at fibrillating Mr. Daniels." Of course, if you're going to be all that picky, you're going to miss a lot.

In due time I began to realize that I no longer enjoyed the high 18 regard that my age and my position in the community entitle me to. I was an idiot, is what I was. So I swore off, which you too may be able to do by following my simple prescriptions. If, however, by any chance one of you is still backward enough to be watching "One Life to Live," would you please write and tell me if Joe and Viki still have a security guard for the baby? And how *is* that marriage?

Study Questions

1. What does the personal tone contribute to Kerr's essay?
2. How many paragraphs make up Kerr's introduction?
3. Comment on the arguments presented in paragraph 8.
4. What are the major structural divisions in this essay?
5. What special use does Kerr make of the final sentence in most of her paragraphs?
6. What creates the humor in the line addressed to Dorian in paragraph 16?

Television: The Splitting Image
MARYA MANNES

Marya Mannes (1904–   ) was born in New York City. She holds an honorary L.H.D. from Hood College, Maryland. From 1942 to 1945 Mannes was an intelligence analyst for the United States government. Her television appearances, university lecture tours, and numerous periodical articles have made her a familiar figure to the American public. She has published *Message from a Stranger,* a novel (1948); *More in Anger* (1958); *Subverse,* satiric verse (1959); *The New York I Know* (1961), *But Will It Sell?* (1964); *They,* a novel (1968); and *Out of My Time* (1971).

A bride who looks scarcely fourteen whispers, "Oh, Mom, 1 I'm so *happy!*" while a doting family adjust her gown and veil and a male voice croons softly, "A woman is a harder thing to be than a man.

She has more feelings to feel." The mitigation of these excesses, it appears, is a feminine deodorant called Secret, which allows our bride to approach the altar with security as well as emotion.

Eddie Albert, a successful actor turned pitchman, bestows his 2 attention on a lady with two suitcases, which prompt him to ask her whether she has been on a journey. "No," she says, or words to that effect, as she opens the suitcases. "My two boys bring back their soiled clothes every weekend from college for me to wash." And she goes into the familiar litany of grease, chocolate, mud, coffee, and fruit-juice stains, which presumably record the life of the average American male from two to fifty. Mr. Albert compliments her on this happy device to bring her boys home every week and hands her a box of Biz, because "Biz *is* better."

Two women with stony faces meet cart to cart in a supermarket as 3 one takes a jar of peanut butter off a shelf. When the other asks her in a voice of nitric acid why she takes the brand, the first snaps, "Because I'm choosy for my family!" The two then break into delighted smiles as Number Two makes Number One taste Jiffy for "mothers who are choosy."

If you have not come across these dramatic interludes, it is because 4 you are not home during the day and do not watch daytime television. It also means that your intestinal tract is spared from severe assaults, your credibility unstrained. Or, for that matter, you may look at commercials like these every day and manage to ignore them or find nothing—given the fact of advertising—wrong with them. In that case, you are either so brainwashed or so innocent that you remain unaware of what this daily infusion may have done and is doing to an entire people as the long-accepted adjunct of free enterprise and support of "free" television.

"Given the fact" and "long-accepted" are the key words here. Only 5 socialists, communists, idealists (or the BBC) fail to realize that a mass television system cannot exist without the support of sponsors, that the massive cost of maintaining it as a free service cannot be met without the massive income from selling products. You have only to read of the unending struggle to provide financial support for public, noncommercial television for further evidence.

Besides, aren't commercials in the public interest? Don't they help 6 you choose what to buy? Don't they provide needed breaks from programming? Aren't many of them brilliantly done, and some of them funny? And now, with the new sexual freedom, all those gorgeous chicks with their shining hair and gleaming smiles? And if you didn't have commercials taking up a good part of each hour, how on earth would you find enough program material to fill the endless space/time void?

Tick off the yesses and what have you left? You have, I venture to 7 submit, these intangible but possibly high costs: the diminution of human worth, the infusion and hardening of social attitudes no longer valid or desirable, pervasive discontent, and psychic fragmentation.

Should anyone wonder why deception is not an included detriment, 8

I suggest that our public is so conditioned to promotion as a way of life, whether in art or politics or products, that elements of exaggeration or distortion are taken for granted. Nobody really believes that a certain shampoo will get a certain swain, or that an unclogged sinus can make a man a swinger. People are merely prepared to hope it will.

But the diminution of human worth is much more subtle and just 9 as pervasive. In the guise of what they consider comedy, the producers of television commercials have created a loathsome gallery of men and women patterned, presumably, on Mr. and Mrs. America. Women liberationists have a major target in the commercial image of woman flashed hourly and daily to the vast majority. There are, indeed, only four kinds of females in this relentless sales procession: the gorgeous teen-age swinger with bouncing locks; the young mother teaching her baby girl the right soap for skin care; the middle-aged housewife with a voice like a power saw; and the old lady with dentures and irregularity. All these women, to be sure, exist. But between the swinging sex object and the constipated granny are the millions of females never shown in commercials. These are—married or single—intelligent, sensitive women who bring charm to their homes, who work at jobs as well as lend grace to their marriage, who support themselves, who have talents or hobbies or commitments, or who are skilled at their professions.

To my knowledge, as a frequent if reluctant observer, I know of only 10 one woman on a commercial who has a job; a comic plumber using Comet. Funny, heh? Think of a dame with a plunger.

With this one representative of our labor force, which is well over 11 thirty million women, we are left with nothing but the full-time housewife in all her whining glory: obsessed with whiter wash, moister cakes, shinier floors, cleaner children, softer diapers, and greaseless fried chicken. In the rare instances when these ladies are not in the kitchen, at the washing machine, or waiting on hubby, they are buying beauty shops (fantasy, see?) to take home so that their hair will have more body. Or out at the supermarket being choosy.

If they were attractive in their obsessions, they might be bearable. 12 But they are not. They are pushy, loud-mouthed, stupid, and—of all things now—bereft of sexuality. Presumably, the argument in the tenets of advertising is that once a woman marries she changes overnight from plaything to floor-waxer.

To be fair, men make an equivalent transition in commercials. The 13 swinging male with the mod hair and the beautiful chick turns inevitably into the paunchy slob who chokes on his wife's cake. You will notice, however, that the voice urging the viewer to buy the product is nearly always male: gentle, wise, helpful, seductive. And the visible presence telling the housewife how to get shinier floors and whiter wash and lovelier hair is almost invariably a man: the Svengali in modern dress, the Trilby (if only she were!), his willing object.

Woman, in short, is consumer first and human being fourth. A wife 14 and mother who stays home all day buys a lot more than a woman who lives alone or who—married or single—has a job. The young girl hellbent on marriage is the next most susceptible consumer. It is entirely understandable, then, that the potential buyers of detergents, foods, polishes, toothpastes, pills, and housewares are the housewives, and that the sex object spends most of *her* money on cosmetics, hair lotions, soaps, mouthwashes, and soft drinks.

Here we come, of course, to the youngest class of consumers, the 15 swinging teen-agers so beloved by advertisers keen on telling them (and us) that they've "got a lot to live, and Pepsi's got a lot to give." This affords a chance to show a squirming, leaping, jiggling group of beautiful kids having a very loud high on rock and—of all things—soda pop. One of commercial TV's most dubious achievements, in fact, is the reinforcement of the self-adulation characteristic of the young as a group.

As for the aging female citizen, the less shown of her the better. 16 She is useful for ailments, but since she buys very little of anything, not having a husband or any children to feed or house to keep, nor—of course—sex appeal to burnish, society and commercials have little place for her. The same is true, to be sure, of older men, who are handy for Bosses with Bad Breath or Doctors with Remedies. Yet, on the whole, men hold up better than women at any age—in life or on television. Lines on their faces are marks of distinction, while on women they are signatures of decay.

There is no question, in any case, that television commercials (and 17 many of the entertainment programs, notably the soap serials that are part of the selling package) reinforce, like an insistent drill, the assumption that a woman's only valid function is that of wife, mother, and servant of men: the inevitable sequel to her earlier function as sex object and swinger.

At a time when more and more women are at long last learning to 18 reject these assumptions as archaic and demeaning, and to grow into individual human beings with a wide option of lives to live, the sellers of the nation are bent upon reinforcing the ancient pattern. They know only too well that by beaming their message to the Consumer Queen they can justify her existence as the household Mrs. America: dumber than dumb, whiter than white.

The conditioning starts very early: with the girl child who wants 19 the skin Ivory soap has reputedly given her mother, with the nine-year-old who brings back a cake of Camay instead of the male deodorant her father wanted. (When she confesses that she bought it so she could be "feminine," her father hugs her, and, with the voice of a child-molester, whispers, "My little girl is growing up on me, huh.") And then, before long, comes the teen-aged bride who "has feelings to feel."

It is the little boys who dream of wings, in an airplane commercial; 20 who grow up (with fewer cavities) into the doers. Their little sisters turn into *Cosmopolitan* girls, who in turn become housewives furious that their neighbors' wash is cleaner than theirs.

There is good reason to suspect that this manic obsession with 21 cleanliness, fostered, quite naturally, by the giant soap and detergent

interests, may bear some responsibility for the cultivated sloppiness of
so many of the young in their clothing as well as in their chosen
hideouts. The compulsive housewife who spends more time washing
and vacuuming and polishing her possessions than communicating to,
or stimulating her children creates a kind of sterility that the young
would instinctively reject. The impeccably tidy home, the impeccably
tidy lawn are—in a very real sense—unnatural and confining.

Yet the commercials confront us with broods of happy children, 22
some of whom—believe it or not—notice the new fresh smell their
clean, white sweatshirts exhale, thanks to Mom's new "softener."

Some major advertisers, for that matter, can even cast a benign eye 23
on the population explosion. In another Biz commercial, the genial
Eddie Albert surveys with surprise a long row of dirty clothes heaped
before him by a young matron. She answers his natural query by
telling him gaily they are the products of her brood of eleven "with one
more to come!" she adds as the twelfth turns up. "That's great!" says
Mr. Albert, curdling the soul of Planned Parenthood and the future of
this planet.

Who are, one cannot help but ask, the writers who manage to 24
combine the sales of products with the selling-out of human dreams
and dignity? Who peoples this cosmos of commercials with dolts and
fools and shrews and narcissists? Who know so much about quirks and
mannerisms and ailments and so little about life? So much about
presumed wants and so little about crying needs?

Can women advertisers so demean their own sex? Or are there no 25
women in positions of decision high enough to see that their real selves
stand up?

Do they not know, these extremely clever creators of commercials, 26
what they could do for their audience even while they exploit and
entertain them? How they could raise the levels of manners and
attitudes while they sell their wares? Or do they really share the
worm's-eye view of mass communication that sees, and addresses, only
the lowest common denominator?

It cannot be argued that commercials are taken too seriously, that 27
their function is merely to amuse, engage, and sell, and that they do
this brilliantly. If that were all to this wheedling of millions, well and
good. But it is not. There are two more fallouts from this chronic sales
explosion that cannot be measured but that at least can be expected.
One has to do with the continual celebration of youth at the expense of
maturity. In commercials only the young have access to beauty, sex,
and joy in life. What do older women feel, day after day, when love is
the exclusive possession of a teenage girl with a bobbing mantle of
hair? What older man would not covet her in restless impotence?

The constant reminder of what is inaccessible must inevitably 28
produce a subterranean but real discontent, just as the continual sight
of things and places beyond reach has eaten deeply into the ghetto soul.
If we are constantly presented with what we are not or cannot have,
the dislocation deepens, contentment vanishes, and frustration reigns.
Even for the substantially secure, there is always a better thing, a

better way, to buy. That none of these things makes a better life may be consciously acknowledged, but still the desire lodges in the spirit, nagging and pulling.

This kind of fragmentation works in potent ways above and beyond 29 the mere fact of program interruption, which is much of the time more of a blessing than a curse, especially in those rare instances when the commercial is deft and funny: the soft and subtle sell. Its overall curse, due to the large number of commercials in each hour, is that it reduces the attention span of a people already so conditioned to constant change and distraction that they cannot tolerate continuity in print or on the air.

Specifically, commercial interruption is most damaging during 30 that 10 percent of programming (a charitable estimate) most impor- tant to the mind and spirit of a people: news and public affairs, and drama.

To many (and among these are network news producers), commer- 31 cials have no place or business during the vital process of informing the public. There is something obscene about a newscaster pausing to introduce a deodorant or shampoo commercial between an airplane crash and a body count. It is more than an interruption; it tends to reduce news to a form of running entertainment, to smudge the edges of reality by treating death or disaster or diplomacy on the same level as household appliances or a new gasoline.

The answer to this would presumably be to lump the commercials 32 before and after the news or public affairs broadcasts—an answer unpalatable, needless, to say, to the sponsors who support them.

The same is doubly true of that most unprofitable sector of 33 television, the original play. Essential to any creative composition, whether drama, music, or dance, are mood and continuity, both inseparable from form and meaning. They are shattered by the periodic intrusion of commercials, which have become intolerable to the serious artists who have deserted commercial television in droves because the system allows them no real freedom or autonomy. The selling comes first, the creation must accommodate itself. It is the rare and admirable sponsor who restricts or fashions his commercials so as to provide a minimum of intrusion or damaging inappropriateness.

If all these assumptions and imponderables are true, as many 34 suspect, what is the answer or alleviation?

One is in the course of difficult emergence: the establishment of a 35 public television system sufficiently funded so that it can give a maximum number of people an alternate diet of pleasure, enlighten- ment, and stimulation free from commercial fragmentation. So far, for lack of funds to buy talent and equipment, this effort has been in terms of public attention a distinctly minor operation.

Even if public television should, hopefully, greatly increase its 36 scope and impact, it cannot in the nature of things and through long public conditioning equal the impact and reach the size of audience now tuned to commercial television.

Enormous amounts of time, money, and talent go into commer- 37 cials. Technically they are often brilliant and innovative, the product not only of the new skills and devices but of imaginative minds. A few of them are both funny and endearing. Who, for instance, will forget the miserable young man with the appalling cold, or the kids taught to use—as an initiation into manhood—a fork instead of a spoon with a certain spaghetti? Among the enlightened sponsors, moreover, are some who manage to combine an image of their corporation and their products with accuracy and restraint.

What has to happen to mass medium advertisers as a whole, and **38** especially on TV, is a totally new approach to their function not only as sellers but as social influencers. They have the same obligation as the broadcast medium itself: not only to entertain but to reflect, not only to reflect, not only to reflect but to enlarge public consciousness and human stature.

This may be a tall order, but it is a vital one at a time when **39** Americans have ceased to know who they are and where they are going, and when all the multiple forces acting upon them are daily diminishing their sense of their own value and purpose in life, when social upheaval and social fragmentation have destroyed old patterns, and when survival depends on new ones.

If we continue to see ourselves as the advertisers see us, we have no **40** place to go. Nor, I might add, has commercial broadcasting itself.

Study Questions

1. Explain the use of *splitting*.
2. What is the tone of this essay? How is it established?
3. How and why does Mannes use rhetorical questions?
4. Is there evidence that this article was based on research, or does it represent educated opinion?

Prufrock Before the Television Set
MICHAEL ARLEN

Michael Arlen (1930–   ) was born in London, moved to the
United States in 1940, and attended Harvard University. He
served as a reporter for *Life* and in 1956 joined the *New Yorker* staff
where he has been ever since. Among the awards Arlen has
received is one for television criticism from the Screen Directors
Guild, and the National Book Award for contemporary affairs. His
publications include *The Living-Room War* (1969), *An American
Verdict* (1973), and *The View from Highway 1: Essays on Television*
(1976). Arlen has also contributed to *Cosmopolitan, Holiday,
Saturday Review,* the *Atlantic Monthly,* and other periodicals.

A few days ago, while seated snugly in an airplane seat on   1
my way back to New York from Chicago, with a drink in front of me,
and last week's copy of *Sports Illustrated* on my lap, and the soothing
hum of the engines washing over my ears (and with the memory of the
taxi ride and traffic jam and ticket-counter chaos already receding), it
occurred to me that there was a rather striking similarity between
what I was experiencing then, flying in a modern airliner, and what
I've felt often happens as I watch television. To begin with, both are
largely passive experiences; or, rather, they have been made into
passive experiences. But this passivity is, itself, interesting and
complicated, for not only does it involve obvious conditions of quietude
and inaction, as well as the illusion of privacy; it also implies, and
sometimes makes explicit, a quite formal undertaking of non-
aggressive behavior on the part of the passenger or viewer. In fact,
there is something to be said for the notion that much of the "pleasure"
involved with riding in a commercial airliner, or in watching an
evening's television schedule, has to do as much with this subjective
state of non-aggression (in contrast with the aggressions of the
"outside world") as it has with the supposedly greater and more
evident pleasure of the trip or the actual programs.

Consider, for example, the airplane journey. In many ways, levels   ,2
of ordinary comfort for passengers have been, if anything, decreasing
since the days of the old Pan American "Yankee Clipper." Even so,
there is undoubted pleasure to be had in a routine jetliner trip of

reasonable length (and admittedly one without crying babies or furious grandparents on one's lap). As an extreme example of this, I mention the experience of a friend who, being harried to exhaustion by a project in New York, determined suddenly to fly to California for a few days by the sea. As soon as he was airborne on the way out, he began to relax. Five hours later in California, however, as soon as he was on the ground, dealing with baggage and car rentals and freeways and finally his motel-by-the-sea, he began again to unravel. The same evening, he drove back to the airport, took a return flight to New York, and, after five more hours of airplane massage, was in a suitable condition for resuming work.

People still talk of the romance of travel, and perhaps it is still   3 romance for fashionable visitors to Ethiopian ruins, or even for cruise-ship passengers. Indeed, travel was once an active and difficult undertaking, with the pleasure therein consisting in actively engaging in the difficulties and surmounting them—though even surmounting them wasn't always all that important. The important thing was to participate, to experience. But in much travel nowadays, it seems to me, the key element is non-participation. Not only is aggressive behavior discouraged or proscribed but non-aggressive behavior is formally encouraged as the norm. Thus, the pleasure of much of modern travel lies in the restful illusion that non-aggressive behavior is "being oneself."

On an airplane, for instance, the passenger lumpishly settles into   4 his narrow seat, usually dishevelled in mind or spirit from the hurly-burly of the outside world, sometimes still quivering from the hazards of actually getting to the airplane. The stewardess has already relieved him of his coat and briefcase, his downtown symbols. Sometimes, wifelike, she will have given him an initial, token reward for having reached her: a cup of coffee, a ginger ale, a Bloody Mary. Prufrock has arrived home. Prufrock need do nothing more, except buckle himself to his seat, and follow modest instructions "for his own safety," and act unaggressively. In fact, for doing so, he will be rewarded: by great speed and forward motion (i.e., by progress), by the benign smiles of the stewardess, by the loan of a magazine, by the outright gift of an airline magazine ("Yours to keep"), by drinks, by the hospitality of a meal, even by the appurtenances of an overnight guest—a pillow and blanket. A shower of benefits is rained upon the passenger by the authorities of the airplane (including periodic descriptions of the unseen ground being traversed, delivered over loudspeaker by the unseen captain), who ask in return only that the passenger do nothing, stay quiet, keep still. Bathroom privileges are given, but can easily be revoked. Primary addictive substances, such as cigarettes, are permitted the passengers more rapidly and easily than secondary substances, such as alcohol, which might cause disquiet or might "spill." When all the right conditions are met, modest walking about is allowed, but since there is usually no place to walk to, it is a privilege rarely accepted. Even when the seat-belt sign has been turned off, so the captain has announced, one would do well to keep buckled.

In short, passivity reigns in the modern airliner. And when   5
aggression reappears, it is sternly chastised. For example, after the
plane has landed but before it has arrived at the gate, several
passengers—doubtless summoned again to aggressive behavior by the
imminence of the outside world—will leap to their feet and begin
reaching for coats and bags like children who have been held too long
in school. At this point, the formerly benign stewardess becomes severe
and quickly reprimands the aggressive passengers. If these passengers
do not abandon their aggressive behavior and return to the passivity of
their seats, she says, they will be deprived of the one thing they still
lack: further forward motion. Thereupon, the misbehaving passengers
feign non-aggressive behavior until the second the plane has docked at
the gate and they have been released from passivity. Immediately,
aggression returns and now all the passengers push past each other
down the airport corridors and once again start fighting over baggage,
taxis, buses, or parking space.

The experience of watching most commercial television seems to   6
involve a similar voyage and a similar stylized passivity. Here, of
course, the seat belts are figurative rather than actual, though I notice
that there are a variety of "TV lounge chairs" now on the market,
whose chief function seems to be safety to enclose the viewer during his
nightly journey. Also, it is an interesting (if taste-numbing) coinci-
dence that the TV dinner and the standard airline meal are made the
same way, with the same technology and the same results. With
television, the forward motion is through time, not space; but the effect
is somewhat the same, since in the modern world final destinations
rarely exist. The end of each day's program schedule, as with O'Hare
Airport, is as much a beginning as a terminus.

Rewards for good behavior flow ceaselessly throughout the eve-   7
ning, according to a set routine. In return for sitting still in front of his
television set, the viewer is rewarded not only by the vague, general,
forward-seeming flow of the entertainment but, more specifically, by
periodic "messages" from the authority of the television station which
promise him two levels of benefits. On the higher, symbolic level, there
is the romantic promise of an upward alteration or enhancement of his
life, by the acquisition of a new car, or a new deodorant, or a new kind
of floor tile. This is deeply moving but it is remote, as is the promise of
romance in travel. On a more immediate level, then, the viewer is
rewarded by a trip to the bathroom or another bottle of beer from the
refrigerator: these are stand-ins for the larger, dreamlike rewards.

Aggressive behavior is not actively prohibited, but it is discour-   8
aged. There are almost no viewer phone-in programs, as on radio. Live
audiences are few. Real audience participation is almost nonexistent,
save for the inflated hysteria of a few game shows. Indeed, even some of
the new game shows have become quite stylized and remote, with
earnest, sedate couples trying to guess the authorship of *Hamlet* in the
company of a lonely host and much electronic paraphernalia. On what
are described as comedy or drama or adventure programs, there
remains scarcely any nourishment of the viewer's active participation,

in the form of emotionally involving stories. Thus, a middling detective series such as "Baretta" becomes oddly noticeable, as if it contained a certain gritty substance that somehow spoke to the still-awake part of the viewer's mind—that part persistently untouched by the noisiest bang-bang of cop-show revolvers or even by the sight of artillery explosions in foreign lands. In recent years, many news programs have taken steps toward greater informality and a semblance of involvement on the part of the newscasters. But the involvement of these newsmen has been mostly with each other. The audience continues voyaging, buckled into its Barcaloungers, attending no longer to the voice of a single, solemn captain but to the equally distant, cheery chitchat of two or three of them.

What is strange about this new passivity, regarding both travel **9** and broadcasting, is that not so long ago the reverse was considered normal. That is, flying was once a highly participatory activity—as was automobile driving, as was broadcasting. Thirty-five years ago, the driver of an ordinary car was intimately involved with the event of driving, by means of direct access to his steering wheel, brakes, transmission, and the outside environment. In the same period, a listener to Edward R. Murrow's broadcasts from London was directly involved with the event of broadcasting as well as the events of the Second World War that Murrow was describing. Since then, however, the automobile driver has given up his direct involvement in favor of power controls, automatic transmission, and sealed-in passenger interiors, while the television audience has largely given up its involvement with drama and news in favor of undemanding, mechanical entertainment and uninvolving news. Nowadays, only aggressive people insist on direct, or participatory, driving, by means of sports cars; at least, they are owned by people who are willing to appear aggressive. And only an aggressive minority, perhaps of a different cultural nature, appears to prefer participatory television, such as the music and serious drama programs that now and then are shown on public television.

The question remains: Have we somehow demanded this period of **10** passivity for ourselves (one in which we may, so to speak, draw a breath in order to reach the summit of this peculiar century), or has it been foisted upon us by the onrush of technical systems? Certainly it's true that technical systems assert a logic of their own, as well as clearly seeming to "prefer" a passivity on the part of their components, whether semiconductors or passengers or viewers. At the same time, if fear of flying evoked the seat belt and the stewardess, then fear of another kind has surely evoked our present uninvolving programs, news and entertainment both. Is it fear of communication, of "too much"? Or fear of ourselves? Are we the people meekly buckled in by seat belts or the people rushing pell-mell down the airport corridors and fighting over taxis? Or is there any difference?

At least, nowadays when one has something to think about, one **11** can usually find the time and space for it, either by flying to Chicago or by turning on the television set.

Study Questions

1. Arlen's opening sentences are long. Comment on their construction and their effectiveness.
2. Where does Arlen make the transition from travel to television? What is the basis for the comparison?
3. Who is Prufrock, and what is the basis for the title and the remarks in paragraph 4?
4. Find examples of Arlen's using figurative language. How does the language add to the desired effect?
5. Comment on the opening sentence of paragraph 9 in terms of how Arlen supports that statement about the travel and broadcasts of "not so long ago."
6. Could one fairly consider Arlen's conclusion to be the thesis of his essay?

Do the Arts Inspire Violence in Real Life?

LESLIE BENNETTS

Leslie Bennetts (1949–   ) was born in New York City. She studied art in New York at both the Art Students League and the School of Visual Arts, attended the Philadelphia College of Art, and received a B.A. from the University of Pennsylvania. Bennetts was an editor for *City Center Magazine*, executive editor for *Popular Dogs*, and editor for *On-Tape Magazine* before joining *The Philadelphia Bulletin* staff. Her work on the *Bulletin* led to a position in the Living/Style Department of *The New York Times*. She has also served as host and coproducer for "Changes," a radio show in Philadelphia; and as on-camera talent for WHYY-TV, also in Philadelphia. She has won numerous awards for her work as a news reporter, both for individual pieces and for her part in a team investigation series.

In film as in other media, violence has long since become commonplace, with people dismembered, impaled, incinerated, blown up, machine-gunned or otherwise annihilated with numbing regularity. Social scientists have long debated the effects of such depictions of violence upon viewers, and recently the controversy flared anew with reports that Federal investigators believe John Hinckley, who has been charged with the attempted assassination of President Reagan, was influenced by the 1976 movie "Taxi Driver."

That film explored the pathological progress of Travis Bickle, a   2
human time bomb who plans to murder a political candidate but ends up slaughtering a group of pimps and pushers in an orgiastic massacre. He is then hailed by the news media as a hero.

Such bloody scenes are far from unique in contemporary movies   3
and television programs. But although psychologists have published reams of research on the impact of such violence, opinion remains sharply divided on the conclusions that can be drawn. However, the assassination attempt was not the first to raise the issue in a public forum; it had been foreshadowed in the growing number of trials that have focused on the effect of media violence, with defense lawyers contending that exposure to such stimuli prompted specific crimes.

In 1977, attorneys for a 15-year-old Florida youth argued that six   4
to eight hours' worth of daily television viewing had so inured him to violence that he had lost the ability to distinguish right from wrong, and therefore should not be convicted of fatally shooting his next-door neighbor, an 82-year-old woman, during a robbery attempt. Elements of one episode of the boy's favorite television show, "Kojak," were said to resemble the actual slaying. The boy's attorney, Ellis Rubin, told the jury, "If you judge Ronny Zamora guilty, television will be an accessory ... Ronny is a victim of shows that are on television, depicting violence and breaking the law." The prosecution called the defense "hogwash," and the boy was found guilty.

The following year, NBC broadcast a television movie in which a   5
girl was sexually assaulted by a group of reform-school classmates who raped her with a mop handle. Four days later a gang of teen-agers similarly molested a 9-year-old girl on a San Francisco beach, and lawyers for the girl sued NBC for "negligence," claiming that the network should have known that such a scene might be imitated. One judge ruled that the plaintiff had to prove the network intended to "incite" violence in order to collect damages; the case is still pending before the California Court of Appeals.

And when a 9-year-old boy robbed a midtown Manhattan bank last   6
month, his lawyer said that the child had been influenced by television crime programs and that he had only been "playing" when he pointed a toy gun at a bank teller and demanded money. The boy is scheduled for a Family Court trial on Wednesday.

Whatever the merits of such individual defenses, the issue con-   7
tinues to preoccupy many social scientists. But despite innumerable experiments, psychologists still argue among themselves almost as fiercely as some of their findings are disputed by civil libertarians, First Amendment experts, film industry people and television network officials, to name only a few of the interested parties.

The one thing almost everyone seems to agree upon is that the   8
question is a complicated one. "I think there are lots of different
processes that determine the consequences of observed violence," says
Leonard Berkowitz, a psychology professor at the University of Wisconsin who has done considerable research on aggression. "There is no
one factor at work, but one of the things that happens is that people get
ideas as well as inclinations, and if their inhibitions happen to be weak
at the time, these ideas or inclinations can be translated into open
behavior."

Dr. Berkowitz's studies have focused on the immediate influence of   9
movie violence upon adults, because, he says, "I think adults are more
dangerous than kids, and that adults can be stimulated by what they
see for a short time. I also think that the effect is by no means confined
to movies or television; anything in the mass media can give people
ideas. News reports of widely publicized crimes can have many of the
same effects. For instance, we investigated the after-effects of President Kennedy's assassination and of the Richard Speck killings of the
Chicago nurses, and found there was a rise in violent crimes in the
month following each of those events, among others."

Like a number of other researchers, Dr. Berkowitz has also found   10
that when college students view a violent film and are then given an
opportunity to administer electric shocks to other students, they inflict
more severe punishment than do students who have not witnessed
such violence.

Other inquiries have addressed the long-term effects of observed   11
violence on children. Dr. Leonard Eron, a psychologist at the University of Illinois at Chicago Circle, conducted a study which first
examined a group of 8-year-olds and then followed up their development ten years later. "We found that the best single predictor we had
on how aggressive these people were at 18 was the violence in the
programs they viewed at age 8," Dr. Eron reports.

"Now, it could have been said that aggressive youngsters like   12
violent programs to begin with," he says. "But because of the methodology we used to control the experiment, we were fairly certain this
was a cause-and-effect relationship, with television viewing preceding
the aggressive behavior. The highly aggressive youngsters who were
watching non-violent programs were significantly less aggressive by
age 18 than the youngsters who were not aggressive at 8 but who had
watched violent programs; they turned out to be more aggressive in the
end. We later repeated the study, and found the same thing. Furthermore, the more violent the programs, the more aggressive the children
became."

Dr. Eron believes that such exposure conditions children to be   13
casual about violence. "They grow up seeing this stuff, and they think
it's socially acceptable to do these things," he says. "They think this is
the way life is, that this is the norm."

Others question such conclusions. "I don't share the prevailing   14
view among behavioral psychologists that violence in media plays a
significant role in violence and criminal behavior in the United States,

and has been an important factor in the increasing violence we see in our society," says Seymour Feshbach, chairman of the psychology department at the University of California at Los Angeles.

"I think that violence in the media can be a contributing factor, but 15 that it depends on a lot of other factors, including the age of the viewer," Dr. Feshbach adds. "The younger the viewer, the more vulnerable they are. The more realistic the violence, the more it approaches an instructional, how-to-do-it kind of experience. And the more the violence is the central and only theme, the more likely it is to stimulate aggressive behavior. Many dramatic experiences are clearly fantasies and do not meet these criteria."

However, Dr. Feshbach believes that the combination of erotic and 16 violent elements is particularly potent, stimulating aggression far more readily than violence alone. He finds the possible social consequences of such fare extremely worrisome: "If you vicariously identify with the characters, you can get a very strong conditioned effect, and the violent act becomes attached to sexual arousal," he explains. "The cognitive message is, this is okay, people do this. And obviously rape is the more severe form of sex mixed with violence."

In considering violence and its portrayal, some analysts pose a 17 chicken-and-egg question about which came first. "In a violent society, there may be an appetite for violence, in which case the media wouldn't be the cause—they'd be the effect, simply reflecting back on us who we are and what we do," suggests Robert Liebert, a professor of psychology at the State University of New York at Stonybrook. "Unquestionably, if we did not have a bent toward being a somewhat violent people, the kind of entertainment you see on television wouldn't be there."

Many critics point out that the malignant has exerted a powerful 18 lure since ancient times. "Violence partakes of evil and evil has always been more interesting than good, unfortunately," says Richard Gilman, a professor at the Yale School of Drama and drama critic of *The Nation.* "Great sinners are generally more interesting than great saints. It's useless and silly to protest against the prevalence of violence in art; what's legitimate is to protest against gratuitous violence that has no esthetic or literary point, that's done just for effect."

Others note that although dramatic conventions have varied from 19 civilization to civilization, violence has always constituted a major element of art. "There was a time, particularly with the Greeks, when violence was always kept off the stage; it was reported onstage by messengers," notes Robert Brustein, artistic director of the American Repertory Theater and director of the Loeb Drama Center at Harvard University.

"But the Greeks were the last time, outside of French neoclassical 20 imitations, that violence was absent from the stage," Dr. Brustein says. "Roman drama was extremely bloody and violent, Elizabethan drama was bloody and violent, Jacobean drama was bloody and violent, and 19th-century Romantic drama was also bloody and violent. So is 20th-century drama, not to mention movies, reflecting a world that is bloody and violent. An honest artist is compelled to represent what is happening. I don't believe that outside of pathological people, violent movies or plays cause violence in society; they simply reflect it. The violence is there already."

Moviemakers echo such assertions. "Film is about life, and vio- 21 lence is a part of life," says Martin Poll, a producer whose most recent film is a police thriller about international terrorism called "Nighthawks." "Unless you're going to do totally escapist entertainment, you can't ignore the subject of violence today, because it's prevalent in our lives."

Paul Schrader, who wrote the screenplays for "Taxi Driver" and for 22 "Raging Bull," adds: "Every artist since pre-history has thought that violence and conflict were within the proper realm of art, from cave artists to the Greeks to the present." But he disputes suggestions that the bloody climax of "Taxi Driver" might have precipitated the recent assassination attempt upon President Reagan.

"It isn't the violence that's the problem, it's the depth of the 23 psychological portrait," contends Mr. Schrader, who has also directed such films as "Hardcore" and a work currently in production, "Cat People." "The only reason that man connected with that film is that the pathology of the character was so accurate that he identified with it. If you want to stop someone from connecting with violence, either you can't portray criminals on screen at all, so sick people won't identify with them, or you can only do it two-dimensionally, so no one can really get inside the character's head."

Since Aristotle, some scholars have maintained that identification 24 with tragic drama can be cathartic. "There are those who theorize that violent representations in art exteriorize the latent cruelty and blood lust that seem to be indigenous to human beings, and thereby purge it and get rid of it for a while," explains Dr. Brustein.

Whether or not it is cathartic, however, there is little question that many people find violence exciting, a fact which some attribute to a jaded society whose ability to appreciate more complex art has been wrecked by the fast-paced superficiality of television. "The extent to which we're seeing violence in the arts reflects the increasing hunger for sensation in general," says Dr. Bennetts. "I think that everyone's very bored; they're so used to being able to switch the dial that the people who cater to the hunger for sensation resort to more and more violent devices in order to satisfy the desire."

In trying to defend such practices, television executives often claim 25 that they are just giving the audience what it wants. "People in jeopardy and people being saved are inherently dramatically interesting," says Ronald Milavsky, vice president for news and social research at NBC television. "The more vulnerable the person is—say a child being in danger—the more dramatic the situation would be. It's good television material. People like to see victims get saved. That's never going to change; why should it? I don't see that it does any harm."

Among those who strongly disagree is George Gerbner, dean of the 26 Annenberg School of Communications at the University of Pennsylvania. Dr. Gerbner holds that while violent dramas may influence a small number of people to identify with the perpetrators, they influence a far larger number who identify with the victims.

"Those who are exposed to this kind of violence develop an 27 exaggerated sense of fear, anxiety, insecurity, dependence, paranoia and mistrust," says Dr. Gerbner who has found that the great majority of those victimized in television drama are women and minorities. "Therefore general exposure to a high level of violence cultivates a 'mean world' syndrome, a sense that the world is a very dangerous place in which to live and that you're going to be hurt."

Debate over such findings will doubtless continue, but even those 28 most convinced that media violence is harmful hesitate to suggest what to do about it. "I saw more violence on network news programs during the Vietnam War than I have seen in a lifetime," says Jack Valenti, president of the Motion Picture Association of America, which assigns ratings to films based on their levels of violence and obscenity.

"What are you going to do, shut the news off?" Mr. Valenti asks. 29 "Where do you draw the line? A movie might jolt a psychotic into action—or somebody might jostle him on the subway, or be rude to him, and that might also precipitate an action by someone teetering on the precipice. Anything could set him off. We lose tens of thousands of people a year to automobile accidents: should we ban the automobile? We don't even ban handguns, and look at all the people who are killed every year by handguns."

Many legal experts say that whatever the conclusions of research- 30 ers, any attempt to translate experimental data into regulatory curbs will run afoul of the Constitution. "Any kind of government regulation which tried either to shift the time at which programs were aired, or which banned them altogether because of the fear that they would encourage aggressive action on the part of children, would be unconstitutional under the First Amendment," declares Thomas Krattenmaker, a constitutional scholar and professor of law at Georgetown University. "That's because the government is required to demonstrate the presence of a clear and present danger that violence will immediately and irreparably ensue from the viewing of such programs by children, and because the government has no right to deny to adults the right to receive information, expression, entertainment or other similar speech protected by the First Amendment on the theory that it may harm children."

Others add that one such regulatory step would lead to others in a 31 succession profoundly antithetical to democratic ideals. "The threat to freedom of expression in the imposition of sanctions in such cases is a clear and direct one," says Floyd Abrams, an attorney who has specialized in cases involving the First Amendment. "Every artist, filmmaker or author would have to consider before putting pen to paper what someone could say later on what the social effect of his expression was. Once they start importing into their creative efforts that kind of guesswork about how people might react to what they do, we would inevitably have a diminution of the vigor of public expression. That's not a price that's worth paying—nor is it one, as a purely legal matter, which the First Amendment allows to be paid."

Mr. Valenti, the official spokesman for the Hollywood film indus- 32 try, concludes, "You pay a price for a democratic society. But I wonder whether those people who clamor for the banning of violent shows might find the Russian model attractive, where the state tells you what you can put on television. You pay another price for the absence of what some people find offensive, and that price is that you give over to the state or another authority the right to make judgments about what should be banned."

Dr. Gerbner disagrees that official censorship represents the only 33 possible remedy for the current levels of media violence. "The question is not one of more censorship or less," he says. "The networks are 100 percent self-censored as it is. The question is, on whose behalf is this process operating? Right now it's on behalf of the advertisers who pay the bill to get the maximum audience at the minimum cost, and cater to every existing prejudice. The networks should be censoring themselves according to a different value system."

Study Questions

1. What is the thesis of Bennetts's essay? What does she conclude?
2. What is accomplished by Bennetts's use of the examples in the paragraphs which immediately follow the thesis?
3. To what extent does Bennetts demonstrate that "almost everyone" agrees that the question is a complicated one? What does she accomplish by that sentence at the beginning of paragraph 8?
4. In paragraph 25, Bennetts refers to "debate." How does she create the debate in the course of her essay?
5. At what point does Bennetts begin to discuss the Constitutional issue? What effect is created by ending the essay with a quotation? With that particular quotation?

The Great American Barbe-Queue

CHARLES KURALT

Charles Kuralt (1934–   ) was born in North Carolina and attended the University of North Carolina at Chapel Hill. He went from reporter and columnist for the *Charlotte News* to CBS, where he has worked since 1957 and where he is currently the "On the Road" correspondent. The essay reprinted here is an example of his reporting, which he tries to keep "unimportant, irrelevant, and insignificant." Kuralt and his crew travel approximately 50,000 miles a year. Among other awards, Kuralt has received the Ernie Pyle Memorial Award, two George Foster Peabody Awards, and two Emmys. His books include *To the Top of the World* (1968) and *Dateline America* (1979). He is a frequent contributor to *Saturday Review, Family Circle,* and other periodicals.

An old refrigerator shelf was all you really needed. 1

That was your grill. You laid it on a circle of stones surrounding a 2 bare spot on the lawn in the North Carolina backyard of my youth, started a charcoal fire under it, unwrapped a sirloin from the A & P, iced down a few bottles of beer in the wheelbarrow, and invited the neighbors over. After supper you sat talking quietly in the dusk until the mosquitoes got too bad. Contentment was within the grasp of anybody with an old refrigerator shelf.

I should have known something was going wrong when I came 3 home from college to find that my own father had built a brick fireplace in the backyard, with a chimney. The neighbors admired it and set out to exceed it. That was twenty years ago.

You, too, have noticed, I assume, how it all turned out. In this 4 summer of our celebration, the electrical hum of the three-speed spit is heard in the land. It is revolving majestically over a four-wheel, gas-fired, smoke-controlled Adjustable Grid Patio Grill with a copper hood and a warming oven. The chef is wearing an apron with a funny saying on it. He is frowning over his *caneton rôti aux pêches flambées,* trying to decide whether the sauce needs more Madeira. Contentment is not his.

For many years I have been traveling around America mooching 5 meals from friends where possible and observing the decline of suburban serenity. I think the outdoor cooking machine has a lot to do with it. If we are ever going to win back our innocence, we have to rediscover the refrigerator shelf.

The pleasure of outdoor cooking used to be the simplicity of it. This is the ancestral secret of generations of American males that is in danger of being lost. *Nothing you can do to a steak cooked outdoors can ruin it.*   6

A man (outdoor cooks are invariably men, for atavistic reasons having to do, I imagine, with knives and fire and ego) can thoughtfully marinate his steak for hours in a mixture of his own invention—wine vinegar, soy sauce, secret herbs, and tequila; then patiently wait for the coals to reach just the right color and temperature; then quickly sear the steak on both sides to contain its juices; then cook it by feel and by experience; he can do all these things—*or not*—and be certain of triumphant approval. "Good steak, George." "You cooked it just right, Daddy." They will say the same if he unwraps it half frozen, drops it on the grill, and remembers to pause in his drinking to turn it once.   7

But let this same man begin to believe himself a chef, acquire, in his pride, an outdoor cooking machine, and attempt dishes having to do with delicate sauces or, worse, flaming swords, and we would all be better off staying indoors. Indoors, Daddy disdains to help with the cooking. It is not cooking he loves; it is his machine.   8

There is still some good outdoor cooking going on in this country, but none of it needs machinery, and none of it comes from Escoffier.   9

The first meal that comes to mind as I ruminate happily through my own recent memories of outdoor eating is a clambake last summer in Maine. Here is the authentic recipe for a clambake: dig a big hole in a beach. If you have a Maine beach to dig your hole in, so much the better, but any beach will do. Line the hole with rocks. Build a big fire on the rocks and take a swim. When the fire is all gone, cover the hot rocks with seaweed. Add some potatoes just as they came from the ground; some corn just as it came from the stalk; then lobsters, then clams, then another layer of seaweed. Cover the whole thing with a tarp and go for another swim. Dinner will be ready in an hour. It will make you very happy. No machine can make a clambake.   10

If there is a next-best thing to a Maine clambake, it is a Mississippi fish fry. I have a friend in Mississippi who is trying to keep Yankees from finding out that beneath the slimy hide of the catfish is concealed the flakiest, most delicate of all gifts from sea, stream, or farm pond. He is trying to keep it secret because there are not enough catfish to go around. I know he is my friend because he took me to a fish fry. You dip your catfish in seasoned flour, then in eggs, then in cornmeal, then into a bubbling pot of fat—that's all. Catfish fry happiest when accompanied in the pot by hush puppies. Hush puppies are cornmeal, flour, salt, baking powder, chopped onion, and ham fat, with enough beer worked in to hold them together. A few Baptists use water instead of beer. A fish fry is wonderful, with either wet or dry hush puppies.   11

Clambakes and fish fries are for fun. I went on a cattle roundup in West Texas this spring and found another brand of outdoor cooking that survives by necessity. Camp cooks are still much honored. They   12 live by the principle that anything that can't be cooked in a heavy black iron skillet over live coals isn't worth eating. Any of the good ones, given a campsite and one hour, can supply from one of those skillets beans, chili, stew, coffee, and even bread baked over the hot coals with additional coals heaped on the skillet lid. It is simple fare, always delicious, and more welcome to a hungry cowhand than anything Paul Bocuse ever created for jaded palates of the Continent.

I know some trout fishermen on the Upper Peninsula of Michigan 13 who meet frequently at streamside to tell lies, play cribbage, and occasionally persuade some young brook trout that a fanciful floating speck of fur and feathers is actually a mayfly. They succeed often enough to eat well. Their speciality is mushrooms, grilled until their caps fill up with juices, served with a little salt, and washed down with bourbon out of an old tin cup. This is a meal I remember with reverence—mushrooms and bourbon—noble in its simplicity.

From *barbe* to *queue,* the French said, to describe the roasting of a 14 whole hog, from whiskers to tail. And thereby started an argument. Barbecue is one of those things Americans can't agree on, like nuclear power or Ronald Reagan. Midwesterners, to whom barbecue is any roasted meat with ketchup on it, think Midwestern barbecue is best. The best barbecue comes from a genius I know in Lexington, N.C., who merely anoints his hog with salt, pepper, garlic, sage, and a mysterious sauce, wraps it in burlap, buries it in coals, covers it with earth, and serves it in precious shreds hours later with hot corn bread and Brunswick stew. It's simple, he says.

There are Southerners transplanted to New York who achieve 15 almost the same result working with a hibachi on an apartment balcony. They know enough not to get too fancy with their barbecue sauce, whether swabbing it on a whole hog with a new broom in Lexington, N.C., or touching up a little pork tenderloin with a watercolor brush twenty-three floors above Lexington Avenue.

North, South, East, or West, cooking outdoors is a healing and a 16 renewal for those smart enough to keep it simple. Hot dogs and hamburgers, than which nothing is more boring when cooked in the kitchen, become magical delights when grilled outdoors and eaten with your back against an oak tree. Spareribs, sausages, lamb chops, or chicken wings smoked indolently over a section of old stovepipe become greater than they are. Just being outdoors, it is truly said, enhances the flavor of just about everything, but it's not just that. *Is* there a better way of cooking fish than sautéing it, freshly caught, in butter, over a campfire? I have never discovered it. All you need is a fire, a fork, and a frying pan.

What you don't need is a machine. 17

But I know I am too late. You probably already have one. This is 18 how far the al fresco escalation has gone: a man of my acquaintance, grown rueful and contemplative over the bigger and better outdoor cooking machines of his neighbors, watching their parties grow in size and sophistication, recently came upon a description of an Arab barbecue. A chicken, it seems, is stuffed into the stomach of a lamb, the lamb into the stomach of a cow, and the cow into the stomach of a camel. Roasting takes three days.

He's thinking about it. He says there's a machine at the hardware 19 store that would do the job, but he can't find a camel in Scarsdale.

Study Questions

1. What is Kuralt's thesis? Where does it occur?
2. On what basis does Kuralt choose the meals he discusses? How does he order them?
3. How do the meals in paragraphs 10 and 11 differ from that in paragraph 12? Comment then on paragraph 13.
4. Why does Kuralt use only one sentence in paragraph 17?
5. How does the anecdote in the last two paragraphs reinforce Kuralt's thesis?

Author-Title Index